PREPARING COSTS

PREPARING COMPANY ACCOUNTS 2009-10

Small companies accounting under the Companies Act 2006

Ray Mayes BA, FCA

BUZZACOTT

Seventeenth Edition

CCH
a Wolters Kluwer business

Wolters Kluwer (UK) Limited
145 London Road
Kingston upon Thames
Surrey KT2 6SR
Tel: 0844 561 8166
Fax: 020 8247 1184
E-mail: customerservices@cch.co.uk
www.cch.co.uk

Disclaimer
This publication is sold with the understanding that neither the publisher nor the authors, with regard to this publication, are engaged in rendering legal or professional services. The material contained in this publication neither purports, nor is intended to be, advice on any particular matter.

Although this publication incorporates a considerable degree of standardisation, subjective judgment by the user, based on individual circumstances, is indispensable. This publication is an 'aid' and cannot be expected to replace such judgment.

Neither the publisher nor the authors can accept any responsibility or liability to any person, whether a purchaser of this publication or not, in respect of anything done or omitted to be done by any such person in reliance, whether sole or partial, upon the whole or any part of the contents of this publication.

Telephone Helpline Disclaimer Notice
Where purchasers of this publication also have access to any Telephone Helpline Service operated by Wolters Kluwer (UK), then Wolters Kluwer's total liability to contract, tort (including negligence, or breach of statutory duty), misrepresentation, restitution or otherwise with respect to any claim arising out of its acts or alleged omissions in the provision of the Helpline Service shall be limited to the yearly subscription fee paid by the Claimant.

© 2009 Wolters Kluwer (UK) Ltd

Accounting Standards Board material is reproduced with the permission of the Accounting Standards Board Limited.

Auditing Practices Board material is reproduced with the permission of the Auditing Practices Board Limited.

ISBN – 978-1-84798-143-1

All rights reserved. No part of this publication may be reproduced or transmitted in any form or by any means or stored in any retrieval system of any nature without prior written permission, except for permitted fair dealing under the Copyright, Designs and Patents Act 1988 or in accordance with the terms of a licence issued by the Copyright Licensing Agency in respect of photocopying and/or reprographic reproduction. Application for permission for other use of copyright material, including permission to reproduce extracts in other published works shall be made to the publisher. Full acknowledgement of author, publisher and source must be given.

Material is contained in this publication for which copyright is acknowledged. Permission to reproduce such material cannot be granted by the publisher and application must be made to the copyright holder.

Crown copyright material is reproduced with the permission of the Controller of HMSO and the Queen's Printer for Scotland.

No responsibility for loss occasioned to any person acting or refraining from action as a result of any material in this publication can be accepted by the author or publisher.

Views expressed in this publication are the author's and are not necessarily those of his firm or of the publisher.

British Library Cataloguing-in-Publication Data

A catalogue record for this book is available from the British Library.

Typeset by RefineCatch Limited, Bungay, Suffolk
Printed and bound in the UK by TJ International Ltd, Padstow, Cornwall

Preface

Implementation of the Companies Act 2006 has arrived at last!

During 2009 and 2010, accountants will increasingly prepare financial statements in accordance with the new Act and under new statutory references. Small company accounts produced for filing purposes will be shorter and more relevant. Many more companies within the 'small companies regime' will also take the opportunity of audit exemption.

Nevertheless, despite clearer and more relevant legislation, familiarisation of the law can still be difficult and the detailed legislation often remains complex – exemptions and opportunities for small companies (or the rules to take advantage of them) can be easy to miss.

The FRSSE (Financial Reporting Standard for Smaller Entities) is now widely adopted. The recently revised version (FRSSE (effective April 2008)), which reflects the impact of relevant company legislation under the Companies Act 2006, is likely to remain in force for the foreseeable future.

Overall, however, the playing field for company accounting remains confusing.

There are some five million companies in Europe that may be regarded as 'small and private'. The IASB (International Accounting Standards Board) is currently developing a set of international accounting standards (IFRS) for smaller private companies and there are also European proposals to exempt very small 'micro' companies from EU accounting directives. For companies generally, UK accounting standards (FRSs) are steadily 'converging' with international standards (IFRSs). A consensus of application for the 'IFRS for Non-publicly Accountable Entities', however, is not proving easy.

It is possible to envisage a scenario, therefore, where we have the following framework of four tiers of reporting practice:

- International Financial Reporting Standards – for publically accountable entities
- International Financial Reporting Standard for Non-publicly Accountable Entities – for SMEs
- UK Financial Reporting Standard for Smaller Entities – within the UK
- European exemption for 'micros' – exempt from EU accounting directives.

Such a scenario, with a variety of GAAPs, would hardly suggest simplification

Preparing Company Accounts is now in its seventeenth edition. After nearly thirty years, I believe that a book such as this, which focuses totally on the small company, continues to have a role in easing the burden of producing small company accounts and promoting the quality of appropriate statutory compliance.

My objective remains the same as when I originally set out to illustrate (in colour!) the Companies Act 1981. The book has always intended to be a companion rather than a comprehensive technical treatise in its own right – a quick and relatively straightforward guide, simplifying where possible, concentrating on basic principles, suggesting appropriate tools, and illustrating changes and opportunities. In concentrating on the small company, the book seems to have found its own niche.

Preface

I am always grateful to readers for their kind comments and helpful suggestions. Whilst any deficiencies will always remain entirely my own, I am indebted to many people over the years who have contributed to the book's success. My professional colleagues at Buzzacott have always encouraged me. On this edition, I have enjoyed working with Chris Harrison and the editorial team at CCH Wolters Kluwer (UK) Limited.

Finally, as ever, I thank my wife Sue for her support and encouragement.

Ray Mayes
February 2009

Contents

	page
Preface	v
Abbreviations	xi
Summary of implementation dates	xiii
Small company thresholds	xv
Note on scope of book	xvi

PART I GENERAL 1

1 Introduction 3
  1.1 Purpose of the book 3
  1.2 Legislation – Accounting regimes under the Companies Acts 2006 and 1985 5
  1.3 Financial Reporting Standard for Smaller Entities (FRSSE) 6
  1.4 International accounting standards 7
  1.5 'WebFiling' – electronic filing of accounts 7

2 Companies Act 2006 and transition 9
  2.1 Company law reform 9
  2.2 Annual accounts under Companies Act 2006 11
  2.3 Main changes affecting small companies' accounts 13
  2.4 Auditing and audit reports 15
  2.5 Contents of annual accounts and reports 16

3 General accounting provisions 17
  3.1 Introduction 17
  3.2 Accounts 17
  3.3 'True and fair' view 18
  3.4 Format of accounts 19
  3.5 Accounting principles 20
  3.6 Notes to accounts – disclosures 21
  3.7 Directors' report – contents and requirements 21
  3.8 Group accounts 22
  3.9 Audit reports 23
  3.10 Adequate accounting records 23
  3.11 Approval and signature of accounts 24
  3.12 Publication of non-statutory accounts 24

4 Accounts and accounting standards 27
  4.1 Basic contents of financial statements 27
  4.2 Primary statements 27
  4.3 Cash flow statements 28
  4.4 Accounting standards 28
  4.5 Application of accounting standards to smaller companies 31
  4.6 International Accounting Standards 34

Contents

PART II	**SMALLER COMPANIES**	**39**
5	**Qualifying as a small company**	**41**
5.1	The 'small companies regime'	41
5.2	Qualifying conditions – 'small' and 'medium-sized' companies	41
5.3	Parent companies and small groups	42
5.4	Decision chart to determine size qualification	42
6	**Contents of small company accounts**	**45**
6.1	Introduction	45
6.2	Accounts – provisions for small companies	45
6.3	'True and fair' view	46
6.4	Format of small company accounts	46
6.5	Small company balance sheet	49
6.6	Small company profit and loss account	52
6.7	Notes to the accounts – small company	53
6.8	Directors' report of a small company	55
6.9	Directors' statements	57
6.10	Small dormant companies	60
6.11	Disclosure of directors' remuneration – small companies	60
6.12	Disclosure of auditor's remuneration: small audited companies	61
7	**Dormant companies**	**63**
7.1	Dormant companies	63
7.2	Definition of 'dormant company'	63
7.3	Conditions for exemption from audit	63
7.4	Companies excluded from dormant companies' exemption	64
7.5	Directors' statements – entitlement to exemption	64
7.6	Dormant company acting as agent	65
7.7	CA 2006 sections 480–481 – Dormant company exemption from audit	65
7.8	Dormant companies – e-filing	66
8	**Abbreviated accounts**	**67**
8.1	Abbreviated accounts	67
8.2	Contents of abbreviated accounts	67
8.3	Filing abbreviated accounts	67
8.4	Abbreviated balance sheet	70
8.5	Directors' statements	71
8.6	Notes to abbreviated accounts	72
8.7	Approval and signing of abbreviated accounts	73
8.8	Parent companies	73
8.9	Special auditors' report (CA 2006 s. 449)	73
8.10	Medium-sized companies	74
8.11	Small company abbreviated accounts checklist	75
9	**Group accounts – small groups**	**79**
9.1	Small companies – option to prepare group accounts	79
9.2	Qualifying conditions – group accounts exemptions	79
9.3	Exempt small groups – related undertakings disclosures	80
9.4	Group accounts filing	80
9.5	Preparing small group accounts	81
9.6	Medium-sized companies – group accounts	82
9.7	Entitlement to group exemption – auditors' report	83
9.8	Group companies – availability of small audit exemption	83

10	**Essentials of the FRSSE – Financial Reporting Standard for Smaller Entities**		**85**
	10.1	Development of the FRSSE	85
	10.2	Essentials of the 'FRSSE (effective April 2008)'	88
	10.3	The FRSSE in outline	93
	10.4	Cash flow statements	107
	10.5	Small groups	109
	10.6	FRS 3 and the FRSSE	109
	10.7	Reporting the substance of transactions	109
	10.8	Related party transactions	110
	10.9	Pensions and retirement benefits	113
	10.10	Foreign currency translation	116
	10.11	Provisions and discounting	117
	10.12	Revenue recognition	118
	10.13	Share based payments	118
	10.14	Going concern and the FRSSE	119
11	**Determining small company audit exemption**		**121**
	11.1	Introduction – preparation of accounts irrespective of audit	121
	11.2	Small companies – conditions for exemption from audit	121
	11.3	Companies excluded from small companies' audit exemption	122
	11.4	Group companies – availability of small audit exemption	122
	11.5	Right to require an audit	123
	11.6	Determining audit exemption	123
	11.7	Audit or assurance reports on accounts of small companies	124
	11.8	Audit exemption – Director's statement	125
PART III	**GUIDELINES AND DEFINITIONS**		**127**
12	**Guidelines and definitions**		**129**
	12.1	Accounts	129
	12.2	Profit and loss account	132
	12.3	Balance sheet	137
	12.4	Financial instruments	141
	12.5	Alternative bases of accounting	143
	12.6	Groups – parent and subsidiary undertakings	144
	12.7	Groups – related undertakings disclosure	146
	12.8	The substance of transactions	149
	12.9	Revenue recognition	150
	12.10	Dividends	152
PART IV	**EXAMPLE ACCOUNTS**		**155**
13	**Example accounts**		**157**
	13.1	Accounts of Small Company Limited	157
	13.2	Abbreviated accounts of Small Company Limited	158
	13.3	Unaudited accounts of Dormant Small Company Limited	158
	13.4	Auditors' reports	158
	13.5	FRC guidance: Going concern and the FRSSE	158
14	**Small company audit reports**		**189**
	14.1	Auditors' reports	189
	14.2	ISA (UK and Ireland) 700 The Auditor's Report on Financial Statements	191
	14.3	Example Auditors' Report of a small company	192
	14.4	Special Auditors' Report – abbreviated accounts	194
	14.5	Duty of care to third parties	197
	14.6	Non-statutory audit and assurance reports	197
	14.7	Reports on accounts prepared for unaudited companies	200

Contents

APPENDICES 203

Appendix A	Company accounts sections – Companies Act 2006	205
Appendix B	Companies Act 2006 Part 15 – Accounts and Reports (Sections 380–474)	213
Appendix C	Statutory formats of accounts – SI 2008 No. 409 Schedule 1	265
Appendix D	Form and content of abbreviated accounts of small companies delivered to Registrar – Companies Act 2006 (SI 2008 No. 409 Schedule 4)	277
Appendix E	SI 2008 No. 409 – The Small Companies and Groups (Accounts and Directors' Report) Regulations 2008	281
Appendix F	Selected reading and reference material	347

Index 351

Abbreviations

ACT	Advance corporation tax
APB	Auditing Practices Board
ARC	Accounting Regulatory Committee of the EU
ASB	Accounting Standards Board
BERR	Department for Business Enterprise and Regulatory Reform (formerly DTI)
CA 1985	Companies Act 1985 (as amended by CA 1989 and subsequent statutory instruments)
CA 1989	Companies Act 1989
C(AICE) 2004	Companies (Audit, Investigations and Community Enterprise) Act 2004
CA 2006	Companies Act 2006
CCAB	Consultative Committee of Accountancy Bodies
DTI	former Department of Trade and Industry (now BERR)
EC	European Commission
EEA	European Economic Area
ESOP	Employee share ownership plan
EU	European Union
EU Regulation	Regulation (EC) No. 1606/2002 of the European Parliament (dated 19 July 2002) on the application of international accounting standards
FA	Finance Act
FASB	US Financial Accounting Standards Board
FRC	Financial Reporting Council
FRED	Financial Reporting Exposure Draft
FRRP	Financial Reporting Review Panel
FRS	Financial Reporting Standard
FRSSE	Financial Reporting Standard for Smaller Entities (being the 'FRSSE (effective April 2008)' unless otherwise indicated or 'FRSSE (effective January 2007)' as the circumstances dictate
FSMA 2000	Financial Services and Markets Act 2000
GAAP	Generally accepted accounting practice (or principles)
IAASB	International Auditing and Assurance Standards Board
IAS	International accounting standards issued or adopted by IASB
IAS Regulation	Regulation (EC) No. 1606/2002 of the European Parliament (dated 19 July 2002) on the application of international accounting standards
IASB	International Accounting Standards Board
ICTA	Income and Corporation Taxes Act 1988
IFRIC	International Financial Reporting Interpretations Committee (an IASB committee)
IFRS	International Financial Reporting Standards (including IAS and interpretations adopted by IASB)
ISA	International Standard on Auditing ('ISA (UK and Ireland)': an ISA applicable within UK and Ireland).
NIC	National Insurance contribution
MiFID	MiFID investment firm – an investment firm within the meaning of Article 4.1.1 of Directive 2004/39/EC of the European Parliament and of the Council of 21 April 2004 on markets in financial instruments (but see CA 2006 s. 474)
OFR	Operating and Financial Review
OPSI	Office of Public Sector Information
P & L account	Profit and loss account
PAYE	Pay as you earn

Abbreviations

PN	APB Practice Note
POB	Professional Oversight Board (Part of the FRC)
Reg.	Regulation (for example, SI 2008 No. 409 reg. 4(2) means regulation 4(2) of SI 2008 No. 409)
s.	section (unless otherwise stated, section references refer to CA 2006, as amended or inserted from time to time)
SAS	Statement of Auditing Standards
Sch	Schedule (for example: 'CA 2006 Sch 7.7(2)' means Companies Act 2006 Schedule 7, paragraph 7(2); or for SI 2008 No. 409, 'SI 2008 No. 409 Sch 4.5(2)' or simply 'Sch 4.5(2)' means Schedule 4 paragraph 5(2))
SI	Statutory instrument
SIC	Standing Interpretation Committee of IASB (or an interpretation of SIC e.g., 'SIC-1').
SME	Small or medium-sized entity (or enterprise)
SORP	Statement of Recommended Practice
SSAP	Statement of Standard Accounting Practice
SSRA	Statement of Standards for Reporting Accountants
STRGL	Statement of total recognised gains and losses
UCITS	Undertaking for Collective Investment in Transferable Securities (see CA 2006 s. 471(1)).
UITF	ASB Urgent Issues Task Force
VAT	Value added tax

Statutory instruments

SI 2008 No. 2860	The Companies Act 2006 (Commencement No. 8, Transitional Provisions and Savings) Order 2008
SI 2007 No. 3495	The Companies Act 2006 (Commencement No. 5, Transitional Provisions and Savings) Order 2007
SI 2008 No. 374	The Companies (Summary Financial Statement) Regulations 2008
SI 2008 No. 393	The Companies Act 2006 (Amendment) (Accounts and Reports) Regulations 2008
SI 2008 No. 409	The Small Companies and Groups (Accounts and Directors' Report) Regulations 2008
SI 2008 No. 410	The Large and Medium-sized Companies and Groups (Accounts and Reports) Regulations 2008
SI 2008 No. 489	The Companies (Disclosure of Auditor Remuneration and Liability Limitation Agreements) Regulations 2008
SI 2007 No. 2932	The Markets in Financial Instruments Directive (Consequential Amendments) Regulations 2007
SI 2004 No. 2947	The Companies Act 1985 (International Accounting Standards and Other Accounting Amendments) Regulations 2004

EC Regulations and Directives

EC 707/2004	Adoption of certain IASs in accordance with regulation EC 1606/2002 (amending regulation EC 1725/2003) (6 April 2004)
EC 1725/2003	Adoption of certain IASs in accordance with regulation EC 1606/2002 (23 September 2003)
EC 1606/2002	Requirement for use of ISAs by listed companies (by 2005) (19 September 2002)
2003/51/EC	The 'Modernisation Directive' amending earlier Directives on annual and consolidated accounts (18 June 2003)
2001/65/EC	The 'Fair Value Directive' on valuation rules for annual and consolidated accounts of certain companies (21 September 2001)

Summary of implementation dates

Company Law

Companies Act 2006

The Companies Act 2006 received Royal Assent on 8 November 2006. Provisions under the Act are being introduced by commencement orders and regulations, available via the BERR website at:

http://www.berr.gov.uk/whatwedo/businesslaw/co-act-2006/index.html

All parts of the Act will be in force by October 2009.

Accounts and reports – Generally, the requirements on the form and content of accounts and reports in Companies Act 2006 Part 15 (Accounts and reports) and new regulations made under it (including, for example, SI 2008 No. 409 for small companies) are effective for accounts and reports for **periods beginning on or after 6 April 2008**. Accounts and reports for periods beginning before then will continue to be prepared in accordance with the Companies Act 1985 and the Companies (Northern Ireland) Order 1986.

Audit – the provisions of Companies Act 2006 Part 16 (Audit) are effective on 6 April 2008, and, following the approach in Part 15 (accounts and reports) above, most of the provisions are applicable to the audits of accounts for **financial years beginning on or after 6 April 2008**.

The Companies Act 2006 is available via the Office of Public Sector Information (OPSI) website at:

www.opsi.gov.uk/acts/acts2006/ukpga_20060046_en_1

www.opsi.gov.uk/acts/acts2006/pdf/ukpga_20060046_en.pdf

Regulations under Companies Act 2006 are available via the Office of Public Sector Information (OPSI) website at:

SI 2008 No. 409 The Small Companies and Groups (Accounts and Directors' Report) Regulations 2008: *www.opsi.gov.uk/si/si2008/uksi_20080409_en_1*

SI 2008 No. 410 The Large and Medium-sized Companies and Groups (Accounts and Reports) Regulations 2008: *www.opsi.gov.uk/si/si2008/uksi_20080410_en_1*

The Companies Act 1985 – for accounting for small companies under the previous Companies Act 1985 regime, refer to *Preparing Company Accounts 2007/2008* (15th edition).

Abbreviations

Financial Reporting Standard for Smaller Entities (FRSSE)

Directors choosing to adopt the FRSSE must ensure that accounts are prepared in accordance with the appropriate version:

- FRSSE (effective January 2007) – accounts prepared under CA 1985, or
- FRSSE (effective April 2008) – accounts prepared under CA 2006 (must not be adopted early).

The updated FRSSE (effective April 2008) is available free of charge on the ASB website at:

www.frc.org.uk/asb/technical/frsse.cfm.

and hard copies are available (price £10.00 (post-free)) from ASB Publications.

FRSSE (effective April 2008)

The Financial Reporting Standard for Smaller Entities (effective April 2008) updates and supersedes the FRSSE (effective January 2007). It should be regarded as standard for financial statements relating to accounting periods beginning on or after 6 April 2008.

Early adoption is not permissible to be consistent with commencement dates of statutory regulations, including SI 2008 No. 409.

The FRSSE (effective April 2008) introduces no changes to the accounting requirements. The only differences between the FRSSE (effective April 2008) and the FRSSE (effective January 2007) are in respect of the legal requirements which have been updated to reflect the Companies Act 2006, including the increases in the small company accounting and audit thresholds (see below).

A derivation table, available on the ASB website, provides a full cross-reference between the legal requirements set out in the FRSSE (effective April 2008) and the Companies Act 2006.

Small Limited Liability Partnerships (LLPs) adopting the FRSSE are not able to use the updated version (FRSSE (effective April 2008)) until accounting periods beginning on or after 1 October 2008, in compliance with SI 2008 No.1912 *The Small Limited Liability Partnerships (Accounts) Regulations 2008*. LLPs are outside the scope of this book.

FRSSE (effective January 2007)

The previous FRSSE (effective January 2007) updated and superseded the FRSSE (effective January 2005) and effectively remains as standard for financial statements relating to accounting periods beginning on or before 5 April 2008.

International Accounting Standards

In accordance with SI 2004 No. 2947 *The Companies Act 1985 (International Accounting Standards and Other Accounting Amendments) Regulations 2004*, from 1 January 2005 all British companies (other than charities and those automatically covered by the EU IAS Regulation) were permitted (but not required) to use international accounting standards (IAS) as an alternative to the UK domestic reporting accounting framework. Once IAS accounts are adopted by a company, however, all subsequent accounts must continue to be prepared in accordance with international accounting standards except in defined 'relevant changes of circumstance'.

The application of international accounting standards is explained more fully in **Chapter 4**.

Small company thresholds

Accounting and audit exemption thresholds for small and medium-sized companies, as increased by Statutory Instrument SI 2008 No. *393 The Companies Act 2006 (Amendment) (Accounts and Reports) Regulations 2008,* are set out below.

The Regulations came into force on 6 April 2008 and apply in relation to financial years beginning on or after 6 April 2008.

Transitional determination of qualification – In determining whether a company or group qualifies as small or medium-sized under CA 2006 ss. 382(2), 383(3), 465(2) or 466(3) (qualification in relation to subsequent financial year by reference to circumstances in preceding financial years), for financial years ending on or after 6th April 2008, a company or group is treated as having qualified as small or medium-sized (as the case may be) in any previous financial year in which it would have so qualified as if the increased thresholds introduced by the Regulations (SI 2008 No. 393 reg 2(3)) had been in force.

Statutory Instrument SI 2008 No. 393 is available via the Office of Public Sector Information (OPSI) website at:

http://www.opsi.gov.uk/si/si2008/uksi_20080393_en_1

Small companies – see *Chapter 5*

	Current thresholds (CA 2006 accounts)	*Previous thresholds (CA 1985 accounts)*
Small company		
Turnover	£6.5 million	£5.6 million
Balance sheet total	£3.26 million	£2.8 million
Average number of employees (on a monthly basis)	50	50
Small group		
Aggregate turnover	£6.5 million net (£7.8 million gross)	£5.6 million net (£6.72 million gross)
Aggregate balance total sheet	£3.26 million net (£3.9 million gross)	£2.8 million net (£3.36 million gross)
Average number of employees (on a monthly basis)	50	50

Medium-sized Companies – see *Chapter 5*

	Current thresholds (CA 2006 accounts)	*Previous thresholds (CA 1985 accounts)*
Medium-sized company		
Turnover	£25.9 million	£22.8 million
Balance sheet total	£12.9 million	£11.4 million
Average number of employees (on a monthly basis)	250	250
Medium-sized group		
Aggregate turnover	£25.9 million net (£31.1 million gross)	£22.8 million net (£27.36 million gross)
Aggregate balance sheet total	£12.9 million net (£15.5 million gross)	£11.4 million net (£13.68 million gross)
Average number of employees (on a monthly basis)	250	250

Note on scope of book

Companies Act 2006 ('CA 2006 accounts')

Preparing Company Accounts 2009-10 is essentially concerned with the accounts of small companies (that is, 'small companies' as defined by the Companies Act 2006) under the 'small companies regime' for financial years beginning on or after 6 April 2008.

Preparing Company Accounts 2009-10 is solely focussed on the new regime.

The statutory accounting provisions for small companies under the Companies Act 2006 are applicable for financial years beginning on or after 6 April 2008 – they cannot be adopted earlier.

Companies Act 1985 (The old regime – 'CA 1985 accounts')

Preparing Company Accounts 2007/08 (a previous edition of this book) covered the statutory accounting provisions for small companies under the Companies Act 1985 which continue to be applicable for financial years beginning before 6 April 2008.

Accounts prepared throughout 2008 and into 2009 will continue to be subject to the CA 1985 regime. **Table 2.2** in **Chapter 2** identifies which accounts are appropriate to that regime. Refer also to 'Summary of implementation dates'.

Scope and contents of book

This present edition of *Preparing Company Accounts 2009-10* concentrates on matters most relevant to the preparation of small company accounts. Statutory references are to CA 2006 itself (as amended from time to time) or to regulations made under the Act, unless otherwise indicated.

The following topics are considered peripheral to this main objective and are not therefore covered in detail:

International accounting standards: Small companies are increasingly adopting the FRSSE and also preparing abbreviated accounts. At present, international accounting standards (IAS) impinge on small companies only to the extent that 'convergence' (that is, harmonisation) of domestic UK and international financial reporting standards is reflected within the UK FRSSE. A major programme of convergence of UK accounting standards is currently being conducted by the ASB for introduction on a 'big bang' basis. The current version of the FRSSE, however, is likely to remain in force for the foreseeable future.

Chapter 4 at **4.6** provides a brief overview of IAS but international accounting standards are not generally covered in detail.

Medium-sized companies: Although medium-sized companies continue to benefit from certain exemptions, these are generally now more limited and less distinguishable from the requirements for larger companies. A medium-sized parent company is no longer exempt from the requirement to prepare group accounts. Statutory requirements for medium-sized companies may be found in SI 2008 No. 410 'The Large and Medium-sized Companies and Groups (Accounts and Reports) Regulations 2008' at:

www.opsi.gov.uk/si/si2008/uksi_20080410_en_1

Note on scope of book

Chapter 5 at **5.2** provides the qualifying conditions for 'small' and 'medium-sized' companies.

Fair value accounting: Preparing Company Accounts 2009-10 does not cover the subject of fair value accounting as this is rarely adopted by small companies. Further, the FRSSE does not apply to companies preparing individual or group accounts in accordance with the fair value accounting rules for certain assets and liabilities set out in Section D of Schedule 1 of Regulation 2008 No. 409 to Companies Act 2006 (see **Appendix E**). SI 2008 No. 409 may be found at:

www.opsi.gov.uk/si/si2008/uksi_20080409_en_1

Consolidated accounts: Small parent companies (as defined) are not required to prepare group accounts. However, as well as preparing individual accounts for a year, they *may* prepare group accounts if they wish to do so. **Chapter 9** provides details of the exemption opportunities and also the requirements where a small parent company prepares group accounts. *Preparing Company Accounts 2009-10* does not cover the detailed mechanics of consolidations and group accounting

Summary financial statements: All companies subject to audit, including small companies, may be able to send summary financial statements to members and others instead of their full audited accounts (CA 2006 s 426). Small companies rarely produce summary financial statements and such statements are not consequently covered.

The statutory requirements concerning summary financial statements may be found in SI 2008 No. 374 'The Companies (Summary Financial Statement) Regulations 2008' at:

www.opsi.gov.uk/si/si2008/uksi_20080374_en_1

Audit and assurance: Preparing Company Accounts 2009-10 does not purport to provide professional guidance on auditing or the provision of assurance services by auditors. Many small companies are now increasingly able to take advantage of audit exemption. Consequently, the book does not comment on audit exemption, audit reports and on the reporting requirements of auditors in circumstances where an audit may be appropriate. Reference should be made to **Chapter 11** (Determining small company audit exemption) and **Chapter 14** (Small company audit reports).

Charities: Preparing Company Accounts 2009-10 does not cover the requirements of incorporated charities. Accounting for charities (incorporated or otherwise) has generally been brought under one roof by the introduction of the Charities Act 2006, to which reference should be made where appropriate. Further information is available at:

www.charity-commission.gov.uk/ (Charity Commission), or

www.opsi.gov.uk/acts/acts2006/ukpga_20060050_en_1 (Charities Act 2006).

Part I General

Chapter 1 Introduction

1.1 Purpose of the book

1.1.1 Accounts of small companies

This book is essentially concerned with the accounts of small companies (that is, 'small companies' as defined by the Companies Act 2006 under the 'small companies regime') for financial years beginning on or after 6 April 2008.

Preparing Company Accounts 2007/08 (15th edition) covered the statutory accounting provisions for small companies under the Companies Act 1985 which continue to be applicable for financial years beginning before 6 April 2008.

The statutory accounting provisions for small companies under the Companies Act 2006 are applicable for financial years beginning on or after 6 April 2008; they cannot be adopted earlier. *Preparing Company Accounts 2009/2010* is solely focussed on the new regime.

Basically, a company is treated as small (or medium-sized) if it does not exceed more than one of the following criteria:

	Small	Medium-sized
Turnover	£6.5 million	£25.9 million
Balance sheet total	£3.26 million	£12.9 million
Average number of employees (on a monthly basis)	50	250

Criteria amended (increased) by SI 2008 No. 393

Chapter 5 sets out the qualifying criteria in detail.

Certain categories of company, regardless of size, will not be entitled to any exemptions. The following companies are not eligible: *s. 384*

- public companies;
- members of 'ineligible' (basically, public) groups;
- companies carrying on an insurance market activity; and
- companies that are authorised insurance companies, banking companies, e-money issuers, MiFID investment firms or UCITS management companies.

Certain categories of small financial services companies that would otherwise be precluded from taking advantage of the exemptions are however now treated as 'small' companies (unless they are required to have an audit under European directives).

All companies are required to prepare full statutory accounts for shareholders but those for small companies contain less detailed information than medium-sized or large companies.

Small (and, to a lesser extent, medium-sized) companies may also prepare 'abbreviated accounts' for filing.

Certain defined categories of small company are exempt from audit.

Chapter 1 Introduction

The Companies Act 2006 has simplified the approach to small company accounting, adopting a 'think small first' basis of presentation of the legislative requirements; small company provisions are clearly identified and separate from other non-relevant legislation. This approach is evident, for example, in Part 15 of CA 2006 which is reproduced in **Appendix B.**

The book endeavours to simplify the still somewhat complex requirements for small company accounts. While not purporting to give comprehensive coverage of all accounting provisions, the aim of the book is to explain many of the company accounting requirements that affect small companies and the exemptions (both accounting and audit) that are available to them. The book concentrates on those matters of practical relevance as far as accounts are concerned. In essence, it aims to resolve the following issues.

What sort of statutory accounts are required? The Act, together with the regulations under SI 2008 No. 409 *The Small Companies and Groups (Accounts and Directors' Report) Regulations 2008,* sets out the requirements for small company accounts.

Preparing and filing abbreviated accounts. Many companies that are able to do so, now prepare (additional) simplified 'abbreviated accounts' for filing with Registrar of Companies

Adoption of the FRSSE. The simplified FRSSE ('Financial Reporting Standard for Smaller Entities'), avoiding the full rigours of UK accounting standards (and increasingly international standards), has become the basic standard for small companies

Is an audit required or necessary? Many companies, while qualifying as 'audit exempt', nevertheless consider whether a voluntary audit or alternatively some form of assurance or accountants' report is appropriate.

International standards. With an international accounting standard for SMEs on the horizon, the smaller company has the choice of adopting IAS accounts.

The book is written from the perspective of the small company and focuses on matters currently relevant to small companies. It provides the following:

- a summary of statutory company accounts provisions in general – to put 'small companies' in context;
- an explanation of the company accounts provisions for small (and 'medium-sized') companies – for both full statutory and abbreviated accounts;
- an explanation of the audit exemptions available to certain small companies;
- guidelines and definitions – for accounting presentation, disclosure and terminology; and
- illustrative examples – including the full statutory accounts of a 'small company'.

Consolidated accounts and accounting for consolidations and group situations are generally not dealt with in detail, although the basic statutory provisions affecting small group accounts and group audit exemptions are inevitably covered.

1.1.2 Small companies in the 'small companies regime'

Legislation over recent years, of both domestic and European origin, has resulted in a measure of standardisation for company accounts, the codification of accounting rules and principles and, to some extent, the simplification of disclosure. Increasingly, the accounts provisions of company law have been supplemented by guidance in the form of Financial Reporting Standards issued by the UK Accounting Standards Board.

UK company law, nevertheless, has remained comprehensive and complex. Preparers of accounts have to contend with ever-increasing legislation and regulation. It has been particularly difficult to identify readily those provisions that apply to the smaller company.

Over the years, the whole process of accounts production for the small company has gradually been simplified resulting in:

- small company accounts are now much less detailed than those of larger companies;
- 'abbreviated accounts' (as a filing option) afford a measure of further privacy and simplicity for small companies;
- statutory recognition of a dedicated regime of accounting for small companies (together with an accounting standard for such companies – the FRSSE); and
- audit exemption affording the opportunity for many smaller companies to avoid the cost and effort involved in what is often regarded as a 'statutory burden'.

Many more companies are falling into the category of 'small company' (becoming increasingly large!) and are hence taking advantage of the accounting opportunities available – see **6.2** below. Accounting and audit exemption thresholds for small and medium-sized companies have been further increased by Statutory Instrument SI 2008 No. *393 The Companies Act 2006 (Amendment) (Accounts and Reports) Regulations 2008.*

Eighty eight per cent of all annual accounts filed with the Registrar of Companies in 2007/08 were classified as audit exempt accounts. A further three per cent comprised audited small company abbreviated accounts.

Table 1.1 Annual accounts registered at Companies House by type 2007/2008

Great Britain in total

	000s	%
Audited accounts		
Full individual accounts (CA 1985 Sch 4 and Sch 8)	143.6	7.9
Abbreviated accounts		
Small company	55.7	3.1
Medium-sized company	8.1	0.4
Group accounts	15.4	0.9
		12.3
Audit exempt		
Audit exempt accounts (Full and abbreviated)	1,250.1	69.1
Dormant company accounts	335.6	18.6
		87.7
Other		
Interim/Initial accounts	0.6	0.0
	1,809.1	100.0

Source: *Companies House* Statistical Tables on Companies Register Activities 2007–2008 (Table F2)
www.companieshouse.gov.uk/about/companiesRegActivities.shtml

With the advent of comprehensive reform introduced by the Companies Act 2006, the small private company will find relevant company law and accounting more comprehensible, more transparent and easier to apply.

1.2 Legislation – Accounting regimes under the Companies Acts 2006 and 1985

The Companies Act 2006 (originally the Company Law Reform Bill) received Royal Assent on 8 November 2006. Running to 701 pages of primary legislation together with 59 pages of index

Chapter 1 Introduction

and comprising 47 Parts, 1300 sections and 16 Schedules, it is the longest Act ever. It consolidates virtually all existing companies legislation and introduces many reforms. Company law has been re-written and re-presented to make it easier to understand and more flexible – especially for smaller companies. About a third of the new provisions represent a straightforward restatement of existing legislation in clearer and simpler language.

The accounts provisions of Part 15 of the Companies Act 2006, which affect the accounts of small companies, relate to financial years commencing on or after 6 April 2008. As a consequence, the first annual accounts prepared under the new small companies regime will, in general terms, be for the year ending on 30 April 2009. Short period accounts may be affected earlier.

Early adoption of provisions of the new Companies Act 2006 regime is not permitted or appropriate and consequently the Companies Act 1985 will remain the appropriate source of company law for annual accounts prepared under the previous small companies regime for years beginning on or before 5 April 2008.

Reference should always be made to the actual legislation itself (Companies Act 2006 or Companies Act 1985 or as amended by subsequent legislation including statutory instruments), in order to ensure full adherence to current and up-to-date legislation. Part 15 of Companies Act 2006 (Accounts and reports) and SI 2008 No. 409 'The Small Companies and Groups (Accounts and Directors' Report) Regulations 2008' are reproduced in full in **Appendices B** and **E** respectively.

This book brings the legislation currently in force up to date to February 2009, having regard, where possible, to known or anticipated changes in the law or accounting standards and practice.

1.3 Financial Reporting Standard for Smaller Entities (FRSSE)

For the smaller entity, the burden of considering and complying with the whole range of accounting standards has frequently outweighed the benefits of clearer financial reporting. Together with statutory rules and accounting principles, accounting standards are the bedrock upon which annual accounts are prepared. With Financial Reporting Standards becoming more detailed and complex and more exemptions being made for small entities, the need for a more succinct and relevant set of standards tailor-made for small companies had been recognised for some time.

The UK Accounting Standards Board (ASB) responded to this situation by issuing a FRSSE – Financial Reporting Standard for Smaller Entities. Originally issued in November 1997, the FRSSE has been subsequently updated on a number of occasions.

The FRSSE applies to all smaller entities (as defined) – not just companies – which prepare accounts showing a true and fair view and which choose to adopt the stand-alone document containing all the relevant standards. In essence, the FRSSE aims to be a 'one-stop shop FRSSE' in the sense of incorporating all relevant existing requirements of small companies legislation (covering small company accounts and directors' reports) and including, for example, statutory accounts formats.

The FRSSE (effective April 2008) is summarised in outline in **Chapter 10**.

FRSSE (effective January 2007) updated and superseded the previous FRSSE (effective January 2005) and is regarded as standard for financial statements relating to accounting periods beginning on or after 1 January 2007; it is based on CA 1985 legislation.

The ASB issued an amended **FRSSE (effective April 2008)** in June 2008 updating statutory references to Companies Act 2006 and its underlying regulations.

The main changes that have been made to the FRSSE concern:

- Thresholds – increased CA 2006 thresholds for companies and groups to qualify as small;
- Eligibility criteria – limiting the scope for small investment firms and entities such as e-money issuers to use the FRSSE;
- Liability limitation agreements – a new requirement to disclose details of any liability limitation agreement (where the accounts subject to audit);
- Disclosure of authorised share capital – no longer required;
- Transactions with directors – 'Loans, quasi-loans, credit transactions and guarantees' are now referred in CA 2006 to as 'Advances, credit and guarantees';
- Disclosure of 'political donations and expenditure' and 'charitable donations' – new requirement for separate disclosure. (Reporting threshold for these donations in the directors' report has increased to £2,000); and
- Disclosures regarding independent election candidates – new requirement for disclosures in the directors' report.

1.4 International accounting standards

Recent years have seen increasing cooperation between world accounting bodies to achieve harmonisation of financial reporting and globally accepted accounting standards. In 2001 the IASB was re-constituted as the international body responsible for setting financial reporting standards and in 2002 the European Commission introduced a Regulation (Regulation (EC) No. 1606/2002 – the 'IAS Regulation') requiring the adoption of IASs (that is, EU-endorsed IFRSs) in the consolidated accounts of EU quoted (that is, publicly traded) companies. The application of international accounting standards is explained more fully in **Chapter 4**.

In July 2003, the UK government announced its intention to permit (but not require) all British companies (other than those automatically covered by the EU Regulation) to use international accounting standards as an alternative to UK domestic accounting standards. This legislative change was subsequently implemented by statutory instrument SI 2004 No. 2947 *The Companies Act 1985 (International Accounting Standards and Other Accounting Amendments) Regulations 2004*.

Despite the fact that the adoption of international accounting standards in the UK are impacting primarily on listed and AIM-listed parent companies and subsidiaries preparing group accounts, there is inevitability about the cascading effect of international harmonisation, so that all companies will sooner or later have to embrace international accounting practice and principles.

There is currently no international financial reporting standard for smaller enterprises ('International FRSSE') but the IASB is developing a 'set' of standards for SMEs with a project to this end currently on the IASB agenda. An exposure draft of a proposed IFRS for 'Small and Medium-sized Entities' (IFRS for SMEs) was issued in February 2007. The name of the standard was changed in May 2008 to 'IFRS for Private Entities'. The final IFRS for Private Entities is expected to be published later in 2009 but its universal application or adoption within the UK is yet to be determined. The ASB FRSSE is likely to continue its fundamental role as the accounting standard for small entities for some years to come.

The impact of international accounting standards for smaller companies is explained more fully in **Chapter 4** at **4.6.5**.

1.5 'WebFiling' – electronic filing of accounts

1.5.1 Electronic filing of abbreviated and dormant accounts

Increasingly, the unaudited annual accounts of small companies can be filed with the registrar of companies online by using the Companies House website at *www.companieshouse.gov.uk*.

Chapter 1 Introduction

Unaudited abbreviated accounts and dormant company accounts, which together comprise over 75 per cent of all accounts received each year by Companies House, can be filed online via the Companies House 'WebFiling' service or by using certain software packages. Details of the various software packages that are capable of filing electronically are available at the Companies House website.

1.5.2 Using the WebFiling template

Filing via the WebFiling service uses a template that registered users download and complete offline. A key feature of the template is that it contains in-built checks and helptext which assists with avoiding the omission of key information and making calculation errors in the balance sheet and notes.

Once downloaded, the template prompts the user to make choices that define the content of the dormant or abbreviated accounts. The accounts can then be completed offline over a period of time and saved drafts can then, for example, be emailed to colleagues or clients before submitting the final version to Companies House using a company 'authentication code'. This code is the electronic equivalent of a company officer's signature. The completed template is then saved on the computer as a locked copy of the accounts filed with Companies House.

1.5.3 Benefits of WebFiling

Electronic filing is an efficient method of filing accounts.

The main benefit of WebFiling (or, indeed software filing generally at Companies House), is that the registrar emails:

- acknowledgement of receipt; and
- confirmation of correct processing.

Acknowledgement of receipt is emailed immediately back to the filer of the accounts; in contrast to paper filing of accounts, electronic filing spares any doubt surrounding receipt of the document. Once the Companies House systems have processed the accounts, a further confirmation email is sent.

Electronic filing is particularly useful if accounts are filed near to the filing deadline when there is invariably a risk of incurring penalties for late filing in the event that Companies House does not receive the document in time.

Companies House rejects some 10 per cent of paper based accounts filed. An additional benefit of software filing is that Companies House is finding that it rejects only 1 per cent of WebFiled accounts.

To date, Companies House had received over 200,000 sets of dormant and abbreviated accounts and market research confirms that accountants and SME companies are becoming more aware of electronic filing systems and their willingness to use them is also growing.

1.5.4 Electronic filing and the development of XBRL

Electronic filing of accounts data is possible thanks to the development of XBRL (eXtensible Business Reporting Language). This is a language for formatting electronic financial information. It has been developed by the International XBRL Consortium (see *www.xbrl-uk.org* for more details) in conjunction with the international accounting community. At its heart has emerged an extensive XBRL taxonomy which is a comprehensive menu that comprises the thousands of accounting terms and relationships recognised in UK GAAP (Generally Accepted Accounting Principles).

Chapter 2 Companies Act 2006 and transition

2.1 Company law reform

Company law has undergone the most fundamental and wide-ranging scrutiny and reform since the ground-breaking Limited Liability Act of 1855. Converting the various proposals for reform into legislation, however, has proved a daunting task.

2.1.1 Company Law Review

Company law reform has been some ten years in the making. In March 1998, the Department of Trade and Industry launched a review of company law, the aim of which was the modernisation of core company law (that is, company law excluding legislation relating to insolvency, corporate taxation or the regulation of financial services). The review, inter alia, addressed the needs of small and closely held companies, which it recognised were not well served by existing legislation.

A basic principle of the review was that legislation should provide a coherent, self-contained statement of the law for the small and private company to which more detailed provisions could be added for larger and public companies – the so called 'think small first' principle. The review, and resulting reform, recognised a greater distinction between private companies and public companies.

The ultimate result of the review of company law was the Companies Act 2006, which received Royal Assent on 8 November 2006.

The overall achievement has been a much improved and modernised framework of company law, including a major simplification and restructuring for small companies.

2.1.2 Revised regulatory framework for company law

The legislation contained in the Companies Act 2006 is the most radical revision of the law since the mid-nineteenth century and is intended to last for at least a generation. To ensure that the law can be kept up to date and be responsive to change, the Government determined that a revised regulatory and institutional framework for company law should allow much of the technical detail to be amended by 'secondary legislation' (by regulations within statutory instruments), and permit a greater role for non-governmental institutions in keeping company law up to date and effective. The overall Company Law reporting regime may be summarised to include:

- devolved rule-making and enforcement (delegated to bodies such as the FRC and ASB);
- the regulatory and institutional framework under which the reporting and accounting aspects of company law are conducted;

The profession's framework for accountancy and audit regulation, as now established, is described in **2.1.3** and **Table 2.1**.

2.1.3 Framework for accountancy regulation

The framework of independent regulation for the accountancy profession in the UK has now been developed to provide overall arrangements for:

- general 'oversight' (scrutiny, monitoring and supervision) of the profession;
- securing appropriate ethical standards
- setting accounting, reporting and auditing standards; and
- investigation and disciplinary matters.

These reforms have resulted in:

- strengthening the audit and accountancy profession in the UK;
- providing a more effective system of regulation of the profession; and
- raising standards of corporate governance generally (and of listed companies in particular).

Table 2.1 sets out the structure for accountancy regulation under the FRC.

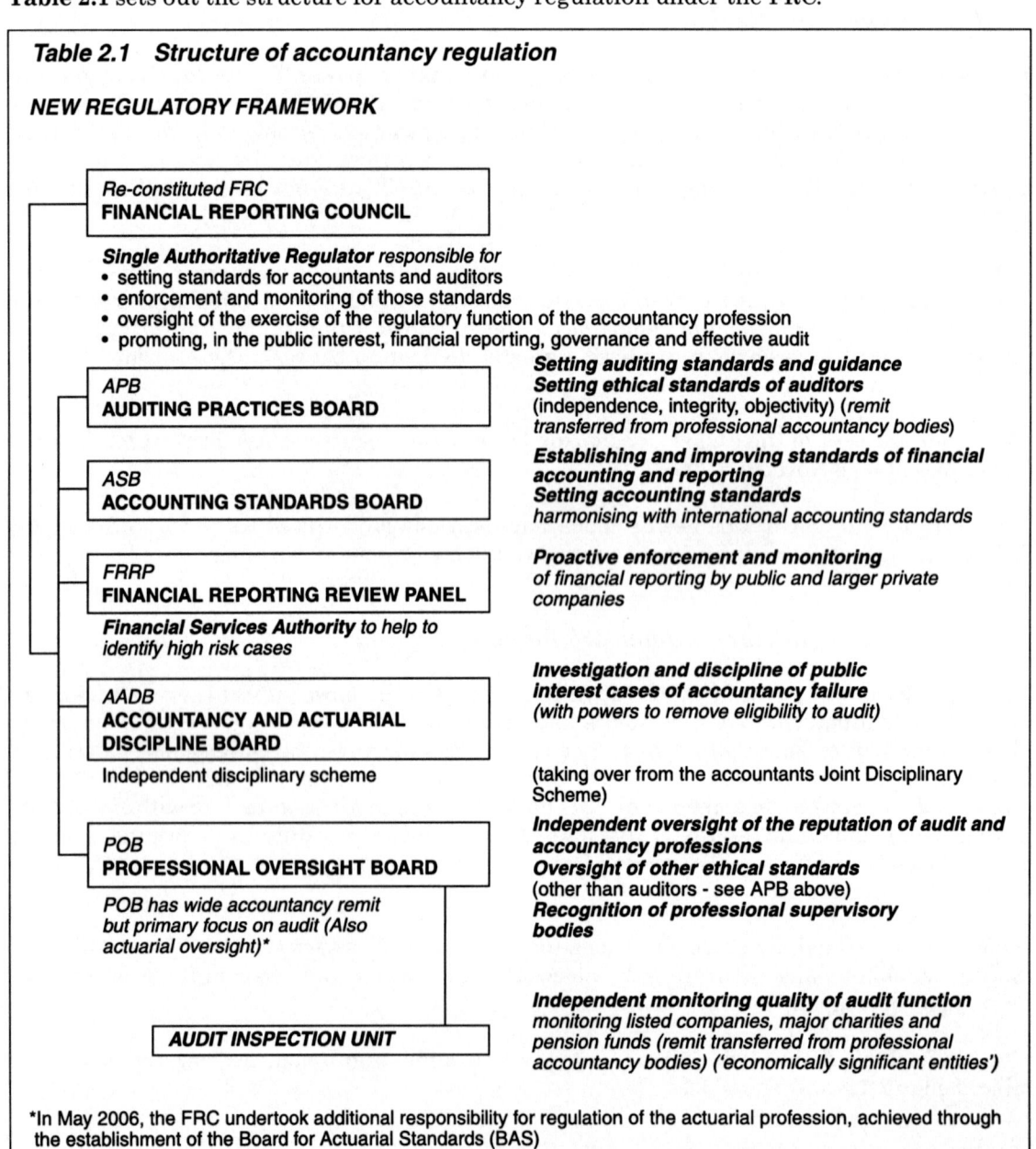

Table 2.1 Structure of accountancy regulation

NEW REGULATORY FRAMEWORK

Re-constituted FRC — FINANCIAL REPORTING COUNCIL

Single Authoritative Regulator responsible for
- setting standards for accountants and auditors
- enforcement and monitoring of those standards
- oversight of the exercise of the regulatory function of the accountancy profession
- promoting, in the public interest, financial reporting, governance and effective audit

APB — AUDITING PRACTICES BOARD
Setting auditing standards and guidance
Setting ethical standards of auditors (independence, integrity, objectivity) (*remit transferred from professional accountancy bodies*)

ASB — ACCOUNTING STANDARDS BOARD
Establishing and improving standards of financial accounting and reporting
Setting accounting standards
harmonising with international accounting standards

FRRP — FINANCIAL REPORTING REVIEW PANEL
Proactive enforcement and monitoring of financial reporting by public and larger private companies

Financial Services Authority to help to identify high risk cases

AADB — ACCOUNTANCY AND ACTUARIAL DISCIPLINE BOARD
Investigation and discipline of public interest cases of accountancy failure (with powers to remove eligibility to audit)

Independent disciplinary scheme
(taking over from the accountants Joint Disciplinary Scheme)

POB — PROFESSIONAL OVERSIGHT BOARD
Independent oversight of the reputation of audit and accountancy professions
Oversight of other ethical standards (other than auditors - see APB above)
Recognition of professional supervisory bodies

POB has wide accountancy remit but primary focus on audit (Also actuarial oversight)*

AUDIT INSPECTION UNIT
Independent monitoring quality of audit function
monitoring listed companies, major charities and pension funds (remit transferred from professional accountancy bodies) ('economically significant entities')

*In May 2006, the FRC undertook additional responsibility for regulation of the actuarial profession, achieved through the establishment of the Board for Actuarial Standards (BAS)

2.2 Annual accounts under Companies Act 2006

2.2.1 Basic approach

The Companies Act 2006 (originally the Company Law Reform Bill) received Royal Assent on 8 November 2006. Running to 701 pages of primary legislation together with 59 pages of index and comprising 47 Parts, 1300 sections and 16 Schedules, it is the longest Act ever. It consolidates virtually all existing companies legislation and introduces many reforms. Company law has been re-written and re-presented to make it easier to understand and more flexible – especially for smaller companies.

About a third of the new provisions represent a straightforward restatement of existing legislation in clearer and simpler language.

Working on the 'think small first' approach, company law is now presented on a basis that clearly recognises each of the following categories of company or group (CA 2006 s. 380):

- Small companies
- Larger private companies
- Public companies (other than quoted companies)
- Quoted public companies
- All companies.

Different provisions apply to different kinds of company; the main distinctions are between:

- companies subject to the 'small companies regime' (CA 2006 s. 381); and companies that are not subject to that regime; and
- quoted companies (CA 2006 s. 385) and companies that are not quoted.

Provisions applying to companies subject to the small companies regime appear in the legislation before the provisions applying to other companies (CA 2006 s. 380(4)).

The small companies regime applies to a company for a financial year in relation to which the company:

- qualifies as small (CA 2006 ss. 382–3); and
- is not excluded from the regime (CA 2006 s. 384).

The law, both within the Act itself and in supporting legislation issued in regulations under it, is clearly presented in its application. Small companies now have their own separate comprehensive code of accounting and reporting requirements, defining the generally accepted accounting practice relevant to them.

2.2.2 Implementation

Provisions of the Companies Act 2006 are being introduced by statutory instrument by means of 'commencement orders' and other supporting regulations in the months leading up to October 2009, the date by which the DTI have announced that all parts of the Act will be in force.

The accounts and report provisions of the Act relate to financial years **commencing on or after 6 April 2008**. As a consequence, the first annual accounts prepared under the new small companies regime will, in general terms, be for the year ending on 30 April 2009. Examples of the requirement to prepare accounts under the new Companies Act regime are set out in **Table 2.2. Early adoption of provisions of the new Companies Act regime is not permitted or appropriate.**

Chapter 2 Companies Act 2006 and Transition

Table 2.2 Implementation of accounting provisions – Examples
Accounts are required to be produced under the appropriate Companies Act framework as follows

Year end 2008	Accounts year to	Accounts regime	First CA 2006 accounts
31 March	31 March 2008	Companies Act 1985	31 March 2010
05 April	05 April 2008	Companies Act 1985	05 April 2009
30 April	30 April 2008	Companies Act 1985	30 April 2009
31 December	31 December 2008	Companies Act 1985	31 December 2009
Year end 2009			
31 March	31 March 2009	Companies Act 1985	31 March 2010
05 April	05 April 2009	Companies Act 2006	05 April 2009
30 April	30 April 2009	Companies Act 2006	30 April 2009
30 June	30 June 2009	Companies Act 2006	30 June 2009
31 December	31 December 2009	Companies Act 2006	31 December 2009

Short period accounts (of less than 12 months) which relate to financial periods **commencing on or after 6 April 2008** will be required to be produced under the appropriate Companies Act 2006 framework.

2.2.3 Small companies accounts regime

The new Act presents the 'small companies regime' (as it is termed) within

- Part 15 (Sections 380 to 474) – 'Accounts and reports', and
- Part 16 (Sections 475 to 539) – 'Audit' (where relevant for the smaller company).

These topics (which are the essence of this book) were to be found with considerable difficulty scattered around Companies Act 1985 (as amended from time to time) in Part VII of the old Companies Act 1985 and various Schedules to that Act (Schedules 4, 4A, 5, 6, 7, 8 and 8A, for example).

Preparing small company accounts will in future be governed by reference to:

- Companies Act 2006 Part 15 (relevant sections) (the 'primary legislation'), and
- Regulations made under statutory instruments for small companies ('secondary legislation'), covering the form and content of accounts and directors' report.

2.2.4 Structure of SI 2008 No. 409

SI 2008 No. 409 *The Small Companies and Groups (Accounts and Directors' Report) Regulations 2008.* These Regulations specify the form and content of the accounts and directors' report of companies subject to the small companies regime under Part 15 of the Companies Act 2006. CA 2006 s. 381 of the Act defines what is meant by "small companies regime".

> **Table 2.3 Contents and structure of SI 2008 No. 409**
>
> The contents and structure of SI 2008 No. 409 *The Small Companies and Groups (Accounts and Directors' Report) Regulations 2008* are as follows:
>
> Schedule 1 – *Companies Act individual accounts*
> - general rules and formats
> - accounting principles and rules
> - notes to the accounts
>
> Schedule 2 – *Information about related undertakings where company not preparing group accounts (Companies Act or IAS individual accounts)*
> - required disclosures
> - interpretation of references to 'beneficial interest'
>
> Schedule 3 – *Information about directors' benefits: remuneration (Companies Act or IAS accounts)*
> - information required to be disclosed
> - supplementary provisions
>
> Schedule 4 – *Companies Act abbreviated accounts for delivery to registrar of companies*
> - required balance sheet formats
> - notes to the accounts
>
> Schedule 5 – *Matters to be dealt with in directors' report*
>
> Schedule 6 – *Group accounts*
> - form and content of Companies Act group accounts
> - information about related undertakings where company preparing group accounts (Companies Act or IAS group accounts)
>
> Schedule 7 – *Interpretation of term 'provisions'*
>
> Schedule 8 – *General interpretation*
>
> SI 2008 No. 409 *The Small Companies and Groups (Accounts and Directors' Report) Regulations 2008* is reproduced in full in **Appendix E**

2.3 Main changes affecting small companies' accounts

For small companies, accounting rules and financial reporting procedure have in practice changed little from previous legislation under Companies Act 1985. However, while in essence the substance of company law as it affects the small company has remained largely unchanged, the manner of presentation within the legislation (and hence accessibility and comprehension) has been made considerably easier.

Although in essence the substance of company law for small companies accounting and reporting has remained unchanged under the new 'small companies regime', there are, nevertheless, changes that should be noted. These changes may be summarised as follows:

Small company thresholds: Following SI 2008 No. 393, the thresholds for determining whether a company qualifies as small under CA 2006 have been increased for financial years beginning on or after 6 April 2008.

'True and fair view' accounts (CA 2006 s. 393): There is a new obligation for the directors of a company (as preparers of accounts) not to approve accounts unless they are satisfied that they give a 'true and fair view'.

The directors of a company must not approve accounts unless they are satisfied that they give a true and fair view of the assets, liabilities, financial position and profit or loss of the company (for its 'individual accounts' (CA 2006 ss. 394–396)), or of the group (comprising the

Chapter 2 Companies Act 2006 and Transition

undertakings included in the consolidation as a whole) (for the company's group accounts). The auditor of a company must have regard to the directors' duty in this regard.

Small company group accounts (CA 2006 s. 398): a parent company subject to the small companies regime *may* prepare group accounts (as well as preparing individual accounts for the year). Previously this was phrased as '*need not* prepare group accounts'.

All other parent companies (unless otherwise exempt) *must* prepare group accounts in addition to individual accounts (CA 2006 s. 399). This means that the previous specific medium-sized company group accounts exemption has therefore been removed. A parent company may nevertheless be exempt as result of the company being included in the EEA or non-EEA accounts of a larger group, or where none of the group's subsidiary undertakings need be included in the consolidation (ss. 400–402).

There is one small modification to the profit and loss account format for group accounts (concerning income from interests in associated undertakings and participating interests).

Medium-sized companies: statutory accounting provisions for medium-sized companies have been separated from those for the 'small companies regime' to make them easier to identify (CA 2006 ss. 465–467 and SI 2008 No. 410 *The Large and Medium-sized Companies and Groups (Accounts and Reports) Regulations 2008*).

A medium-sized parent company is no longer exempt from the requirement to prepare group accounts.

Directors' benefits – advances, credit and guarantees (CA 2006 s. 413): new disclosure requirements of advances and credits granted, and guarantees of any kind entered into, by the company to or on behalf of its directors. These replace previous provisions for transactions with directors (covering loans, quasi-loans, credit transactions and related guarantees and securities). (See **Chapter 6** at **6.11** for small companies.) 'Advances, credit and guarantees' are not defined in CA 2006.

CA 2006 s. 413

Companies will no longer be required to disclose transactions made between the company and officers other than directors.

Directors' report – disclosure of directors' interests: there is no longer a requirement for companies to maintain a register of dealings in their shares by directors and their spouses, civil partners or children. Nor are directors now required to provide details of their other directorships.

Directors' report – liability for false or misleading statements (CA 2006 s. 463): new provisions deal with directors' liability for narrative statements within the directors report (or summary financial statement), in the event of a statement being 'untrue, misleading or reckless' or if an omission could constitute a 'dishonest concealment of a material fact'.

Directors report – Business Review: A company subject to the 'small companies' regime' is *not* required to provide the new enhanced business review in its directors' report (CA 2006 s. 417(1)).

Approval and signing of accounts (CA 2006 s. 414): the copy of the accounts (balance sheet) delivered to the registrar will no longer be required to be actually signed by a director – otherwise approval and signing procedures remain unchanged.

Filing and circulating accounts (CA 2006 s. 442(2)): the 'period for filing' accounts of a private company (including 'abbreviated accounts' of a small company (CA 2006 s. 444(3)), where appropriate) is now reduced to *nine months* after the end of the 'relevant accounting reference period'.

All private companies must send copies of annual accounts and reports to members for whom the company has a 'current address' (CA 2006 s. 423) no later than when the accounts are filed (CA 2006 s. 424(2)).

Audit and limitation of liability: New disclosure requirements for liability limitation agreements (relevant only to audited small companies and where such an agreement is in place for a financial year) (CA 2006 Part 16 – Audit s.534–538).

Charitable companies (CA 2006 s. 1175): Charitable companies will henceforth be required to comply with the requirements of charity law rather company law. Part VII of the Companies Act 1985 (Accounts and audit) are amended in accordance with Schedule 9 to the Companies Act 2006 so as to remove the special provisions about companies that are charities. The provisions relating to the accounts scrutiny of small charities under CA 1985 s. 249A have therefore been removed.

Companies Act 2006 represents UK legislation and is therefore applicable in Northern Ireland.

2.4 Auditing and audit reports

The new company law basically restates the previous requirements under Companies Act 1985 for the audit of company accounts, except for removal of provisions for small charitable companies (see **2.3** above) and new provisions concerning public sector companies (CA 2006 s. 475).

Audit is covered in Part 16 of Companies Act 2006, which contains provisions concerning , for example, the requirement for audited accounts, the appointment of auditors, the auditor's report, the duties and rights of auditors, and removal, resignation, etc.

The statutory sections within Part 16 are outlined in **Appendix A.**

The audit report must henceforth include an introduction identifying the annual accounts and the financial reporting framework under which they are prepared, together with a description of the scope of the audit identifying the auditing standards adopted.

In essence, under CA 2006 s. 495, the auditor will henceforth be required to report his opinion on four elements:

(1) ***True and fair view*** – whether the annual accounts show a 'true and fair view' (having regard to the directors' statutory duty under CA 2006 s. 393(1));
(2) ***Relevant reporting framework*** – whether the accounts have been prepared in accordance with the relevant financial reporting framework;
(3) ***Appropriate legislation*** – whether the accounts have been prepared in accordance with CA 2006 (Part 15) or IAS (IAS Regulation Article 4), if applicable; and
(4) ***Form of report or emphasis*** – whether the report is 'unqualified or qualified' or contains reference to any emphasis of any matters without qualifying the report.

Companies Act 2006 section 495 (Auditor's report on company's annual accounts) is reproduced in full in **Chapter 14** at **Table 14.1.**

The auditor's report must, as previously required, state the name of the auditor and be signed and dated. However, where the auditor is a firm, the report must now be signed by the 'senior statutory auditor' in his own name, for and on behalf of the auditor (CA 2006 s. 504).

Other audit related changes include some significant changes concerning appointment and resignation, eligibility, and limitation of liability.

2.5 Contents of annual accounts and reports

Table 2.6 below compares the contents of the annual reports of small companies, large companies (public and private), and other companies following company law reform:

Table 2.6 Contents of annual reports

Annual reports – Companies Act 2006

	Small Companies	Large Public or Private Companies*	Other Public or Private Companies
Primary Financial Statements Form and content determined by:			
•Statutory regulation	✓	✓	✓
•Accounting Standards and international accounting standards		✓	✓
•FRSSE/Accounting Standards	✓		
Abbreviated Accounts (*Small companies*)	✓		✓ ('Medium sized' private companies only)
Group accounts	[✓] (optional)	✓	✓
Operating and Financial Review (OFR) ASB 'best practice' reporting standard 'Operating and Financial Review (OFR)' (January 2006)		✓ (Quoted Public Companies)	
Directors' Report – including enhanced Business review		✓	✓
Directors' Report **Directors' Remuneration Report**	✓	✓ (Quoted Public Companies)	
Summary Financial Statement (Optional) Summary Financial Statement (extended to include, where appropriate, 'OFR' matters). *Now available to all companies (including audited private companies). Previously available only to listed companies.*	✓	✓	✓

Chapter 3 General accounting provisions

3.1 Introduction

This chapter summarises the company accounts provisions of the Companies Act 2006 which lays down provisions relating to:

- prescriptive formats of accounts;
- the content of accounts, and
- principles and rules for determining amounts included in the accounts.

The chapter summarises accounts provisions of the Companies Act 2006, insofar as they relate to accounts ('individual accounts') that are prepared in accordance with the Companies Act 2006 s. 394. 'Abbreviated accounts' (modified statutory accounts) are considered separately in **Chapter 8**. Matters relating to small groups of companies are covered in **Chapter 9**.

Annual accounts may be prepared:

- as 'Companies Act individual accounts' (CA 2006 s. 396) or 'Companies Act group accounts' (CA 2006 s. 404); or
- in accordance with international accounting standards ('IAS individual accounts' or 'IAS group accounts') (CA 2006 s. 395(1)).

Unless otherwise indicated, this chapter summarises and comments upon the accounts provisions of the Companies Act 2006 insofar as they relate to Companies Act accounts, that is, prepared in accordance with the requirements of the Companies Act 2006.

Appendix B reproduces the whole of Part 15 (ss. 380 to 474 of the Companies Act 2006) – 'Accounts and Reports'.

3.2 Accounts

Full accounts prepared for shareholders must be prepared for all companies, irrespective of size. *s. 394*

The full accounts of a 'small' company, however, are less detailed with reduced disclosure requirements (see **Chapter 6** 'Contents of small company accounts'). A small company may also take advantage of the FRSSE (see **Chapter 10**).

A company qualifying as 'small' or 'medium-sized' (see **Chapter 5**) may, in addition, prepare 'abbreviated' accounts for filing with the Registrar of Companies.

Depending on certain size criteria (see **Chapter 11**), small companies may be exempt from the requirement for audit. Dormant companies may also take advantage of audit exemption.

Company accounts are produced from the company's underlying financial records ('adequate accounting records') as explained at **3.10** below (CA 2006 ss. 386–389).

Chapter 3 General accounting provisions

> **Table 3.1 Individual accounts (Companies Act 2006 s. 396)**
>
> Each financial year, the directors must prepare individual accounts comprising:
>
> - a balance sheet, and
> - a profit and loss account
>
> Showing a true and fair view of:
>
> - the state of affairs at the year end, and
> - the profit or loss for the financial year
>
> Complying (as to form, content and notes) with the provisions of:
>
> - SI 2008 No. 409 *The Small Companies and Groups (Accounts and Directors' Report) Regulations 2008*
> - any additional information (or departure from requirement) necessary to show a true and fair view.
>
> Companies Act 2006 s. 396 is set out in full in **Appendix B**.

3.3 'True and fair' view

s. 393 There is a fundamental requirement for full accounts (individual accounts or group accounts) to show a 'true and fair' view. The directors of a company must not approve accounts unless they are satisfied that they give a true and fair view of the company's assets, liabilities, financial position and profit or loss.

The requirement for full accounts to show a 'true and fair' view applies irrespective of whether or not the accounts are subject to audit. Any decision concerning the method of accounting or means of disclosing information must take this basic requirement into account.

The basic accounting principle is that annual accounts should show a 'true and fair' view, a term that has never been defined in statute or case law (but see 4.4.1).

In essence, accounts are deemed to present a 'true and fair view' if they:

- comply with any relevant legislation or regulatory requirement;
- comply with accounting standards and generally recognised practice (GAAP – see **Chapter 4**);
- comply with recognised and accepted industry based practice;
- provide an unbiased (fair and reasonable) presentation;
- are compiled with sufficient accuracy within the bounds of materiality; and
- faithfully represent the underlying commercial activity (the concept of 'substance over legal form').

The requirement for accounts to give a 'true and fair view' is also embodied within European Accounting Directives. In the case of IAS accounts, there is a requirement under international accounting standards that such accounts must achieve a 'fair presentation'.

'True and fair view accounts' (not a statutory term or specifically defined but used in this book for convenience) are financial statements intended to give a true and fair view of the financial position and profit or loss (or income and expenditure) of an entity.

A 'true and fair view' is required to be given of the state of affairs of the company (and/or consolidated undertakings) as at the end of the financial year and of the profit or loss of the company (and/or consolidated undertakings so far as concerns members of the parent company) for the financial year.

Where compliance with the provisions of CA 2006 as to the matters to be included in 'annual accounts' ('individual accounts' or 'group accounts') or the notes would not be sufficient to give a true and fair view, the necessary additional information must be given in the accounts or in a note to them.

If in *special circumstances* such compliance is inconsistent with the requirement to show a 'true and fair view', the directors must depart from the relevant provision of CA 2006 to the extent necessary to show a 'true and fair view' and must explain such departure in a note to the accounts (the true and fair 'override' principle).

FRS 18

The 'true and fair view' has the ultimate legal override; an entity may override accounting standards only to give a 'true and fair view' and this would be only in exceptional circumstances. A departure from an accounting standard must be justified and explained.

3.4 Format of accounts

The form and content of accounts is governed by regulations made under the Companies Act 2006.

The form and content of Companies Act individual accounts is determined in accordance with:

- SI 2008 No. 409 *The Small Companies and Groups (Accounts and Directors' Report) Regulations 2008* for small companies.
- SI 2008 No. 410 *The Large and Medium-sized Companies and Groups (Accounts and Reports) Regulations 2008* for medium-sized companies and large companies.

SI 2008 No. 409 The *Small Companies and Groups (Accounts and Directors' Report) Regulations 2008* is set out in full in **Appendix E** and is discussed in greater detail in Chapter **6**.

Schedules within SI 2008 No. 409 and SI 2008 No. 410 prescribe the required formats from which companies may choose for Companies Act individual and group accounts. Formats which are most commonly used by small companies are illustrated in **Chapter 6**.

Once a format has been adopted, the company must use the same format for subsequent years unless, in the directors' opinion, there are special reasons for changing; these must be disclosed in the year of change.

Sch 1.2

Every balance sheet and profit and loss account must show the items listed in the adopted format if, of course, they apply either in the financial year or the preceding year.

Sch 1.1

Adopting a particular format is not as restricting as it may seem, as there are a variety of options, for example:

Sch 1.3

- departure is allowed if it is made to ensure a true and fair view (see above);
- certain (Arabic number) headings may be combined (provided combination is disclosed);
- immaterial items may be disregarded;
- information can be given in greater detail than prescribed and items not listed in a format may be included, if directors so wish; and
- certain information may be given in notes instead of on the face of the accounts.

Sch 1.10(2)
Sch 1.4

A company's accounts may include other items not listed in the various formats but there are three specific items which may not be treated as assets in a company's balance sheet:

(a) preliminary expenses;
(b) expenses of, and commission on, any issue of shares or debentures; and
(c) costs of research.

Sch 1.3(2)

Where there is no amount to be shown for a format item for the financial year, a heading or sub-heading corresponding to the item must not be included, unless an amount can be shown

Chapter 3 General accounting provisions

Sch 1.5

for the item in question for the immediately preceding financial year under the relevant format heading or sub-heading.

Sch 1.7

For every balance sheet or profit and loss account item, the corresponding amount for the immediately preceding financial year must also be shown. Where that corresponding preceding year amount is not comparable, the current year amount may be adjusted, but particulars of the non-comparability and of any adjustment must be disclosed in a note to the accounts.

Sch 1.6

Every profit and loss account must show the amount of a company's profit or loss on ordinary activities before taxation. (See **Chapter 6** at **6.6**.)

3.5 Accounting principles

Company accounts are required to be prepared in accordance with the principles set out in:

- Schedule 1 of SI 2008 No. 409 – small companies
- Schedule 6 of SI 2008 No. 409 – small company groups
- Schedule 1 of SI 2008 No. 410 – medium-sized (and large) companies
- Schedule 6 of SI 2008 No. 410 – medium-sized (and large company) groups

Sch 1.10–15

These principles are the fundamental accounting concepts that underlie accounts and are also incorporated within accounting standards (FRSs and SSAPs) generally and (for small companies adopting it) the FRSSE.

The basic statutory accounting principles are as follows:

- *Going concern* – The company or reporting entity is to be presumed to be carrying on business as a going concern.
- *Consistency* – Accounting policies must be applied consistently within the same accounts and from one financial year to the next.
- *Prudence* – The amount of any item must be determined on a prudent basis and in particular:
  (a) only profits realised at the balance sheet date must be included in the profit and loss account, and
  (b) all liabilities having arisen in respect of the financial year (or preceding financial year) must be taken into account (including those liabilities becoming apparent up to the date of approval of the accounts (in accordance with CA 2006 s. 414)).
- *Accruals* – All income and charges relating to the financial year to which the accounts relate must be taken into account, without regard to the date of receipt or payment.
- *Individual determination* – In determining the aggregate amount of any item, the amount of each individual asset or liability that is taken into account must be determined separately.

Sch 1.15
Sch 1.8

- *Netting* – Amounts in respect of items representing assets or income must not be set off against amounts in respect of items representing liabilities or expenditure (as the case may be), or vice versa.
- *Substance of transactions* – In determining how amounts are presented within the accounts, regard should be had to the substance of the reported transaction or arrangement in accordance with GAAP.

Sch 1.9

If it appears to the company's directors that there are special reasons for departing from any of the accounting principles in preparing the company's accounts in respect of any financial year they may do so. Particulars of the departure, the reasons for it and its effect must be given in a note to the accounts.

FRS 18
FRSSE

Accounting standards (FRSs generally) enhance the above principles by determining that accounting policies adopted should be relevant, reliable, comparable and understandable.

Sch 1.16–29

For fixed assets, stocks, investments and goodwill, rules regarding valuation, accounting and disclosure are laid down.

Historical cost principles are stated as the normal method of accounting but alternative bases (eg revaluation and current cost) are allowed provided that details and related historical cost figures are disclosed. The 'alternative accounting rules' are illustrated in **12.5**.

Sch 1.30–35

Only 'realised' profits can be included in the profit and loss account.

Sch 1.13(a)

In determining for accounting purposes 'realised profits' (and 'realised losses'), such profits or losses mean profits or losses of the company that fall to be treated as realised in accordance with principles generally accepted at the time when the accounts are prepared, unless the Companies Act 2006 specifies some other treatment.

ss. 853(4)–(5)

Financial instruments, including derivatives, may be included under the Companies Act 2006 at fair value.

Sch 1.36–41

It should be noted, however, that companies adopting 'fair value accounting' rules cannot apply the FRSSE, although this does not preclude accounting for fixed assets and investments at valuation.

3.6 Notes to accounts – disclosures

For small companies, Schedule 1 of SI 2008 No. 409 *The Small Companies and Groups (Accounts and Directors' Report) Regulations 2008* sets out the information required to be disclosed in the notes to a small company's accounts, covering the following heads:

Sch 1.42–63

- reserves and dividends;
- disclosure of accounting policies;
- share capital and redeemable shares;
- fixed assets;
- financial instruments valued at fair value;
- investment property and living animals and plants at fair value;
- reserves and provisions;
- details of indebtedness (including payments by instalments and nature of security);
- guarantees and other financial commitments;
- particulars (analysis) of turnover;
- preceding year items include in profit and loss account – effect of inclusion;
- exceptional items – the effect of transactions (within ordinary activities) that are exceptional by size or incidence;
- sums denominated in foreign currencies – basis of translation into sterling; and
- dormant companies acting as agent.

Schedule 1 of SI 2008 No. 409 ('The form and content of accounts prepared by small companies') is set out in **Appendix E**.

The enhanced disclosures for medium-sized companies are contained in SI 2008 No. 410 *The Large and Medium-sized Companies and Groups (Accounts and Reports) Regulations 2008*.

3.7 Directors' report – contents and requirements

The directors of a company must prepare a directors' report for each financial year of the company.

s. 415

Where the company is a parent company, and the directors of the company prepare group accounts, the directors' report must be a consolidated report (a 'group directors' report') covering all the undertakings included in the consolidation. A group directors' report may, where appropriate, give greater emphasis to matters that are significant to the undertakings included in the consolidation, taken as a whole.

Chapter 3 General accounting provisions

Small companies, however, are permitted to prepare a directors' report that is much reduced in content, omitting much of the information otherwise required to be included in the directors' report of a medium-sized or large company. (See **Table 6.6** at **6.8**.)

Basically, the directors of larger companies are required to prepare a directors' report complying with CA 2006 provisions as follows:

- general matters (s. 416) including SI 2008 No. 410 disclosures;
- business review (s. 417);
- matters covering company and subsidiaries (SI 2008 No. 410)) (parent company preparing group accounts); and
- statement as to disclosure of information to auditors (audited accounts) (s. 418).

s. 420 Quoted companies are also required to prepare:

- a directors' remuneration report (s. 421), covering aspects of directors' remuneration such as remuneration details, company policy, service contracts, share options and pension disclosures, and
- operating and financial review (OFR).

The directors' report of a small company is covered in **Chapter 6** at **6.8**.

3.8 Group accounts

A parent company (other than a small parent company (see **9.1**)) which has 'subsidiary undertakings' is required (with certain exceptions) to prepare group accounts in the form of consolidated accounts of the company and its subsidiary undertakings, as if they were a single company. Consolidation is not restricted to subsidiaries which are companies.

Group accounts (when prepared) are required to comply with the provisions of the Companies Act 2006 as to the form and content of consolidated accounts and additional information to be given. Regulations under CA 2006 provided by SI 2008 No. 409 Schedules 6 and 3 (Small companies) and SI 2008 No. 410 Schedules 6, 4 and 5 (large and medium-sized companies), require *inter alia* the following accounting for consolidations:

- elimination of group transactions;
- provisions for acquisition and merger accounting;
- treatment and disclosure of 'minority interests';
- non-consolidated subsidiary undertakings;
- joint ventures and associated undertakings; and
- preparation 'as if' the group were a single company.

s. 405(2) A subsidiary may be excluded from consolidation on the grounds of immateriality and *must* be excluded in the following circumstances:

FRS 2 - severe long-term restrictions;
FRS 2 - temporary control – holding with a view to subsequent resale;

The statutory format amendments for group accounts are included in **Appendix C**.

The exemptions available for small and medium-sized groups are explained in **Chapter 9**.

Exemptions otherwise available for groups generally are under:

- CA 2006 s. 400 (company included in EEA accounts of larger group);
- CA 2006 s. 401 (company included in non-EEA accounts of larger group); and

- CA 2006 s. 402 (company none of whose subsidiary undertakings need be included in the consolidation).

3.9 Audit reports

Full statutory accounts (together with an audit, if appropriate) are required for shareholders for all companies (see **6.2**).

For companies other than those applying provisions for companies subject to the small companies regime, the availability or otherwise of audit exemption will determine whether the accounts should be accompanied by an auditors' report (see **Chapter 11**).   *s. 475*

The auditors must consider whether the information given in the directors' report is consistent with the accounts and must state that fact in their report. There is no requirement to state in what respect it is inconsistent.   *s. 496*

Where abbreviated accounts are prepared (under the 'small' and 'medium-sized' company filing provisions), a special auditors' report is required stating that in the auditors' opinion: *s. 449(2)*

- the company is entitled to deliver abbreviated accounts; and
- the abbreviated accounts have been properly prepared.

3.10 Adequate accounting records

Companies are required to keep 'adequate accounting records' (previously referred to as 'proper accounting records') in accordance with Companies Act 2006 s. 386. Company accounts are produced from these underlying financial records.

Companies Act 2006 s. 386 is summarised in **Table 3.2** and is set out in full in **Appendix B**.

Table 3.2 Adequate accounting records

A company is required to keep accounting records ('adequate accounting records') which are sufficient to show and explain the company's transactions. The accounting records must:

- disclose with reasonable accuracy, *at any time*, the financial position of the company *at that time*;
- enable the directors to ensure that any accounts required to be prepared comply with the requirements of CA 2006 (and, where applicable, of Article 4 of the IAS Regulation) and, for example, that the balance sheet and profit and loss accounts comply in form and content;
- contain entries from day to day of all receipts and expenditure (with sufficient identifying detail); and
- contain a record of company assets and liabilities.

If the company deals in goods, the accounting records must also contain statements of:

- stock held at the year end;
- stocktaking (records and procedures) underlying the year end stock; and
- all goods sold and purchased (except for retail sales), in sufficient detail to identify the goods and the buyers and sellers.

A parent company must ensure that any subsidiary undertaking keeps such accounting records as ensure compliance with CA 2006 or IAS.

Comment:
Directors should be constantly aware of the company's financial position and progress. The exact nature and extent of the accounting systems and management information needed to exercise adequate control will depend on the nature and extent of the company's business.

Chapter 3 General accounting provisions

> Adequate control over records and transactions involves monitoring:
>
> - cash;
> - debtors and creditors;
> - stock and work in progress;
> - capital expenditure;
> - contractual arrangements, and
> - plans and budgets.

Accounting records are required by Companies Act 2006 s. 388(4)) to be preserved for:

- 3 years (private company); or
- 6 years (public company),

from the date on which they are made although, having regard to other legislation, it is generally considered that documents should be kept for at least six years (and 12 years in the event of contracts under seal).

3.11 Approval and signature of accounts

The directors' report, statutory accounts and the auditors' report all require appropriate approval and signature.

s. 414

A company's annual accounts must be approved by the board of directors and signed on behalf of the board by a director of the company. The signature must be on the company's individual balance sheet and the name of the signatory must be stated.

s. 419(2)

The directors' report must also be approved by the board of directors and signed on their behalf by a director *or* the secretary of the company; the name of the signatory must be similarly stated.

s. 503

The auditors' report must state the names of the auditors and be signed and dated. Where the auditor is an individual, the report must be signed by him. Where the auditor is a firm, the report must be signed by the senior statutory auditor in his own name, for and on behalf of the firm of auditors.

ss. 444(5) 450(3)

The above requirements also apply to the approval and directors' signature of abbreviated accounts.

ss. 414(3) 419(2)

The balance sheet and directors' report of a small company which have been prepared in accordance with the special provisions for companies subject to the small companies regime must each contain a statement by the directors to that effect in a prominent position above the signature (see **6.9**).

If the accounts are prepared in accordance with the provisions applicable to companies subject to the small companies regime, the balance sheet must contain a statement to that effect in a prominent position above the signature.

3.12 Publication of non-statutory accounts

s. 434

If a company publishes any of its statutory accounts (as required under s. 441) (other than a summary financial statement under s. 426), they must be accompanied by the auditor's report on those accounts (unless the company is exempt from audit and the directors have taken advantage of that exemption). A company that prepares statutory group accounts for a financial year must not publish its statutory individual accounts for that year without also publishing with them its statutory group accounts.

Publication of non-statutory accounts

If a company publishes non-statutory accounts, it must publish with them a statement indicating: *s. 435(1)*

- that they are not the company's statutory accounts;
- whether statutory accounts dealing with any financial year with which the non-statutory accounts purport to deal have been delivered to the registrar; and
- whether an auditor's report has been made on the company's statutory accounts for any such financial year, and if so whether the report:

    (a) was qualified or unqualified, or included a reference to any matters to which the auditor drew attention by way of emphasis without qualifying the report; or
    (b) contained a statement under CA 2006 s. 498(2) (accounting records or returns inadequate or accounts or directors' remuneration report (where applicable) not agreeing with records and returns), or CA 2006 s. 498(3) (failure to obtain necessary information and explanations).

A company must not publish with any non-statutory accounts the auditor's report on the company's statutory accounts. *s. 435(2)*

'Non-statutory accounts' are accounts or other published financial information that are not the company's statutory accounts. Simplified accounting information, abridged accounts, announcements of company results to employees or the press, might be classified non-statutory accounts. *s. 435(3)*

A full audit report under CA 2006 s. 495 must *not* to be published with non-statutory accounts.

Chapter 4 Accounts and accounting standards

4.1 Basic contents of financial statements

'Financial statements are a structured financial representation of the financial position of and transactions undertaken by an enterprise.'

In its *Statement of Principles for financial reporting*, issued in December 1999, the Accounting Standards Board set out the concepts that underlie the preparation and presentation of financial statements. The ASB states that the objective of financial statements is:

> 'to provide information about the reporting entity's financial performance and financial position that is useful to a wide range of users for assessing the stewardship of management and for making economic decisions.'

To meet this objective, accounting information is normally presented in the form of a structured set of financial statements comprising:

- primary statements, and
- supporting notes, related to the primary statements.

Together these will form the true and fair view 'accounts' (as the term is used in this book).

4.2 Primary statements

Primary statements comprise the profit and loss account (income statement); the statement of total recognised gains and losses (if necessary in addition to the profit and loss account); the balance sheet (assets, liabilities, and equity), and the cash flow statement. Notes to the financial statements amplify or explain items in the primary statements (for example, accounting policies).

The formats of the primary statements, as they apply to small companies, are determined as in **Table 4.1**.

Table 4.1 Formats of the primary statements

Primary statements	Format
Financial performance	
Profit and loss account	CA 2006 under SI 2008 No. 409 Sch 1 (Small companies) amplified by FRSSE/relevant FRSs.
Statement of total recognised gains and losses (STRGL)	FRSSE/FRS 3 *Reporting financial performance*.
Financial position	
Balance sheet	CA 2006 under SI 2008 No. 409 Sch 1 (Small companies) amplified by FRSSE/relevant FRSs.
Cash flow	
Cash flow statement	FRSSE (voluntary)/FRS 1 *Cash flow statements*.

Chapter 4 Accounts and accounting standards

A statement of total recognised gains and losses includes those items, being gains or losses that are recognised in the period, which do not pass through the profit and loss account. Gains, such as revaluation surpluses which are recognised but not necessarily realised in the period, are dealt with in the statement.

4.3 Cash flow statements

FRS 1 *Cash flow statements* requires, with exceptions, all entities producing true and fair view accounts to include a cash flow statement within the accounts drawn up in accordance with the FRS.

Small companies and other equivalent sized entities are exempt from the requirement to produce a cash flow statement (but are, nevertheless 'encouraged' by the FRSSE to provide such a statement on a voluntary disclosure basis). Wholly-owned subsidiary undertakings are also generally exempted.

Medium-sized and larger companies, and small ineligible companies (including, for example, a public, banking or insurance company or certain authorised entities under FSMA 2000), are required to prepare cash flow statements in accordance with FRS 1.

The form of cash flow statement indicated as voluntary disclosure by the FRSSE for smaller entities is set out in **Chapter 10 (Table 10.4)**.

The parent company of a small group, entitled to the exemption from preparing group accounts, is (subject to the voluntary provisions of the FRSSE, if applicable) exempted from preparing a cash flow statement (whether its own individual statement or a consolidated one), whether or not group accounts are actually prepared.

4.4 Accounting standards

4.4.1 True and Fair

The basic accounting principle is that annual accounts should show a 'true and fair' view, a term that has never been defined precisely in statute or case law, although eminent authority has been given over the years in the form of legal opinion.

In essence, accounts are deemed to present a 'true and fair view' if they:

- comply with any relevant legislation or regulatory requirement;
- comply with accounting standards and generally recognised practice (GAAP – see below);
- comply with recognised and accepted industry based practice;
- provide an unbiased (fair and reasonable) presentation;
- are compiled with sufficient accuracy within the bounds of materiality; and
- faithfully represent the underlying commercial activity (the concept of 'substance over legal form').

Companies that prepare Companies Act accounts in accordance with UK (ASB) accounting standards are subject to the overriding requirement of CA 2006 (and regulations made under it) that accounts give a 'true and fair view', which, in all but highly exceptional cases, requires compliance with UK accounting standards.

Those companies adopting international accounting standards (IAS) are required to present accounts that are 'fairly presented'. Although in essence this may constitute a 'true and fair' view, unlike ASB accounting standards, IAS are explicitly part of the law rather than deriving from it. The true and fair override (referred to in **4.4.2**) no longer applies to companies which prepare their accounts in accordance with IAS.

UK tax legislation (Finance Act 1998 s. 42 as amended by Finance Act 2002) now requires that the profits of a trade, profession or vocation be computed in accordance with generally accepted accounting practice on an accounting basis which gives a true and fair view, subject to any adjustment required by tax law in computing those profits. *FA 2005 s. 80(1)*

FA 1998 s. 42

In the absence of statutory definition, the FRC (Financial Reporting Council) commissioned further legal opinion to confirm the continued relevance of the 'true and fair' concept to the preparation and audit of financial statements following the enactment of the Companies Act 2006 and the introduction of international accounting standards. The opinion received is available at:

http://www.frc.org.uk/documents/pagemanager/frc/T&F%20Opinion%2021%20April%202008.pdf

This recent legal opinion (May 2008) has endorsed the analysis of previous opinions and confirmed the centrality of the 'true and fair view' concept in UK financial reporting.

4.4.2 Company law and 'true and fair view'

The requirement for accounts to give a 'true and fair view' is now embodied within the UK Companies legislation and also European accounting directives. The principles derive from and are laid down in CA 2006 s. 393.

Companies Act accounts must show a 'true and fair view'. The directors of a company must not approve these statutory accounts unless they are satisfied that the accounts give a true and fair view of the assets, liabilities, financial position and profit or loss:

- of the company (in the case of the company's individual accounts); and
- of the undertakings included in the consolidation as a whole, so far as concerns members of the company (in the case of the company's group accounts). *s. 393(1)*

For a company that is subject to audit, the auditor of the company in carrying out his functions in relation to the company's annual accounts under CA 2006 must have regard to the directors' statutory duty in this respect. *s. 393(2)*

The 'true and fair view' has the ultimate legal override; an entity may override accounting standards only to give a 'true and fair view' and this would be only in exceptional circumstances. A departure from an accounting standard must be justified and explained.

The 'true and fair view' override no longer applies to companies which (from the 1 January 2005) prepare their accounts in accordance with IAS. Nevertheless, although the application of IAS (including IFRS) is presumed to result in a 'fair presentation', in extremely rare circumstances it may be necessary for a company to depart from strict compliance with IFRS in the interests of fair presentation.

4.4.3 Accounting standards

Accounting standards are defined as 'such standards as are, in accordance with their terms, relevant to the company's circumstances and to the accounts'. *s. 464*

For the purposes of Part 15 of CA 2006 (Accounts and Reports) the term 'Accounting standards' means statements of standard accounting practice issued by such body or bodies as may be prescribed by regulations or the Secretary of State. Accounting standards applicable to a company's annual accounts are such standards as are relevant to the company's circumstances and to the accounts.

Chapter 4 Accounts and accounting standards

The Accounting Standards Board (ASB) is the prescribed standard setting body for the purposes of CA 2006 s. 464.

'Accounting standards', in the context of this chapter, are UK (ASB) accounting standards considered on the basis discussed in **4.4.1** above, particularly the requirement to show a 'true and fair' view.

The UK Accounting Standards Board, in its foreword to *Accounting Standards,* has stated that:

> 'Accounting standards are authoritative statements of how particular types of transaction and other events should be reflected in financial statements and accordingly compliance with accounting standards will be necessary for financial statements to give a true and fair view'.

Accounting standards are applicable to financial statements of a reporting entity which are intended to give a true and fair view of its state of affairs at the balance sheet date and of its profit or loss (or income and expenditure) for the financial period ending on that date.

Accounting standards do not need to be applied to items judged to be immaterial.

In preparing accounts giving a true and fair view, a company should therefore follow any applicable accounting standard (FRS or SSAP) unless there are good reasons for not doing so.

Accounting standards may comprise:

- Financial Reporting Standards (FRSs including the FRSSE) and UITF Abstracts;
- Statements of Standard Accounting Practice (SSAPs) (that is, accounting standards adopted by the ASB but issued prior to its formation); and
- International Financial Reporting Standards (IFRSs including IASs and SIC interpretations) (for those companies adopting them – primarily, in UK, quoted or publicly traded groups of companies only).

Recent years have seen a programme of increasing convergence (that is, harmonisation) of domestic UK and international (including US) financial reporting on the basis of globally accepted accounting standards (see **4.6** below).

FRSs issued and SSAPs adopted by the Accounting Standards Board are 'accounting standards' for the purposes of the Companies Act legislation. The Companies Act 2006 requires individual accounts, other than those prepared by small or medium-sized companies (as defined by the Act), to state whether they have been prepared in accordance with applicable accounting standards and to give particulars of any material departure from those standards and the reasons for it. References to accounting standards in the Act are contained in paragraph 45 of SI 2008 No. 410 Sch. 1 *The Large and Medium-sized Companies and Groups (Accounts and Reports) Regulations 2008* Sch. 4, with the exemptions for medium-sized companies to be found in regulation 4(2) of SI 2008 No. 410.

UITF Abstracts are published consensus pronouncements of the Urgent Issues Task Force, a committee of the ASB, which deals with accounting issues and treatments requiring early authoritative interpretation. The pronouncements are made within the framework of the law and the principles established in accounting standards, and have a standing similar in authority to accounting standards. Once accepted by the ASB, a UITF Abstract is to be regarded as accepted practice in the area in question and therefore effectively has the force of an accounting standard. Amplification of accounting principles and treatment introduced by UITF Abstracts are invariably reflected within existing or subsequently revised FRSs.

A small company may choose to adopt the FRSSE instead of the whole range of FRSs and SSAPs which are more appropriate to larger entities (see **Chapter 10**).

4.4.4 Generally accepted accounting practice (GAAP)

There is no precise technical or legal definition of 'GAAP' in the UK. 'Generally accepted' means a practice that is accepted by accountants generally as being permissible in the particular circumstances of a business – the practice may not necessarily be the 'best' or 'only' accounting method available. GAAP may therefore be regarded as encompassing:

- accounting principles contained in 'Accounting Standards';
- Companies Acts and listing rules of quoted companies;
- industry-specific accounting treatments, including SORPs; and
- any other acceptable accounting treatment, including treatments for which there is currently no adopted Accounting Standard (for example, methods of 'revenue recognition').

'GAAP' as an overarching caption, is frequently referred to in terms of:

- 'Big GAAP', or
- 'Little GAAP'.

Fundamentally, basic accounting methods and techniques (for example, measurement and estimation criteria or bases of revenue recognition) apply irrespective of the size of an enterprise. Scale and complexity may differ, however, and the extent of disclosure is determined by stakeholder interest, economic significance or regulatory requirement. Big GAAP, therefore, is concerned with those principles, rules and requirements governing large or economically significant companies or businesses. Little GAAP represents the same or consistent basic principles but simplified for the smaller enterprise. The 'small companies regime' of the Companies Act 2006 or the FRSSE (Financial Reporting Standard for Smaller Entities) are examples of parts of the overall framework of Little GAAP.

The basic accounting principle that annual accounts should show a 'true and fair' view applies equally to Big GAAP and Little GAAP.

4.5 Application of accounting standards to smaller companies

It is frequently recognised that the burden of complying with accounting standards falls more heavily upon the smaller company. While it is correct that the *principles* of accounting (in terms of accounting methods and treatment, measurement criteria and estimation techniques) should apply equally to *all* companies, the application of certain accounting standards (particularly their disclosure requirements) is seen as inappropriate, cost-inefficient, immaterial or simply not applicable to small companies. Alleviation is achieved in three ways:

- exemptions and concessions,
- CA 2006 small companies regime; and
- the FRSSE.

Table 4.2 gives an indication of the concessions that may be available to small or medium-sized companies in the application of the various Accounting Standards (SSAPs, FRSs and UITF Abstracts). A particularly significant example of exemption is that afforded to small (but not medium-sized) companies from the requirement to prepare a cash flow statement under FRS 1 *Cash flow statements,* although such exemption may not be available under the FRSSE if voluntary disclosure is adopted.

A small company can alternatively choose to adopt the stand-alone FRSSE.

Chapter 4 Accounts and accounting standards

A small company is not required to state in its Companies Act individual accounts whether they have been prepared in accordance with applicable accounting standards and to give particulars of and reasons for any material departure from those standards. However, this exemption relates only to disclosure – it does not diminish in any way the obligation of a small company to adopt and comply with appropriate accounting standards.

As stated in **4.4.3** above, a medium-sized company is also exempt from the requirement (under SI 2008 No. 410 Sch. 1(45) to state whether its Companies Act individual accounts have been prepared in accordance with applicable accounting standards or give particulars of any material departure from those standards.

SI 2008 No. 410 reg. 4(2)

Table 4.2   UK Accounting standards

This table shows the whole range of FRSs and SSAPs and comments on their application to and relevance for small and medium-sized companies. Exceptions and comments are made in the 'Application' column.

A small company can alternatively choose to adopt the stand-alone FRSSE (see **Chapter 10**), although many of the accounting principles and measurement criteria may still be relevant.

'Applicable from 2006 (or 2007)' in the 'Application' column refers to application with effect from accounting periods beginning on or after 1 January 2006 (or 2007) as appropriate. 'Applicable as FRS 26' means application with effect from a company's application of FRS 26 (accounting periods beginning on or after 1 January 2006).

In December 2008, the ASB issued a Financial Reporting Standard (FRS) entitled 'Improvements to Financial Reporting Standards' setting out a variety of amendments. The amendments mainly reflect consequential updating of UK IFRS-based standards and also improvements deriving from the IASB's annual improvements project. The FRS's affected are indicated by boxing below.

Statement	Accounting standard	Application
ASB Financial Reporting Standards (FRSs)		
FRS 1 revised 1996	Cash flow statements	Not applicable to small companies and entities and most wholly-owned subsidiaries (but see FRSSE)
FRS 2	Accounting for subsidiary undertakings	Applicable to parent undertakings preparing consolidated financial statements. However, a small parent undertaking exempted from preparing consolidated financial statements is required to provide disclosures in its individual accounts in accordance with SI 2008 No. 409 Sch. 2.
FRS 3	Reporting financial performance	
FRS 4	*Capital instruments*	*Substantially replaced by FRS 25 and FRS 26*
FRS 5	Reporting the substance of transactions	Applicable for specific (generally more complex) transactions
FRS 6	Acquisitions and mergers	Applicable where appropriate for consolidated accounts
FRS 7	Fair values in acquisition accounting	Applicable where appropriate for acquisitions
FRS 8	Related party disclosures	Applicable (but see FRSSE)
FRS 9	Associates and joint ventures	Where applicable
FRS 10	Goodwill and intangible assets	Where applicable
FRS 11	Impairment of fixed assets and goodwill	
FRS 12	Provisions, contingent liabilities and contingent assets	

Statement	Accounting standard	Application
FRS 15	Tangible fixed assets	
FRS 16	Current tax	
FRS 17	Retirement benefits	
FRS 18	Accounting Policies	
FRS 19	Deferred tax	
FRS 20 *(IFRS 2)*	Share-based payment	
FRS 21 *(IAS 10)*	Events after the balance sheet date	
FRS 22 *(IAS 33)*	Earnings per share	Not applicable
FRS 23 *(IAS 21)*	The effect of changes in foreign exchange rates	Not applicable–but adoption permitted. Application as FRS 26
FRS 24 *(IAS 29)*	Financial reporting in hyperinflationary economies	Rarely applicable–but adoption permitted. Application as FRS 26.
FRS 25 *(IAS 32)*	Financial instruments: disclosure and presentation	Presentation–applicable Disclosure–replaced by FRS 29
FRS 26 *(IAS 39)*	Financial instruments: measurement	Not applicable–other than listed companies or companies applying 'fair value accounting'
FRS 27	Life Assurance	Not applicable
FRS 28	Corresponding amounts	
FRS 29 *(IFRS 7)*	Financial instruments: disclosures	Not applicable–other than entities applying FRS 26.
–	Improvements to Financial Reporting Standards	

Statements of Standard Accounting Practice (SSAPs) adopted by ASB

SSAP 4	Accounting for Government grants	
SSAP 5	Accounting for value added tax	
SSAP 9	Stocks and work-in-progress	
SSAP 13	Accounting for research and development	Applicable but with disclosure exemptions
SSAP 19	Accounting for investment properties	
SSAP 21	Accounting for leases and hire-purchase contracts	
SSAP 24	*Accounting for pension costs*	*Superseded by FRS 17*
SSAP 25	Segmental reporting	Not generally applicable

Urgent Issues Task Force (UITF) Abstracts
Reporting entities applying the FRSSE are exempt from UITF Abstracts.
(With the exception of UITFs 21, 24 and 28, no UITF Abstract is addressed or reflected within the FRSSE (see **Chapter 10**).)

UITF 4	Presentation of long-term debtors in current assets	
UITF 5	Transfers from current assets to fixed assets	
UITF 11	*Capital instruments: issuer call options*	*Adopted within FRS 26.* Rarely applicable
UITF 15	Disclosure of substantial acquisitions	Rarely applicable
UITF 19	Tax on gains and losses on foreign currency borrowings that hedge an investment in a foreign enterprise	Rarely applicable
UITF 21	Accounting issues arising from the proposed introduction of the euro	Principles apply but disclosure exemption
UITF 22	The acquisition of a Lloyds business	Rarely applicable
UITF 23	Application of the transitional rules in FRS 15	
UITF 24	Accounting for start-up costs	Principles apply but disclosure exemption

Chapter 4 Accounts and accounting standards

Statement	Accounting standard	Application
UITF 25	National Insurance contributions on share option gains	Rarely applicable
UITF 26	Barter transactions for advertising	
UITF 27	Revision to estimates of the useful economic life of goodwill and intangible assets	
UITF 28	Operating lease incentives	Applicable (but see FRSSE)
UITF 29	Website development costs	
UITF 31	Exchanges of business or other non-monetary assets for an interest in a subsidiary, joint venture or associate	
UITF 32	Employee benefit trusts and other intermediate payment arrangements	
UITF 34	Pre-contract costs	
UITF 35	Death-in-service and incapacity benefits	
UITF 36	Contracts for sales of capacity	Rarely applicable
UITF 38	*Accounting for ESOP trusts*	*Rarely applicable Amended within FRS 20*
UITF 39	Members' shares in cooperative entities and similar instruments	
UITF 40	Revenue recognition and service contract	
UITF 41	Scope of FRS 20 (IFRS2)	
UITF 42	Reassessment of embedded derivatives	Rarely applicable
UITF 43	The interpretation of equivalence for the purposes of S 228A of the Companies Act 1985	
UITF 44	FRS 20 (IFRS2) – Group and Treasury share transactions	
UITF 45	Liabilities arising from Participating in a Specific Market – Waste Electrical and Electronic Equipment	Rarely applicable
UITF 46 (IFRIC Interpretation 16)	Hedges of a Net Investment in a Foreign Operation	Rarely applicable

In December 2008, FRS 8 *Related Party Disclosures* was amended to reflect certain changes to the law (implementing EU Directive 2006/46/EC) introduced by SI 2008 No. 410 'The Large and Medium-sized Companies and Groups (Accounts and Reports) Regulations'. The amendments were effective for accounting periods beginning on or after 6 April 2008. **Reporting entities applying the FRSSE currently applicable are exempt from FRS 8 (as amended).** See **10.8**.

4.6 International Accounting Standards

4.6.1 Arrival of IAS

The year 2005 saw the arrival of an EU requirement to adopt international accounting standards (IAS). Recent years have seen a continuing programme aiming at convergence (that is, harmonisation) of domestic UK, international and US financial reporting on the basis of globally accepted accounting standards.

Despite the fact that changes from 2005 onwards (in the UK) will initially impact primarily on the consolidated accounts of quoted (that is, publicly traded) groups of companies, there is an inevitability about the cascading effect of international harmonisation so that all companies, including small companies, will sooner or later have to embrace new procedures or principles.

4.6.2 IAS accounts and the option to choose

Within the UK, SI 2004 No. 2947 (The Companies Act 1985 (International Accounting Standards and Other Accounting Amendments) Regulations 2004) implemented changes to bring UK accounting into line with EU requirements. The changes applied to financial years beginning on or after 1 January 2005 and the adoption of IAS can now be broadly illustrated as in **Table 4.3**.

Table 4.3 The adoption of IAS accounts by British companies

	IAS accounts	CA 1985/CA 2006 accounts
Publicly traded companies (trading on an EU regulated market)	Required	Not permitted
Other publicly traded companies	Permitted (if not otherwise required by EU regulation)	Required (unless IAS accounts adopted)
Non-publicly traded companies	Permitted	Required (unless IAS accounts adopted)
Incorporated charities	Not permitted	Required

A change to IAS accounts is (with certain exceptions) irrevocable. All companies within a group must consistently adopt the same accounting framework (that is, IAS or UK GAAP). Upon adopting IAS accounts, a company will still need to apply a variety of provisions of CA 2006 where the scope is beyond IAS (for example, disclosures of staff or directors' remuneration, or the directors' report).

Small companies (as defined) should be alert to various factors when considering a move to IAS accounts:

- no equivalent exemptions as afforded by CA 2006 or the FRSSE are available under IAS;
- the determinants to define a 'small company' are different within IAS formats;
- abbreviated accounts are not available for filing (although a small company is not required to file its IAS profit and loss account); and
- exemptions concerning audit exemption, the directors' report, and group accounts continue to be available.

4.6.3 IASB standards

IFRSs are the financial reporting standards issued or adopted by the IASB (International Accounting Standards Board). The IASB is an independent body, formed in 2001 to succeed the International Accounting Standards Committee.

IASB and ASB standards have over the years been very similar in many cases (although there were significant differences), having been developed on the basis of the application of general principles and the use of professional judgment. US accounting standards have traditionally incorporated a more rigid adherence to specific accounting rules and consequently convergence of IASB and US standards have posed a considerable challenge. Nevertheless, the IASB and the US Financial Accounting Standards Board (FASB) are currently working together on joint projects to achieve substantial harmonisation in the next few years.

Chapter 4 Accounts and accounting standards

Table 4.4 *International accounting standards issued or adopted by the IASB as 'International Financial Reporting Standards'.*

IASB standards are endorsed by the EU to enable adoption within IFRS-compliant accounts in 2005 and subsequently (in accordance with Regulation (EC) No. 1725/2003).

Information on up to date endorsement status of IASB standards are available at:

www.europa.eu.int/comm/internal_market/accounting/ias_en.htm#status-adoption

---

4.6.4 The EU Regulation on the Application of IAS

In July 2002, Member States of the EU adopted a Regulation (Regulation (EC) No. 1606/2002)* on the application of accounting standards. Applying from financial years commencing 1 January 2005, the Regulation requires publicly traded companies (that is, companies whose securities are traded on a regulated market within the EU) to prepare their consolidated accounts on the basis of accounting standards issued by the International Accounting Standards Board that are adopted by the European Commission. The Regulation only applies to the detailed accounting provisions; domestic law implementing EU Accounting Directives where relevant will continue to apply in other areas such as the requirement to prepare individual accounts, auditing, enforcement and directors' reports.

In order to be 'adopted' by the EU for the purposes of the Regulation, individual accounting standards issued by the IASB must be endorsed in accordance with a laid down adoption procedure, based on advice from the EU Accounting Regulatory Committee (ARC) – an accounting technical committee of representatives of Member States. The reason for this endorsement requirement is to preclude accounting setting being effectively delegated to a private organisation (the IASB) and to ensure that the European Commission retains ultimate control and influence over financial reporting standards throughout the EU. Regulation (EC) No. 1725/2003 (29 September 2003) endorsed certain standards in accordance with this procedure in time for the introduction of IFRS-compliant accounts in 2005.

EU Directive 2003/51/EC was issued in June 2003 to modernise existing Accounting Directives (for example, the fourth and seventh Directives on annual and consolidated accounts) and remove inconsistencies between the Directives and IASB standards.

Two main impacts of Regulation (EC) No. 1606/2002 for those UK companies affected are:

- such companies have to comply with adopted IASB accounting standards, rather than much of the Companies Acts 1985 and 2006 and UK domestic standards issued by the ASB; and
- those IASB accounting standards have direct legal force within the UK, without the requirement for legislative action to turn them into UK statute law.

The EU Regulation applies directly to the preparation of consolidated accounts of publicly traded companies. In addition, the Regulation also permits each Member State to extend application to:

- the individual accounts of publicly traded companies; and
- the individual and/or consolidated accounts of some or all non-publicly traded companies.

Legislative change by statutory instrument was introduced by SI 2004 No. 2947 to permit (but not require) all British companies (other than those automatically covered by the EU Regulation) to use international accounting standards (IASs – that is, EU-adopted IFRSs) as an alternative to UK domestic accounting standards.

International Accounting Standards

> Until such time as the EU Regulation is applied, by UK adoption, to private companies, the accounting requirements of such companies will continue to be governed by relevant UK GAAP determined by UK legislation (Companies Act 2006) and ASB standards.
>
> There is currently no IASB standard for smaller entities (or 'international FRSSE') although such a project is on the IASB agenda (see **4.6.5** below) and an exposure draft issued. Until an international standard for smaller entities is adopted, the lighter touch regime for smaller companies will continue to be available in the form of the existing ASB FRSSE. The FRSSE will inevitably be revised over time to reflect the increasing convergence of mainstream ASB standards incorporating the principles and practices of IAS.

* The IAS Regulation may be downloaded from: www.ec.europa.eu./internal_market/accounting/ias_en.htm#regulation

4.6.5 The IASB SME project and exposure draft

There is currently no IASB financial reporting standard for smaller enterprises ('International FRSSE'). The IASB has, however, developed a 'set' of standards for SMEs as a separate stand-alone document and published an Exposure Draft of a proposed international standard (*Small and Medium-sized Entities*) ('IFRS for SMEs'). The name of the standard was changed in January 2009 to 'IFRS for Non-publicly Accountable Entities'.

The IASB intend that the IFRS for Non-publicly Accountable Entities would apply to entities that are 'not publicly accountable' and that publish 'general purpose financial statements for external users'. It is intended that the IFRS will focus on financial reporting for those entities that have external users of their financial statements, that is, users other than owner managers. 'Public accountability' would be indicated by filing financial statements with regulatory organisations or securities commissions, or holding assets in a fiduciary capacity for a broad range of outsiders (for example: banks, insurance entities, pension funds or mutual finds).

SME standards would be based on principles from the fully adopted IFRSs and would:

- preserve recognition and measurement principles, but simplified as necessary;
- simplify burden of presentation and disclosure;
- simplify the standards only where a case had been made on cost/benefit grounds;
- be adopted wholesale (that is, individual SME standards could not be cherry-picked or individual IFRSs adopted standard-by-standard);
- permit easy transition to the adoption of full IFRSs; and
- be written in 'plain English' and organised topically in balance sheet and income statement order.

The need for globally recognised SME standards continues to be enthusiastically endorsed by national accounting setters and the IASB project is considered to be of considerable importance. The 'IFRS for Non-publicly Accountable Entities', based on generally accepted IASB accounting principles for SMEs, is scheduled for completion for mid-2009, although transitional adoption (if any) may be much later.

IASB have said that it will be up to national jurisdictions to determine which entities are required to permit or adopt IASB SME standards. In the meantime, until the IFRS for SME standards is adopted, the lighter touch regime for smaller companies in the UK continues to be available in the form of the revised 'one stop shop' FRSSE revised in 2008 (FRSSE (effective April 2008) see **10.1.3 Chapter 10**).

Part II Smaller companies

Chapter 5 Qualifying as a small company

5.1 The 'small companies regime'

The Companies Act 2006 provides for different provisions to apply in certain respects to different kinds of company. As far the smaller (and unquoted) company is concerned, the main distinction is between:

- companies subject to the 'small companies regime'; and *s. 381*
- other companies (companies that are not subject to that regime). *s. 380(3)*

The small companies regime applies to a company for a financial year in relation to which the company:

- qualifies as small; and *ss. 382–383*
- is not excluded from the regime. *s. 384*

The small companies regime does not apply to the following companies: *s. 384(1)*

(a) public companies;
(b) authorised insurance companies, banking companies, e-money issuers, MiFIDs, investment firms or UCITS management companies;
(c) companies carrying on insurance market activity; or
(d) members of an ineligible group (being, basically, companies within (a) to (c) above, other than companies qualifying as 'small' under the small companies regime, CA 2006 s. 384(3)).

5.2 Qualifying conditions – 'small' and 'medium-sized' companies

Two classifications of companies – 'small' and 'medium-sized' – are entitled to certain special provisions with regard to the contents of the statutory accounts for filing with the Registrar of Companies.

Companies Act 2006 ss. 382(3) and 465(3) set out the conditions to be met by a company to qualify as 'small' or 'medium-sized' as appropriate.

Basically, under the Companies Act 2006, a company is treated as small or medium-sized if it does not exceed more than one of the following criteria: *s. 382 and s. 465*

	Small	*Medium-sized*
Turnover	£6.5 million	£25.9 million
Balance sheet total	£3.26 million	£12.9 million
Average number of employees (on a monthly basis)	50	250

CA 2006 criteria amended (increased) by SI 2008 No. 393

Turnover figures should be proportionately adjusted where the financial 'year' is not in fact 12 months. *s. 382(4)*

Chapter 5 Qualifying as a small company

s. 382(5)   'Balance sheet total' means the aggregate of the amounts shown as assets in the company's balance sheet (basically, gross assets before deduction of liabilities, accruals and provisions; that is, the aggregate of headings A to D in Format 1 or the 'Assets' headings in Format 2).

As a general rule, for a company to qualify as small or medium-sized, the criteria must be met for the current and previous year. If the criteria are not met for the following year, a company may continue to be treated as small or medium-sized, as appropriate, for that year. However, if the criteria are not met in the year after that, then the company must file accounts according to its size.

5.3 Parent companies and small groups

Companies Act 2006 ss. 383(4) and 466(4) set out the conditions to be met by a group for the parent company to qualify as 'small' or 'medium-sized' as appropriate.

s. 383   A parent company qualifies as a small company in relation to a financial year only if the group headed by it qualifies as a small group.

The size classification of a parent company is determined with regard to the aggregate qualifying criteria of the group taken as a whole (parent company and subsidiary undertakings), irrespective of the actual size qualification of the parent company itself (see **Chapter 9**).

5.4 Decision chart to determine size qualification

The decision chart in **Figure 5.1** is designed to determine whether a company qualifies in any particular year to be treated as small or medium-sized, and hence whether it is entitled to special provisions in the preparation of its annual accounts, and whether it is entitled to prepare and file abbreviated accounts. The chart may also be used, as a separate consideration, to determine whether a company is entitled to small company audit exemption (see **Chapter 11**).

Figure 5.1 Decision chart to determine size qualification

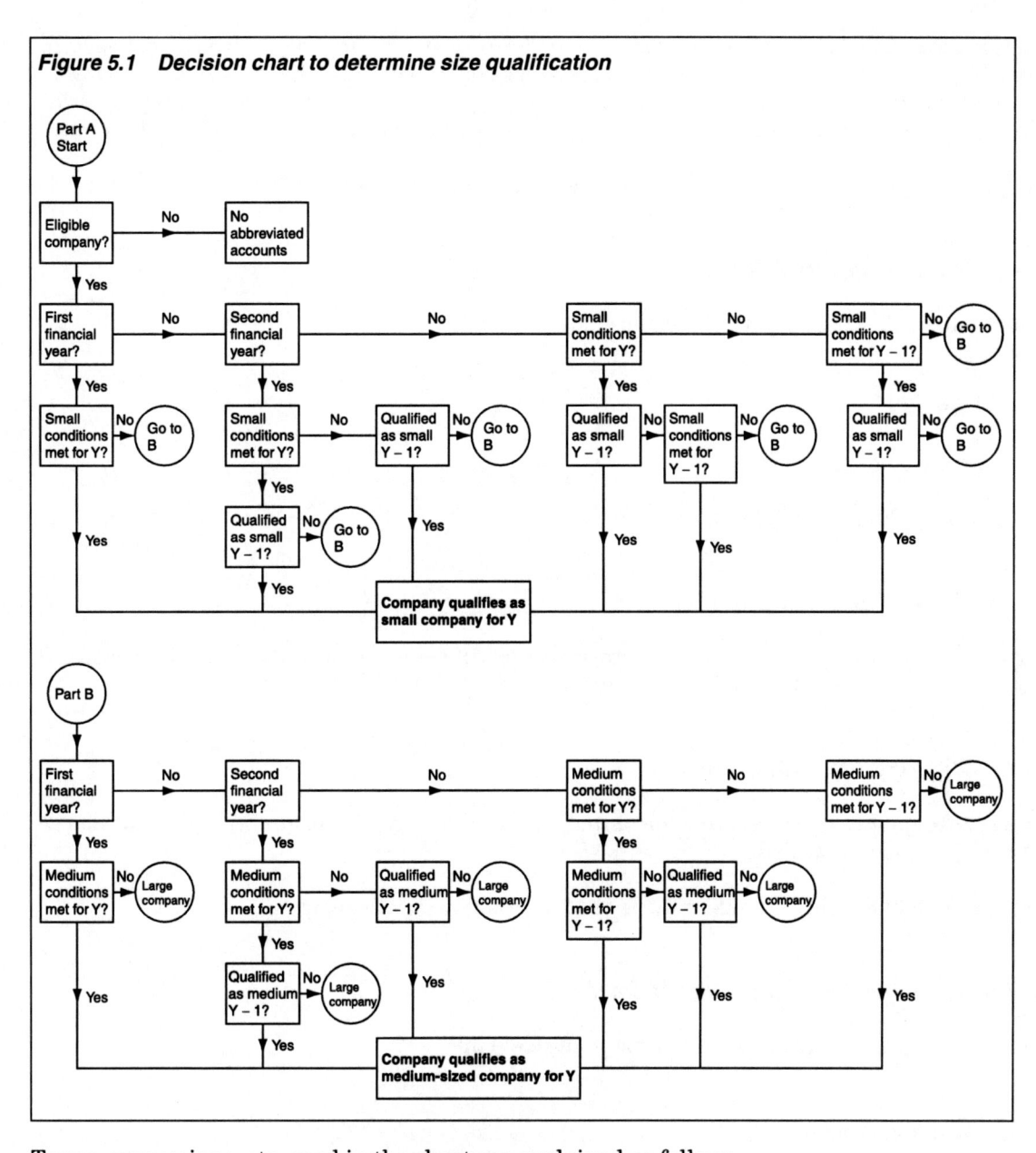

[Decision flowchart with Part A and Part B determining small and medium-sized company qualification]

Terms, expressions, etc. used in the chart are explained as follows.

5.4.1 'Eligible company?'

The following companies are not eligible and are not therefore entitled to prepare small company accounts or to file abbreviated accounts, irrespective of size: *s. 384*

- public companies;
- members of 'ineligible' (basically, public) groups;   *s. 384(2)*
- a company carrying on an insurance market activity; and
- a company that is an authorised insurance company, a banking company, an e-money issuer, a MiFID investment firm or a UCITS management company (but see **5.1**).   *s. 384(1)*

A group is 'ineligible' if any of its members is a public company; a body corporate (other than a company) whose shares are admitted to trading on a regulated market in an EEA State; a person (other than a small company) who has permission under Part 4 of the FSMA 2000 to carry on a regulated activity; a small company that is an authorised insurance company, a

Chapter 5 Qualifying as a small company

banking company, an e-money issuer, an MiFID investment firm or a UCITS management company; or a person who carries on insurance market activity (CA 2006 384(2)). A company is a 'small company' for this purpose of ineligibility if it qualified as small in relation to its last financial year ending on or before the end of the financial year to which the accounts relate.

s. 480(2)   A dormant company member of an ineligible group may prepare small company accounts.

5.4.2 'No abbreviated accounts'

The company is not entitled to file abbreviated accounts.

5.4.3 Years

Y = current financial year

Y – 1 = preceding financial year

5.4.4 'First financial year?'

In a company's first year of incorporation, it will qualify as small or medium-sized, as appropriate, provided it meets the qualifying conditions in its first financial year.

5.4.5 Qualifying conditions

In order to qualify as small or medium-sized, as the case may be, the qualifying conditions set out in **5.2** must be satisfied.

Note: Part B of the chart should only be used after following the logic route of Part A.

5.4.6 'Qualified as small (medium)?'

Did the company qualify as small (or medium-sized) in Y – 1?

5.4.7 'Large company'

s. 246
s. 246A   The company, being neither small nor medium-sized, is not entitled to prepare accounts in accordance with the relevant special provisions. The term 'large' is not used in the legislation.

Chapter 6 Contents of small company accounts

6.1 Introduction

This chapter summarises the company accounts provisions of the Companies Act 2006 as they affect companies under the 'small companies regime'. The Companies Act 2006 lays down provisions relating to:

- prescriptive formats of accounts;
- the content of accounts; and
- principles and rules for determining amounts included in the accounts.

This chapter summarises accounts provisions of the Companies Act 2006, insofar as they relate to accounts ('Companies Act individual accounts') that are prepared in accordance with the Companies Act 2006 s. 396. 'Abbreviated accounts' (modified statutory accounts for filing purposes) are considered separately in **Chapter 8**. Small company 'group accounts' under Companies Act 2006 s. 398 and s. 404 are considered separately in **Chapter 9**.

All companies are required to keep 'adequate accounting records' in accordance with Companies Act 2006 s. 386. Small company accounts are produced from the company's underlying financial records, as explained at **3.10 (Chapter 3)**. Companies Act 2006 s. 386 is set out in full in **Appendix B**.

6.2 Accounts – provisions for small companies

Full accounts prepared for shareholders must be prepared for all companies, irrespective of size.

s. 394 et seq

The full accounts of a 'small' company, however, are less detailed with reduced disclosure requirements. A small company may also take advantage of the FRSSE (see **Chapter 10**). In addition, a company qualifying as 'small' or 'medium-sized' (see **Chapter 5**) may prepare 'abbreviated' accounts for filing with the Registrar of Companies (see **Chapter 8**).

Certain small companies may be exempt from the requirement for audit, as explained in **Chapter 11**. Dormant companies may also take advantage of audit exemption.

By virtue of the special provisions for small companies under the Companies Act 2006, a small company is therefore entitled to prepare:

- annual accounts for shareholders – with a balance sheet and reduced disclosure requirements for the notes to the accounts and the directors' report (as determined by SI 2008 No. 409 – see **Chapter 3**); and
- abbreviated accounts for filing and delivery to the Registrar of Companies – under Companies Act 2006 s. 444.

Small company accounts with simplified provisions and reduced disclosure provided by Companies Act 2006 s. 396 and Regulations contained in Sch. 1 of SI 2008 No. 409 are referred to as 'small company accounts' in this book.

Chapter 6 Contents of small company accounts

Abbreviated accounts are explained in **Chapter 8**. A company wishing to file abbreviated accounts with the Registrar of Companies has to produce two sets of accounts: annual accounts for shareholders and abbreviated accounts.

The Companies Act 2006 s. 396 and SI 2008 No. 409 together determine the minimum disclosure required in a small company's annual accounts. However, a small company does not have to take advantage of all the exemptions and modifications permitted if it does not wish to do so.

SI 2008 No. 409 reg 3(3)

For example, SI 2008 No. 409 provides that Companies Act individual accounts 'are treated as having complied with any provision of Schedule 1 to these Regulations [i.e. the 'Small Companies Accounts Regs' SI 2008 No. 409] if they comply instead with the corresponding provision of Schedule 1 to the Large and Medium-Sized Companies and Groups (Accounts and Reports) Regulations 2008 [SI 2008 No. 410]'.

SI 2008 No. 409 reg 8(2)

Similarly, Companies Act group accounts 'are treated as having complied with any provision of Part 1 to Schedule 6 [of SI 2008 No. 409 – "form and content of Companies Act group accounts] if they comply instead with the corresponding provision of Schedule 6 to the Large and Medium-Sized Companies Accounts Regs [SI 2008 No. 410]'.

s. 399

The special provisions for small companies apply not only to the individual accounts of such companies but also to the group accounts where a small company produces them. If at the end of a financial year a company subject to the small companies regime is a parent company the directors, as well as preparing individual accounts for the year, have the option to prepare group accounts for the year, if they so wish.

6.3 'True and fair' view

s. 393

There is a fundamental requirement for full accounts (Companies Act individual accounts or group accounts) other than abbreviated accounts to show a 'true and fair' view.

The Companies Act 2006 provides that the directors of a company must not approve annual accounts unless they are satisfied that the accounts give a true and fair view of the assets, liabilities, financial position and profit or loss of the company (in the case of the company's individual accounts) or of the undertakings included in the consolidation taken as a whole), so far as concerns members of the company (for group accounts).

The requirement to show a 'true and fair' view applies irrespective of whether or not the accounts are subject to audit or other independent review. Any decision concerning the method of accounting or means of disclosing information must take this basic requirement into account.

s. 393(2)

The Companies Act 2006 now also specifically requires auditors to have regard to the directors' duty as explained above to approve annual accounts only if they (the directors) are satisfied that the accounts give a true and fair view.

The concept of 'true and fair' is discussed in **Chapter 4** (at **4.4**).

6.4 Format of small company accounts

6.4.1 SI 2008 No. 409

Under the small companies regime of the Companies Act 2006, the form and content of:

- Companies Act individual accounts for small companies;
- Companies Act group accounts for small companies; and
- Companies Act abbreviated accounts

Format of small company accounts

are determined in accordance with SI 2008 No. 409 'The Small Companies and Groups (Accounts and Directors' Report) Regulations 2008'.

The Regulations in SI 2008 No. 409 prescribe the required formats from which small companies may choose. Formats which are most commonly used are illustrated in **Tables 6.2** and **6.3** below and in **Appendix C**.

Once a format has been adopted, the company must use the same format for subsequent years unless, in the directors' opinion, there are special reasons for changing; these must be disclosed in the year of change.

Sch 1.2(1)

6.4.2 Form and content of accounts prepared by small companies

The form and content of individual accounts prepared by small companies are determined in accordance with regulations provided by SI 2008 No. 409 'The Small Companies and Groups (Accounts and Directors' Report) Regulations 2008' and in particular Schedule 1.

Schedule 1 to SI 2008 No. 409 (Companies Act individual accounts) is structured as in **Table 6.1**.

Table 6.1 **Schedule 1 Companies Act individual accounts – SI 2008 No. 409 'The Small Companies and Groups (Accounts and Directors'Report) Regulations 2008'**

Part 1 General rules and formats

Section A	General rules
Section B	Required formats for accounts

- Balance sheet formats (Formats 1 and 2) and notes thereon
- Profit and loss account formats (Formats 1, 2, 3 and 4) and notes thereon

Part 2 Accounting principles and rules

Section A	Accounting principles

- Accounting principles

Section B	Historical cost accounting rules

- Fixed assets
- Depreciation and diminution in value
- Development costs
- Goodwill
- Current assets
- Miscellaneous and supplementary provisions *(including determination of purchase price and production cost, and assets included at a fixed amount)*

Section C	Alternative accounting rules

- Alternative accounting rules
- Application of the depreciation rules
- Additional information to be provided in case of departure from historical cost account rules
- Revaluation reserve

Section D	Fair value accounting

- Inclusion of financial instruments at fair value
- Determination of fair value
- Inclusion of hedged items at fair value

Chapter 6 Contents of small company accounts

> - Other assets that may be included at fair value
>   - Accounting for changes in value
>   - The fair value reserve
>
> Part 3 Notes to the accounts
>
> - Reserves and dividends
> - Disclosure of accounting policies
> - Information supplementing the balance sheet *(Share capital, fixed assets, investments, fair values, reserves and provisions, indebtedness, and guarantees and other financial commitments)*
> - Information supplementing the profit and loss account *(including particulars of turnover)*
> - Miscellaneous matters *(including foreign currencies and dormant companies as agents)*
>
> Schedule 1 is reproduced in full in Appendix **E**.

6.4.3 The statutory formats

The accounts formats from which a small company may choose are given in SI 2008 No. 409 Schedule 1 (Part 1 Section B – 'The required formats for accounts').

There is a choice of:

- *four* profit and loss account formats; and
- *two* balance sheet formats.

Two profit and loss account formats and one of the balance sheet formats are in the 'vertical' styling in which most accounts are prepared. The two 'horizontal' styles of profit and loss account (Formats 3 and 4) and balance sheet (Format 2) are considered 'old-fashioned'.

The statutory formats are reproduced in full in **Appendix C**.

Less detailed balance sheet

A small company must adopt in its annual (individual) accounts one of the formats of balance sheet set out in SI 2008 No. 409 Schedule 1 (Part 1 Section B). It must show the items listed in either of the formats, as set out in **Tables 6.2** and **6.3** below. The individual balance sheet of a small company which adopts Format 1 would be as set out in **Table 6.4**. This amended format is also reproduced in **Appendix C**.

Profit and loss account

The choice of profit and loss account formats for a small company is set out in SI 2008 No. 409 Schedule 1 (Part 1 Section B) and is reproduced in **Appendix C**. They are also illustrated in **Table 6.5**. The principles governing the formats are as set out in **3.4**.

Accounting principles

Sch 1.9–15

Small company accounts are prepared in accordance with the principles set out in SI 2008 No. 409 Schedule 1 (Part 2 Section A) These principles are the fundamental accounting concepts that underlie accounts and are also incorporated within FRSs and SSAPs generally, including the FRSSE for small companies.

Accounting principles are explained further in **3.5 (Chapter 3)**.

6.5 Small company balance sheet

The formats of balance sheet set out in SI 2008 No. 409 Schedule 1 (Part 1 Section B) from which a small company must choose for its annual (individual) accounts are set out in **Table 6.2**. Table 6.2 illustrates the differences between the two balance sheet formats available.

Table 6.2 Small company balance sheets – the two formats compared

The items boxed need not be disclosed in Format 2. For illustrative purposes, the Arabic number sub-headings (which are common to both formats) are not reproduced in this table but are set out in **Table 6.3**. The balance sheet formats with notes are given in **Appendix C**.

Format 1 *Format 2*

ASSETS

Format 1	Format 2
A Called up share capital not paid	A Called up share capital not paid
B Fixed assets	B Fixed assets
I Intangible assets	I Intangible assets
II Tangible assets	II Tangible assets
III Investments	III Investments
C Current assets	C Current assets
I Stocks	I Stocks
II Debtors	II Debtors
III Investments	III Investments
IV Cash at bank and in hand	IV Cash at bank and in hand
D Prepayments and accrued income	D Prepayments and accrued income
E Creditors: amounts falling due within one year	
F Net current assets (liabilities)	
G Total assets less current liabilities	

LIABILITIES

Format 1	Format 2
H Creditors: amounts falling due after more than one year	A Capital and reserves
	I Called up share capital
	II Share premium account
	III Revaluation reserve
	IV Other reserves
	V Profit and loss account
	[ ] Minority interests
I Provisions for liabilities	B Provisions for liabilities
J Accruals and deferred income	
[ ] Minority interests [*Alternative* (1)]	
K Capital and reserves	C Creditors
I Called up share capital	[*'Amounts falling due within one year' and 'amounts*
II Share premium account	*falling due after more than one year' should be shown*
III Revaluation reserve	*separately, both in year' should be shown separately,*
IV Other reserves	*both in aggregate and for each of the constituent*
V Profit and loss account	*(Arabic number) items of this heading.*]
[ ] Minority interests [*Alternative (2)*]	D Accruals and deferred income

The dotted line above in Format 1 illustrates the usual 'break-point' in the balance sheet, although in practice the balance sheet total could be 'struck' after item G. Format 2 requires balance sheet totals of ASSETS and LIABILITIES to be given.

Chapter 6 Contents of small company accounts

Table 6.3 Small company balance sheets – Arabic number sub-headings

INTANGIBLE ASSETS

1 Goodwill
2 Other intangible assets

TANGIBLE ASSETS

1 Land and buildings
2 Plant and machinery etc.

INVESTMENTS

1 Shares in group undertakings and participating interests
2 Loans to group undertakings and undertakings in which the company has a participating interest
3 Other investments other than loans
4 Other investments

STOCKS

1 Stocks
2 Payments on account

DEBTORS

1 Trade debtors
2 Amounts owed by group undertakings and undertakings in which the company has a participating interest
3 Other debtors

INVESTMENTS

1 Shares in group undertakings
2 Other investments *

CREDITORS: AMOUNTS FALLING DUE WITHIN ONE YEAR

1 Bank loans and overdrafts
2 Trade creditors
3 Amounts owed to group undertakings and undertakings in which the company has a participating interest
4 Other creditors

CREDITORS: AMOUNTS FALLING DUE AFTER MORE THAN ONE YEAR

1 Bank loans and overdrafts
2 Trade creditors
3 Amounts owed to group undertakings and undertakings in which the company has a participating interest
4 Payments received on account
5 Other creditors

For group balance sheets, the format headings are as set out in SI 2008 No. 409 Schedule 6 (Part I paragraph 1(2) see Table 6.4).

The balance sheet format of a small company which adopts balance sheet Format 1 would be a set out in **Table 6.4**. Small company balance sheet

---

Table 6.4 Small company balance sheet (Format 1)

CALLED UP SHARE CAPITAL NOT PAID

FIXED ASSETS
Intangible assets
Goodwill
Other intangible assets

Tangible assets
Land and buildings
Plant and machinery, etc.

Investments *(Note 1)*
Shares in group undertakings and participating interests
Loans to group undertakings and undertakings in which the company has a participating interest
Other investments other than loans
Other investments

Small company balance sheet

CURRENT ASSETS
Stocks
Stocks
Payments on account

Debtors (*Note 2*)
Trade debtors
Amounts owed by group undertakings and undertakings in which the company has a participating interest
Other debtors

Investments
Shares in group undertakings
Other investments

Cash at bank and in hand

PREPAYMENTS AND ACCRUED INCOME

CREDITORS: amounts falling due within one year
Bank loans and overdrafts
Trade creditors
Amounts owed to group undertakings and undertakings in which the company has a participating interest
Other creditors (*Note 3*)

NET CURRENT ASSETS (LIABILITIES)

TOTAL ASSETS LESS CURRENT LIABILITIES

CREDITORS: amounts falling due after more than one year (*Note 3*)
Bank loans and overdrafts
Trade creditors
Amounts owed to group undertakings and undertakings in which the company has a participating interest
Other creditors (*Note 3*)

PROVISIONS FOR LIABILITIES

ACCRUALS AND DEFERRED INCOME (*Note 3*)

CAPITAL AND RESERVES
Called up share capital
Share premium account
Revaluation reserve
Other reserves
Profit and loss account

Note 1   Where a small company prepares small group accounts, in a consolidated balance sheet the format for 'Investments' is:
  1 shares in group undertakings;
  2 interests in associated undertakings;
  3 other participating interests;
  4 loans to group undertakings and undertakings in which a participating interest is held;
  5 other investments other than loans, and
  6 others
  SI 2008 No. 409 Sch. 6.1(2)

Note 2   A small company must disclose the aggregate total of 'debtors falling due after more than one year' but such disclosure (if the amount is not material) may be in the notes to the accounts rather than in the balance sheet.

Note 3   Where a small company adopts balance sheet Format 2, if it discloses in the notes to its accounts the aggregate amounts included under 'Creditors' which fall due within one year and which fall due after one year respectively, it is not required to disclose the amounts falling due within one year and after one year separately for each item under 'Creditors'.

The amount of any creditors in respect of taxation and social security and convertible loans should be shown separately.

Chapter 6 Contents of small company accounts

Appendix C reproduces balance sheet Format 1 (as above) (and also Format 2) provided by SI 2008 No. 409 Schedule 1 (Part 1 Section B).

6.6 Small company profit and loss account

The choice of profit and loss account formats for a small company, as set out in SI 2008 No. 409 Sch. 1 (Part 1 Section B), is illustrated in **Table 6.5**. The formats are also reproduced in **Appendix C**.

In practice, care needs to be taken in the choice of format and presentation of the profit and loss accounts. **Table 6.5** presents a comparison of the two formats (Formats 1 and 2) showing the differences in presentation and disclosure. It is particularly relevant to note:

- *gross profit or loss* is specifically disclosed only in Format 1 (it may also be readily ascertained from Format 3); and
- *depreciation* requires allocation over various cost headings in Formats 1 (and 3) but needs only to be shown as one item in a Format 2 (or 4) profit and loss account.

Sch 1.6

> One item *must* be shown on the *face* of the profit and loss account.
>
> 'The amount of a company's profit or loss on ordinary activities before taxation'.
>
> (This item is not specified in the formats).

All formats require identical information, except that Formats 3 and 4 require separate totals of 'charges' and 'income'.

Following SI 2004 No. 2947, with regard to companies' financial years beginning on or after 1 January 2005, there is no requirement to show 'dividends: aggregate amounts paid and proposed' as a separate item in the profit and loss account.

All other items in the profit and loss account formats (being represented by Arabic numbers) could be combined and given in the notes to the accounts, provided the profit and loss account contains a summarised linking figure.

For small companies which are able and intend to file abbreviated accounts, the choice of profit and loss account formats may be of less consequence.

Table 6.5   Small company profit and loss account formats (SI 2008 No. 409 Schedule 1 (Part I Section B))

Items boxed show the differences in disclosure required by the formats.

Full profit and loss account formats are given in **Appendix C**. Formats 3 and 4 are not recognised under the FRSSE (see **Chapter 10**).

Expenses classified by function	Expenses classified by type
Format 1	Format 2
Format 3 requires the same information in a different presentation	Format 4 requires the same information in a different presentation
1 Turnover	1 Turnover
2 Cost of sales	2 Change in stocks of finished goods and work in progress
3 Gross profit or loss	3 Own work capitalised

Notes to the accounts – small company

4 Distribution costs 5 Administrative expenses	
6 Other operating income	4 Other operating income
	5 (a) Raw materials and consumables (b) Other external charges

Staff costs disclosure – not applicable for small companies (CA 2006 s. 411)	6 Staff costs:
	   (a) Wages and salaries
	   (b) Social security costs
	   (c) Other pension costs

Depreciation must be allocated over items 2, 4 and 5 (Sch 1 Part I Section B note 11) and disclosed separately in Notes (Sch 1.19)	7 (a) Depreciation and other amounts written off tangible and intangible fixed assets
	(b) Exceptional amounts written off current assets 8 Other operating charges
7 Income from shares in group undertakings 8 Income from participating interests 9 Income from other fixed asset investments 10 Other interest receivable and similar income 11 Amounts written off investments 12 Interest payable and similar charges	9 Income from shares in group undertakings 10 Income from participating interests 11 Income from other fixed asset investments 12 Other interest receivable and similar income 13 Amounts written off investments 14 Interest payable and similar charges
12A Profit or loss on ordinary activities before taxation *(Sch. 1.6 and FRSSE)*	14A Profit or loss on ordinary activities before taxation *(Sch 1.6 and FRSSE)*
13 Tax on profit or loss on ordinary activities 14 Profit or loss on ordinary activities after taxation	15 Tax on profit or loss on ordinary activities 16 Profit or loss on ordinary activities after taxation
15 Extraordinary income 16 Extraordinary charges 17 Extraordinary profit or loss 18 Tax on extraordinary profit or loss	17 Extraordinary income 18 Extraordinary charges 19 Extraordinary profit or loss 20 Tax on extraordinary profit or loss
19 Other taxes not shown under the above items 20 Profit or loss for the financial year	21 Other taxes not shown under the above items 22 Profit or loss for the financial year

Extraordinary items, although included within the statutory formats, are now viewed by the FRSSE (and FRS 3 Reporting financial performance) as being extremely rare.

'Profit and loss on ordinary activity before taxation' must also be disclosed – see SI 2008 No. 409 Sch. 1.6 and FRSSE.

Where a small company prepares group accounts, the items in **Table 6.5** headed 'Income from participating interests' in the above formats (item 8 (Format 1 and item 10 (Format 2) become two items:

- Income from interests in associated undertakings; and
- Income from other participating interests.

SI 2008 No. 409 Sch 6.1(3)

6.7 Notes to the accounts – small company

A small company must set out in the notes (if not given in the company's accounts) the following information specified in SI 2008 No. 409 Sch. 1 paragraphs 42–63):

- *Reserves and Dividends.*
  Movements and transfers from reserves.
  Aggregate dividends paid and payable or proposed.
  Aggregate dividend proposed before date of approval of accounts.
- *Disclosure of accounting policies.*

Sch 1.43

Sch 1.44

Chapter 6 Contents of small company accounts

Information supplementing the balance sheet:

Sch 1.46–47	• *Share capital* Allotted share capital; redeemable shares; share allotments during the year.
Sch 1.48–49	• *Fixed assets* Movements; revaluation; depreciation.
Sch 1.50	• *Investments* Listed investments; market valuation.
Sch 1.51–52	• *Fair value of assets and liabilities* Assumptions; fair value; derivatives; transfers to/from reserves.
Sch 1.53	Investment property and living animals and plants at fair value
Sch 1.54	• *Reserves and provisions* Movements and transfers to/from reserves and provisions. Details of 'other provisions'
Sch 1.55–56	• *Details of indebtedness* Creditors payable or repayable more than five years; security; arrears of fixed cumulative dividends.
Sch 1.57	• *Guarantees and other financial commitments* Charges on assets; contingent liabilities; capital commitments not provided for; pension commitments; and other financial commitments.
Sch 1.58	• *Substituted price or cost of assets* Ascribed purchase price or production cost.

Information supplementing the profit and loss account:

Sch 1.60	• *Turnover** Percentage attributable to geographical markets outside UK.
Sch 1.61	• *Miscellaneous** Effect of prior year adjustments and exceptional transactions, and particulars of extraordinary charges or income.

* *Information not required where group accounts exemption applies (CA 2006 s. 408)*

General:

Sch 1.62	• *Sums in foreign currencies* Basis of translation of foreign currencies.
Sch 1.63	• *Dormant companies acting as agents* Audit exempt dormant companies acting as agents.

Information about related undertakings (small groups):

Where the parent company of a small company does not prepare group accounts, it must set out in the notes to the company's accounts the information about related undertakings specified in SI 2008 No. 409 Sch. 2 as specified by regulation 4. Required disclosures include:

- Subsidiary undertakings–details, share holdings, financial information;
- Shares of company held by subsidiary undertakings;
- Significant holdings in other undertakings; and
- Ultimate parent company and parent undertakings for larger group.

Schedule 2 ('Information about related undertakings where company not preparing group accounts (Companies Act or IAS individual accounts)') contained within SI 2008 No. 409 'The Small Companies and Groups (Accounts and Directors' Report) Regulations 2008' is set out in **Appendix C**.

Other information:

- *Directors' benefits – advances credit and guarantees*

    Companies Act 2006 Section 413 provides for the disclosure of advances and credits granted by a company to its directors, and guarantees of any kind entered into by a company on behalf of its directors (see **6.11** below).

- *Liability limitation agreements*

    A company (subject to audit) which has entered into a liability limitation agreement limiting an auditor's liability must disclose in the notes:

- the principal terms of the agreement; and
- the date of the resolution approving the agreement (or its principal terms) or (for a private company) the date of the resolution waiving the need for such approval.

(CA 2006 s 538 and SI 2008 No. 489 reg 8).

6.8 Directors' report of a small company

6.8.1 Small company directors' report – entitlement

A company is entitled to small companies exemption in relation to the directors' report for a financial year if:

- it is entitled to prepare accounts for the year in accordance with the small companies regime; or
- it would be so entitled but for being or having been a member of an ineligible group (see **9.2**). *s. 415A*

The exemption enables a small company not to provide:

- a business review (otherwise required by s. 417).
- a statement of the amount recommended by way of dividend) (under s. 416(3)).
- matters required by ss. 444 to 446 (being the filing obligations of medium-sized or unquoted companies.

6.8.2 Small company directors' report – contents

The directors' report of a small company is only required to provide the following information:

Companies Act 2006 s. 416

- names of directors during the year; and
- principal activities;

SI 2008 No. 409 Sch. 5

- political donations and expenditure (exceeding £2,000);
- charitable donations (exceeding £2,000);
- company acquiring own shares; and
- employment of disabled persons (where employees exceed 250).

Companies Act 2006 s. 236

- qualifying third party indemnity provision.

Chapter 6 Contents of small company accounts

For a small company to take advantage of the exemptions and disclosure concessions provided by CA 2006 s. 415A with respect to the preparation of a directors' report, the report must contain a statement to that effect under s. 419. This is explained in **6.9** below.

s. 496

Where the accounts are audited, the auditors must state in their report whether in their opinion the information given in the directors' report for the financial year for which the annual accounts are prepared is consistent with those accounts (see **Chapter 14**). For small companies, the directors' report is not in other respects subject to audit scrutiny.

Table 6.6 compares the contents of a small company directors' report with the requirements for other companies, including medium-sized companies.

Table 6.6   Contents of directors' report (Section 415)

'Small companies'	*Companies other than 'small companies'*
Section 416	*Section 416*
Names of directors during the financial year.	Names of directors during the financial year.
Principal activities of the company and its subsidiary undertakings and any significant changes during the year.	Principal activities of the company and its subsidiary undertakings and any significant changes during the year.
	Amount of dividend payment, if any, recommended.
	Section 417
	Business review – a fair review of the business, development and performance of the company and its subsidiary undertakings during the financial year (including key performance indicators) and of their position at the end of it.
SI 2008 No. 409 Sch. 5	*SI 2008 No. 410 Sch. 7*
	Asset values – any significant and substantial difference in market value of interests in land at the year end from balance sheet amount.
Political and charitable gifts exceeding £2,000 (not applicable for wholly-owned subsidiaries).	Political and charitable gifts exceeding £2,000 (not applicable for wholly-owned subsidiaries).
	Particulars of any important post balance sheet events affecting the company and its subsidiary undertakings.
	Indication of likely future developments in the business of the company and its subsidiary undertakings.
	Indication of research and development activities (if any), of the company and its subsidiary undertakings.
	Indication of the existence of branches outside UK (unless company is unlimited company).
Particulars of any purchase by the company of its own shares.	Particulars of any purchase by the company of its own shares.

Statement of policy of the company concerning the employment of disabled persons. (*Small companies with 250 or more employees only.*)	Statement of policy of the company concerning the employment of disabled persons. (*Companies with 250 or more employees only.*)
	Statement of arrangements adopted concerning employee involvement. (*Companies with 250 or more employees only.*) Statement of policy and practice on the payment of creditors. (*Public company and large (ie. other than small or medium-sized) subsidiaries only.*) Disclosures relating to the use of financial instruments Disclosures required by certain publicly traded companies

Disclosure of information to auditors (Section 418) – Unless a company is exempt for the financial year in question from the requirements of CA 2006 Part 16 as to audit of accounts (and the directors take advantage of that exemption), the directors' report must also contain a statement as to disclosure of relevant audit information to auditors in accordance with CA 2006 s. 418.

6.8.3 Drafting considerations

When drafting a small company's directors' report for full shareholders' (Companies Act individual) accounts, it is worth bearing in mind whether abbreviated accounts are going to be prepared.

In 'small company' abbreviated accounts, no directors' report is filed.

The directors' report of a 'medium-sized company' is reproduced in full in abbreviated accounts and should be drafted with this in mind. Gross margin and turnover analysis details are not disclosed in abbreviated accounts and the directors' report of a medium-sized company should not therefore be drafted so as to provide such information.

SI 2008 No. 410 reg 4(3)

6.9 Directors' statements

A company which qualifies as a small company in relation to a financial year (other than a dormant company) and takes advantage of the special provisions with respect to the preparation of annual accounts and/or directors' report must include statements in its accounts, where appropriate, on the balance sheet, and in the directors' report confirming preparation in accordance with the small company special provisions.

For small (unquoted) companies, every copy of any balance sheet and directors' report that is published by or on behalf of the company must state the name of the person who signed it on behalf of the board.

s. 433

6.9.1 Directors' statement – small company accounts preparation: Section 414

A company's annual accounts must be approved by the board of directors and signed on behalf of the board by a director of the company. The signature must be on the company's balance sheet.

Chapter 6 Contents of small company accounts

s. 414

If the accounts are prepared in accordance with the provisions applicable to companies subject to the small companies regime, the balance sheet must contain a statement to that effect in a prominent position above the signature.

The balance sheet therefore must contain (in a 'prominent position' above the signature of a director required by s. 433) a statement that the accounts have been prepared in accordance with the provisions applicable to companies subject to the small companies regime within Part 15 of Companies Act 2006 relating to small companies. Reference to the FRSSE (effective April 2008) should also be made in this statement, but only if applicable, as indicated by the tinted text in **Example 6.1** below.

> *Example 6.1*
>
> **Section 414 Directors' statement – balance sheet**
>
> These accounts have been prepared in accordance with the special provisions relating to small companies within Part 15 of the Companies Act 2006 *[and with the Financial Reporting Standard for Smaller Entities (effective April 2008)]*.

The directors' report must be approved by the board of directors and signed on behalf of the board by a director or the secretary of the company.

s. 419

If the report is prepared in accordance with the small companies regime, it must contain a statement to that effect in a prominent position above the signature.

The directors' report must therefore contain (in a 'prominent position' immediately above the signature of a director or secretary required by s. 433) a statement that the report has been prepared in accordance with special provisions of Part 15 of Companies Act 2006 relating to small companies.

> *Example 6.2*
>
> **Section 419 Directors' statement – directors' report**
>
> The above report has been prepared in accordance with the special provisions relating to small companies within Part 15 of the Companies Act 2006.

6.9.2 Directors' statement – small company audit exemption entitlement: Section 475

A small company eligible for audit exemption is required to provide a statutory statement in accordance with CA 2006 s. 475(2) to appear in the balance sheet above the director's signature of approval.

> *Example 6.3*
>
> **Section 475 Directors' statement – entitlement to exemption from audit (Balance sheet)**
>
> For the financial year ended 30 April 2009 the company was entitled to exemption from audit under ss. 475 and 477 [*small company exemption*] [or s. 480] [*dormant company*] [*as the case may be*] Companies Act 2006; and no notice has been deposited under s. 476 [*member or members requesting an audit*].
>
> The directors acknowledge their responsibilities for ensuring that the company keeps accounting records which comply with s. 386 [of the Act] and for preparing accounts which give a true and fair view of the state of affairs of the company as at the end of the financial year and of its profit or loss for the financial year in accordance with the requirements of ss. 394 and 395 and which otherwise comply with the requirements of the Companies Act 2006 relating to accounts, so far as applicable to the company.

6.9.3 Directors' statement – Directors' responsibilities

A small company subject to audit is required (in accordance with international auditing standards) to prepare a more detailed statement appearing, generally, within the directors' report. The APB ISA (UK and Ireland) 700 *The auditors' report on financial statements* requires the financial statements or accompanying information (for example, the directors' report) to include an adequate statement of directors' responsibilities. Where the accounts omit such a statement of responsibilities, the auditors' report must include one.

Example 6.4 reproduces the example directors' responsibilities statement provided in APB Bulletin 2006/6 *Auditors' reports on financial statements in Great Britain and Northern Ireland* (APB Bulletin Appendix 5).

An independent accountants' report on unaudited (audit-exempt) accounts, should, on the same basis, include a statement that the directors are responsible for the preparation of the accounts.

Example 6.4

Example Directors' Responsibilities Statement
Auditors' reports on financial statements in Great Britain and Northern Ireland
APB Bulletin 2006/6 *Appendix 5* [Amended for CA 2006]

'Statement of directors' responsibilities

The directors are responsible for preparing the Annual Report and the financial statements [*accounts*] in accordance with applicable law and regulations.

Company law requires the directors to prepare financial statements [*accounts*] for each financial year. Under that law, the directors have elected to prepare the financial statements [*accounts*] in accordance with United Kingdom Generally Accepted Accounting Practice (United Kingdom Accounting Standards and applicable law). The financial statements [*accounts*] are required by law to give a true and fair view of the state of affairs of the company and of the profit or loss of the company for that period. In preparing these financial statements [*accounts*], the directors are required to:

- select suitable accounting policies and then apply them consistently;
- make judgments and estimates that are reasonable and prudent;
- state whether applicable UK Accounting Standards have been followed, subject to any material departures disclosed and explained in the financial statements [*accounts*] *[Not applicable for small companies;, and*
- prepare the financial statements [*accounts*] on the going concern basis unless it is inappropriate to presume that the company will continue in business.

The directors are responsible for keeping **adequate** accounting records that disclose with reasonable accuracy at any time the financial position of the company and enable them to ensure that the financial statements [*accounts*] comply with the [Companies Act 2006]. They are also responsible for safeguarding the assets of the company and hence for taking reasonable steps for the prevention and detection of fraud and other irregularities.

[*Where the financial statements are published on the internet*] The directors are responsible for the maintenance and integrity of the corporate and financial information included on the company's website. Legislation in the United Kingdom governing the preparation and dissemination of financial statements may differ from legislation in other jurisdictions.'

6.9.4 Directors' statement – Disclosure of information to auditors

For audited companies, the directors' report must contain a statement that so far as each of the directors at the time the report is approved are aware:

- there is no relevant audit information of which the company's auditors are unaware; and
- the directors have taken all steps that they each ought to have taken to make themselves aware of any relevant audit information and to establish that the auditors are aware of that information.

s. 418(2)

Chapter 6 Contents of small company accounts

> **Example 6.5**
>
> **Section 418 Directors' statement as to disclosure of information to auditors (Directors' report)**
>
> The directors confirm that so far as they are aware, there is no relevant audit information of which the company's auditors are unaware. They have taken all the steps that they ought to have taken as directors in order to make themselves aware of any relevant audit information and to establish that the company's auditors are aware of that information.

In practice the directors' statements provided in accordance with APB Bulletin 2006/6 Appendix 5 and CA 2006 s. 418(2) (**Examples 6.3** and **6.4** above) may be combined into one statement.

6.10 Small dormant companies

s. 480 Provided they comply with certain conditions, the Companies Act 2006 permits dormant companies to be exempt from audit. Dormant companies are defined and explained in **7.2** (**Chapter 7**).

Dormant companies which are exempt from audit may file 'small company' abbreviated accounts (an abbreviated balance sheet and notes), without an auditors report, provided the balance sheet contains a statement by the directors in accordance with s. 475(2) (see Example accounts in **Chapter 13**).

6.11 Disclosure of directors' remuneration – small companies

Companies Act 2006 s. 412 provides for regulations to be made about the disclosure of directors' remuneration. These are contained in SI 2008 No. 409 'The Small Companies and Groups (Accounts and Directors' Report) Regulations 2008'.

For small companies, as defined, the only details in respect of directors' remuneration and benefits that are required are as set out in Sch. 3 of SI 2008 No. 409 and summarised in **Table 6.7** below.

Schedule 3 of SI 2008 No. 409 ('Information about Directors' Benefits: Remuneration (Companies Act or IAS accounts)') is set out in **Appendix E**.

> **Table 6.7 Small companies – directors' remuneration**
>
> A small company is required to disclose the overall total amounts of:
>
> - directors' remuneration in respect of qualifying services (paid to or receivable by directors), being the total of the aggregates of: *Sch 3.1*
>   (a) directors' remuneration (including salaries, fees, bonuses, expense allowances and estimated non-cash benefits receivable);
>   (b) money or assets received or receivable (other than shares or share options) under long-term incentive schemes;
>   (c) company contributions paid to money purchase pension schemes;
> - compensation to directors or past directors for loss of office (CA 2006 s. 215); *Sch 3.2*
> - sums paid to third parties in respect of directors' services. *Sch 3.3*
>
> Disclosure is also required of the number of directors (if any) to whom retirement benefits are accruing in respect of qualifying services for: *Sch 3.1*
>
> - money purchase schemes, and
> - defined benefit schemes.

Companies Act 2006 Section 413 provides for the disclosure of directors' benefits: advances credit and guarantees.

In the case of a company that does not prepare group accounts, details of:

- advances and credits granted by the company to its directors; and
- guarantees of any kind entered into by the company on behalf of its directors,

must be shown in the notes to the company's individual accounts.   *s. 413*

Companies Act 2006 ss. 412 and 413 are set out in full in **Appendix B**.

6.12 Disclosure of auditor's remuneration – small audited companies

Requirements for the disclosure of auditors' remuneration in respect of small and medium-sized companies are provided by SI 2008 No. 489 'The Companies (Disclosure of Auditor Remuneration and Liability Limitation Agreements) Regulations 2008'.

Remuneration receivable by a small company's auditor for auditing the accounts must be disclosed in a note to the annual accounts. Remuneration includes benefits in kind and the nature and estimated money-value of those benefits must also be disclosed.

Where more than one person has been appointed as a company's auditor in respect of any financial period, separate disclosure is required in respect of the remuneration of each such person.   *SI 2008 No. 489 reg 4(1)–(3)*

For a medium-sized company, disclosure of remuneration may be required in respect of assurance services (other than auditing), tax advisory services, and other services.   *SI 2008 No. 489 reg 4(4)*

A small eligible parent company preparing audited group accounts must disclose consolidated auditors' remuneration information on the basis of SI 2008 No. 489 regulation 6, in which case neither the parent company's individual accounts nor those of its subsidiaries need disclose auditors' remuneration.   *SI 2008 No. 489 reg 6*

Chapter 7 Dormant companies

7.1 Dormant companies

For the purposes of the Companies Acts, a company is 'dormant' during any period in which it has no significant accounting transaction. – ('significant accounting transaction' is explained below in **7.2**).

s.1169(1)

Dormant companies (as defined) are no longer required to pass a special resolution in order to qualify for exemption from audit but qualify automatically provided ten per cent of the members do not request an audit, as explained in **7.3** below.

Dormant companies which are exempt from audit may file abbreviated accounts under the small companies regime (an abbreviated balance sheet and notes), without an auditors' report, provided the balance sheet contains a statement by the directors in accordance with Companies Act 2006 s. 475. (See Example accounts in **Chapter 13** and abbreviated accounts in **Chapter 8**).

Conditions for exemption are subject to:

- the requirement for a statement to be contained in the balance sheet (see **7.5**);
- the right of members to require audit (see **7.3**); and
- companies excluded from dormant companies exemption (see **7.4**).

7.2 Definition of 'dormant company'

A dormant company is a company which (during any period) has no 'significant accounting transaction'.

s. 1169(2))

A 'significant accounting transaction' means a transaction which is required by CA 2006 s. 386 to be entered in the company's accounting records, *other than* transactions:

- consisting of penalties or payments to the Registrar for
    (a) change of name fee;
    (b) re-registration fee (*on the re-registration of a company's status, e.g. to public company*);
    (c) penalty for failure to deliver accounts (*under s. 453*);
    (d) annual return registration fee, or
- arising from the taking of shares by a subscriber to the memorandum, on the formation of the company.

7.3 Conditions for exemption from audit

A company is exempt from the requirements for audit of its accounts in respect of a financial year if:

- it has been dormant since its formation, or
- it has been dormant since the end of the previous financial year.

s. 480

Further, to be exempt the company must also:

Chapter 7 Dormant companies

ss. 381–384
- be entitled to prepare its individual accounts in accordance with the small companies regime, and
- not be required to prepare group accounts for that year.

s. 479 (3)
A public company or a member of an ineligible group which are dormant and would otherwise be entitled to prepare individual accounts in accordance with the small companies regime are nevertheless exempt from the requirements for audit. A company that is both a subsidiary undertaking and dormant is, therefore, not excluded from exemption throughout the whole of the period or periods during the financial year when it is a group company.

Companies Act 2006 section 476 states that members of a company that would otherwise be entitled to exemption from audit may require it to obtain an audit of its accounts for a financial year by giving notice under the section. The notice must be given by members representing not less than

s. 476
- 10 per cent in total of the nominal value of the company's issued share capital (or any class of it); or
- 10 per cent in number of the members of the company (for a company not having a share capital).

The notice may not be given before the financial year to which it relates and must be given not later than one month before the end of that year.

A dormant company is not entitled to audit exemption unless its balance sheet contains a statement or statements under Companies Act 2006 s. 475(2) as explained in **7.5** below.

A dormant company is not exempt from audit (and an audit of the accounts is, therefore necessary) if there is a specific requirement in the company's articles of association to appoint auditors.

7.4 Companies excluded from dormant companies' exemption

A company is not entitled to the exemption from audit (conferred by Companies Act 2006 s. 480) if:

(a) it was at any time within the financial year one of the following:

SI 2007
No. 2932
- an authorised insurance company;
- a banking company;
- an e-money issuer;
- an MiFID investment firm;
- a UCITS management company; or

s. 481
(b) the company carries on insurance market activity.

7.5 Directors' statements – entitlement to exemption

s. 480(3)
A dormant company is not entitled to audit exemption unless its balance sheet contains a statement or statements by the directors to that effect that:

- the company is entitled to exemption from audit by virtue of Companies Act 2006 s. 480;
- the members have not required the company to obtain an audit of its accounts for the year in question in accordance with Companies Act 2006 s. 476; and
- the directors acknowledge their responsibilities for complying with the requirements of the Companies Act 2006 with respect to accounting records and the preparation of accounts.

s. 475(3)

The statements required to entitle audit exemption as above must appear on the balance sheet above the signature required to approve the accounts under Companies Act 2006 s. 414.

7.6 Dormant company acting as agent

Where the directors of a dormant company take advantage of audit exemption (conferred by Companies Act 2006 s. 480) and the company has during the financial year acted as an agent for any person, the accounts (small company individual accounts and abbreviated accounts) are required to disclose that fact (SI 2008 No. 409 Schedule 1.63).

Sch 1.63

7.7 CA 2006 sections 480–481 – Dormant company exemption from audit

Sections 480 and 481 are reproduced in **Table 7.1**

Table 7.1   CA 2006 ss. 480–481 Exemption from audit: dormant companies

480 Dormant companies: conditions for exemption from audit

(1) A company is exempt from the requirements of this Act relating to the audit of accounts in respect of a financial year if—

   (a) it has been dormant since its formation, or
   (b) it has been dormant since the end of the previous financial year and the following conditions are met.

(2) The conditions are that the company—

   (a) as regards its individual accounts for the financial year in question—
       (i) is entitled to prepare accounts in accordance with the small companies regime (see sections 381 to 384), or
       (ii) would be so entitled but for having been a public company or a member of an ineligible group, and
   (b) is not required to prepare group accounts for that year.

(3) This section has effect subject to—

   section 475(2) and (3) (requirements as to statements to be contained in balance sheet),
   section 476 (right of members to require audit), and
   section 481 (companies excluded from dormant companies exemption).

481 Companies excluded from dormant companies exemption

A company is not entitled to the exemption conferred by section 480 (dormant companies) if it was at any time within the financial year in question a company that—

   (a) is an authorised insurance company, a banking company, an e-money issuer, a MiFID investment firm or a UCITS management company, or
   (b) carries on insurance market activity.

7.8 Dormant companies – e-filing

Dormant company accounts (and also unaudited abbreviated accounts) can be filed with the Registrar of Companies by online WebFiling via the Companies House website at: *www.companieshouse.gov.uk*

See **Chapter 8** at **8.3** and also **Chapter 1** at **1.5** for further comment on e-filing dormant company accounts and unaudited abbreviated accounts.

Chapter 8 Abbreviated accounts

8.1 Abbreviated accounts

A company classified as small and preparing Companies Act (but not IAS) accounts, is permitted to deliver 'abbreviated accounts', in place of full statutory accounts ('individual accounts'), to the Registrar of Companies. Accounts abbreviated in such a way are statutory accounts and are then filed as 'annual accounts' with the Registrar of Companies in accordance with the Companies Act 2006 s. 444 for small companies.

Abbreviated accounts are accounts prepared in accordance with:

Small company
(a) SI 2008 No. 409 Schedule 4 (Part 1) – abbreviated balance sheet
(b) SI 2008 No. 409 Schedule 4 (Part 2) – limited disclosures

Medium-sized company
SI 2008 No. 410 Schedule 1 and Regulation 4 – minimal disclosure exemptions within medium-sized company profit and loss account.

8.2 Contents of abbreviated accounts

Abbreviated accounts are not required to give a true and fair view; they are a form of accounts containing less information and disclosure than the full individual annual accounts for shareholders and basically comprise:

Small company – 'an abbreviated balance sheet', being an abbreviated version of the full balance sheet, and certain notes.

Medium-sized company – full statutory accounts (to accord with SI 2008 No. 410) *except* that analysis of turnover and derivative of gross profit or loss may be omitted.

A summary of the options available for filing small company accounts with the registrar of companies is set out in **8.3**. Abbreviated accounts will usually comprise the elements shown in **Table 8.2**.

Abbreviated accounts, in practice, can be prepared on the basis of minimal or selective amendments from full annual accounts prepared under SI 2008 No. 409 Sch. 1, remembering that abbreviated accounts must be copies of those elements of the company's (full shareholders) annual accounts and reports that are required under SI 2008 No. 409 Sch. 4. (See **8.3** below)

8.3 Filing abbreviated accounts

The filing requirements for abbreviated accounts are set out in CA 2006 s. 444(3) (small companies) and CA 2006 s. 445 (3) (medium-sized companies).

The directors of a company subject to the small companies regime **must** deliver to the registrar for each financial year a copy of a balance sheet drawn up as at the last day of that year.

A small company preparing Companies Act accounts is required to send a copy of its full

Chapter 8 Abbreviated accounts

annual accounts and directors' report to its members. It must also deliver to the Registrar of Companies one of the following:

- Full annual accounts – full individual or group annual accounts prepared in accordance with CA 2006 and SI 2008 No. 409, or full IAS accounts;
- Abbreviated accounts – prepared in accordance with SI 2008 No.409 Regulation 6;
- Copy of the full balance sheet as sent to its members – prepared in accordance with CA 2006 and SI 2008 No. 409; or
- Copy of the full balance sheet and profit and loss account as sent to its members – prepared in accordance with CA 2006 and SI 2008 No. 409.

There is no provision for filing (delivering) either "abbreviated group accounts" or IAS accounts as abbreviated accounts.

Eligible small companies that are subject to the small companies regime are able to choose whether or not to file a profit and loss account or directors' report. **Table 8.1** below summarises the options available.

Table 8.1 Filing accounts on public record – summary of options available

FILING OPTION	**Full annual accounts** *Companies Act and IAS accounts*	**Full balance sheet only** *Companies Act and IAS accounts*	**Abbreviated accounts** *Companies Act accounts only*	**Abbreviated balance sheet only** *Companies Act accounts only*
Copy full balance sheet	Yes	Yes	n/a	n/a
Balance sheet statement – *under s. 444(5)*	No – n/a	Yes – *where P&L account and /or Directors' report not filed*	n/a	Yes – *where P&L account and /or Directors' report not filed*
Balance sheet statement – *under s. 414*	Yes	No – n/a	No – n/a	No – n/a
Copy full P&L account	Yes	No – *filing optional*	Optional	No – n/a
Copy Directors' report	Yes	No – *filing optional*	Optional	No – n/a
Auditors' report *(if applicable)*				
– under s. 495	Yes – *if accounts audited*	Yes (full s. 495 auditors' report) * – *if full accounts audited*	No – n/a	Yes (full s. 495 auditors' report) * – *if full accounts audited*
– statement under s. 496 (where directors' report filed)	Yes – *if accounts audited*	No – n/a	Yes – *if full accounts audited*	No – n/a
Companies Act (UK GAAP) accounts preparation – *under SI 2008 No. 409* regulations	Yes *(Sch 1)*	Yes *(Sch 1)*	Yes *(Sch 4)*	Yes *(Sch 4)*
Prescribed notes (including accounting policies)	Yes	Yes	Yes – *Per SI 2008 No. 409 (including Sch 4)*	Yes – *Per SI 2008 No. 409 (including Sch 4)*
Special Auditors' report – *under s. 449*	n/a	No – n/a	Yes – *if full accounts audited*	No – n/a
Approval, signature and balance sheet statement – *under s. 450 (abbreviated accounts)*	n/a	No – n/a	Yes	Yes

Filing abbreviated accounts

The accounts of a small company may be audited in circumstances where it is either:

- Not exempt from audit, or
- If exempt from audit, advantage is not taken of that exemption.

Where accounts delivered are audited but neither abbreviated accounts nor full annual accounts, the auditors' report delivered with them is the full report under CA 2006 s. 495 notwithstanding that the accounts themselves may be restricted in content, for example, to simply a balance sheet. (This is indicated in **Table 8.1** above by *). In these circumstances, APB in its Bulletin 2008/4 (April 2008) suggests that the auditors' report should be accompanied by a textual explanation on the following lines:

> *Although the company is only required to file a balance sheet, the Companies Act 2006 requires the accompanying auditor's report to be a copy of our report to the members on the company's full annual accounts and directors' report. Readers are cautioned that the profit and loss account and certain other primary statements and the directors' report, referred to in the copy of our auditor's report, are not required to be filed with the Registrar of Companies.*

Table 8.2 Abbreviated accounts

	Small company SI 2008 No. 409 Sch. 4	Medium-sized company SI 2008 No. 410 Sch. 1
Directors' report	No report	Full report
Profit and loss account	No profit and loss account	Profit and loss account must disclose 'turnover' but may combine items to disclose 'gross profit or loss'
Balance sheet	Abbreviated balance sheet – SI 2008 No. 409 Sch. 4 format Debtors and creditors falling due after more than one year	Full balance sheet – SI 2008 No. 410 Sch. 1 format
Cash flow and other primary statements	Not required[(1)]	Full statements required
Notes	Limited information only SI 2008 No. 409 Sch. 4 disclosures No information on directors' or employees' remuneration No disclosure of auditors' remuneration	Full notes, including disclosure of turnover (but omitting turnover analysis) (SI 2008 No. 410 reg. 4(2))
Auditors' report	Special report	Special report

[(1)] *Although the voluntary disclosure of a cash flow statement is 'encouraged' by the FRSSE*

The directors **may** also file (deliver to the registrar):

- a copy of the company's profit and loss account for that year; and
- a copy of the directors' report for that year.

Chapter 8 Abbreviated accounts

They **must** also deliver to the registrar a copy of the auditor's report on those accounts and on the directors' report (unless the company has taken advantage of exemption from audit).

The copies of accounts and reports delivered to the registrar must be copies of the company's (full shareholders) annual accounts and reports (that is, reproducing the contents of the annual accounts and report), *except* that (where the company prepares Companies Act accounts) the directors *may* deliver to the registrar 'abbreviated accounts' drawn up in accordance with statutory regulations; these regulations are the SI 2008 No. 409 for small companies and SI 2008 No. 410 for medium-sized companies.

If abbreviated accounts are delivered to the registrar, and the company is not exempt from audit (or the directors have not taken advantage of any such exemption), the accounts must be delivered together with a copy of the special auditor's report required by s. 449.

Approval and signing obligations generally, for Companies Act accounts that are not abbreviated accounts or where the directors of a company subject to the small companies regime deliver to the registrar IAS accounts, are dealt with in **Chapter 3** at **3.11**.

The balance sheet delivered to the registrar must contain in a prominent position a statement that the company's annual accounts and reports have been delivered in accordance with the provisions applicable to companies subject to the small companies regime. (See **8.5**)

The copies of the balance sheet and any directors' report delivered to the registrar under this section must state the name of the person who signed it on behalf of the board.

The decision whether or not to take advantage of the exemptions to prepare abbreviated accounts will be a commercial one. Full statutory accounts have to be prepared in any case for shareholders; the directors of small or medium-sized companies will have regard to:

- the additional costs involved in the preparation of an additional set of accounts,
- the financial information omitted in abbreviated accounts; and
- the sensitivity or confidentiality of financial information required for public disclosure.

A decision can only be reached after a comparison is made of full and limited disclosure and after the relative costs and benefits have been considered. Many small companies now chose to produce abbreviated accounts (see **Chapter 1** at **1.1.2**).

8.4 Abbreviated balance sheet

The balance sheet format and contents in abbreviated accounts of a small company are set out in regulations under SI 2008 No. 409 Sch. 4.

Sch 4.1(1) A small company may deliver to the registrar a copy of the balance sheet showing the items listed in either of the balance sheet formats set out in the regulations, in the order and under the headings and sub-headings given in the format adopted, but in other respects corresponding to the full balance sheet of the company.

The abbreviated balance sheet formats provided by SI 2008 No. 409 Schedule 4 are set out in **Table 8.3**. Schedule 4 is reproduced in full in **Appendix D**.

> **Table 8.3 Form and content of abbreviated accounts of small companies delivered to Registrar (SI 2008 No. 409 Sch. 4)**
>
> BALANCE SHEET FORMATS
>
> The items listed in either of the balance sheet formats set out below must be shown in the order and under the headings and sub-headings given in the format adopted, but in other respects corresponding to the full balance sheet.
>
> **Balance sheet formats**
>
> | Format 1 | Format 2 |
> |---|---|
> | | ASSETS |
> | A. Called up share capital not paid | A. Called up share capital not paid |
> | B. Fixed assets
　I　Intangible assets
　II　Tangible assets
　III　Investments | B. Fixed assets
　I　Intangible assets
　II　Tangible assets
　III　Investments |
> | C. Current assets
　I　Stocks
　II　Debtors
　III　Investments
　IV　Cash at bank and in hand | C. Current assets
　I　Stocks
　II　Debtors
　III　Investments
　IV　Cash at bank and in hand |
> | D. Prepayments and accrued income | D. Prepayments and accrued income |
> | E. Creditors: amounts falling due within one year | LIABILITIES |
> | F. Net current assets (liabilities) | A. Capital and reserves
　I　Called up share capital
　II　Share premium account
　III　Revaluation reserve
　IV　Other reserves
　V　Profit and loss account |
> | G. Total assets less current liabilities | |
> | H. Creditors: amounts falling due after more than one year | |
> | I. Provisions for liabilities | B. Provisions for liabilities |
> | J. Accruals and deferred income | C. Creditors |
> | K. Capitals and reserves
　I　Called up share capital
　II　Share premium account
　III　Revaluation reserve
　IV　Other reserves
　V　Profit and loss account | D. Accruals and deferred income |
>
> **Debtors (both formats)** – *the aggregate amount of debtors falling due after more than one year must be shown separately unless it is disclosed in the notes to the accounts.*
>
> **Creditors (format 2)** – *the aggregate amount of creditors falling due after more than one year must be shown separately unless it is disclosed in the notes to the accounts.*

8.5 Directors' statements

Abbreviated accounts must include a statement in a prominent position on the balance sheet (above the signature of the director) that the accounts have been prepared in accordance with the provisions applicable to companies subject to the small companies regime (SI 2008 No. 409 Sch. 4.1(2)).

The requirement can be illustrated as follows:

Chapter 8 Abbreviated accounts

> 'The [abbreviated] accounts have been prepared in accordance with the provisions applicable to companies subject to the small companies regime of the Companies Act 2006'.

or

> 'These [abbreviated] accounts have been prepared in accordance with the special provisions relating to small companies within Part 15 of Companies Act 2006'.

Accounts that are subject to audit exemption are also required to have additional statements as explained in **Chapter 11** and illustrated in **Example 11.1**.

8.6 Notes to abbreviated accounts

Sch. 4.2

Any information required for the purposes of the abbreviated accounts of a small company must (if not given in the accounts themselves (that is, the balance sheet or profit and loss account, as appropriate)) be given by way of a note to the accounts.

The information required to be given by way of a note is set out in **Table 8.4**.

SI 2008 No. 409 Sch. 4 is reproduced in **Appendix D**.

Table 8.4   Notes to abbreviated accounts

	SI 2008 No.409 Sch. 4 paragraph	Illustrated in example abbreviated accounts by
Accounting policies	3	Note 1
Share capital and redeemable shares	4	Note 5
Particulars of share allotments	5	Note 5
Fixed assets movements, valuation and depreciation [for letter or Roman number format headings only]	6	Note 2
Financial fixed assets in excess of fair value	7	—
Debtors: amounts falling due after more than one year (aggregate)	Formats footnote (1)	Note 3
Creditors: amounts falling due within one year or after more than one year for each category of creditors (Format 2)	Formats footnote (2)	—
Particulars of creditors:		Note 4
Debts falling due after five years	8(1)	
Secured debts	8(2)	
Basis of translation of foreign currencies	9	Note 1
Comparative figures [required by FRSSE/accounting standards]		Accounts
	SI 2008 No.409 Sch. 2 paragraph	
Subsidiary undertakings	1–3/11	Note 2
Other significant (20% or more) undertakings	5–7/11	—
Membership of certain qualifying undertakings (being a partnership or unlimited company)	8	—
Parent undertakings and ultimate parent company	9–11	—
	CA 2006 section	
Directors' benefits: advances, credits and guarantees	413	Note 6

8.7 Approval and signing of abbreviated accounts

Companies Act 2006 s. 450 sets out the provisions for the approval and signing of abbreviated accounts.

Abbreviated accounts must be approved by the board of directors and signed on behalf of the board by a director of the company. The signature must be on the balance sheet.

s. 450(1)–(2)

The balance sheet must contain in a prominent position above the signature, a statement to the effect that it is prepared in accordance with the special provisions of the Companies Act relating (as the case may be) to companies subject to the small companies regime or to medium-sized companies.

s. 450(3)

There are provisions dealing with penalties if abbreviated accounts are approved that do not comply with the statutory requirements of the Companies Act 2006.

s. 450(4)–(5)

8.8 Parent companies

As noted in **Chapter 9** at **9.4**, there is no statutory provision to file abbreviated group accounts. A parent company which files its own abbreviated individual accounts includes within those accounts considerable disclosure relating to subsidiaries and other significant holdings in undertakings (see **Chapter 9** and **Chapter 12** at **12.7**).

A parent company wishing to produce group accounts will need to prepare these as statutory accounts in addition to its own statutory individual abbreviated accounts.

8.9 Special auditors' report (CA 2006 s. 449)

Abbreviated accounts prepared by an audit-exempt company are not required to contain an auditors' report (but see the requirement for directors' statement in **8.5** above).

Where the directors of a company deliver abbreviated accounts to the registrar and the company is not exempt from audit (or the directors have not taken advantage of any such exemption), they must also deliver to the registrar a copy of a special report of the company's auditor stating that in his opinion:

- the company is entitled to deliver abbreviated accounts in accordance with the relevant section s. 444(3) (small companies) or 445(3) (medium-sized companies) (as appropriate); and
- the abbreviated accounts to be delivered are properly prepared in accordance regulations under SI 2008 No. 409 Sch. 4 (small companies) or regulations under SI 2008 No. 410 Schedule 1 (medium-sized companies).

Where produced, a special auditors' report is not required to include the full auditors' report under s. 495, reproduced in full, except where:

s. 449(3)

- the s. 495 report was qualified; or
- the s. 495 report contained a statement under s. 498(2)(a) or (b) (accounts, records or returns inadequate or accounts not agreeing with records or returns) or s. 498(3) (failure to obtain necessary information and explanations).

The legislation does not envisage a qualified opinion; if the auditor cannot give the positive statements of opinion required as above, the directors are not entitled to deliver abbreviated accounts.

APB guidance has been provided in APB Bulletin 2008/4 *The special auditor's report on abbreviated accounts in the United Kingdom* (April 2008) and is reflected in the example reports on abbreviated accounts in **Chapter 14**.

Chapter 8 Abbreviated accounts

In Bulletin 2008/4, the APB recommend, where the CA 2006 s. 495 report is unqualified but contains an explanatory paragraph regarding a fundamental uncertainty (for example, concerning the going concern basis), the special auditors' report should also include the explanatory paragraph, within a section entitled 'Other information'. The auditor should include whatever information is considered important for a proper understanding of the report.

8.10 Medium-sized companies

8.10.1 *Annual accounts – medium-sized companies*

The directors of a company that *qualifies* as a medium-sized company in relation to a financial year (see ss. 465 to 467) *must* deliver to the registrar a copy of:

- the company's annual accounts;
- the directors' report; and
- the auditor's report on the accounts and directors' report (as applicable).

8.10.2 *Medium-sized company abbreviated accounts*

Where medium-sized company prepares Companies Act accounts, the directors *may* deliver to the registrar 'abbreviated accounts', these being a copy of the company's annual accounts for the financial year that includes a profit and loss account in which items are combined in accordance with regulations under SI 2008 No. 410 *The Large and Medium-sized Companies and Groups (Accounts and Reports) Regulations 2008*, and where any items whose omission is authorised by the regulations are omitted.

The copies of the accounts and reports delivered to the registrar as the 'abbreviated accounts' must be **copies** of the company's annual accounts and reports, except that where the company prepares Companies Act accounts, the directors may deliver to the registrar a copy of a balance sheet drawn up in accordance with statutory regulations; these regulations are the SI 2008 No. 410 for medium-sized companies.

8.10.3 *Medium-sized company – abbreviated profit and loss account*

SI 2008 No. 410 reg. 4(3)

A medium-sized company may prepare abbreviated accounts in which the profit and loss account includes items that are combined; these items are (in format 1 'cost of sales', 'gross profit or loss', and 'other operating income' as in **Table 8.5**.

The combination does not result in a figure of 'gross profit or loss' and it will be appreciated that the combination depends on which format is adopted and the inclusion of 'other operating income'. 'Staff costs' and 'depreciation charges' are excluded in Formats 2 and 4.

Table 8.5 Profit and loss account items combined as 'Gross profit or loss' (SI 2008 No. 410 Regulation 4(3))

Format 1	Format 2	Format 3	Format 4
2 Cost of sales		A1 Cost of sales	
	2 Change in stocks of finished goods and work-in-progress		A1 Reduction in stocks of finished goods and work-in-progress
			B2 Increase in stocks of finished goods and work-in-progress
3 Gross profit or loss			

6 Other operating income	3 Own work capitalised 4 Other operating income 5 (a) Raw materials and consumables (b) Other external charges	B2 Other operating income	B3 Own work capitalised B4 Other operating income A2 (a) Raw materials and consumables (b) Other external charges

*References are to item numbers in the statutory formats of **SI 2008 No. 410 Sch. 1***

8.11 Small company abbreviated accounts checklist

This checklist provides a guide to the appropriate disclosure requirements in producing 'abbreviated accounts' for delivery to the Registrar of Companies. This applies where the company prepares Companies Act accounts. Abbreviated accounts are not available for filing where IAS accounts are prepared, although a small company is not required to file its IAS profit and loss account.

s. 444(3)

This checklist does not purport to be a complete checklist, detailing the disclosure requirements applicable where individual full accounts are prepared. For this purpose one of the accounts checklists suggested in **Appendix F** should be used.

Special provisions may additionally apply where a company is a 'dormant company' under the Companies Act 2006 s. 480 (see also **Chapter 7**).

References in this checklist to 'full accounts' include 'small company individual accounts' (in accordance with SI 2008 No. 409 Sch. 1 – see **6.1**)).

Where the small company is audit-exempt, there is no requirement for a special auditors report (see **7** in checklist below).

Table 8.6 Checklist for the preparation of abbreviated accounts

A company which qualifies as small or medium-sized is entitled to deliver abbreviated accounts to the Registrar of Companies (CA 2006 s. 444). A medium-sized company is also entitled to deliver abbreviated accounts to the Registrar in accordance with CA 2006 s. 445 (see **8.10**).

Company classification — *ss. 244–445*

1. Complete the following information:				
	2009	2008	2007	
Turnover	£	£	£	
Balance sheet total	£	£	£	
Employees				
Dormant?	Yes/No	Yes/No	Yes/No	*s. 1169*

Refer to 'Decision chart to determine size qualification' (**Figure 5.1**).

Two of the following three criteria must be met:

		Small company	Medium-sized company	
Turnover	Under	£6.5 million	£25.9 million	*s. 382–4* *s. 465–7*
Balance sheet total (gross assets before deducting liabilities, ie A–D (Format 1) or total of 'assets' (Format 2))	Under	£3.26 million	£12.9 million	*SI 2008* *No. 393*
Employees (average number)	Under	50	250	

75

Chapter 8 Abbreviated accounts

s. 383	Companies that are: (a) public companies; (b) authorised insurance companies, banking companies, e-money issuers, MiFID investment firms or UCITS management companies; (c) companies carrying on insurance market activity; or (d) members of an ineligible group (basically, containing companies within (a) to (c)) are not entitled to prepare abbreviated accounts. (Refer to Chapter 5 at **5.1**). A parent company is not treated as small or medium-sized unless the group headed by it is small or medium-sized respectively. Transitional determination of qualifying criteria: see note at end of checklist.	

	Are abbreviated accounts appropriate?	✓ or N/A
	2. Based on the above information	

	(a) The company qualifies as:
	    (i) small (if so, answer **3** to **11**) } abbreviated accounts
	    (ii) medium-sized (if so, answer **3** to **7** and **13**) } may be prepared
	(b) The company qualifies as dormant (if so, answer **5, 6** and **8** to **12**)
	(c) The company is:
	    (i) ineligible } if so, abbreviated
	    or accounts *not*
	    (ii) other (ie neither 'small' nor 'medium-sized') appropriate	

	Directors' statements and signature	
s. 414(3)	3. Directors are required to state in a prominent position above approval signature on the balance sheet that the accounts are prepared in accordance with the special provisions of CA 2006 relating to small companies.	
s. 475–476	4. Where advantage is taken of audit exemption, the directors are required to confirm or acknowledge: (a) company's entitlement to audit exemption (b) members have not required the company to obtain an audit (s. 476 CA 2006) (c) duty to keep accounting records (s. 386 CA 2006) (d) duty to prepare true and fair view accounts (ss. 393–394 CA 2006).	
s. 475(2) s. 480	5. If the company is dormant and is exempt from the provisions relating to the audit of accounts, a statement is required as in **4** above.	
s. 414	6. Abbreviated balance sheet (small company) or full balance sheet (medium-sized company) must be signed by a director (in accordance with CA 2005 s. 414) on behalf of the board.	
	Special auditors' report **(Not applicable where 'dormant company' under CA 2006 s. 480 or advantage taken of small company audit exemption)**	
s. 449(1) s. 449(2)	7. Where abbreviated accounts are filed, the special auditors' report is required to state that in the auditors' opinion: (a) the company is entitled to deliver abbreviated accounts prepared in accordance with the relevant provision (s. 444(1)–(3) [small companies] or s. 445(1)–(3) [medium-sized companies]); (b) the accounts are properly prepared in accordance with that relevant provision.	
s. 449(3)	If the auditors' report on the full shareholders' accounts was qualified, the special report must reproduce the text in full (with further material necessary to understand a qualification).	
s. 449(3)	The special auditors' report must also reproduce any statement contained in the full auditors' report under s. 498 (2) or (3) (proper accounting records or failure to obtain necessary information, etc.).	
s. 246(5) SI 2008 No. 409 3(3)	*Small company* Note: Small company Companies Act individual accounts exceeding the basic SI 2008 No. 409 Sch. 1 minimum requirements may be presented as abbreviated accounts.	
	8. No directors' report.	
s. 444(3)	9. No profit and loss account.	

76

Small company abbreviated accounts checklist

10. Balance sheet – abbreviated version	
(a) Only format headings with letter or Roman number need be shown (in the order and presentation of Sl.2008 No. 409 Sch 4).	*Sch 4.1(1)*
(b) For debtors *and* creditors, show aggregate amounts falling due: *formats*	*Sch 4*
(i) within one year;	
(ii) after more than one year,	
(unless shown in notes).	
(c) The signature of a director (see **6** above).	*s. 444(6)*
11. Notes – show only:	*Sch 4.2*
(a) Accounting policies adopted – including:	*Sch 4.3*
• depreciation and diminution in value of assets, and	
• statement of preparation in accordance with the FRSSE (if applicable).	
(b) Share capital:	*Sch 4.4*
(i) number and aggregate nominal value of allotted shares of each class;	*Sch 4.4(1)*
(ii) share allotments during the year- – state classes allotted and reason for allotment and for each class of shares, the number allotted, their aggregate nominal value and the consideration received by the company;	*Sch 4.5*
(iii) redeemable shares – redemption dates and option details *(Preference shares as financial liabilities).*	*Sch 4.4(2)*
(c) Fixed assets –	
• movements – only format headings with letter or Roman number (i.e., movements in tangible fixed assets, intangible fixed assets, and fixed asset investments for the categories in total) need be shown, including cost or valuation and accumulated depreciation at beginning and end of year; additions, disposals, revaluations, and depreciation provisions,	*Sch 4.6(1)–(3)*
• fair value disclosure of financial fixed assets.	*Sch 4.7*
(d) Creditors and indebtedness	
(i) liabilities repayable in more than five years	*Sch 4.8*
(1) amount due for repayment, other than by instalments, after more than five years from the balance sheet date;	
(2) amount repayable by instalments, after more than five years;	
(ii) aggregate amount of *secured* liabilities.	*Sch 4.8(2)*
(e) Foreign currencies – basis for translating sums denominated in foreign currencies.	*Sch 4.9*
(f) Comparative figures (in accordance with accounting standards). Where corresponding amounts are not comparable, adjust and give particulars of and reasons for adjustment.	
(g) Particulars of subsidiary undertakings. For disclosure details see **Chapter 12** at **12.7** *(Details of shares of the company held by subsidiary undertakings (SI 2008 No. 409 Sch. 2.4) are **not** required to be disclosed in abbreviated accounts)*	*Sch 2.1–3*
(h) Particulars of holdings in undertakings (other than subsidiary undertakings) where holdings exceed 20 per cent ('significant holdings'). (For disclosure details see **Chapter 12** at **12.7**.)	*Sch 2.5–8*
(i) Parent undertakings (name and country of incorporation or principal business address if unincorporated).	*Sch 2.9*
(j) Ultimate parent company.	*Sch 2.10*
(k) Directors benefits: advances, credits and guarantees. *(Details of directors remuneration (SI 2008 No. 409 Sch. 3) are **not** required to be disclosed in abbreviated accounts)*	*s. 413*
Dormant company – acting as agent	
12. Where an audit-exempt dormant company (under s. 480) has acted as agent for any person during the financial year, that fact must be disclosed in the notes to the accounts.	*Sch 4.10*
Medium-sized company	*s. 465 s. 445(3)*
13. Full shareholders' (Companies Act) accounts, including directors' report, should be reproduced as abbreviated accounts *except*:	
(a) Profit and loss account may combine items. (Turnover requires disclosure) 'Gross profit or loss' is achieved by combining items 2, 3 *and* 6 (Format 1) items 2 to 5 (Format 2) items A1 and B2 (Format 3) items A1, A2 and B1 to B4 (Format 4)	*SI 2008 No. 410 reg. 4*
(b) Notes may omit information required by SI 2008 No. 410 Sch. 1.68: turnover analysis by class of business and geographical market.	
(c) Director's report – 'Business review' and non-financial information (otherwise required by s. 417(6)) may be omitted	*s. 417 (7)*

Chapter 8 Abbreviated accounts

Transitional determination of qualification – In determining whether a company or group qualifies as small or medium-sized under CA 2006 ss. 382(2), 383(3), 465(2) or 466(3) (qualification in relation to subsequent financial year by reference to circumstances in preceding financial years), for financial years ending on or after 6th April 2008, a company or group is treated as having qualified as small or medium-sized (as the case may be) in any previous financial year in which it would have so qualified as if the increased thresholds introduced by the Regulations (SI 2008 No. 393 reg 2(3)) had been in force.

Chapter 9 Group accounts – small groups

9.1 Small companies – option to prepare group accounts

If at the end of a financial year a company subject to the small companies regime is a parent company the directors, as well as preparing individual accounts for the year, *may* prepare group accounts for the year. On this basis, a small parent company (as defined) is not, therefore, required to prepare group accounts.

All other parent companies (being companies that are ineligible or excluded from the small companies regime under CA 2006 s. 384) *must* prepare group accounts for the year *unless* the company is otherwise exempt from that requirement under exemptions set out in CA 2006 s. 399(3).

Notwithstanding the above, a small parent company may prepare group accounts for its own management accounting purposes and not submit them to the Registrar of Companies but file instead its own individual statutory accounts with appropriate disclosures. If group accounts are not prepared because of the group accounts exemption entitlement, the company may, if it wishes, file abbreviated accounts provided it qualifies as a small (or medium-sized) company.

A medium-sized parent company is no longer exempt from the requirement to prepare group accounts.

9.2 Qualifying conditions – group accounts exemptions

Companies Act 2006 ss. 383(4) and 466(4) set out the conditions to be met by a group for the parent company to qualify as 'small' or 'medium-sized' as appropriate.

A parent company qualifies as a small company in relation to a financial year only if the group headed by it qualifies as a small group. *s. 383*

The size classification of a parent company is determined with regard to the aggregate qualifying criteria of the group taken as a whole (parent company and subsidiary undertakings), irrespective of the actual size qualification of the parent company itself.

A group qualifies as small in relation to the parent company's first financial year if the qualifying conditions are met in that year. In subsequent years, a group qualifies as small if the qualifying conditions:

- are met in that year and the preceding financial year;
- are met in that year and the group qualified as small in relation to the preceding financial year; or
- were met in the preceding financial year and the group qualified as small in relation to that year. *ss. 383(2)–(3)*

Basically, a group meets the qualifying conditions (and is, therefore, exempt from producing group (consolidated) accounts as a small group) if it does not exceed more than one of the following criteria on one or other of the following two bases: *s. 383(4)–(7)*

Criteria	Net basis	(The bases may be mixed)	Gross basis
Small group (CA 2006 s. 383 (4))			
Turnover	£6.5 million		£7.8 million
Balance sheet total	£3.26 million		£3.9 million
Average number of employees (on a monthly basis)	50		50
Medium-sized group			
Turnover	£25.9 million		£31.1 million
Balance sheet total	£12.9 million		£15.5 million
Average number of employees (on a monthly basis)	250		250

Criteria amended (increased) by SI 2008 No. 393

The aggregate figures are ascertained by aggregating the relevant figures from individual statutory accounts (determined in accordance with CA 2006 s.382) for each member of the group. (See **5.2**)

The alternative bases for turnover and balance sheet totals (as qualifying conditions for exemption) are:

- *'Net' basis* – Aggregate figures arrived at with set-offs and consolidation adjustments (elimination of group transactions, etc.) and in accordance with CA 2006 s. 404 and SI 2008 No. 409 Sch. 6 (Companies Act group accounts) or international accounting standards (IAS group accounts); and
- *'Gross' basis* – Aggregate figures arrived at without such set-offs and consolidation adjustments.

CA 2006 under SI 2008 No. 409 Sch. 6 consolidation adjustments include:

- elimination of intra-group transactions and assets and liabilities;
- elimination of intra-group unrealised profits or losses; and
- adjustments to effect uniform accounting policies within the group.

9.3 Exempt small groups – related undertakings disclosures

The information to be given in notes to a small company's annual accounts in relation to related undertakings, **where group accounts are not required** are provided by Part 1 of Schedule 2 to SI 2008 No. 409 (The Small Companies and Groups (Accounts and Directors' Report) Regulations 2008) 'Information about related undertakings where company not preparing Group accounts (Companies Act or IAS individual accounts)').

Details of required disclosures are set out in **Chapter 12** at **12.7.1**. Schedule 2 to SI 2008 No. 409 is provided in full in **Appendix E**.

9.4 Group accounts filing

There is no statutory provision to prepare and submit abbreviated group accounts.

A small group is required to file at Companies House either:

- individual accounts of the parent company, if no group accounts are filed where the group qualifies as exempt; or
- consolidated (small or medium-sized company) accounts of the group. **See Chapter 8** at **8.8**

Companies Act group accounts delivered to the registrar of companies under CA 2006 s. 444

need not give the information otherwise required (in the full Companies Act group accounts) concerning:

- directors' benefits: remuneration–in accordance with SI 2008 No. 409 Sch. 3, or
- shares of company held by subsidiary undertakings)–in accordance with SI 2008 No. 409 Sch. 6 paragraph 25.

SI 2008 No. 409 reg. 11

The Companies Act group accounts delivered to the registrar constitute the 'abbreviated accounts' of the group. Where the group accounts are audited but abbreviated accounts are delivered to the registrar, the accounts must be delivered together with a copy of the special auditor's report required by CA 2006 s. 449. See **Chapter 8** at **8.8**

9.5 Preparing small group accounts

9.5.1 Companies Act small group accounts

Where the directors of a parent company which is subject to the small companies regime and has prepared Companies Act individual accounts prepare Companies Act group accounts under CA 2006 s. 398 (Option to prepare group accounts), those group accounts must comply with the provisions of:

- SI 2008 No. 409 Schedule 6 (Part 1) – Form and content of Companies Act group accounts (consolidated balance sheet and consolidated profit and loss account, and additional information to be provided by way of notes to the accounts).
- SI 2008 No. 409 Schedule 6 (Part 2) – Information about related undertakings to be given in notes to the company's accounts.
- SI 2008 No. 409 Schedule 3 – Information about directors' benefits: remuneration to be given in notes to the company's accounts.

Information about related undertakings may be omitted from the notes to a company's accounts in certain circumstances where the undertaking is established under the law of a country outside the United Kingdom, or carries on business outside the United Kingdom (CA 2006 s. 409(4)).

SI 2008 No. 409 reg. 10(2)

A parent company of a small or medium-sized group was previously not entitled to the exemption from preparing group accounts unless the company's auditors provide a report stating that in their opinion the company was so entitled. Following SI 1996 No. 189, this is no longer required.

The group accounts of a small company are treated as having complied with any provision of SI 2008 No. 409 Schedule 6 (Part 1) (Form and content of Companies Act group accounts) if they comply instead with the corresponding (additional) provisions of SI 2008 No. 410 Schedule 6 (Part 1) *The Large and Medium-Sized Companies and Groups (Accounts and Reports) Regulations 2008.*

9.5.2 Small groups and the FRSSE

A small group voluntarily preparing group accounts may take advantage of the provisions and exemptions afforded by the FRSSE (effective April 2008) (see **10.5**) but must have regard to the legal requirements reflected in the FRSSE and CA 2006 under SI 2008 No. 409 Sch. 6. (See **9.5.1** above). When considering SI 2008 No. 409 Sch. 6, any references in that Schedule to compliance with the provisions of 'Part 1 of Schedule 6' are to be construed as references to the legal requirements reflected in the FRSSE. As a consequence, where a small reporting entity is preparing consolidated financial statements, it should regard as standard the accounting practices and disclosure requirements set out in:

Chapter 9 Group accounts – small groups

FRS 2	Accounting for subsidiary undertakings	
FRS 6	Acquisitions and mergers	
FRS 7	Fair values in acquisition accounting	
and, as they apply in respect of consolidated accounts:		
FRS 5	Reporting the substance of transactions	
FRS 9	Associates and joint ventures	
FRS 28	Corresponding amounts	
FRS 10	Goodwill and intangible assets	(Only in respect of purchased goodwill on consolidation)
FRS 11	Impairment of fixed assets and goodwill	

Where the reporting entity is part of a group that prepares publicly available consolidated accounts, it is entitled under the FRSSE to the exemptions provided by FRS 8 paragraph 3(a)–(c), being:

- transactions or balances between group entities that have been eliminated on consolidation (consolidated accounts);
- disclosure in the parents' own accounts when presented together with consolidated accounts; and
- transactions with group entities in the accounts of 90 per cent subsidiary undertakings.

Where group accounts are prepared, the balance sheet should contain in a prominent position on the balance sheet, above the director's approval signature, that they are prepared in accordance with the special provisions in Part 15 of the Companies Act 2006 relating to small companies (see **Chapter 6** at **6.9**).

9.5.3 Small group accounts – balance sheet format heading ('Investments')

SI 2008 No. 409 Sch 6.1(2)

Where small group accounts are prepared, Schedule 6 ('Group Accounts') of SI 2008 No. 409 amends the balance sheet format headings for 'Investments'.

For item B.III in each of the balance sheet formats, the sub-headings of 'Investments' are modified as follows:

'B. III. Investments
1. Shares in group undertakings
2. Interests in associated undertakings
3. Other participating interests
4. Loans to group undertakings and undertakings in which a participating interest is held
5. Other investments other than loans
6. Others'.

9.6 Medium-sized companies – group accounts

Medium-sized parent companies (being companies that are ineligible or excluded from the small companies regime under CA 2006 s. 384) *must* prepare group accounts for the year *unless* the company is otherwise exempt from that requirement under exemptions set out in CA 2006 s. 399(3).

The exemptions available are under:

- CA 2006 s. 400 (company included in EEA accounts of larger group);
- CA 2006 s. 401 (company included in non-EEA accounts of larger group); and
- CA 2006 s. 402 (company none of whose subsidiary undertakings need be included in the consolidation).

A medium-sized parent company to which these exemptions apply can nevertheless prepare group accounts. CA 2006 s. 399(4).

9.7 Entitlement to group exemption – auditors' report

A parent company of a small (or medium-sized) group was previously not entitled to the exemption from preparing group accounts unless the company's auditors provide a report stating that in their opinion the company was so entitled. This is no longer required.

If the directors of a company have prepared accounts and reports in accordance with the small companies regime and in the auditor's opinion they were not entitled so to do, the auditor must state that fact in the auditors' report; the auditors are now required to refer to the exemption and make a statement of non-entitlement only if in their opinion the directors were not entitled to the exemption.

s. 498(5)

Notwithstanding the above, a parent company may prepare group accounts for its own management accounting purposes and not submit them to the Registrar of Companies but file instead its own individual statutory accounts with appropriate disclosures. If group accounts are not prepared because the group accounts exemptions are met, the company may, if it wishes, file abbreviated accounts provided it qualifies as a small or medium-sized company.

9.8 Group companies – availability of small audit exemption

A company is exempt from the requirements for the audit of its accounts in respect of a financial year if it meets the conditions set out in CA 2006 s. 477 (see **Chapter 11** at **11.2**). Whether a group qualifies as small is determined in accordance with CA 2006 s. 383 (companies qualifying as small: parent companies) (see **9.2** above).

A company which is a group company (being a parent company or a subsidiary undertaking) is only entitled to audit exemption (in accordance with CA 2006 s. 477(2)) if the following conditions are met:

- the group qualifies as a small group in relation to the financial year (during any part of which it was a group company);
- the group was not at any time in the year an 'ineligible' group (as defined by CA 2006 s. 384(2) and (3));
- the group's aggregate turnover in the year is not more than £6.5 million net (or £7.8 million gross); and
- the group's aggregate balance sheet total for that year is not more than £3.26 million net (or £3.9 million gross).
  *A group's aggregate turnover and aggregate balance sheet total are determined as for the purposes of CA 2006 s. 383 on the bases as set out in **5.2**.*

s. 479(2) amended by SI 2008 No. 393 reg 5(2)

Audit exemption, including the availability of small company audit exemption for group companies, is covered in **Chapter 11**.

Chapter 10 Essentials of the FRSSE – Financial Reporting Standard for Smaller Entities

10.1 Development of the FRSSE

10.1.1 Introduction

The Financial Reporting Standard for Smaller Entities (FRSSE) is the Financial Reporting Standard which brings together, in one document, all accounting requirements applicable to smaller entities. The FRSSE prescribes the basis for preparing and presenting the accounts of small entities (as defined in the standard–basically on the same criteria as 'small companies') and incorporates all relevant companies legislation and accounting standards.

A small company may choose not to adopt the FRSSE, in which case all accounting standards (UK or international) and UITF Consensus Abstracts apply in full where appropriate or not otherwise specifically exempted.

A small company preparing true and fair view accounts which chooses to adopt the FRSSE is exempt from all other accounting standards (FRSs and SSAPs) and UITF Abstracts (except those relevant to the production of consolidated accounts, that is FRSs 2, 5, 6, 7 and 9, and also FRSs 10 and 11 only in respect of the application of purchased goodwill arising on consolidation).

For accounts produced under the new Companies Act 2006 regime (see **10.1.4** below), the applicable FRSSE will be the FRSSE (effective April 2008). The FRSSE (effective January 2007) remains appropriate for CA 1985 regime accounts.

The FRSSE presents, in one self-contained FRS document, definitions, accounting treatments and measurement criteria that are consistent with existing accounting standards but in a simplified version. Some disclosure requirements are also simplified or excluded. In the absence of specific guidance within the FRSSE, accepted accounting practice should be interpreted and adopted having regard to FRSs, SSAPs and UITF Abstracts generally. Industry – or sector – specific SORPs may indicate the circumstances in which the current FRSSE is to be adopted.

The FRSSE is not available to and does not apply to large or medium-sized companies or to large or medium-sized groups or other entities; it also does not apply to:

- public companies;
- companies preparing IAS accounts (individual or group);
- companies preparing accounts (individual or group) under fair value accounting rules (SI 2008 No. 409 Sch 1 Section D Part 2).
- companies being an authorised insurance company, a banking company, an e-money issuer, a MiFID investment firm or a UCITS management company or a company that carries on insurance market activity;
- certain authorised persons under FSMA 2000, being persons (other than small companies) who have permission under Part 4 of FSMA 2000 (in the UK) to carry on a regulated activity *(or, notwithstanding the definition of a small company in the legislation, companies authorised under the Investment Intermediaries Act 1995 (in the Republic of Ireland));*
- members of an ineligible group. *(A group is ineligible if any of its members is: a public company; a body corporate (other than a company) whose shares are admitted to trading on a*

regulated market in an EEA State; a person (other than a small company) who has permission under Part 4 of FSMA 2000 to carry on a regulated activity; a small company that is an authorised insurance company, a banking company, an e-money issuer, a MiFID investment firm or a UCITS management company; or a person who carries on insurance market activity).

A 'small' subsidiary within a 'large' or 'medium-sized' group (which is not otherwise excluded) is entitled to choose to adopt the FRSSE if it so wishes.

A small company which chooses to adopt the FRSSE should disclose which version of the FRSSE it is adopting, for example:

Accounts year end	*FRSSE version*
31 March 2007	Either version FRSSE (effective January 2005) or FRSSE (effective January 2007)
31 December 2007	FRSSE (effective January 2007)
31 December 2008	FRSSE (effective January 2007)
31 March 2009	FRSSE (effective January 2007)
30 April 2009	FRSSE (effective April 2008)

This disclosure of version statement may be included with the accounts note of accounting policies or in the statement required by companies legislation on the balance sheet. For example, the statement could read as follows:

> 'These accounts have been prepared in accordance with the special provisions relating to small companies within Part 15 of the Companies Act 2006 and with the Financial Reporting Standard for Smaller Entities (effective April 2008).'

If abbreviated accounts are also prepared, the statement referring to the Financial Reporting Standard for Smaller Entities (effective April 2008) should be included with the note of accounting policies so that it is reproduced within the abbreviated accounts.

10.1.2 The 'one-stop shop' FRSSE'

The ASB originally issued the FRSSE in November 1997. As an FRS specifically for small entities, it was anticipated that it would be reissued and updated annually. The ASB has subsequently revised the FRSSE on four occasions when there had been sufficient accounting developments to incorporate.

In April 2005, the ASB issued a revised 'stand-alone' FRSSE (entitled the 'FRSSE (effective January 2005))' to be effective for accounting periods beginning on or after 1 January 2005.

Much of the effect of the changes in the 'FRSSE (effective January 2005)' represented re-presentation rather than substance in the approach to accounting for small companies. The main impact of the changes was that it:

- became a 'one-stop shop FRSSE' – in the sense of incorporating all relevant companies legislation within the main body of the text of the FRSSE (including, for example, accounting formats and accounting treatments for small companies);
- incorporated existing and new requirements of companies legislation; and
- reflected relevant aspects of recent FRSs and UITF abstracts issued since the previous version of the FRSSE.

Development of the FRSSE

The FRSSE has subsequently been revised and updated in:

- Financial Reporting Standard for Smaller Entities (effective January 2007) – for CA 1985 regime accounts; and
- Financial Reporting Standard for Smaller Entities (effective April 2008) – for CA 2006 regime accounts only.

Further changes in the form and content of the FRSSE, following the January 2007 revisions and the CA 2006 updating, will be inevitable in due course in the light of the gradual convergence of UK accounting standards with international accounting standards. The ASB continues to monitor developments in international accounting provision for smaller entities – the proposed 'IFRS for Non-publicly Accountable Entities' – **see 4.6.5**).

10.1.3 The 'FRSSE (effective January 2007)'

The FRSSE (effective January 2007) is effective for accounting periods commencing on or after 1 January 2007, although early adoption was permitted. The main change (although perhaps of marginal practical relevance to most small companies) concerned share-based payments; otherwise there were no significant changes.

The key matters covered in the revised FRSSE were:

- share-based payments – representing a major simplification of the terms of FRS 20;
- scope – whereby the FRSSE (a) precluded use by companies using the 'fair value accounting 'rules, but (b) permitted adoption by certain small authorised persons under FSMA 2000;
- revenue recognition (contracts for services) – incorporating the requirements of UITF 40 for service contracts within the main body of the FRSSE;
- companies legislation – incorporating changes to reflect (a) new requirements for corresponding amounts (following FRS 28), and (b) including the statutory definition of 'subsidiary undertakings' (now CA 2006 s. 1162); and
- accounting for pension costs – including a revised guidance example following withdrawal of SSAP 24 and full implementation of FRS 17.

The revised FRSSE also became a more manageable document by removing derivation tables (showing the source of the FRSSE provisions) but providing access on the ASB website (*www.frc.org.uk/asb/technical/frsse.cfm*)

10.1.4 CA 2006 – the 'FRSSE (effective April 2008)' update

The Financial Reporting Standard for Smaller Entities (effective April 2008) updated and superseded the FRSSE (effective January 2007) for CA 2006 regime accounts. The FRSSE 2008 is to be regarded as standard for financial statements relating to accounting periods ***beginning on or after 6 April 2008***. The FRSSE (effective January 2007) otherwise remains in force for financial statements relating to accounting periods beginning on or after 1 January 2007.

The FRSSE (effective April 2008) introduced no changes to the accounting requirements. The only differences between the 2008 version of the FRSSE and the FRSSE (effective January 2007) are in respect of the legal requirements set out in the FRSSE which reflect company law, including the Companies Act 2006, together with amendments and regulations issued under the Act which are effective from 6 April 2008.

The main change relates to increases in the thresholds for companies to qualify as small. Other changes are not considered significant and do not impact upon the accounting requirements for small companies preparing FRSSE accounts.

The main changes that have been made to the FRSSE may be summarized as follows:

- Qualifying thresholds – increased CA 2006 thresholds for companies and groups to qualify as small;
- Eligibility criteria – limiting the scope for small investment firms and entities such as e-money issuers to use the FRSSE;
- Liability limitation agreements – a new requirement to disclose details of any liability limitation agreement (where the accounts subject to audit)
- Disclosure of authorised share capital – no longer required;
- Transactions with directors – 'Loans, quasi-loans, credit transactions and guarantees' are now referred in CA 2006 to as 'Advances, credit and guarantees';
- Disclosure of 'political donations and expenditure' and 'charitable donations' – new requirement for separate disclosure. (Reporting threshold for these donations in the directors' report has increased to £2,000); and
- Disclosures regarding independent election candidates – new requirement for disclosures in the directors' report.

The ASB has prepared a derivation table (available on the ASB website) that provides a full cross-reference between the legal requirements set out in the FRSSE (effective April 2008) and the Companies Act 2006.

> **'FRSSE (effective April 2008)': Derivation tables for legal requirements**
>
> Derivation tables for all the legal requirements referred to in the FRSSE, indicating the source of company law, are available from the ASB website at:
>
> *www.frc.org.uk/asb/technical/frsse.cfm*
>
> The derivation table provides a full cross-reference between the Companies Act 2006 and the legislative requirements set out in the FRSSE. It is presented in columnar format with separate columns showing the equivalent references to the Companies Act 1985 and relevant legislation in Northern Ireland and the Republic of Ireland. (There have been no changes to relevant Republic of Ireland legislation).

10.2 Essentials of the 'FRSSE (effective April 2008)'

10.2.1 Essentials of the FRSSE – contents of chapter

This chapter provides the essential elements and requirements of the FRSSE by summarising its main contents and making cross references to the FRSSE itself. The essential elements and requirements relate to the FRSSE (effective April 2008) although most of the content will be equally applicable to the FRSSE (effective January 2007) except for legislative reference.

The FRSSE in the context of accounting standards generally and in particular the requirement for small company accounts to give a true and fair view are explained in **10.2.2** and **10.2.3** below.

A summary of the whole FRSSE in outline is provided in **10.3** and **Table 10.3**.

Further commentary on a variety of aspects of the FRSSE covers:

- cash flow statements (**10.4** and **Table 10.4**);
- small groups (**10.5**);
- FRS 3 and the FRSSE (**10.6**);
- reporting the substance of transactions (**10.7**);
- 'related party' requirements (including transactions with directors) (**10.8**);
- pensions and retirement benefits (**10.9**);

- foreign currency translation (**10.10**);
- provisions and discounting (**10.11**);
- revenue recognition (**10.12**), and
- share based payments (**10.13**).

The whole FRSSE is available on the ASB website as follows:

http://www.frc.org.uk/asb/technical/frsse.cfm

FRSSE (effective April 2008):
http://www.frc.org.uk/documents/pagemanager/asb/FRSSE/FRSSE%20Web%20optimized%20FINAL.pdf

FRSSE Derivation tables (Accounting standards):
http://www.frc.org.uk/documents/pagemanager/asb/Derivation%20tables%20in%20respect%20of%20accounting%20standards.pdf

FRSSE Derivation tables (Legislation):
http://www.frc.org.uk/documents/pagemanager/asb/FRSSE/company%20law%20derivation%20table%20(June%202008)%20doc.pdf

---

10.2.2 Small companies – true and fair view

Accounts are required under CA 2006 s. 393 to give a true and fair view within the accounting framework set out in the Companies Act 2006.

Accounts drawn up in compliance with the FRSSE incorporating the requirements of SI 2008 No. 409 Sch 1 are deemed to be 'true and fair' as required under the small companies regime of the Companies Act 2006. To achieve a true and fair view, regard must be had to the actual substance of any transaction or arrangement, and adequate explanation made (in the notes to the accounts) of the treatment adopted. Full and appropriate disclosure of any transaction should be made wherever there is doubt in presenting a true and fair view.

Table 10.1   Preparing small company accounts under the FRSSE

The FRSSE prescribes the basis of preparing small company true and fair view accounts:

	FRSSE Basis
Accounting standards:	
Financial reporting/accounting standards	Adoption of FRSSE affords exemption from all SSAPs, FRSs and UITF Abstracts.
Accounting:	
Accounting treatments	Simplified version consistent with existing financial reporting/accounting standards.
Measurement criteria	
Estimation techniques	
Definitions	
Disclosure:	
Accounts formats	Consistent with SI 2008 No. 409 Sch 1 (Individual accounts)
Disclosure requirements	Simplified or excluded.
GAAP:	
Guidance on specific issues or topics where FRSSE silent	Generally accepted accounting practice to be interpreted and adopted consistent with existing financial reporting/accounting standards.

Chapter 10 Essentials of the FRSSE – Financial Reporting Standard for Smaller Entities

10.2.3 Accounting standards and the FRSSE

While the principles of accounting standards explained in **Chapter 4** apply to companies generally, small companies can have regard to the single Financial Reporting Standard (FRSSE) covering all relevant accounting standards in one stand-alone document.

The FRSSE is designed to provide smaller entities (not just companies) with a single accounting standard that is focused on their particular circumstances. The FRSSE applies to all smaller entities (as defined) which prepare true and fair view accounts and which choose to adopt the FRSSE. Accounts complying with the SORP of a particular industry or sector should not, however, be prepared in accordance with the FRSSE, other than in the circumstances specified in the SORP.

With certain exceptions, for example small groups, exemption is granted from other accounting standards and UITF Abstracts. Nevertheless, in the absence of guidance on a particular accounting practice within the FRSSE, the ASB has stated that the preparers and auditors of accounts of small entities should have regard to SSAPs, FRSs and UITF Abstracts, not as mandatory documents, but as a means of establishing current accepted accounting practice.

Table 10.2 shows the effect for a small company of adopting the FRSSE. Small reporting entities applying the FRSSE are exempt from FRSs or UITF consensus interpretations issued subsequent to the latest version.

Table 10.2 The FRSSE and FRSs 1 to 29

	Small company adopting the FRSSE	Small company not adopting the FRSSE
FRS 1 Cash flow statements	FRSSE encourages, but does not require, a cash flow statement See **10.4** and **Table 10.4**	Cash flow statement required, applies in full, except most wholly owned subsidiaries
FRS 2 Accounting for subsidiary undertakings	FRS 2 applies in full for small parent preparing consolidated financial statements	FRS 2 applies in full for small parent preparing consolidated financial statements
FRS 3 Reporting financial performance	Only key elements of FRS 3 included in FRSSE See **10.6**	FRS 3 applies in full See **3.5**
FRS 4 Capital Instruments	Only basic elements (classification of capital instruments, finance cost allocation, carrying amount of borrowings, etc.) included in FRSSE See **Table 10.3**	FRS 4 applies in full (but see FRS 25) See **12.4** (and FRS 25)
FRS 5 Reporting the substance of transactions	Only basic principles of FRS 5 included in FRSSE	FRS 5 applies in full See **10.7**
FRS 6 Acquisitions and mergers	FRS 6 applies in full for small parent preparing consolidated financial statements	FRS 6 applies in full for small parent preparing consolidated financial statements
FRS 7 Fair values in acquisition accounting	FRS 7 applies in full for small parent preparing consolidated financial statements	FRS 7 applies in full for small parent preparing consolidated financial statements

Essentials of the 'FRSSE (effective April 2008)'

FRS 8 *Related party disclosures*	FRSSE adopts basic principles of FRS 8 but only those related party transactions material to the reporting entity require disclosure See **10.8**	FRS 8 applies in full, requiring full disclosure of transactions and balances and additional judgement of materiality in relation to related parties
FRS 9 *Associates and joint ventures*	FRSSE cross-refers to FRS 9 in entirety where group accounts are prepared.	Applies in group accounts, where prepared.
FRS 10 *Goodwill and intangible assets*	FRSSE includes basic measurement requirements but most presentation and disclosure requirements of FRS 10 are omitted. Annual impairment reviews avoided.	Applies in full, involving: (a) annual impairment reviews required for asset lives of over 20 years, and (b) recognition and revaluation provisions of intangible assets (including internally developed intangible assets) with a market value.
FRS 11 *Impairment of fixed assets and goodwill*	Only key principles of FRS 11 included in FRSSE. See **Table 10.3**.	Applies in full, involving: (a) full note disclosures; (b) calculation of 'value in use', and (c) monitoring of cash flows for five years following an impairment review involving 'value in use'
FRS 12 *Provisions, contingent liabilities and contingent assets*	FRSSE includes basic principles but most disclosure requirements of FRS 12 are omitted Detailed rules for discounting omitted	Applies in full, involving: (a) reference to risk in measuring a provision; (b) detailed rules for discount rates, and (c) full note disclosures.
FRS 13 *Derivatives and other financial instruments: disclosures*	Not applicable	Not applicable
FRS 15 *Tangible fixed assets*	FRSSE includes basic principles consistent with FRS 15 but most detailed disclosure requirements are omitted. See **Table 10.3**.	Applies in full, involving: (a) detailed bases of valuation; (b) annual reviews of impairment and residual values for certain assets; (c) renewals accounting, and (d) detailed disclosure requirements.
FRS 16 *Current tax*	FRSSE includes main requirements of FRS 16 involving recognition of dividends: (a) excluding attributable tax credits or underlying tax, and (b) including withholding taxes	Applies in full.
FRS 17 (IAS 19) *Retirement benefits*	FRSSE follows FRS 17 and continues to adopt the basic principles (of SSAP 24) for defined contribution schemes	Applies in full (with effect from 6 April 2007 for FRS 17 amendments implementing alignment with IAS19) For defined benefit schemes:

Chapter 10 Essentials of the FRSSE – Financial Reporting Standard for Smaller Entities

	FRS 17 principles for defined benefit schemes apply in full with effect from 22 June 2006 year end	(a) greater disclosures required (following IAS 19); (b) market value approach to accounting (move from actuarial approach).
FRS 18 *Accounting policies*	FRSSE adopts the basic principles of FRS 18 involving accounting policies that are relevant, reliable, comparable and understandable	Applies in full involving more detailed disclosures of: (a) true and fair view override departures; (b) significant appropriate estimation techniques; (c) non-adoption of going concern basis, and (d) provisions of any SORP
FRS 19 *Deferred tax*	FRSSE follows FRS 19 Discounting not required. Disclosure of 'material components' of charge only required.	Applies in full involving: (a) full provision for deferred tax; (b) deferred tax recognised on 'incremental liability' approach, (ie when it meets the definition of an asset or liability in its own right), and (c) discounting permissible for deferred tax assets and liabilities
FRS 20 (IFRS 2) *Share-based payment*	Not applicable (but FRSSE includes simplified disclosures)	Applies in full covering accounting treatment and disclosures for share-based payment transactions (shares and share options)
FRS 21 (IAS 10) *Events after the balance sheet date*	Not applicable (but main principles of FRS 21 adopted by FRSSE)	Applies in full
FRS 22 (IAS 33) *Earnings per share*	Not applicable	Voluntary but not mandatory.
FRS 23 (IAS 21) *The effects of changes in foreign exchange rates*	Not applicable	Applies in full with effect from application of FRS 26
FRS 24 (IAS 29) *Financial reporting in hyperinflationary economies*	Not applicable	Applies in full with effect from application of FRS 26.
FRS 25 (IAS 32) *Financial instruments: disclosure and presentation*	Not applicable	Applies in full (Presentation) [with effect from application of FRS 26 (Disclosure)]
FRS 26 (IAS 39) *Financial instruments: measurement*	Not applicable	Applies in full covering fair value accounting treatment and disclosures for financial instruments and hedge accounting
FRS 27 *Life Assurance*	Not applicable	Not applicable
FRS 28 *Corresponding amounts*	Key principles apply (UK GAAP) within FRSSE	Applies in full
FRS 29 (IFRS 7) *Financial instruments: disclosures*	Not applicable	Applies in full (with effect from accounting periods beginning on or after 1 January 2007

10.3 The FRSSE in outline

Table 10.3 presents an outline summary of the FRSSE reflecting FRSSE (effective April 2008). It does not constitute a complete checklist of the FRSSE requirements. *References to 'FRSSE paragraph' are to paragraphs of the FRSSE (effective April 2008). Significant changes from the previous version (resulting from CA 2006 and SI 2008 No. 409) are indicated as* **bold text**. References to 'FRS' or 'SSAP' are to indicate principal derivations.

Table 10.3 The FRSSE in outline

	FRSSE paragraph
GENERAL	
Objective To provide useful and relevant information about the financial position, performance and stewardship of a small entity.	A
Scope True and fair view accounts of:	1.1
• small companies under companies legislation, Companies adopting 'fair value accounting' rules cannot apply the FRSSE: *this does not preclude accounting for fixed assets and investments at valuation.* • small unincorporated entities (on same criteria)	Scope
Comprising: • balance sheet; and • profit and loss account.	2.1
True and fair view (FRS 5 / FRS 18) Requirement to present a true and fair view, having regard to the substance of any transaction or arrangement, in accordance with GAAP.	2.2–2.5
Adequate explanation of transaction or arrangement and treatment adopted should be given, whenever doubt in showing true and fair view.	2.2
Any true and fair view override (departure from the requirements of the FRSSE or Companies Act to give a true and fair view) should be explained fully in accordance with disclosures of SI 2008 No. 409 Sch 1.10(2) • description of treatment; • reasons for treatment; • quantification of difference resulting from override; and • comparative figures for continuing override.	2.3–2.4
Adequate explanation of transaction or arrangement and treatment adopted should be given, whenever doubt in showing true and fair view.	2.5
Accounting principles and policies (FRS 18) Accounts must disclose preparation (as applicable) 'in accordance with: • FRSSE (effective April 2008)', or • FRSSE (effective January 2007)' 'Accounting policies' are the principles, bases, conventions, rules and practices applied by an entity that specify how transactions and other events are reflected (or 'recognised') in financial statements. 'Estimation techniques' implement the measurement aspects of accounting policies, being the methods adopted to arrive at estimated monetary amounts. Accounts must include: • description of each material accounting policy; • details (explanation and effect) of changes of accounting policies and prior period adjustments; and • details (description and effect) of material changes to estimation techniques.	2.6 2.7–2.8

An entity must select accounting policies and estimation techniques most appropriate to its particular circumstances for the purpose of giving a true and fair view (consistent with the requirements of the FRSSE and relevant legislation). Accounting policies and estimation techniques should be selected with the objective of being relevant, reliable, comparable and understandable. — 2.9–2.10

Accounting policies must be reviewed regularly to ensure that they remain the most appropriate to the entity's particular circumstances. A change in accounting policy should result in the amounts for the current and corresponding periods being restated on the basis of the new policy. — 2.10

Amounts reported for each item of asset or liability / income or expenditure should be determined separately, with no netting off. — 2.11

Going concern — 2.12
Accounts must be prepared on the presumption of the business as a going concern, unless there is an intention (after balance sheet date) to liquidate or cease trading.

Directors should assess whether there are significant doubts about the entity's ability to continue as a going concern. Any material uncertainties, of which the directors are aware in making their assessment, should be disclosed. Where the period considered by the directors in making this assessment has been limited to a period of less than one year from the date of approval of the financial statements, that fact should be stated.

Prudence — 2.13
Under conditions of uncertainty, the exercise of judgement in determining the amount of any item must be made on a prudent basis (that is, with a degree of caution). It is not appropriate to use prudence as a reason to understate deliberately assets or gains or to overstate liabilities or losses.

Accruals — 2.14
Preparation of accounts must be on the accruals basis (except for cash flow information) without regard to the date of payment or receipt.

Prior period adjustments — 2.15
Prior period adjustments must be accounted for by restating the comparative figures for the preceding period in the primary statements and notes and adjusting the opening balance of reserves for the cumulative effect. The cumulative effect of the adjustments should also be noted at the foot of the STRGL of the current period. The effect of prior period adjustments on the results for the preceding period should be disclosed where practicable.

Format of accounts — 2.16–2.29

General rules
Requirement to comply with the formats and format rules set out in the FRSSE (following SI 2008 No. 409 Sch 1 Companies Act 2006), including: — 2.16

- consistency of adoption; — 2.17
- additional information, where necessary, to give a 'true and fair view'; — 2.18
- greater detail than required by formats permitted, where necessary; — 2.19
- rules for arrangement and headings; — 2.20–2.22
- **comparative figures (corresponding amounts); — 2.23**
- details of movements to and from reserves; — 2.24
- disclosure of secured creditors and creditors falling due for payment after more than five years. — 2.25–2.26

Refer to chapters above:

- *Chapter 6 (Small companies)* **(6.4–6.5)**
- *Chapter 3 (Companies generally) (3.4–3.5)*

Balance sheet format — 2.27
FRSSE specifies Format 1 (following SI 2008 No. 409 Sch 1) format of balance sheet but Format 2 may be adopted.

The FRSSE in outline

> *Refer to:*
>
> - *Chapter 6 above (Small companies)* **(6.4–6.5** including **Table 6.4)**
> - **Appendix C** *below (Small company balance sheet formats)*

Profit and loss account formats   2.28–2.29
FRSSE specifies Formats 1 and 2 (Sch 8) formats of profit and loss account (but Formats 3 and 4 may be adopted)

> *Refer to:*
>
> - *Chapter 7 (Small companies)* **(7.4–7.5** including **Table 7.2)**
> - **Appendix C** *below (Profit and loss account formats)*

Approval and signing of accounts   2.30–2.34
Requirement to comply with the accounts approval rules of Companies Act 2006 (ss. 433(1), 414 and 441), including:

- approval by board and signature on its behalf by a director;
- dating of approval;
- penalties for 'reckless' or non-compliant accounts approval (all directors); and
- Directors statements (small company provisions) (CA 2006 ss.414(3), 419(2), 444(5),and 450(3)). See *Chapter 6 (Small companies)* **(6.9)** above

Delivery of accounts to registrar   2.35–2.36
Accounts delivered to registrar must:

- state the registered number in a prominent position;
- be signed by, and state name of, the directors and registered auditors (as appropriate); and
- enable registrar to make clear copies

Exemptions from audit
Requirement to comply (where relevant) with the audit exemption provisions of Companies Act 1985, including:

- CA 2006 s. 475(2) statement (audit exemption); and   2.37
- dormant company acting as agent disclosure   2.38

Requirement to disclose principal terms and date of approval of any liability limitation agreement with auditors (other than audit exempt companies).   2.39

> *Refer to:*
>
> - *Chapter 6 (Small companies)* **(6.9)** and *Chapter 11 (Small company audit exemption)* **(11.8)**

PROFIT AND LOSS ACCOUNT *(FRS 3)*   3.1–3.2
All realised gains and losses recognised in the accounts for the financial period **(or previous period)** must be included in:

- the profit and loss account; or
- the statement of total recognised gains and losses

including all liabilities arising in respect of the period.

Disclosure must include:

- the effect of any amount included relating to the preceding financial period; and   3.3
- percentage of turnover attributable to markets outside the UK.   3.4

Exceptional items – to be included within relevant statutory headings, giving description, effect and amounts.   3.5–3.6

Determination of profit or loss on disposal of assets (as the difference between net sales proceeds and net carrying amount)   3.7
Auditors' remuneration, including expenses and benefits in kind.   3.8

Chapter 10 Essentials of the FRSSE – Financial Reporting Standard for Smaller Entities

REVENUE RECOGNITION *(UITF 40)* Basic principles of how, when and whether to recognise revenue, including the sale of goods and services resulting in 'Turnover'.	4.1–4.9
Contracts for services – including consideration of contractual obligations, 'critical events' and rights to consideration; revenue accounting and performance over time; and payment uncertainties.	4.10–4.15

See *Chapters 10 and 12 below (Revenue recognition)* **(10.12 and 12.9.3)**

STATEMENT OF TOTAL RECOGNISED GAINS AND LOSSES (STRGL) *(FRS 3)* (See **Tables 4.5** and **10.5**.)	5.1

A primary statement should be presented, with the same prominence as the profit and loss account, showing the total of recognised gains and losses and its components. The components should be the gains and losses that are recognised in the period insofar as they are attributable to shareholders, excluding transactions with shareholders. Where the only recognised gains and losses are the results included in the profit and loss account, no separate statement to this effect need be made.

FIXED ASSETS AND GOODWILL

Disclosures Statutory disclosures of cost or valuation, acquisition or disposal, revaluation or transfers, together with provision for depreciation or diminution in value.	6.1–6.2
Research and development *(SSAP 13)* The cost of fixed assets acquired or constructed in order to provide facilities for research and development activities over a number of accounting periods should be capitalised and written off over their useful lives through the profit and loss account.	6.3
Expenditure on pure and applied research should be written off in the year of expenditure through the profit and loss account.	6.4
In certain circumstances, development expenditure may be deferred to the extent that its recovery can reasonably be regarded as assured; otherwise, development expenditure should be written off in the year of expenditure except in certain defined circumstances when it may be deferred to future periods.	6.5–6.7
If development costs are deferred to future periods, such costs must be amortised and the amount of deferred development expenditure (and the reasons for capitalisation and period of depreciation) disclosed.	6.8–6.10
Other intangible assets and goodwill *(FRS 10)* Positive purchased goodwill and purchased intangible assets should be capitalised. Internally generated goodwill and intangible assets should not be capitalised. An intangible asset purchased with a business should be recognised separately from the purchased goodwill if its value can be measured reliably.	6.11–6.12
Capitalised goodwill and intangible assets should be depreciated on a straight-line (or more appropriate) basis over their useful economic lives, which should not exceed 20 years (with reason for period chosen explained). The residual value assigned to goodwill should be zero. A higher residual value may be assigned to an intangible asset only when this value can be established reliably, for example when it has been agreed contractually.	6.13–6.14
Useful economic lives should be reviewed at the end of each reporting period and revised if necessary, subject to the constraint that the revised life should not exceed 20 years from the date of acquisition. The carrying amount at the date of revision should be depreciated over the revised estimate of remaining useful economic life.	6.15
Goodwill and intangible assets should not be revalued.	6.16
If an acquisition appears to give rise to negative goodwill, fair values should be checked to ensure that those of the acquired assets have not been overstated and those of the acquired liabilities have not been understated. Once this has been done, remaining negative goodwill up to the fair values of the non-monetary assets acquired should be released in the profit and loss account over the lives of those assets. Any additional negative goodwill should be recognised in the profit and loss account over the period expected to benefit from it. The amount of negative goodwill on the balance sheet and the period(s) in which it is being written back should be disclosed.	6.17

Goodwill that was eliminated against reserves in accordance with an accounting policy permitted until 23 March 1999 may remain eliminated against reserves thereafter (unless, in its first accounting period beginning on or after that date, an entity reinstated by prior period adjustment all goodwill previously so eliminated).	19.2
Tangible fixed assets (other than investment properties) *(FRS 15)*	6.18–6.29
A tangible fixed asset should initially be measured at its cost, then written down to its recoverable amount if necessary. The initial carrying amount of a tangible fixed asset received as a gift or donation by a charity should be its current value, (ie the lower of replacement cost and recoverable amount) at the date it is received.	6.19
Costs that are directly attributable to bringing the tangible fixed asset into working condition for its intended use should be included in its measurement. Other costs should not be included.	6.20

Capitalising finance costs:

Where an entity adopts an accounting policy of capitalising finance costs (such as interest), finance costs that are directly attributable to the construction of tangible fixed assets should be capitalised as part of the cost of those assets (and the fact noted in the accounts). The total amount of finance costs capitalised during a period should not exceed the total amount of finance costs incurred during that period.	6.20
Capitalisation of directly attributable costs, including finance costs, should be suspended during extended periods in which active development is interrupted. Capitalisation should cease when nearly all the activities that are necessary to get the tangible fixed asset ready for use are complete, even if the asset has not yet been brought into use.	6.21
Subsequent expenditure should be capitalised only if:	6.22

- it represents an 'improvement'; or
- it replaces or restores a component that has been separately depreciated over its useful economic life.

Revaluations:

Where an entity adopts an accounting policy of revaluation in respect of a tangible fixed asset, the carrying amount of a revalued tangible fixed asset should be its market value (or the best estimate thereof) as at the balance sheet date. Where the directors believe that market value is not an appropriate basis, current value (ie the lower of replacement cost and recoverable amount) may be used instead.	6.23

Where a tangible fixed asset is revalued all tangible fixed assets of the same class, (ie having a similar nature, function or use in the business) should be revalued, but a policy of revaluation need not be applied to all classes of tangible fixed assets.

Such valuations should be made:	6.24

- certain assets (other than properties) – by reference (with reasonable reliability) to active second-hand markets or appropriate publicly available indices;
- other tangible fixed assets, including properties – (at least every five years) by an experienced valuer, (ie one who has recognised and relevant recent professional experience (but not necessarily qualified). A material change in value in the intervening years should be updated by an experienced valuer.

Where, for its first accounting period ending on or after 23 March 2000, an entity does not adopt an accounting policy of revaluation, but the carrying amount of its tangible fixed assets continues to reflect previous revaluations, it is permitted to:	19.3

- retain the book amounts – disclosing the fact that the valuation has not been updated and giving the date of the last revaluation; or
- restate the carrying amount of the tangible fixed assets to historical cost (less restated accumulated depreciation) as a change in accounting policy.

Revaluation losses caused only by changing market prices should be recognised in the statement of total recognised gains and losses until the carrying amount of the asset reaches its depreciated historical cost. Other revaluation losses should be recognised in the profit and loss account.	6.25

Chapter 10 Essentials of the FRSSE – Financial Reporting Standard for Smaller Entities

Revaluation gains should be recognised in the statement of total recognised gains and losses, except to the extent (after adjusting for subsequent depreciation) that they reverse revaluation losses on the same asset that were previously recognised in the profit and loss account. To that extent they should be recognised in the profit and loss account. The adjustment for subsequent depreciation is to achieve the same overall effect that would have been reached had the original downward revaluation reflected in the profit and loss account not occurred.	6.26
Disclosures include comparable historical cost amounts for revalued tangible fixed assets, the option to include fixed assets at fixed quantity and amount, and details of valuers and valuation bases.	6.27–6.29

Fixed asset investments

Fixed asset investments must initially be measured at cost, or alternatively at a market value (determined at date of last valuation or on other basis deemed by the directors as appropriate in the circumstances and disclosed as such).	6.30
Gains and losses must be recognised (in the P&L account or statement of total recognised gains and losses) using the same basis applied to tangible fixed assets in paragraphs 6.25 and 6.26.	
Other disclosures include comparable historical cost amounts for revalued fixed asset investments; the aggregate amount and valuation (market value/Stock Exchange) of listed investments; and significant investment holdings (20 %+).	6.31–6.33

Revaluation reserve

Gains and losses arising on the revaluation of assets that have been recognised in the Statement of total recognised gains and losses should be credited, or debited, to a separate revaluation reserve. Amounts may be transferred from the revaluation reserve to the P&L account when they are realised. Disclosure of tax treatment.	6.34–6.36

Depreciation (other than investment properties) (FRS 15)

The cost (or revalued amount) less estimated residual value of a tangible fixed asset should be depreciated on a systematic basis over its useful economic life.	6.37–6.43 6.38
The depreciation method used should reflect as fairly as possible the pattern in which the asset's economic benefits are consumed by the entity. The depreciation charge for each period should be recognised as an expense in the profit and loss account unless it is permitted to be included in the carrying amount of another asset.	
Where a tangible fixed asset comprises two or more major components with substantially different useful economic lives, each component should be accounted for separately for depreciation purposes and depreciated over its individual useful economic life.	6.39
With certain exceptions, such as sites used for extractive purposes or landfill, land has an unlimited life and therefore is not depreciated.	
The useful economic lives and residual values of tangible fixed assets should be reviewed regularly and, when necessary, revised. On revision, the carrying amount of the tangible fixed asset at the date of revision less the revised residual value should be depreciated over the revised remaining useful economic life. Such revisions are not the result of a change in accounting policy and are not therefore prior period adjustments.	6.40
However, where, for its first accounting period ending on or after 23 March 2000, an entity separates tangible fixed assets into different components with significantly different useful economic lives for depreciation purposes, the changes should be dealt with as a prior period adjustment, as a change in accounting policy.	19.4
A change from one method of providing depreciation to another is permissible only on the grounds that the new method will give a fairer presentation of the results and of the financial position. Such a change does not, however, constitute a change of accounting policy; the carrying amount of the tangible fixed asset is depreciated using the revised method over the remaining useful economic life, beginning in the period in which the change is made.	6.41
Disclosures should be made of:	6.42–6.43

- depreciation methods;
- useful economic lives or depreciation rates; and
- changes (with reasons) in the above or residual values.

Write-downs to recoverable amount (capitalised goodwill and all fixed assets except investment properties and financial instruments) (other than investments in subsidiaries, associates and joint ventures). (FRS 11)   6.44–6.49

Fixed assets and goodwill should be carried in the balance sheet at no more than recoverable amount.   6.45

If the net book amount of a fixed asset or goodwill is considered not to be recoverable in full at the balance sheet date (perhaps as a result of obsolescence or a fall in demand for a product), the net book amount should be written down to the estimated recoverable amount, which should then be written off over the remaining useful economic life of the asset.

If the recoverable amount of a tangible fixed asset or investment subsequently increases as a result of a change in economic conditions or in the expected use of the asset, the net book amount should be written back to the lower of recoverable amount and the amount at which the asset would have been recorded had the original write-down not been made.   6.46

If, on the other hand, the recoverable amount of an intangible asset or capitalised goodwill subsequently increases, the net book amount should be written back *only* if an external event caused the original write-down and subsequent external events clearly and demonstrably reverse the effects of that event in a way that was not foreseen when the original write-down was calculated.   6.47

Write-downs (and any reversals) to recoverable amount should be charged (or credited) in the profit and loss account for the period. However, write-downs of revalued tangible fixed assets that reverse previous revaluation gains simply as a result of changing market prices should instead be recognised in the statement of total recognised gains and losses, to the extent that the carrying amount of the asset is greater than its depreciated historical cost.   6.48

Disclosure must be made where fixed assets are not actually revalued but their value considered by the directors (to ensure that the aggregate value is not less than stated).   6.49

Investment properties (SSAP 19)   6.50–6.53

Investment properties should be included in the balance sheet at their open market value and should not be subject to periodic charges for depreciation except for properties held on lease which should be depreciated over the period when the unexpired term is 20 years or less. Changes in market value should be taken to the statement of total recognised gains and losses unless a deficit (or its reversal) on an individual property is expected to be permanent in which case it should be charged (or credited) to the profit and loss account of the period.   6.50–6.51

Disclosures include the names and qualifications of valuers and the bases of valuation. Where the valuer is an employee or officer of the company or group that owns the property, this fact must be disclosed.   6.52

Changes in the market value of investment properties should not be taken to the P&L account but to the statement of total recognised gains and losses (being a movement on an investment revaluation reserve), unless a deficit (or its reversal) on an individual investment property is expected to be permanent, in which case it shall be charged (or credited) in the P&L account of the period.   6.53

Government grants (SSAP 4)   6.54–6.57

Government grants should be recognised in the profit and loss account so as to match them with the expenditure towards which they are intended to contribute.   6.54

To the extent that the grant is made as a contribution towards expenditure on a fixed asset, the amount of a grant so deferred should be treated as deferred income; a UK company may not deduct such grants from the purchase price or production costs of fixed assets.

A government grant should not be recognised in the P&L account until the conditions for its receipt have been complied with and there is reasonable assurance that the grant will be received.   6.55

Repayment of a government grant (in whole or in part and where probable) should be accounted for by setting off the repayment against any unamortized deferred income relating to the grant. Any excess should be charged immediately to the P&L account.	6.56
Disclosures include the effect of grants on results and the effect of other government assistance.	6.57

LEASES (HP AND LEASING) *(SSAP 21)*

Lessees — 7.1–7.7

A finance lease should be recorded in the balance sheet of a lessee as an asset and as an obligation to pay future rentals. At the inception of the lease, the sum to be recorded both as an asset and as a liability should normally be the fair value of the asset unless present value of minimum lease payments is a more realistic estimate.

An asset leased under a finance lease should be depreciated over the shorter of the lease term or its useful life. However, in the case of a hire purchase contract that has the characteristics of a finance lease, the asset should be depreciated over its useful life.

Rentals payable under operating leases and finance charges payable under finance leases should be charged on a straight-line basis over the lease term even if the payments are not made on such a basis, unless another systematic and rational basis is more appropriate.

Incentives to sign a lease, in whatever form they may take, should be spread by the lessee on a straight-line basis over the lease term or, if shorter than the full lease term, over the period to the review date on which the rent is first expected to be adjusted to the prevailing market rate.

Lessors — 7.8–7.11

The total gross earnings under finance leases and rental income from operating leases should be recognised on a systematic and rational basis. This will normally be a constant periodic rate of return on the lessor's net investment.

The amount due from the lessee under a finance lease should be recorded in the balance sheet of a lessor as a debtor at the amount of the net investment in the lease after making provisions for items such as bad and doubtful rentals receivable.

An asset held for use in operating leases by a lessor should be recorded as a fixed asset and depreciated over its useful life.

Manufacturer/dealer lessor — 7.12

A manufacturer or dealer lessor should not recognise a selling profit under an operating lease. The selling profit under a finance lease should be restricted to the excess of the fair value of the asset over the manufacturer's or dealer's cost less any grants receivable by the manufacturer or dealer towards the purchase, construction or use of the asset.

Other transactions, (eg sale and leaseback) and disclosures — 7.13–7.18

CURRENT ASSETS

Stocks and long-term contracts (SSAP 9) — 8.1–8.8

The amounts at which stocks are stated in the financial statements should be the total of the lower of cost and net realisable value of the separate items of stock or of groups of similar items. — 8.1–8.5

Cost may include 'purchase price' or 'production cost' and 'finance costs' (eg interest) directly attributable to acquisition, construction or production. 'Distribution costs', however, should not be included in production costs.

Immaterial stocks may be included at a fixed quantity and value.

Long-term contracts should be assessed on a contract-by-contract basis and reflected in the profit and loss account by recording turnover and related costs as contract activity progresses. Turnover is ascertained in a manner appropriate to the stage of completion of the contract, the business and the industry in which it operates. — 8.6–8.8

The FRSSE in outline

Where it is considered that the outcome of a long-term contract can be assessed with reasonable certainty before its conclusion, the prudently calculated attributable profit should be recognised in the profit and loss account as the difference between the reported turnover and related costs for that contract.

Long-term contracts should be disclosed in the balance sheet as follows:

- amounts recoverable on contracts – recorded turnover in excess of payments on account (as 'Debtors');
- balance of payments on account (as 'Creditors');
- long-term contract balances – costs incurred after transfers to cost of sales (as 'Stocks') – net of foreseeable losses and payments on account (separately disclosed); and
- provision or accrual for foreseeable losses (as 'Creditors' or 'Provisions for liabilities and charges')

Consignment stock (see **10.7.2 below**) *(FRS 5)* 8.9
Where consignment stock is, in substance, an asset of the dealer, the stock should be recognised as such on the dealer's balance sheet, together with a corresponding liability to the manufacturer.

Any deposit should be deducted from the liability and the excess classified as a trade creditor. Where stock is not, in substance, an asset of the dealer, the stock should not be included on the dealer's balance sheet until the transfer of title has crystallised. Any deposit should be included under 'other debtors'.

Debt factoring/invoice discounting *(FRS 5)* 8.10–8.12
Non-recourse debts/debts removed from seller:
Where there is no obligation to repay the factor, debts or liability in respect of proceeds received from the factor should not be reflected in the balance sheet. The profit or loss recognised is the difference between the carrying amount of the debts and the proceeds received.

Seller retains significant benefits and risks:
Factored debts should be shown separately on balance sheet as:

> *Gross debts* (after provision for bad debts, credit protection charges and any accrued interest)
> less:
> *amounts received from factor* (in respect of those debts)
> (Linked presentation).

Interest element of factor's charges should be included in profit and loss account as it accrues.

Factored debts subject to full recourse:
Balance sheet should show

> *Gross debts* as assets, (ie remain assets of seller)
> *Proceeds received from factor* as corresponding liability within liabilities.

Factoring costs including interest charges should be included in profit and loss account as they accrue.

Current asset investments
Current asset investments must initially be stated at the lower of cost and net realisable value or alternatively, may be measured at their current cost. Gains and losses should be recognised (in the P&L account or Statement of total recognised gains and losses) using the same basis applied to tangible fixed assets (FRSSE paragraphs 6.25–6.26). 8.13

Disclosure of listed shares held as current asset investments must include: the aggregate market value (where it differs from balance sheet amount); and market value and stock exchange value of any investments (where the market value is taken as being higher than the stock exchange value). 8.14

Start-up costs *(UITF 24)* 8.15
Start-up costs should generally be expensed as incurred, on a basis consistent with the accounting treatment of other similar costs incurred as part of the entity's on-going activities. Start-up costs should not be carried forward as an asset, unless they specifically meet the criteria for recognition as assets under another specific requirement of the FRSSE.

Chapter 10 Essentials of the FRSSE – Financial Reporting Standard for Smaller Entities

Pre-contract costs should be expensed as incurred, except that directly attributable costs should be recognised as an asset when it is virtually certain that a contract will be obtained and the contract is expected to result in future net cash inflows with a present value no less than all amounts recognised as an asset. Costs incurred before the asset recognition criteria are met should not be recognised as an asset.	8.16

TAXATION *(FRS 16)*

General

Tax (current and deferred) should be recognised in the profit and loss account, except to the extent that it is attributable to a gain or loss that is or has been recognised directly in the statement of total recognised gains and losses (in which case the tax should also be recognised directly in that statement).	9.1–9.3

The following should be disclosed separately:

- the material components of the (current and deferred) tax charge (or credit) for the period;
- any special circumstances that affect the overall tax charge or credit for the period, or may affect those of future periods; and
- the effects of a fundamental change in the basis of taxation (included in the tax charge or credit for the period).

Deferred tax (FRS 19)

Deferred tax should be recognised in respect of all timing differences that have originated but not reversed by the balance sheet date.	9.4–9.12 9.4

Deferred tax should not be recognised on permanent differences, nor should it be recognised on:

- revaluation gains and losses (unless, by the balance sheet date, the entity has entered into a binding agreement to sell the asset and has revalued the asset to the selling price); or
- taxable gains arising on revaluations or sales if it is more likely than not that the gain will be rolled over into a replacement asset.

Unrelieved tax losses and other deferred tax assets should be recognised only to the extent that it is more likely than not that they will be recovered against the reversal of deferred tax liabilities or other future taxable profits.	9.5
Deferred tax should be recognised when the tax allowances for the cost of a fixed asset are received before or after the depreciation of the fixed asset is recognised in the profit and loss account. However, if and when all conditions for retaining the tax allowances have been met, the deferred tax should be reversed.	9.6–9.7

Deferred tax should not be recognised on permanent differences.

Deferred tax should be measured at the average tax rates that would apply when the timing differences are expected to reverse, based on tax rates and laws that have been enacted by the balance sheet date.	9.8
The discounting of deferred tax assets and liabilities is not required. (However, if an entity does adopt a policy of discounting, all deferred tax balances that have been measured by reference to undiscounted cash flows and for which the impact of discounting is material should be discounted. Where discounting is used, the unwinding of the discount should be shown as a component of the tax charge and disclosed separately.)	9.9
The following should be disclosed separately:	9.10–9.12

- the deferred tax balance and its material components;
- the movement between the opening and closing net deferred tax balances, and the material components of this movement; or
- the amount of tax that would be payable or recoverable if revalued assets were sold at values shown in the financial statements.

Tax on dividends (FRS 16)

Outgoing dividends, etc. payable should exclude attributable tax credits but include any withholding tax.	9.13

Incoming dividends and similar income receivable should exclude attributable tax credits but include any withholding tax. Any withholding tax suffered should be shown as part of the tax charge.	9.14

Value Added Tax (VAT) *(SSAP 5)*   9.15
Turnover shown in the profit and loss account should exclude VAT on taxable outputs or VAT imputed under the flat rate VAT scheme. Irrecoverable VAT allocated to fixed assets and to other items disclosed separately in the financial statements should be included in their cost where practicable and material.

PENSIONS (see 10.9 (Pensions and retirement benefits) below including Table 10.7) *(FRS 17)*	10.1–10.4

The basic accounting objective is to ensure that the cost of providing pensions and other post-retirement benefits is recognised in the accounting period during which they arise.

For a defined contribution scheme, the charge against operating profits within the profit and loss account should be the cost of contributions payable to the pension scheme in respect of the accounting period.	10.1

For defined benefit schemes, the pension cost should be calculated using actuarial methods where, basically:

- scheme assets are valued at fair value; and
- scheme liabilities (discounted as appropriate) are measured on the projected unit method.

The FRSSE deals with the accounting of defined benefit schemes in an Appendix 'Accounting for retirement benefits: defined benefit schemes'; this is reproduced in **Table 10.7**.	10.4
Pension disclosures include scheme details (type of scheme) and cost for the period; outstanding or prepaid contributions; pension commitments provided in the company's balance sheet and any such commitments for which no provision has been made. Separate particulars should be given for commitments relating to pensions payable to past directors of the company.	10.2 – 10.3
PROVISIONS, CONTINGENT LIABILITIES AND CONTINGENT ASSETS (OTHER THAN PENSIONS, DEFERRED TAX AND LEASES)	11.1

Provisions *(FRS 12)*   11.2–11.6
A provision is a liability of uncertain timing or amount.

Provisions should be reviewed at each balance sheet date and adjusted to reflect the current best estimate. A provision should be used only for expenditures for which the provision was originally recognised.	11.4–11.5
A provision should be recognised when, and only when, it is probable, (ie more likely than not) that a present obligation exists, as a result of a past event, and that the likely settlement amount can be estimated reliably. The amount of the provision should be the best estimate of the expenditure required to settle the obligation at the balance sheet date.	11.2

An obligation may be either:

- a legal obligation – derived, for example, from a contract or legislation; or
- a constructive obligation – where the entity has indicated to other parties that it will accept certain responsibilities and has created valid expectations in those other parties that it will discharge those responsibilities.

Where the effect of the time value of money is material, the amount of a provision should be the present value of the expenditures expected to be required to settle the obligation. Where discounting is used, the unwinding of the discount should be shown as finance costs adjacent to interest. The FRSSE provides an example of discounting when making a provision **(See 10.11 and Table 10.7)**.	11.2
Where some or all of the expenditure required to settle a provision may be reimbursed by another party (for example, through an insurance claim), the reimbursement should be recognised as a separate asset only when it is virtually	11.3

certain to be received if the entity settles the obligation. In the profit and loss account, the expense relating to the provision may be presented net of the recovery. Gains from the expected disposal of assets should be excluded from the measurement of a provision.

Disclosure of provisions is required (except where movement consists of the application of a provision for the purpose for which it was established) comprising: the amount (at beginning and end of year); amounts transferred during the year; source and application of the amounts transferred; and particulars of each material provision included under 'other provisions' in the balance sheet.   11.6

Contingent liabilities and contingent assets (FRS 12)   11.7–11.11
Contingent liabilities (except where their existence is remote) and probable   11.7–11.9
contingent assets must be disclosed (but not 'recognised' or numerically incorporated) in accounts, giving a brief description of the nature of the contingent item (including legal nature and security) and, where practicable, an estimate of its financial effect.

A contingent asset is a possible asset that arises from past events and whose existence will be confirmed only by the occurrence of one or more uncertain future events not wholly within the entity's control.

A contingent liability is:
- a possible obligation that arises from past events and whose existence will be confirmed only by the occurrence of one or more uncertain future events not wholly within the entity's control; or
- an obligation at the balance sheet date that arises from past events but is not recognised as a provision because:
    (i) settlement of the obligation is unlikely; or
    (ii) the amount of the obligation cannot be measured with sufficient reliability.

    11.10–11.11

Disclosures include: aggregate amount of contracts for capital expenditure not provided for; other relevant financial commitments not provided for; and amount of any charge on the assets of the company to secure the liabilities of any other person.

FINANCIAL INSTRUMENTS (FRS 25 / FRS 26)   12.1–12.5
A financial instrument may be classified as a 'financial liability', a 'financial asset' or   12.1
an 'equity instrument' depending upon the substance of the contractual arrangement (rather than its legal form). A financial instrument is any contract that gives rise to a financial asset of one entity and a financial liability or equity instrument of another entity.

An 'equity instrument' is any contract that evidences a residual interest in the assets of an entity after deducting all of its liabilities (for example, an 'equity share'). A preference share, however, (providing for mandatory redemption by the issuer for a fixed or determinable amount at a fixed or determinable future date, or giving the holder the right to require the issuer to redeem the instrument at or after a particular date for a fixed or determinable amount) is a 'financial liability'.

Capital instruments other than shares should be classified as liabilities if they contain an obligation to transfer economic benefits (including a contingent obligation to transfer economic benefits). Shares and other capital instruments that do not contain an obligation to transfer economic benefits should be reported within shareholders' funds.

The finance costs of borrowings (included arrangement fees regarded as   12.2
significant additional cost) should be allocated to periods over the term of the   12.4
borrowings at a constant rate on the carrying amount. All finance costs should be charged in the P&L account.

Borrowings should be initially stated at the fair value of consideration received. The   12.3
carrying amount of borrowings shall be increased by the finance cost and reduced by any relevant payments made in respect of the reporting period.

The amount of any convertible debt issued should be separately disclosed from   12.5
other liabilities.

The FRSSE in outline

Dividends relating to financial instruments that are financial liabilities should be recognised as expense in profit or loss. Distributions to holders of an equity instrument should be debited directly to equity, net of any related income tax benefit. If an entity declares dividends after the balance sheet date, the dividends should not be recognised as a liability at the balance sheet date.	12.6
Disclosures include:	12.7–12.8

- aggregate amount of dividends paid in the year (other than those for which a liability existed at the immediately preceding balance sheet date);   12.7
- aggregate amount of dividends that the company is liable to pay at the balance sheet date;
- aggregate amount of dividends that are proposed before the date of approval of the accounts, and not otherwise disclosed;
- amount of arrears of any fixed cumulative dividends in arrears and the period for which each class of dividends is in arrears;   12.8
- the company's share capital (number and aggregate nominal value of shares of each class allotted; redeemable shares (terms and basis of redemption; earliest and latest dates and premium details, if any); and   12.9
- allotted share capital (allotments; amount of allotted and called up share capital; shares held by subsidiary undertakings).   12.10–12.12

Share based payments   12.13–12.15

Share-based payment arrangements (including employee share option schemes, SAYE arrangements and transactions with employees or others) should be accounted for them as either:

- cash-settled share-based payments – as an expense at the best estimate of the expenditure required to settle the liability; or
- equity-settled share-based payments – to be reported on a disclosure basis only.

(See **10.13 below**).

FOREIGN CURRENCY TRANSLATION (SSAP 20)   13.1–13.12
Method and basis of translation and determination of gains and losses (see **10.10 below**).

Denomination of foreign equity investments financed by foreign currency borrowings.

Incorporating accounts of foreign entities.

POST BALANCE SHEET EVENTS (FRS 21)   14.1–14.4
Post balance sheet events are those events, both favourable and unfavourable, that occur between the balance sheet date and the date when financial statements are authorised for issue. Post balance sheet events may be:

- adjusting events (those that provide evidence of conditions that existed at the balance sheet date); or
- non-adjusting events (those that are indicative of conditions that arose after the balance sheet date).

Adjusting post balance sheet events (but not non-adjusting events) should be reflected in amounts recognised in the financial statements. Each material category of non-adjusting event should be disclosed, giving the nature and financial effect of each such event.   14.1–14.3

The financial statements should disclose:

- date of approval of the financial statements, and
- who gave that approval.   14.4

RELATED PARTY DISCLOSURES (FRS 8)   15.1–15.5
(see **10.8 below**)
Financial statements should disclose material transactions undertaken by the reporting entity with a related party. Disclosure should be made irrespective of whether a price is charged. The materiality of a related party transaction should be judged in terms of its significance to the reporting entity.   15.1

Personal guarantees given by directors in respect of borrowings by the reporting entity should be disclosed in the notes to the financial statements.	15.2
Disclosure of controlling (or ultimate controlling) party or the fact if unknown (irrespective of whether any related party transactions have taken place).	15.8
Disclosure, where the company is a subsidiary undertaking, of the name of the company (if any) regarded by the directors as being the company's ultimate parent company and its country of incorporation (if outside **United Kingdom** and if known).	15.9

Separate statutory disclosures concerning group undertakings include:

• investment income, interest receivable or payable;	15.3–15.4
• commitments undertaken on behalf of parent or subsidiary undertakings;	15.5
• subsidiary undertaking of parent drawing up accounts for larger group;	15.10
• related undertakings disclosures (CA 2006 SI 2008 No. 409 Schedule 2): Subsidiary undertakings (name, incorporation, shareholdings and membership, financial information, capital and reserves (see **Chapter 12** at **12.7** below).	15.16–15.24

Directors' benefits: advances, credit and guarantees

Disclosure is required of advances and credits granted by the company to its directors and guarantees of any kind entered into by the company on behalf of its directors; including amounts, terms, conditions and totals (CA 2006 s. 413).	15.11–15.14
'Directors' and 'advances, credit and guarantees' apply to those (respectively) at any time in the financial year to which the accounts relate.	15.15

(see **10.8** below).

CONSOLIDATED FINANCIAL STATEMENTS

Where the reporting entity is preparing consolidated financial statements, it should regard as standard the accounting practices and disclosure requirements set out in:	16.1–16.8

FRS 2   *Accounting for subsidiary undertakings*
FRS 6   *Acquisitions and mergers*
FRS 7   *Fair values in acquisition accounting*

and, as they apply in respect of consolidated accounts:

FRS 5   *Reporting the substance of transactions*
FRS 9   *Associates and joint ventures*

FRS 10   *Goodwill and intangible assets*   ⎫   Only in respect of
FRS 11   *Impairment of fixed assets and goodwill* ⎬   purchased goodwill on
FRS2 28   *Corresponding amounts*   consolidation

Where the reporting entity is part of a group that prepares publicly available consolidated financial statements, it is entitled to exemptions concerning transactions and balances eliminated on consolidation; disclosures in a parent company's accounts; and intra-group related party transactions in the accounts of 90 per cent controlled subsidiaries (FRS 8 paragraph 3(a)–(c)).	16.2
Small group accounts – preparation of small group accounts must have regard to the legal requirements reflected in the FRSSE (effective April 2008) and the provisions of SI 2008 No. 409 Sch 6 (Part 1) (see **Chapter 9** at **9.5.3**).	16.3–16.4
Disclosure in small group accounts of advances and credits granted to parent company directors and guarantees of any kind entered into on behalf of those directors.	16.5
Balance sheet format heading for 'Investments' (BIII)	16.6
Profit and loss account format headings for income from 'interests in associated undertakings' and from 'other participating interests'	16.7
Group accounts–directors' balance sheet statement (above signature–preparation in accordance with special provisions in CA 2006 Part 15 relating to small companies).	16.8

DIRECTORS' REMUNERATION   17.1–17.3
Directors' **remuneration: overall** total of the following must be disclosed:

- **overall** amount of **remuneration** paid to or receivable by directors in respect of qualifying services;
- **overall** amount paid to or receivable by directors and the net value of assets (other than money, share options and shares) received or receivable by directors under long term incentive schemes in respect of qualifying services;
- **overall** value of any company contributions paid (or treated as paid) to a pension scheme in respect of directors' qualifying services, or by reference to which any money purchase benefits payable will be calculated; (SI 2008 No. 409 Sch 3.1)
- aggregate amount of compensation to directors or past directors in respect of loss of office, including **'benefits otherwise than in cash'** – CA 2006 s. 215. (SI 2008 No. 409 Sch 3.2) and
- aggregate amount of any consideration (including **'benefits otherwise than in cash'**) paid to, or receivable by, third parties for making available the services of any person as a director of the company or while director of the company, as director of any subsidiary undertaking, or otherwise in connection with the management of the affairs of the company or any of its subsidiary undertakings. The estimated money value of such benefits and their nature should be disclosed). (SI 2008 No. 409 Sch 3.3)

For money purchase schemes and defined benefit schemes, the number of directors (if any) to whom such retirement benefits are accruing in respect of qualifying services should be disclosed (for each type of scheme).

THE DIRECTORS' REPORT Disclosures include: principal activities; **names** of directors; **political donations and expenditure; charitable donations;** acquisition of own shares; and employment of disabled persons (see **Chapter 6** above at **6.8.2** and **Table 6.6**).	18.1–18.16
Approval and signature of directors' report: the directors' report must be approved by the board and signed on their behalf, and state the name of the person who has signed the report.	18.13–18.14
Third party indemnity provision: if any qualifying third party indemnity provision (whether made by the company or otherwise) is in force or was in force during the financial year for the benefit of one or more directors of the company (or an associated company or of its directors), the report must disclose the fact of such provision. (CA 2006 s. 236)	18.6
The directors' report shall contain a statement that the accounts have been prepared in accordance with the special provisions in Part 15 of the Companies Act 2005 relating to small companies (see **Chapter 6** above at **6.9**). Non-compliance is a criminal offence.	18.15–18.16
Disclosure of information to auditors: for audited companies, the directors' report must contain a statement that, so far as each of the directors at the time of approval of the report are aware: - there is no relevant audit information of which the company's auditors are unaware, and - the directors have taken all steps that they ought to have taken to make themselves aware of any relevant audit information and to establish that the auditors are aware of that information.	18.12

10.4 Cash flow statements

The FRSSE does not include a requirement for a cash flow statement, since small entities are already exempt from the requirements of FRS 1 (Revised 1996). Nevertheless, the ASB 'strongly encourages', within a non-mandatory 'voluntary disclosures' section of the FRSSE, smaller entities to present a simplified cash flow statement using the indirect method.

The indirect method starts with operating profit (normally profit before income from shares in group undertakings) and adjusts it for non-cash charges and credits to reconcile it with cash generated from operations. Other sources and applications of cash are shown to arrive at total cash generated (or utilised in the period).

Chapter 10 Essentials of the FRSSE – Financial Reporting Standard for Smaller Entities

Disclosures are recommended to include the following:

- cash, being 'cash at bank and in hand' less overdrafts repayable on demand – reconciled to the balance sheet;
- cash flows, being net of any attributable VAT or other sales tax, unless the tax is irrecoverable; and
- material transactions not resulting in movements of cash, which should be disclosed by way of note where necessary for a proper understanding of the underlying transactions.

The form of cash flow statement indicated as voluntary disclosure by the FRSSE is set out in **Table 10.4**.

Table 10.4 Small company cash flow statement for the year ended 30 April 2009

	2009 £ 0,000	2009 £ 0,000	2008 £ 0,000	2008 £ 0,000
CASH GENERATED FROM OPERATIONS				
Operating profit/(loss)	(5,050)		4,400	
Reconciliation to cash generated from operations:				
Depreciation	245		240	
Increase in stocks	(194)		(270)	
Decrease in trade debtors	67,440		19,090	
Decrease in trade creditors	(4,678)		1,240	
Increase in other creditors	3,127		100	
		60,890		24,800
CASH FROM OTHER SOURCES				
Interest received	150		100	
Issues of shares for cash	5,500		–	
New long-term bank borrowings	4,500		–	
Proceeds from sale of tangible fixed assets	50		940	
		10,200		1,040
APPLICATION OF CASH				
Interest paid	(3,000)		(1,000)	
Tax paid	(29,220)		(2,100)	
Dividends paid	(10,000)		(10,000)	
Purchase of fixed assets	(10,500)		(5,600)	
Repayment of amounts borrowed	(3,000)		–	
		(55,720)		(18,700)
NET INCREASE IN CASH		**15,370**		**7,140**
Cash at bank and in hand less overdrafts at beginning of year		(4,321)		(11,461)
CASH AT BANK AND IN HAND LESS OVERDRAFTS AT END OF YEAR		**11,049**		**(4,321)**
Consisting of:				
Cash at bank and in hand		11,549		1,909
Overdrafts included in 'bank loans and overdrafts falling due within one year'		(500)		(6,230)
		11,049		**(4,321)**

Major non-cash transactions: finance leases
During the year, the company entered into finance lease arrangements in respect of assets with a total capital value at the inception of the leases of £2,850 (2008 – Nil).

Entities are encouraged, but not required, to report cash flow information using the indirect method. The above statement, prepared on the indirect method of cash flow, is an indication of the type of statements that smaller entities may wish to include in their accounts. This example has been based on and amplified from the example contained in the FRSSE (effective April 2008) (Appendix III).

10.5 Small groups

A small eligible parent company (as defined – see **9.1**) is not required to prepare group accounts. If at the end of a financial year a company subject to the small companies regime is a parent company the directors, as well as preparing individual accounts for the year, *may* prepare group accounts for the year–but they are not required to do so.

Those small groups that voluntarily prepare group accounts may nevertheless take advantage of the provisions in FRSSE (effective April 2008 or January 2007) (see **Table 10.3** – 'Consolidated financial statements' FRSSE paragraphs 16.1–16.5). Entities preparing group accounts must have regard to the legal requirements reflected in the FRSSE and Schedule 6 of SI 2008 No. 409 under the Companies Act 2006 (see **9.5**)

Where the reporting entity is part of a group that prepares publicly available consolidated accounts, it is entitled under the FRSSE to the exemptions provided by FRS 8 paragraph 3(a)–(c), being:

- transactions or balances between group entities that have been eliminated on consolidation (consolidated accounts);
- disclosure in the parents' own accounts when presented together with consolidated accounts, and
- transactions with group entities in the accounts of 90 per cent subsidiary undertakings.

10.6 FRS 3 and the FRSSE

Table 10.5 indicates how the requirements of FRS 3 have been reflected in the FRSSE (effective April 2008).

Table 10.5   FRS 3 and the FRSSE

FRS 3 para	FRSSE para	
13	5.1	Primary statement of total recognised gains and losses (no separate statement required if gains and losses all recognised in profit and loss account).
19–20	3.5–3.6	Exceptional items: include as charge or credit within statutory headings (with separate disclosure if prominence required for true and fair view).
19		No reference to continuing or discontinued operations.
21	3.7	Profit or loss on disposal accounted for in period of disposal (net sales proceeds less net carrying amount).
22		No reference to extraordinary items.
29	2.15	Prior period adjustments.
23	9.3	Disclosure of special circumstances affecting overall tax charge (but no specific requirement to disclose tax on exceptional items).
5–6	C	Definitions of 'exceptional items', 'ordinary activities' and 'prior period adjustments', 'total recognised gains and losses'.
		No reference to 'extraordinary items'.

10.7 Reporting the substance of transactions

10.7.1 Substance over form

In order to ensure that accounts show a true and fair view, the FRSSE requires that any arrangement, transaction or series of transactions into which a company has entered should be accounted for not merely in accordance with their legal form but with their substance, that is, their true commercial effect. While this basic principle of FRS 5 is reflected in the FRSSE, the FRS is not generally covered in detail, other than setting out requirements for consignment stock and debt factoring (FRSSE paragraphs 8.9 to 8.12 – **Table 10.3**). The FRSSE's guidance on consignment stock is summarised below.

10.7.2 Consignment stock

Consignment stock is an important element of some small businesses. The guidance in the FRSSE follows the application notes provided within FRS 5 *Reporting the substance of transactions*.

Consignment stock is stock held by one party (the 'dealer') but legally owned by another (the 'manufacturer'), on terms that give the dealer the right to sell the stock in the normal course of its business or, at its option, to return it unsold to the legal owner.

Where consignment stock is in substance an asset of the dealer, the stock should be recognised as such in the dealer's balance sheet, together with a corresponding liability to the manufacturer. Any deposit should be deducted from the liability and the excess classified as a trade creditor.

Where stock is not in substance an asset of the dealer, the stock should not be included on the dealer's balance sheet until the transfer of title has crystallised. Any deposit should be included under 'other debtors'.

10.8 Related party transactions

The FRSSE requires the disclosure of:

- information on related party transactions;
- the name of the controlling party (if any) and ultimate controlling party (if different), whether or not any transactions between the parties have taken place;
- personal guarantees given by directors in respect of borrowings by the reporting entity; and
- transactions with directors.

10.8.1 Related party disclosures

Material related party transactions that require disclosure are those where the reporting entity:

- purchases, sells or transfers goods or other assets or liabilities;
- renders or receives services, or
- provides or receives finance or financial support.

Aggregated disclosures are allowed subject to certain restrictions.

Related party disclosures within accounts should identify material transactions undertaken by the reporting entity with a related party. Disclosure should be made irrespective of whether a price is charged.

> **Table 10.6 Related parties – FRSSE definition**
>
> Two or more parties are related parties when at any time during the financial period:
>
> - one party has direct or indirect control of the other party;
> - the parties are subject to common control from the same source; or
> - one party has 'significant' influence over the financial and operating policies of the other party, to an extent that the other party might be inhibited from pursuing its own separate interests.
>
> For the avoidance of doubt, the FRSSE definition states that related parties of the reporting entity include the following:
>
> - parent undertakings, subsidiary and fellow subsidiary undertakings;
> - associate and joint ventures;
> - investors with significant influence and their close families; and
> - directors of the reporting entity and of its parent undertakings.
>
> Parties that, in entering a transaction, are subject to influence from the same source to such an extent that one of the parties to the transaction has subordinated its own separate interests are not 'related parties' for the purposes of the FRSSE.

The disclosures should include:

- the names of the transacting related parties;
- a description of the relationship between the parties;
- a description of the transactions;
- the amounts involved;
- any other elements of the transactions necessary for an understanding of the accounts;
- the amounts due to or from related parties at the balance sheet date and provisions for doubtful debts due from such parties at that date, and
- amounts written off in the period in respect of debts due to or from related parties.

No disclosure is required in consolidated accounts of intra-group transactions and balances eliminated on consolidation. A parent undertaking is not required to provide related party disclosures in its own accounts when those accounts are presented with consolidated accounts of the group.

Under the FRSSE, the materiality of a related party transaction need be judged only in terms of its significance to the reporting entity (and not in relation to the other related party as is required by FRS 8 even where (for example) that related party is an individual).

Transactions with related parties may be disclosed on an aggregated basis (aggregation of similar transactions by type of related party) unless disclosure of an individual transaction, or connected transactions, is necessary for an understanding of the impact of the transactions on the accounts of the reporting entity or is required by law.

Disclosure is not required of:

- pension contributions paid to a pension fund, nor
- emoluments in respect of services as an employee of the reporting entity.

Nor is disclosure required of the relationship and transactions between the reporting entity and the following parties simply as a result of their role as:

- providers of finance in the course of their business;
- utility companies;
- government departments and their sponsored bodies; or
- a customer, supplier, franchiser, distributor or general agent.

When the reporting entity is controlled by another party, there should be disclosure of the related party relationship, the name of the controlling party and, if different, that of the ultimate controlling party. If the controlling party or ultimate controlling party of the reporting entity is not known, that fact should be disclosed. (These disclosures are irrespective of whether any transactions have taken place between the controlling parties and the reporting entity.)

10.8.2 Loans and transactions with directors

For a small company, when preparing accounts and having determined the legality of a loan, the directors need to consider the extent of disclosure. It is important to recognise that, notwithstanding that a transaction (other than a loan) may be legal, it may still nevertheless require disclosure in the accounts.

CA 2006 s. 197(1) ('Loans to directors: requirement of members' approval') makes a general prohibition on loans to directors, together with related guarantees or provision of security for loans without the approval of the members of the company. However, for small loans CA 2006 s. 207(1) ('Loans: exceptions for minor and business transactions') provides that such approval is not required if the aggregate value of the transaction (together with other relevant transactions or arrangements) does not exceed £10,000.

A company is therefore not prohibited from making a loan to a director of the company or its holding company if the aggregate value of the transaction does not exceed £10,000.

Expenditure on company business is permitted under CA 2006 s. 204 ('Loans: exception for expenditure on company business') for anything done by a company to provide a director of the company or of its holding company (or a person connected with any such director) with funds to meet expenditure incurred for the company or to enable the proper performance of the director's duties as an officer of the company, provided the aggregate of the value of the transaction (and the value of any other relevant transactions or arrangement) does not exceed £50,000.

The 'value of a transaction or arrangement' referred to above is defined in detail (and some complexity) in CA 2006 s. 211.

Factors determining disclosure may include:

- CA 2006 requirements–section 197 ('Loans to directors: requirement of members' approval') et seq;
- FRS 8 *Related Party Disclosures* or, for small companies adopting it, the FRSSE; and
- requirements of the company's memorandum and articles of association.

Reference should be made to these sources, and a reliable disclosure requirements checklist, for detailed consideration.

10.8.3 Transactions with directors – FRSSE disclosures

The requirements of the FRSSE covering transactions with directors, now referred to as 'Directors' benefits: advances, credit and guarantees', are based on Companies Act 2006 section 413 and are summarised below.

Companies Act 2006 section 413 provides for the provision of information about 'Directors' benefits: advances, credit and guarantees'. The following details must, where appropriate, be shown in the notes to accounts (individual or group accounts):

- advances and credits granted to directors, and
- guarantees of any kind entered into on behalf of directors,

For group accounts, 'directors' are 'parent company directors' and advances, credit and guarantees relate to those granted by the parent company or by any of its subsidiary undertakings to the directors of the parent company. 'Directors' are persons who were a director of the company (or parent company) at any time in the financial year to which the accounts relate.

The details required of an advance or credit are: its amount; an indication of the interest rate; its main conditions; and any amounts repaid. The details required of a guarantee are: its main terms; the amount of the maximum liability that may be incurred by the company (or its subsidiary); and any amount paid and any liability incurred by the company (or its subsidiary) for the purpose of fulfilling the guarantee (including any loss incurred by reason of enforcement of the guarantee).

Companies Act 2006 section 413 is set out in full in **Appendix B** to which reference should be made.

10.9 Pensions and retirement benefits

10.9.1 Accounting for retirement benefits

The FRSSE (effective April 2008) incorporates the relevant aspects of FRS 17 'Retirement Benefits', modified and simplified where appropriate for smaller entities.

Two types of pension schemes are defined within the FRSSE. A 'Defined contribution scheme' is a pension or other retirement benefit scheme into which an employer pays regular contributions, fixed as an amount or as a percentage of pay. The employer has no legal or constructive obligation to pay further contributions in the event of the scheme having insufficient assets to pay all employee benefits relating to employee service in the current and prior periods. Any scheme other than a defined contribution scheme is defined as a 'Defined benefit scheme', the rules of which define benefits independently of the contributions payable (and the benefits are not directly related to scheme investments).

FRS 17 has not significantly changed the accounting for defined contribution pension schemes and as a result accounting for such schemes is essentially the same as under former SSAP 24 'Accounting for pension costs' (and the previous versions of the FRSSE).

Accounting for defined benefit schemes, however, has changed significantly and far more demanding requirements are being introduced for these schemes. FRS 17 applied in full with effect from accounting periods beginning on or after 1 January 2005. Further amendments implementing alignment with IAS19 applied with effect from accounting periods beginning on or after 6 April 2007.

Even though comparatively few smaller entities use defined benefit retirement schemes, implementation of the new accounting rules concerning these schemes is likely to be onerous and warrants careful consideration. Actuarial advice will be essential.

The requirements for accounting for retirement benefits under the FRSSE are in essence as follows:

Defined contribution schemes – scheme contributions payable for the period are charged (or 'recognised') in the profit and loss account for the period.

Defined benefit schemes – scheme assets and liabilities are measured:
- scheme assets – at fair value, and
- scheme liabilities (discounted as appropriate) – on the projected unit method, with the resulting net asset or liability recognised in the balance sheet.

Chapter 10 Essentials of the FRSSE – Financial Reporting Standard for Smaller Entities

Example 10.1 contains example pension scheme disclosures, reproduced (and adapted) from an appendix in the FRSSE (effective April 2008).

Example 10.1 Example pension scheme disclosures

Defined contribution pension scheme
The company operates a defined contribution pension scheme. The assets of the scheme are held separately from those of the company in an independently administered fund. The pension cost charge represents contributions payable by the company to the fund and amounted to £50,000 (2008 – £45,000). Contributions totalling £2,500 (2008 – £1,500) were payable to the fund at the year end and are included in creditors.

Defined benefit pension scheme
(NOTE [Example FRSSE (effective April 2008)]):

The example below (taken from Appendix III of the FRSSE (effective April 2008)) reflects the disclosure requirements for financial statements ending on or after 22 June 2006. See 10.9.2 below.

The company operates a pension scheme providing benefits based on final pensionable pay. The assets of the scheme are held separately from those of the company, being invested with insurance companies.

The contributions are determined by a qualified actuary on the basis of triennial valuations using the projected unit method. The most recent valuation was as at 31 December 2005 which has been updated to reflect conditions at the balance sheet date. The assumptions that have the most significant effect on the results of the valuation are those relating to the rate of return on investments and the rate of increase in salaries and pensions. It was assumed that the investment returns would be 6 per cent per year, that salary increases would average 4 per cent per year and that present and future pensions would increase at the rate of 3 per cent per year.

The pension charge for the year was £46,000 (2005 £25,000). This included £12,000 (2005 £nil) in respect of past service costs. The contributions of the company and employees will remain at 10 per cent and 5 per cent of earnings respectively.

The defined benefit scheme is closed to new members and so under the projected unit method the current service cost would be expected to increase over time as members of the scheme approach retirement.

Value of scheme assets and liabilities	2006 £	2005 £
Market value of assets	1,488,000	962,000
Present value of scheme liabilities	(1,009,000)	(758,000)
Pension scheme surplus/(deficit)	479,000	204,000
Related deferred tax asset/(liability)	(144,000)	(61,000)
Net pension scheme asset/(liability)	335,000	143,000

Movements in year	2006 £	2005 £
Pension scheme surplus/(deficit) at beginning of year	204,000	92,000
Current service cost	(34,000)	(25,000)
Cash contribution	25,000	35,000
Past service costs	(12,000)	0
Other finance income	20,000	11,000
Actuarial gain	276,000	91,000
Pension scheme surplus/(deficit) at end of year	479,000	204,000

10.9.2 The FRSSE and defined benefit retirement schemes

Relatively few small companies run defined benefit pension schemes. Indeed, in drafting the FRSSE, the ASB considered that the number of smaller entities using such schemes was

Pensions and retirement benefits

insufficient to justify including the requirements of FRS 17 relating to such schemes within the main body of the FRSSE itself. The detailed small company requirements for accounting for defined benefit retirement schemes are therefore set out in Appendix II of the revised FRSSE (effective April 2008).

FRSSE (effective **April 2008**) Appendix II is reproduced in full in **Table 10.7** with minor presentational amendments only, primarily caption headings represented in *emboldened italicised text* to aid clarification. FRSSE (effective January **2007**) reproduces only the relevant text of Appendix II that is applicable for accounting periods ending on or after 22 June 2006. Further amendments implementing alignment of FRS 17 with IAS 19 (which apply with effect from accounting periods beginning on or after 6 April 2007) are not reflected in the revised FRSSE.

Table 10.7   Accounting for retirement benefits: defined benefit schemes

Accounting periods ending on or after 22 June 2006
1. The following requirements should be regarded as standard in respect of financial statements relating to accounting periods ending *on or after* 22 June 2006, although earlier adoption is encouraged:

Assets at fair value
(a)   Assets in a defined benefit scheme should be measured at their fair value at the balance sheet date.

Scheme liabilities
(b)   Defined benefit scheme liabilities should be measured on an actuarial basis using the projected unit method. The scheme liabilities comprise both any benefits promised under the formal terms of the scheme and any constructive obligations for further benefits.
(c)   The assumptions underlying the valuation should be mutually compatible and lead to the best estimate of the future cash flows that will arise under the scheme liabilities. The assumptions are ultimately the responsibility of the directors (or equivalent) but should be set upon advice given by an actuary. Any assumptions that are affected by economic conditions (financial assumptions) should reflect market expectations at the balance sheet date.
(d)   Defined benefit scheme liabilities should be discounted at the current rate of return on a high quality corporate bond of equivalent currency and term.

Actuarial valuations
(e)   Full actuarial valuations by a professionally qualified actuary should be obtained for a defined benefit scheme at intervals not exceeding three years. The actuary should review the most recent actuarial valuation at the balance sheet date and update it to reflect current conditions.

Scheme surplus or deficit
(f)   The surplus/deficit in a defined benefit scheme is the excess/shortfall of the value of the assets in the scheme over/below the present value of the scheme liabilities. The employer should recognise an asset to the extent that it is able to recover a surplus either through reduced contributions in the future or through refunds from the scheme. The employer should recognise a liability to the extent that it reflects its legal or constructive obligation.

Balance sheet format presentation
(g)   Any unpaid contributions to the scheme should be presented in the balance sheet as a creditor due within one year. The defined benefit asset or liability should be presented separately on the face of the balance sheet:
   (i)   in balance sheets of the type prescribed for small companies in **the United Kingdom by The Small Companies and Groups (Accounts and Directors' Report) Regulations 2008**, format 1: after item J 'Accruals and deferred income' but before item K 'Capital and reserves', and
   (ii)   in balance sheets of the type prescribed for small companies in **the United Kingdom by The Small Companies and Groups (Accounts and Directors' Report) Regulations 2008**, format 2: any asset after ASSETS item D 'Prepayments and accrued income' and any liability after LIABILITIES item D 'Accruals and deferred income'.

Related deferred tax
(h)   The deferred tax relating to the defined benefit asset or liability should be offset against the defined benefit asset or liability and not included with other deferred tax assets or liabilities.

> **Performance statement presentation**
> (i) The components of the change in the defined benefit asset or liability (other than those arising from contributions to the scheme) should be presented separately in the performance statements as follows:
>   (i) the current service cost should be included within operating profit in the profit and loss account;
>   (ii) the net of the interest cost and the expected return on assets should be included as other finance costs (or income) adjacent to interest;
>   (iii) actuarial gains and losses should be recognised in the statement of total recognised gains and losses;
>   (iv) past service costs should be recognised in the profit and loss account in the period in which the increases in benefit vest; and
>   (v) losses arising on a settlement or curtailment should be recognised in the profit and loss account when the employer becomes demonstrably committed to the transaction (gains should only be recognised once all parties whose consent is required are irrevocably committed).
>
> **Disclosures**
> (j) The following disclosures should be made in respect of a defined benefit scheme:
>   (i) the nature of the scheme, (ie defined benefit);
>   (ii) the date of the most recent full actuarial valuation on which the amounts in the financial statements are based. If the actuary is an employee or officer of the reporting entity, or of the group of which it is a member, this fact should be disclosed;
>   (iii) the contribution made in respect of the accounting period and any agreed contribution rates for future years, and
>   (iv) for closed schemes and those in which the age profile of the active membership is rising significantly, the fact that under the projected unit method the current service cost will increase as the members of the scheme approach retirement.
> (k) The fair value of the scheme assets, the present value of the scheme liabilities based on the accounting assumptions and the resulting surplus or deficit should be disclosed in a note to the financial statements. Where the asset or liability in the balance sheet differs from the surplus or deficit in the scheme, an explanation of the difference should be given. An analysis of the movements during the period in the surplus or deficit in the scheme should be given.

10.10 Foreign currency translation

Each asset, liability, revenue or cost arising from a transaction denominated in a foreign currency should be translated into the local currency at the exchange rate in operation on the date on which the transaction occurred; if the rates do not fluctuate significantly, an average rate for a period may be used as an approximation. Where the transaction is to be settled at a contracted rate, that rate should be used.

Where a trading transaction is covered by a related or matching forward contract, the rate of exchange specified in that contract may be used.

Except for the treatment of foreign equity investments financed by foreign currency borrowings, no subsequent translations should normally be made once non-monetary assets have been translated and recorded.

At each balance sheet date, monetary assets and liabilities denominated in a foreign currency should be translated by using the closing rate or, where appropriate, the rates of exchange fixed under the terms of the relevant transactions. Where there are related or matching forward contracts in respect of trading transactions, the rates of exchange specified in those contracts may be used.

All exchange gains or losses on settled transactions and unsettled monetary items should be reported as part of the profit or loss for the year from ordinary activities.

Where a company has used foreign currency borrowings to finance, or to provide a hedge against, its foreign equity investments and the conditions set out in the FRSSE apply, the equity investments may be denominated in the appropriate foreign currencies and the carrying amounts translated at the end of each accounting period at closing rates for inclusion in the investing company's financial statements. Where investments are treated in this way, any exchange differences arising should be taken to reserves and the exchange gains or losses on the foreign currency borrowings should then be offset, as a reserve movement, against these exchange differences.

10.11 Provisions and discounting

A provision (for a liability of uncertain amount or timing) should be the best estimate of the expenditure required to settle the obligation at the balance sheet date (see **Table 10.3** and FRSSE (effective April 2008) paragraph 11.2).

Where the effect of the time value of money is material, a provision should be determined by discounting the amount to the present value of the expenditures expected to be required to settle the obligation. Discounting is also required in circumstances where it is necessary to show a true and fair view. The FRSSE requires the unwinding of the discount to be disclosed as 'other finance costs' adjacent to interest.

The example set out in **Table 10.8** below is based on the FRSSE to show the calculation of the discount and the effect of unwinding.

Table 10.8

A company faces a fine for operating without due regard to safety legislation. It has been notified of the case and expects to lose it but does not expect the fine of £100,000 to be payable for five years.

The amount to be provided for is as follows:

(Assume the market rate on relevant government bonds is five per cent)

The discounted amount for the payment of £100,000 to be made in five years' time is £78,353

ie $£ \dfrac{100{,}000}{(1 + (5/100))^5} = £78{,}353$

This is recorded as an expense and a provision in the company's books, rather than £100,000.

In the subsequent years the discount will unwind and the amount of the provision will increase. A debit to the profit and loss account (shown as a financial expense separate from interest) arises each year as follows:

		Provision made (Debit) £	Total Provision £
Amount originally recorded			78,353
Year 1	78,353 × 5%	3,918	82,271
Year 2	(78,353 + 3,918) × 5%	4,113	86,384
Year 3	86,384 × 5%	4,319	90,703
Year 4	90,703 × 5%	4,535	95,238
Year 5	95,238 × 5%	4,762	100,000
Total provision at end of Year 5			100,000

10.12 Revenue recognition

Application Note G to FRS 5 provides guidance on the principles of revenue recognition and the treatment of turnover. The Application Note codifies existing practice and sets out a consistent treatment of revenue transactions ('exchange transactions' between seller and customer). The guidance explains how, when and whether to recognise revenue, in a variety of circumstances.

Revenue recognition is covered in more detail in **12.9** below.

The FRSSE (effective April 2008) incorporates the essential principles of revenue recognition promoted by Application Note G to FRS 5, incorporating the guidance contained in UITF 40 (see **12.9.3**).

Entities adopting the FRSSE must comply with principles of UITF 40 (despite a statement of exemption within the UITF) as a result of requirements of HM Revenue and Customs (HMRC). All entities should apply UITF 40 (where applicable) for accounting periods ending on or after 22 June 2005.

On 1 November 2005 HMRC issued the following statement.

'Taxpayers are required by law to calculate their taxable profits in accordance with generally accepted accounting practice, subject to any specific tax law overrides. HMRC expects that all entities will adopt the most appropriate accounting policies consistent with current practice. It is clear that non-FRSSE entities should apply UITF 40 for accounting periods ending on or after 22 June 2005 and, in the light of this and the requirement in the FRSSE that entities which follow the FRSSE should have regard to full standards as a means of establishing current practice, we believe that entities which follow the FRSSE should have regard to UITF 40 in preparing their accounts for the same periods.'

10.13 Share based payments

Share-based payment arrangements (such as employee share option schemes or SAYE arrangements) are relatively uncommon for smaller entities. FRS 20 incorporated into UK accounting the requirements of the international standard IFRS 2 with effect (for all unlisted companies) for accounting years beginning on or after 1 January 2006. The revised FRSSE (effective January 2007) introduced requirements for share-based payment arrangements but with major simplifications.

A share-based payment transaction is defined as 'a transaction in which the entity acquires goods or services by incurring a liability to transfer cash or other assets to the supplier of those goods or services for amounts that are based on the price (or value) of the entity's shares or other equity instruments of the entity'.

An entity which undertakes share-based payment arrangements (including transactions with employees or others providing similar services), where liability is based on the price of the entity's shares or other equity instruments, should account for them as either:

- cash-settled share-based payment; or
- equity-settled share-based payment.

In essence, for small companies, the FRSSE (effective April 2008) requires:

- cash-settled share-based payments – to be accounted for as an expense at the best estimate of the expenditure required to settle the liability; and
- equity-settled share-based payments – to be reported on a disclosure basis only.

Cash-settled share-based payment transactions

In a cash-settled arrangement, the entity recognises the goods or services received or acquired ('goods and services') when it (a) obtains the goods, or (b) as the services are received. Goods or services received or acquired are recognised as expenses or as assets, depending on how they qualify; a corresponding liability is also recognised – the best estimate of the expenditure required to settle the liability at the balance sheet date should be used. At each subsequent balance sheet date and at the date of settlement, the liability shall be remeasured. The notes to the accounts should describe (a) the principal terms and conditions of cash settled share-based payment transactions existing during the period, and also (b) their current and potential financial effect.

Equity-settled share-based payment arrangements

For equity-settled arrangements, the notes should describe the principal terms and conditions of any arrangements existing during the period including (a) the number of shares and the number of employees and others potentially involved, (b) the grant date, (c) any performance conditions and over what periods these apply, and (d) any option exercise prices (where applicable).

Choice of settlement method

Where the terms of the arrangement provide the counterparty to the arrangement with the choice of whether the entity settles the transaction in cash (or other assets) or by issuing equity instruments, the transaction is accounted for as a cash settled transaction, measured at the best estimate of the amount required to settle it at the balance sheet date, as if the counterparty were to opt for cash settlement. If the obligation is eventually settled by the issue of equity instruments, the liability previously recognised is treated as the proceeds of issue of those instruments.

10.14 Going concern and the FRSSE

10.14.1 Fundamental accounting principles

The essential elements in the preparation of annual accounts, as explained in **Chapter 3**, include:

- the fundamental requirement to show a 'true and fair view'; *s. 393*
- preparation in accordance with relevant financial reporting standards; *s. 464*
- the adoption of statutory accounting principles and rules. *Sch 1. 10–15*

Accounts must be prepared on the presumption of the business as a going concern, unless there is an intention after balance sheet date to cease trading or liquidate the company.

These principles apply whether or not the company is entitled to audit exemption or files abbreviated accounts.

10.14.2 Going concern: directors' responsibilities

All directors (including directors of smaller companies) are required by the Companies Act 2006 to decide if it is appropriate to prepare annual accounts on a going concern basis.

The FRSSE (effective April 2008) provides that accounts must not be prepared on a going concern basis if the directors determine that they intend to cease trading, or that they have no realistic alternative but to do so. The FRSSE requires directors to:

- assess the ability of the company to continue as a going concern;
- disclose in accounts any material uncertainties indicated by the assessment; and
- disclose the period covered by the assessment (where the period covers less than one year from the date of approval of the annual accounts). *FRSSE para 2.12*

Assessment of the going concern basis of accounting involves the directors making judgments, at a particular time, about future events which are inherently uncertain. The directors must have reasonable grounds for concluding that it is realistic for the company to avoid liquidation within twelve months of the date of approval of the financial statements.

In order to satisfy themselves, the directors need to:

- prepare a budget, trading estimate, cash flow forecast or a similar analysis;
- document any underlying assumptions and identify possible adverse outcomes;
- consider existing bank facilities or credit arrangements made available by suppliers;
- discuss and confirm, where necessary, the adequacy of continuing facilities and arrangements;
- base their analysis on reasoned assumptions, identifying possible adverse outcomes; and
- prepare the forecasts etc. to cover a period up to (at least) twelve months from the date of approval of the accounts.

10.14.3 Going concern and the FRSSE: FRC guidance

In March 2009, the Financial Reporting Council (FRC) published guidance on the 'going concern basis' and financial reporting for smaller companies entitled *Update for directors of companies that adopt the Financial Reporting Standard for Smaller Entities (FRSSE): Going concern and financial reporting*. The guidance was provided in the light of the current economic difficulties being experienced by many companies.

The FRC guidance aims to help directors of smaller companies by summarising the criteria necessary to support the 'going concern basis' and identifying basic procedures needed to support conclusions. It also explains where appropriate accounts disclosure may be necessary.

The extent of forecasting procedures required, as outlined in **10.14.2** above, may vary considerably according particular circumstances. A company with substantial cash balances and a committed order book is very different from one with significant borrowings and uncertainties about future sales.

10.14.4 Going concern: accounts disclosures

In practice it has been very rare for accounts to be prepared on a basis other than as a 'going concern'. Specific reference to 'going concern' within company accounts has generally not been necessary because it is a fundamental presumption unless indicated otherwise.

In the current economic environment it is clear from its guidance that the Financial Reporting Council (FRC) "does expect that many accounts may benefit from a short note explaining how credit market and other economic difficulties have an impact, if any, on the company's particular circumstances".

Many more small company accounts may, therefore, in future contain notes considering the implications of future trading assessments on the adoption the 'going concern' basis of accounting. See example presentation in **Chapter 13**.

In the current economic climate, predicting future trading trends may be difficult. Doubts about the ability of a company to remain as a going concern do not necessarily mean that the company is, or is likely to become, insolvent. For accounts disclosure purposes, as a rule of thumb disclosure would usually be appropriate where there are 'significant doubts' about future trading or there are ' material uncertainties of such significance' about the ability to continue to trade.

Any specific disclosure about going concern in a company's annual accounts should also be included in any abbreviated accounts filed at Companies House. See example in **Chapter 13**.

Chapter 11 Determining small company audit exemption

Companies Act 2006 sections 477(2) and 479(2) set out the conditions to be met by a company or group in order for the company or group company, as appropriate, to be exempt from audit.

11.1 Introduction – preparation of accounts irrespective of audit

Generally speaking, company law requires the directors of *all* companies to prepare annual (statutory) accounts irrespective of the requirement or otherwise for the need for these accounts to be audited. Statutory (annual) accounts for shareholders should: *s. 394*

- give a true and fair view, and
- comply (to the appropriate extent) with Companies Act 2006 and (for small companies) regulations under SI 2008 No. 409 as to form, content and information provided.

Every company must send a copy of its annual accounts and reports for each financial year to every member of the company, every holder of the company's debentures, and every person who is entitled to receive notice of general meetings, for all of whom the company has a 'current address'. A private company must comply with this requirement not later than the end of the period for filing accounts and reports or (if earlier) the date on which the accounts are delivered to the registrar.   *ss. 423–424*

A company does have the option (upon agreement) to provide summary financial statements complying with statutory regulations.   *s. 426*

For each financial year, the directors must also deliver ('file') a copy of the accounts and reports to the Registrar of Companies. Under the Companies Act 2006, the periods allowed for filing have been shortened. The period allowed for filing is nine months for a private company or six months for a public company after the end of the financial year (relevant 'accounting reference date'). If the relevant accounting reference period is the company's first and is a period of more than twelve months, the period is nine months or six months (as the case may be) from the first anniversary of the incorporation of the company, or three months after the end of the accounting reference period, whichever last expires.   *s. 441*
s. 442
s. 442(3)

A company which is small or medium-sized may file abbreviated accounts instead of full accounts.   *s. 444(3)*
s. 445(3)

The directors of an unlimited company are not required to deliver accounts and reports to the Registrar (provided certain conditions are met).   *s. 448*

11.2 Small companies – conditions for exemption from audit

A company is exempt from the requirements for the audit of its accounts in respect of a financial year if it meets the conditions set out below.   *s. 477*

Whether a company qualifies as a small company is determined in accordance with CA 2006 ss. 382(1)–(6), as set out in **Chapter 5** at **5.2**.

Chapter 11 Determining small company audit exemption

To be entitled to audit exemption, a small company must:

- qualify as a small company in relation to that year;
- have a turnover in that year of not more than £6.5 million; and
- have a balance sheet total for that year of not more than £3.26 million.

Where the company's financial year is a period other than a year, the maximum figure for turnover must be proportionately adjusted.

To be entitled to audit exemption, a small company must also:

- provide within its balance sheet a directors' statement (ss. 475(2)–(4));
- not be one of the categories of companies excluded from small companies exemption (s. 478) (see **11.3** below); and
- not have received notice requiring it to obtain an audit from ten per cent or more of members (s. 476).

Small companies audit exemption is available in the case of group companies where the conditions in CA 2006 s. 479 apply as set out in **11.4** below.

Audit exemption is not available where exemption has been vetoed by shareholders holding 10 per cent or more of any class of share capital (or ten per cent of the members) or where it is precluded in accordance with the Articles of Association.

The audit requirements for charitable companies will be governed by the provisions of the Charities Act 2006 (as implemented) rather than company law.

11.3 Companies excluded from small companies' audit exemption

A company is not entitled to the small companies audit exemption conferred by CA 2006 s. 477 if it was at any time within the financial year in question:

- a public company;
- a company that is an authorised insurance company, a banking company, an e-money issuer, a MiFID investment firm or a UCITS management company, or carries on insurance market activity; or
- a special register body (as defined under the Trade Union and Labour Relations (Consolidation) Act 1992) or an employers' association (as defined).

s. 478

11.4 Group companies – availability of small audit exemption

A company is exempt from the requirements for the audit of its accounts in respect of a financial year if it meets the conditions set out in CA 2006 s. 477 (see **11.2** above).

Whether a group qualifies as small is determined in accordance with CA 2006 s. 383 (companies qualifying as small: parent companies). (See **Chapter 9** at **9.2**)

A company which is a group company (being a parent company or a subsidiary undertaking) is only entitled to audit exemption (in accordance with CA 2006 s. 477(2)) if the following conditions are met:

- the group qualifies as a small group in relation to the financial year (during any part of which it was a group company);
- the group was not at any time in the year an 'ineligible' group (as defined by CA 2006 s. 384(2) and (3));

Determining audit exemption

- the group's aggregate turnover in the year is not more than £6.5 million net (or £7.8 million gross); or
- the group's aggregate balance sheet total for that year is not more than £3.26 million net (or £3.9 million gross).

s. 479(2) as amended by SI 2008 No. 393

A group's aggregate turnover and aggregate balance sheet total are determined as for the purposes of CA 2006 s. 383 as set out in **Chapter 5** *at* **5.3**;

A dormant subsidiary undertaking being a group company during the financial year is also entitled to audit exemption.

s. 479(3)

CA 2006 s. 479(4) defines a 'group' as the group company (parent company or subsidiary undertaking) together with all its associated undertakings.

s. 479(4)

11.5 Right to require an audit

The members of a company that would otherwise be entitled to exemption from audit (under CA 2006 s. 475(1)(a) (small or dormant companies)) may by notice require it to obtain an audit of its accounts for a financial year.

s. 476(1)

Any member or members holding not less than ten per cent in aggregate in the nominal value of the company's issued share capital of a company (or any class of it) or (if the company does not have share capital) not less than ten per cent in number of the members of the company may require an audit of the company's accounts.

s. 476(2)

To obtain an audit of the company's accounts, the member or members must deposit a notice in writing at the company's registered office during the financial year but not later than one month before the end of the year. The company is then not entitled to audit exemption for the year to which the notice relates.

s. 476(3))

There is no requirement for a company to advise members of their rights to require an audit (or the manner in which it may be exercised) nor, for example, of their rights to audit when the accounting year end is changed.

11.6 Determining audit exemption

Table 11.1 summarises the position to demonstrate:

- when an audit is required, which accounts may be prepared (and for whom), and
- whether accounts should be filed at Companies House.

The table applies to a company which:

1. Qualifies as a 'small company' (in accordance with CA 2006 s. 382), meets the small companies conditions for exemption from audit contained in CA 2006 s. 477, and has a 'balance sheet total' CA 2006 s. 382 which does not exceed £3.26 million.

2. Is **not** excluded from the small companies audit exemption by CA 2006 s. 478, being:

   (a) a public company;
   (b) a company that is an authorised insurance company, a banking company, an e-money issuer, a MiFID investment firm or a UCITS management company, or carries on insurance market activity;
   (c) a 'special register body' – trade union or employers' association; or
   (d) an incorporated charity following the implementation of provisions of the Charities Act 2006.

Chapter 11 Determining small company audit exemption

s. 479

3. If a parent company or a subsidiary undertaking, is not the member of a small ineligible group.

It assumes that audit exemption has not otherwise been vetoed by shareholders holding ten per cent or more of any class of share capital (or ten per cent of the members) or is precluded in accordance with the Articles of Association.

Notwithstanding the availability of exemption, an audit may nevertheless be voluntarily carried out.

Table 11.1 Small companies – summary of accounts and the need for audit

Turnover	Small company SI 2008 No. 409 Sch. 1 accounts (s. 394) available?	Small company – abbreviated accounts available?	Audit required?	Accounts filing with Registrar of Companies (Companies House) required? (1)	Full accounts to be sent to shareholders? (2)
Companies (other than charities)					
Not more than £6.5 million	Yes	Yes	No	Yes	Yes
Over £6.5 million	No	No	Yes	Yes	Yes

Note 1   Full individual or abbreviated statutory accounts, except for unincorporated companies (where filing is not required).
Note 2   A company does have the option (upon agreement with shareholders) to provide summary financial statements complying with statutory regulations. (CA 2006 s. 426)

11.7 Audit or assurance reports on accounts of small companies

Following the increase in thresholds for audit exemption for small companies in recent years, it is inevitable that many more accounts of small companies may be prepared without any form of audit or assurance report being attached – simply because none is statutorily required. **Table 11.2** sets out the position

Where a company is entitled to audit exemption, the directors may nevertheless wish (or be required by banking terms) to have the assurance of a non-statutory or 'contractual' audit (voluntarily obtained on terms of engagement instructed by the directors) or the comfort of an accountants' report on the proper compilation of the accounts.

Reports on accounts prepared for unaudited companies are illustrated in **Chapter 14**. The special auditors' report under s. 449 is reflected in the example in **Chapter 14**.

Table 11.2 Audit or assurance reports for small companies

Type of accounts	Type of assurance report
Audit exemption – s. 477	
Small company accounts – audit exemption	No audit or other report required
Abbreviated accounts – audit exemption	No audit or other report required
Audit – s. 475	
Small company accounts – audited (if *statutorily required*)	Auditors' report – s. 495
Small company accounts – audited (*at members' request – s. 476*)	Auditors' report – s. 495
Abbreviated accounts – audited	Special auditors' report – s. 449
Audit – Contractual (Agreed upon procedures)	
Small company accounts – audited (*voluntarily at company's option*)	Auditors' report – s. 495
Full accounts – audited (*voluntarily at company's option*)	Auditors' report – in accordance with *directors' instructions* (for example, determined by banking covenants)
Accountants' report – Contractual	Accountants' report – in accordance with *directors' instructions*
(Compilation/agreed upon procedures) Full small company or abbreviated accounts	

11.8 Audit exemption – Directors' statement

A company's annual accounts for a financial year must be audited unless the company is exempt from audit under CA 2006 s. 477 (small companies), s. 480 (dormant companies), or s. 482 (non-profit-making companies subject to public sector audit). *s. 475*

However, to take advantage of audit exemption, the balance sheet of a small or dormant company must contain a statement by the directors to the effect that:

- the company is exempt from audit under CA 2006 s. 477 (small company) or s. 480 (dormant company);
- the members have not required the company to obtain an audit of its accounts for the year in question in accordance with CA 2006 s. 476; and
- the directors acknowledge their responsibilities for complying with the requirements of CA 2006 with respect to accounting records and the preparation of accounts. *s. 475(2)–(3)*

The directors' statement required by CA 2006 s. 475 must appear on the balance sheet above the signature required by CA 2006 s. 414.

Where the directors of a company subject to the small companies regime deliver to the registrar IAS accounts, or Companies Act accounts that are not abbreviated accounts, and do not deliver a copy of the company's profit and loss account or a copy of the directors' report, the copy of the balance sheet delivered to the registrar must contain in a prominent position a statement that the company's annual accounts and reports have been delivered in accordance with the provisions applicable to companies subject to the small companies regime. *s. 444(5)*

Examples of a form of directors' statement covering the above requirements are illustrated in **Example 11.1**. *s. 475*

Chapter 11 Determining small company audit exemption

> **Example 11.1 Small company audit exemption directors' statements: balance sheet**
>
> For the financial year ended [30 April 2009], the company was entitled to exemption from audit [*Note 1*] under [s. 477 (*small company exemption*) or s. 480 (*dormant company exemption*)] [*as the case may be*] Companies Act 2006; and no notice has been deposited under s. 476(1) [*member or members requesting an audit*]. The directors acknowledge their responsibilities for complying with the requirements of the Companies Act 2006 with respect to accounting records and the preparation of accounts.
>
> The [company's annual accounts and report] [abbreviated accounts] have been prepared in [*Note 2*] accordance with the special provisions relating to companies subject to the small companies regime [or to medium-sized companies] within Part 15 of Companies Act 2006.
>
> *Note: [Words in italics are explanatory only]*
> The above statements are applicable as follows:
>
> (1) applicable, where audit exemption applies, in
>   (a) small company (SI 2008 No. 409) balance sheets (individual and group);
>   (b) Sch 1 (SI 2008 No. 409) balance sheets;
>   (c) abbreviated balance sheets.
> (2) applicable where the company's annual accounts and reports have been delivered in accordance with the provisions applicable to companies subject to the small companies regime and where small company accounts (on the basis of Sch 4 (SI 2008 No. 409)) are adopted, for both audited or audit-exempt accounts; also applicable where abbreviated accounts are prepared, for both audited or audit-exempt accounts.

The responsibilities to keep adequate accounting records (under s. 386) and the requirements determining the contents of individual company accounts (under s. 394) are explained more fully in **Chapter 3** at **3.10** and **3.2** respectively. The obligation for directors of a company not to approve accounts unless they are satisfied that they give a true and fair view (of the company's assets, liabilities, financial position and profit or loss) is explained in **Chapter 3** at **3.3**.

Part III Guidelines and definitions

Chapter 12 Guidelines and definitions

This chapter gives guidelines on statutory definitions, interpretation and analysis. Comment is not necessarily comprehensive but aims to cover those headings or terms that have tended to present difficulty in practice.

Definitions are provided by accounting standards, including the FRSSE, as well as the legislation. Although the Companies Acts over the years have provided a measure of standardisation for company accounts (for example, in the form of prescriptive formats and codification of accounting rules and principles), legislation often only provides limited guidance in terms of definition or interpretation.

Most of the problems that arise in practice concern interpretation of statutory intent. Over the years, accounting standards have increasingly provided a measure of guidance and interpretation. Nevertheless, difficulties often concern topics such as: presentation, analysis of expenses, categorisation or composition of statutory headings, or simply accounts presentation.

Where there are no definitions or rules laid down by the Companies Act or provided by accounting standards (including IAS), it is necessary to:

- refer to definitions in accounting standards (FRSSE, FRSs and SSAPs);
- determine a reasonable interpretation of the requirement;
- ensure the proposed interpretation is sensible and appropriate to the business, and
- adopt the interpretation consistently from year to year.

12.1 Accounts

Definitions of statutory terms concerning a company's accounts, prepared to show a 'true and fair view', are set out below.

12.1.1 Annual report

The annual 'directors' report' of a company. *s. 415*

The directors of a company must prepare a directors' report for each financial year of the company. For a financial year in which the company is a parent company (and the directors of the company prepare group accounts), the directors' report must be a consolidated report (a 'group directors' report') relating to the undertakings included in the consolidation.

12.1.2 Annual accounts *s. 471*

Individual accounts – the accounts of a company prepared by the directors, for each financial year: *s. 394*

- comprising a balance sheet (as at the last day of the year), a profit and loss account, and notes to the accounts; *s. 396*
- showing a 'true and fair view'; and *s. 393*

Chapter 12 Guidelines and definitions

s. 396
- complying with the provisions of CA 2006 and SI 2008 No. 409 Sch 1 (small companies) (as to form, content and additional note information).

s. 395
Individual accounts must be prepared in accordance with the appropriate framework and accordingly may be prepared:

- in accordance with CA 2006 s. 396 ('Companies Act individual accounts'), or
- in accordance with international accounting standards ('IAS individual accounts').

ss. 398–399
Group accounts – the accounts prepared, in addition to 'individual accounts', by the directors of a parent company:

- comprising consolidated accounts (consolidated balance sheet and consolidated profit and loss account of the parent and its 'subsidiary undertakings');
- showing a 'true and fair view' of the consolidated undertakings as a whole (so far as concerns members of the parent company), and
- complying with the provisions of SI 2008 No. 409 Sch 6 (Small companies) (as to form, content and additional note information).

Group accounts must (with exceptions) be prepared either:

- in accordance with SI 2008 No. 409 Sch 6 (Small companies) or SI 2008 No. 410 Sch 6 (Large and medium-sized companies) ('Companies Act group accounts'), or
- in accordance with international accounting standards or if required by Article 4 of the IAS Regulation ('IAS group accounts').

Group accounts exemptions – the following exemptions from preparing group accounts are available:

- eligible small groups (CA 2006 s. 384) – see **Chapter 9**;
- parent companies included in accounts of larger EEA group (CA 2006 s. 400);
- parent companies included in accounts of larger non-EEA group (CA 2006 s. 401); and
- all subsidiary undertakings excluded from consolidation (CA 2006 s. 402).

Entitlement to exemptions in all cases is determined upon conditions – see **Chapter 9**.

IAS accounts – accounts ('IAS individual accounts' or 'IAS group accounts') prepared in accordance with international accounting standards adopted by the EU (EC Regulation No. 1606/2002).

s. 471
Annual accounts of small companies – the individual or group accounts of small companies, as defined, prepared in accordance with the special provisions for small companies set out in CA 2006 and SI 2008 No. 409 Schedules 1 and 6.

A company's 'annual accounts', in relation to a financial year, means the company's individual accounts for that year (CA 2006 s. 394) and any group accounts prepared by the company for that year (CA 2006 ss. 398–399). CA 2006 s. 408 provides an option to omit individual profit and loss account from annual accounts where information given in group accounts.

In the case of an unquoted company, its 'annual accounts and reports' for a financial year are:

- its annual accounts,
- the directors' report; and
- the auditor's report on those accounts and the directors' report (unless the company is exempt from audit).

s. 408
Individual profit and loss account of parent company – the profit and loss account of a parent company:

Accounts

- prepared in addition to, but omitted from, 'group accounts', and
- omitting the supplemental information required by CA 2006 s. 411 (information about employee numbers and costs).

The fact of omission and the amount of the parent company's profit or loss for the year must be disclosed, and the individual profit and loss account of the parent company must be approved by the board of directors (in accordance with CA 2006 s. 414(1)).

Notes to the accounts – notes forming part of the annual accounts (or annexed thereto), giving information required by any provision of CA 2006 or international accounting standards. *s. 472*

Income and expenditure account – the equivalent of a profit and loss account in the case of the undertaking not trading for profit. *s. 474(2)*

12.1.3 Statutory accounts

The accounts that must be prepared for shareholders and/or filed with the Registrar of Companies. These will be either:

- annual accounts, together with the directors' repoort and also (if required) auditors' report, or
- abbreviated accounts, prepared in accordance with s. 444(3) or 445(3) CA 2006, together with (if appropriate) special auditors' report, and directors' statement.

s. 444

12.1.4 Abbreviated accounts

The accounts prepared in accordance with special provisions for small (or medium-sized) companies, as the case may be – see **Chapter 8**.

The copies of accounts and reports delivered to the registrar must be copies of the company's annual accounts and reports, except that where a small company prepares Companies Act accounts the directors may deliver to the registrar 'abbreviated accounts', these being a copy of a balance sheet drawn up in accordance with regulations made by the Secretary of State; items as may be specified by the regulations may also be omitted from the copy profit and loss account delivered to the registrar. The relevant regulations are SI 2008 No. 409 for small companies. *s. 444(3)*

Where a medium-sized company prepares Companies Act accounts, the directors may deliver to the registrar 'abbreviated accounts', these being a copy of the company's annual accounts for the financial year but where the profit and loss account includes items combined in accordance with regulations made by the Secretary of State, and where items as authorised by the regulations are omitted. The relevant regulations are SI 2008 No. 410 for medium-sized companies. *s. 445(3)*

12.1.5 Company accounts – charities

The accounts of a charity that is a company must be either:

- 'Companies Act individual accounts', or *s. 394*
- 'Companies Act group accounts'. *s. 398*

An incorporated charity is not able to prepare accounts in accordance with international accounting standards.

Chapter 12 Guidelines and definitions

12.2 Profit and loss account

The headings that tend to pose most difficulty as far as the allocation of costs and overheads are concerned are the Formats 1 and 3 headings of 'Cost of sales', 'Distribution costs' and 'Administrative expenses'. In practice, it has been found that expenses not conveniently or accurately falling under one of these headings have been attributed to additional, more appropriate, headings. A service or retail organisation, for example, may consider most of its overhead expenditure to be of a general nature rather than specifically 'distribution' or 'administrative'. Where the nature of the business is such that a more informative (and, perhaps, more detailed) analysis is considered appropriate, this approach should be adopted.

12.2.1 Formats 1 and 3

Costs and overheads may be attributed to the headings 'Cost of sales', 'Distribution costs' and 'Administrative expenses' on the lines set out below. There is no statutory interpretation of these items.

12.2.2 Cost of sales

- Opening less closing value of stocks and work-in-progress including stock provisions.
- Direct purchases and raw materials.
- Direct (manufacturing) costs.
- Cash discounts received.
- Plant and factory depreciation – depreciation must be allocated to this heading.
- Plant hire.
- Other external charges relating to production.
- Payroll costs of direct labour and subcontract work.
- Direct production overheads.
- Indirect production overheads (to the extent not related specifically to 'distribution' or 'administrative' functions).
- Property costs of factory buildings, eg, rent and rates, repairs, insurance, etc.

12.2.3 Distribution costs (often amended to 'Selling and distribution costs')

- Payroll costs of the sales, marketing and distribution functions.
- Advertising, exhibitions, trade shows, etc.
- UITF 29 — Website costs of promotion or advertising products and services
- Travel and entertaining.
- Transport and delivery costs, including rent and rates, repairs, insurance, etc.
- Warehouse costs for distribution of finished goods.
- Costs of maintaining sales outlets.
- Vehicle or other depreciation – depreciation must be allocated to this heading.
- Cash discounts on sales.
- Agents' commission payable.

12.2.4 Administrative expenses

- General management costs, including central functions, eg, chief executive, accounting (to the extent not allocated elsewhere).
- Payroll costs of general administration.
- Property costs of administrative (as opposed to production) buildings, eg, rent and rates, repairs, insurance, etc. and including depreciation – depreciation must be allocated to this heading.

Profit and loss account

- Bad debts.
- Legal and professional fees, audit and accountancy.
- Bank charges (but *not* bank 'interest payable').
- General administration costs, postage, stationery, etc.

12.2.5 Turnover

'The amounts derived from the provision of goods and services falling within the company's ordinary activities, after deduction of trade discounts, value added tax and any other taxes based on the amounts so derived.' *s. 474(1)*

Commission or rental income, for example, where forming part of the principal activity of the company, would be included in turnover. The heading 'Turnover' could in such cases be amended to a more appropriate title (eg, 'Commission income' or 'Income from investment properties') in view of the 'special nature of the company's business'. *Sch 1.4(3)*

Turnover (or 'sales') is defined by FRS 5 as the revenue resulting from exchange transactions under which a seller supplies to customers the goods and services that it is in business to provide, as part of its 'operating activities'. Sales of fixed assets are not normally revenue transactions giving rise to 'turnover'. *FRS 5*

Application Note G to FRS 5 and UITF 40 provide guidance on the principles of revenue recognition and the treatment of turnover (see **12.9** below).

For the purposes of analysis of turnover, if in the opinion of the directors the company's different classes of business or different geographical markets do not differ substantially from each other, they may be treated as one class or market.

Where such analysis would be seriously prejudicial to the interests of the company, the information need not be disclosed provided the fact of such non-disclosure is stated.

12.2.6 Other operating income

'Other operating income' will include all other income not arising from turnover or the company's principal activities, except income dealt with elsewhere in the formats (eg, dividends or interest, etc. receivable). It might include:

- Commissions.
- Rental income. } Where not main part of principal activities
- Profit on disposal of fixed assets.   Where material (otherwise reduce depreciation charge)
- Foreign currency trading gains.

12.2.7 Own work capitalised (Formats 2 and 4)

(A credit to profit and loss account.)

The gross amount of items capitalised in the construction of a company's own tangible fixed assets, including direct labour, materials and overheads.

12.2.8 Other external charges (Formats 2 and 4)

- Other production-related costs.
- Other costs related directly to generating turnover.
- Subcontractors' costs and costs of self-employed consultants.

12.2.9 Other operating charges (Formats 2 and 4)

- Other overhead expenses, including audit and professional fees.
- Other charges relating to ordinary activities.
- Foreign currency trading losses.
- Cash discounts allowed.

In practice, the two headings 'Other external charges' and 'Other operating charges' have often been interpreted as alternatives; however defined, they should be used consistently.

12.2.10 Staff costs

CA 2006 s. 411 ('Information about employee numbers and costs') applies to companies other than those subject to the small companies regime.

'Staff costs' are wages and salaries, social security costs and other pension costs paid or payable to, or incurred by, the company on behalf of, persons employed under contracts of service, ie, employees of the company (including directors who are employees). This heading will not include subcontractors' costs or consultants, etc.

Social security costs: company (employers') contributions to any compulsory state, social security, National Insurance, or pension scheme, fund or arrangement.

Other pension costs: all other costs incurred by a company towards employee pensions (for example, company pension scheme).

The disclosure of the average number of employees within categories is to be determined by the directors 'having regard to the manner in which the company's activities are organised'. The number of employees included in this disclosure should be correlated with the amount disclosed for 'staff costs'.

12.2.11 Income from shares in group undertakings

- Dividends received and receivable:
    (a) parent company – from subsidiary undertakings;
    (b) fellow subsidiary – from fellow group undertakings, and
    (c) consolidated P & L account – from non-consolidated subsidiaries.
- Group's shares of earnings of non-consolidated (equity accounted) subsidiaries.

12.2.12 Income from participating interests

Individual company – income, (eg dividends received and receivable) from shares in associated companies (FRS 9), share of profits from partnerships, unincorporated associations.

Consolidated P & L account – group share of pre-tax profit (or loss) of associated companies.

12.2.13 Auditors' remuneration

s. 494 Audit fee and related expenses charged in the accounts, including estimated money value of any benefits in kind should be disclosed.

Remuneration paid to auditors for non-audit work must also be disclosed by companies other than small companies – see SI 2008 No. 489 below.

Profit and loss account

SI 2008 No. 489 reg 4 (*Companies (Disclosure of Auditor Remuneration and Liability Limitation Agreements) Regulations 2008*) sets out the disclosure requirements concerning the remuneration of auditors of small and medium-sized companies.

A small or medium-sized company must disclose in a note to the annual accounts the amount of any remuneration receivable by the company's auditor for the auditing of those accounts. Where the remuneration includes benefits in kind, the nature and estimated money-value of those benefits must also be disclosed in a note.

SI 2008 No. 489 reg 4(1–2)

Separate disclosure is required for separate firms of auditors, for example where there is a change of auditors during the year.

SI 2008 No. 489 reg 4(4–3)

The total remuneration receivable by the auditor of a medium-sized company may also be required to disclose remuneration in respect of audit, other assurance services, tax advisory services and other services.

CA s. 1124
SI 2008 No. 489 reg 4(4–3)

12.2.14 Interest payable and similar charges

Bank loan and overdraft interest, interest on other loans, interest on finance leases, hire-purchase interest, commitment fees, factoring charges, group interest (less interest capitalised).

Dividends payable in respect certain shares (for example, preference shares) treated as financial liabilities under FRS 25 (see **12.4** below).

Foreign currency losses arising from financing. (Gains of a similar nature may be included under 'Other interest receivable and similar income'.)

The following definitions (12.2.15–12.2.23) are based on the definitions contained in FRS 3 *Reporting financial performance.*

12.2.15 Ordinary activities

Any activities which are undertaken by a reporting entity as part of its business and such related activities in which the reporting entity engages in furtherance of, incidental to, or arising from, these activities.

Ordinary activities include the effects on the reporting entity of any event in the various environments in which it operates, including the political, regulatory, economic and geographical environments.

Ordinary activities include the effect of any event irrespective of frequency or unusual nature.

12.2.16 Continuing operations

Operations other than 'discontinued operations'.

12.2.17 Acquisitions

Operations of the reporting entity that are acquired in the period.

Chapter 12 Guidelines and definitions

12.2.18 Discontinued operations

Operations of the reporting entity that are sold or terminated and that satisfy *all* of the following conditions:

- the sale or termination is completed either in the period or before the earlier of three months after the commencement of the subsequent period and the date on which the financial statements are approved;
- if a termination, the former activities have ceased permanently;
- the sale or termination has a material effect on the nature and focus of the reporting entity's operations and represents a material reduction in its operating facilities resulting either from its withdrawal from a particular market (whether class of business or geographical) or from a material reduction in turnover in the reporting entity's continuing markets, and
- the assets, liabilities, results of operations and activities are clearly distinguishable, physically, operationally and for financial reporting purposes.

12.2.19 Exceptional items

Material items which derive from events or transactions that fall within the ordinary activities of the reporting entity and which individually or, if a similar type, in aggregate, need to be disclosed by virtue of their size or incidence if the financial statements are to give a true and fair view.

Exceptional items should not be aggregated on the face of the profit and loss account but should each be included within its natural statutory format heading or relevant FRS 3 heading.

Exceptional items should be attributed to continuing or discontinued operations and should be disclosed with adequate description of the nature of the item.

The following exceptional items should be disclosed separately on the face of the profit and loss account:

- profits and losses on the sale or termination of an operation;
- costs of a fundamental reorganisation or restructuring having a material effect on the nature and focus of the reporting entity's operations, and
- profits and losses on the disposal of fixed assets.

These items should be shown after operating profit and before interest, and included under the appropriate heading of continuing or discontinued operations.

12.2.20 Extraordinary items

Material items possessing a high degree of abnormality which arise from events or transactions that fall outside the ordinary activities of the reporting entity and which are not expected to recur. They do not include exceptional items nor do they include prior period items merely because they relate to a prior period.

Extraordinary items are extremely rare. Although it remains a statutory format heading (see **Table 6.5** and **6.6**), the extraordinary item has effectively been abolished by accounting standards.

12.2.21 Prior period adjustments

Material adjustments applicable to prior periods arising from changes in accounting policies or from the correction of fundamental errors. They do not include normal adjustments or corrections of accounting estimates made in prior periods. Prior period adjustments should be accounted for by restating comparative figures and adjusting the opening balance of reserves.

12.2.22 Total recognised gains and losses

The total of all gains and losses of the reporting entity that are recognised in a period and are attributable to shareholders.

12.2.23 Profit or loss on disposal

The profit or loss on the disposal of an asset should be accounted for in the profit and loss account of the period in which the disposal occurs as the difference between the net sale proceeds and the net carrying amount, whether carried at historical cost (less any provisions made) or at a valuation. The profit or loss on disposal of a previously acquired business should include the attributable amount of purchased goodwill where it has previously been eliminated against reserves as a matter of accounting policy and has not previously been charged in the profit and loss account.

12.3 Balance sheet

Commentary on selected balance sheet headings, including guidelines on the analysis of debtors and creditors, is set out below.

12.3.1 Fixed assets

'Assets of a company which are intended for use on a continuing basis in the company's activities.' Assets not intended for such use are 'current assets'.

'Fixed assets' include, on this definition, investments and intangibles in addition to tangible fixed assets.

Assets awaiting disposal: a fixed asset not in use at the balance sheet date and not intended to be used before disposal should be reclassified as a 'current asset' (this does not apply to assets which it is intended to replace in the normal course of business).

'Development costs' may be capitalised in 'special [undefined] circumstances'. Otherwise, 'costs of research' must not be treated as an asset. SSAP 13 provides the definition of these items lacking in CA 2006. *Sch 1.3(2)* *Sch 1.21*

'Preliminary expenses' and 'expenses of, and commission on, any issue of shares or debentures' may not be treated as assets. *Sch 1.3(2)*

12.3.2 Goodwill

'Amounts representing goodwill shall only be included to the extent that goodwill was acquired for valuable consideration' (SI 2008 No. 409 Sch 1 – balance sheet format Note 3). Any goodwill valued and created by the company itself, therefore, cannot be capitalised and included in a company's balance sheet.

Acquired goodwill should be systematically depreciated over a period (chosen by the directors)

Chapter 12 Guidelines and definitions

Sch 1.22

not exceeding the useful economic life of the goodwill. The period of write-off and the reasons for choosing that period must be disclosed.

The above considerations do not apply to goodwill arising on consolidation.

12.3.3 Tangible assets: headings

The SI 2008 No.409 Schedule 1 balance sheet format heading B II 2 for small companies is 'plant and machinery etc.'

Otherwise in practice, there is some latitude in the formats generally, with headings: for example, 'equipment' would not generally be included in 'plant and machinery' but may be aggregated with 'motor vehicles'. Strict interpretation would not allow, for example, 'plant and machinery' to be changed to 'plant and equipment', particularly in a company where the main activity is manufacturing. However, in a situation where 'equipment' is immaterial, this might acceptably be aggregated with plant and machinery under a heading 'plant, machinery and equipment'. Additional headings may be given but doing so increases the amount of disclosure required.

'Payments on account' and 'Assets in course of construction' have to be shown separately from other items but individually may be aggregated.

Grants relating to fixed assets should be accounted for by the deferred credit method, in which case the credit should be included under 'accruals and deferred income' and should *not* be deducted from fixed assets. Reducing the 'cost' of the asset by the grant would be considered to represent an 'offset', which is not permitted under CA 2006.

12.3.4 Cash at bank and in hand; bank loans and overdrafts

The heading 'Cash at bank and in hand' comprises the amounts as recorded in the company's accounting records, not those as shown necessarily in the bank statements.

Bank balances and bank overdrafts, etc. should not be offset to show a net balance *unless* there is a legal right of set-off.

Cash is defined in FRS 1 (revised 1996) *Cash flow statements* as 'cash in hand and deposits repayable on demand with any qualifying financial institution, less overdrafts from any qualifying financial institution repayable on demand. Deposits are repayable on demand if they can be withdrawn at any time without notice and without penalty or if a maturity or period of notice of not more than 24 hours or one working day has been agreed. Cash includes cash in hand and deposits denominated in foreign currencies.'

Notwithstanding the FRS 1 definition, 'cash at bank' may include bank and building society deposits on (say) up to seven days call.

12.3.5 Current assets

'Assets not intended for use on a continuing basis in the company's activities.'

12.3.6 Participating interest

The definitions of 'participating interest' and 'associated undertaking' are set out in **12.6**.

A 'participating interest' basically is an interest in an undertaking (other than one which is a group undertaking) which is held on a long-term basis (generally, an equity interest in excess of

20 per cent) for the purpose of securing a contribution to activities by the exercise of control or influence arising from that interest.

FRS 2

The above definition of a 'participating interest' is consistent with that of an 'associate' in FRS 9 *Associates and joint ventures*:

'*Associate*
An entity (other than a subsidiary) in which another entity (the investor) has a participating interest and over whose operating and financial policies the investor exercises a significant influence.'

'*Participating Interest*
An interest held in the shares of another entity on a long-term basis for the purpose of securing a contribution to the investor's activities by the exercise of control or influence arising from or related to that interest. The investor's interest must, therefore, be a beneficial one and the benefits expected to arise must be linked to the exercise of its significant influence over the investee's operating and financial policies. An interest in the shares of another entity includes an interest convertible into an interest in shares or an option to acquire shares.'

'*Exercise of significant influence*
The investor is actively involved and is influential in the direction of its investee through its participation in policy decisions covering aspects of policy relevant to the investor, including decisions on strategic issues such as:

- the expansion or contraction of the business, participation in other entities or changes in products, markets and activities of its investee, and
- determining the balance between dividend and reinvestment.'

The statutory definitions of 'participating interest' and 'associated undertaking' are set out in **12.6**.

12.3.7 Stocks

The basis of arriving at the value of 'stocks' must be a reasonable approximation to actual cost (appropriate, in the opinion of the directors, to the circumstances of the company), eg FIFO (first in, first out), weighted average or other similar method.

Sch 1.28

12.3.8 Provisions for liabilities

A 'provision' is a liability of uncertain timing or amount.

FRS 12

'Any amount retained as reasonably necessary for the purpose of providing for any liability the nature of which is clearly defined and which is either likely to be incurred, or certain to be incurred but uncertain as to amount or as to the date on which it will arise.'

12.3.9 Taxation

The two balance sheet format headings for 'Other creditors' including taxation and social security (Creditors) and Taxation, including deferred taxation (within 'Provision for liabilities') may be contrasted as follows.

'Other creditors' including taxation and social security must be analysed between:

- taxation and social security – including corporation tax, VAT, ACT payable on proposed dividends, PAYE and social security payable, and excise duties; and

Chapter 12 Guidelines and definitions

- other creditors – including any other sundry creditors (but not proposed dividends, the recognition of which are now prohibited [FRS 21]).

'Provision for liabilities' will include any provision for deferred taxation (separately disclosed).

12.3.10 Analysis of debtors and creditors

The guidelines below indicate how certain of the 'debtors' and 'creditors' headings are made up. *Materiality* should be considered in any attempt to distinguish between the various categories, as excessive accuracy or refinement may not be necessary. Frequently, for example, where the headings 'Prepayments and accrued income' or 'Accruals and deferred income' are immaterial, they are included within other categories such as 'trade debtors' or 'other debtors' and 'trade creditors' or 'other creditors including taxation and social security', respectively.

Amounts owing by group or any associated undertakings should be separately identified and disclosed.

Amounts falling due after more than one year should be separately analysed for each of the headings.

Debtors

Trade debtors
Will generally comprise:

- sales ledger balances (amounts invoiced to customers);
- purchase ledger debit balances;
- sales invoices/credit notes accrued, less
- provision for bad debts or credits for returns, cash discounts, etc.

Prepayments
Prepaid items and accrued income.

Deferred tax asset (ACT recoverable) (unless separately disclosed).

Other debtors
Debtors other than the above and debtors not otherwise separately disclosed; for example:

- debtors arising from non-trading activities;
- loans and advances, and
- proceeds due from sale of fixed assets.

Creditors

Trade creditors

FRS 12 Trade creditors are liabilities to pay for goods or services that have been received or supplied and that have been invoiced or formally agreed with the supplier. They will generally comprise:

- bought ledger (or equivalent) balances;
- sales ledger credit balances, and
- trade invoices (for purchases) accrued.

Generally, 'trade creditor' items will meet both of the following requirements:

- *expenditure has been incurred as part of the normal business activities of the company, (eg purchase of goods, overhead expenditure, capital expenditure, etc.), and*

- *an invoice has been received dated as or before the year end; late invoices (ie, received after year end but dated before it) should therefore be included in this heading.*

Taxation and social security
Includes VAT, NIC, PAYE and excise duties.

Current corporation tax and ACT payable on dividends are normally separately identified under a heading such as 'Corporation tax'.

Accruals
Accruals are liabilities to pay for goods or services that have been received or supplied but that have not been paid, invoiced or formally agreed with the supplier. Examples include: FRS 12

- accrued items of overhead expenditure;
- estimated accruals where invoice not received;
- capital expenditure accruals;
- bonuses, accrued remuneration, and
- accrued holiday pay.

Generally, 'accruals' items will meet both of the following requirements:

- *expenditure has been incurred before year end but the related invoice is not dated until after year end (or due payment date is after year end if no invoice will be received) (compare 'trade creditors'), and*
- *the amount and payment date of the item can be determined with reasonable certainty.*

Other creditors
Creditors, other than above:

- short-term loans, and
- loans from directors (where not shown elsewhere).

Dividends
Normally shown as separate heading.

12.4 Financial instruments

FRS 4 *Capital instruments* dealt with the classification, presentation and disclosure of capital instruments. For accounting periods beginning on or after 1 January 2005, FRS 4 has generally been superseded by FRS 25 (IAS 32) *Financial Instruments: Disclosure and Presentation* (other than entities adopting the FRSSE).

Many of the situations envisaged by FRS 25 (and FRS 4) may not be encountered by small companies and are not covered in the FRSSE.

Basically, every financial instrument or constituent part under FRS25 is recognised as a 'financial asset', a 'financial liability' or an 'equity instrument'. The definitions set out below (in **12.4.1–12.4.5**) are based on those contained in FRS 25 or FRSSE (effective April 2008).

As a result of FRS 25, certain shares (such as Preference shares) that were previously accounted for as 'share capital' will in future be classified as 'financial liabilities'. A preference share will be a financial liability where it provides for redemption for a fixed (or determinable) amount, being either (a) mandatory redemption, or (b) with the right to redemption at or after a particular date. While no longer presented as 'share capital', the legal form, status and terms of such preference shares would remain unaffected.

Chapter 12 Guidelines and definitions

12.4.1 Financial instrument

A financial instrument is any contract that gives rise to a financial asset of one entity and a financial liability or equity instrument of another entity.

12.4.2 Financial asset

A financial asset is any asset that is:

- *cash;*
- *an equity instrument of another entity;*
- *a contractual right to receive cash or another financial asset from another entity* or to exchange financial assets or financial liabilities with another entity under conditions that are potentially favourable to the entity; or
- *a contract that will or may be settled in the entity's own equity instruments* and is either (a) a *non-derivative* for which the entity is or may obliged to receive a variable number of the entity's own equity instruments; or (b) *a derivative* that will or may be settled other than by the exchange of a fixed amount of cash or another financial asset for a fixed number of the entity's own equity instruments. [For this purpose the entity's own equity instruments do not include instruments that are themselves contracts for the future receipt or delivery of the entity's own equity instruments].

12.4.3 Financial liability

A financial liability is any liability that is:

- *a contractual obligation to deliver cash or another financial asset to another entity* or to exchange financial assets or financial liabilities with another entity under conditions that are potentially unfavourable to the entity; or
- *a contract that will or may be settled in the entity's own equity instruments* and is either (a) a *non-derivative* for which the entity is or may obliged to receive a variable number of the entity's own equity instruments; or (b) *a derivative* that will or may be settled other than by the exchange of a fixed amount of cash or another financial asset for a fixed number of the entity's own equity instruments. [For this purpose the entity's own equity instruments do not include instruments that are themselves contracts for the future receipt or delivery of the entity's own equity instruments].

12.4.4 Equity instrument

An equity instrument is any contract that evidences a residual interest in the assets of an entity after deducting all of its liabilities.

12.4.5 Equity instrument granted

The right (conditional or unconditional) to an equity instrument of the entity conferred by the entity on another party, under a share-based payment arrangement.

12.4.6 Fair value

Fair value is the amount for which an asset could be exchanged, or a liability settled, between knowledgeable, willing parties in an arm's length transaction.

12.4.7 Derivative or Derivative Financial Instrument

A 'derivative financial instrument' is a financial instrument that derives its price or rate from some underlying item (for example equities, bonds, commodities, interest rates, exchange rates, and stock market or other indices). Derivative financial instruments include futures, options, forward contracts, interest rate and currency swaps, interest rate caps, collars and floors, forward interest rate agreements, commitments to purchase shares or bonds, note issuance facilities and letters of credit.

12.5 Alternative bases of accounting

Companies Act 2006 permits two bases of accounting – historical cost accounting rules and alternative accounting rules. A company may choose whichever basis it wishes to follow and may use different bases within the same set of accounts; it is common practice, for example, to revalue properties or investments.

Companies may, therefore, prepare accounts:

- on the pure historical cost convention;
- on the historical cost convention modified to include certain assets at valuation; or
- on the current cost convention.

Alternative methods of valuation permitted under the 'alternative accounting rules' are illustrated in **Table 12.1**.

Table 12.1 Alternative methods of valuation

Fixed assets   (Sch 1.17–22)

Primary method of valuation	Alternative method of valuation ('Alternative accounting rules')
Historical cost of purchase or production, less any provision for depreciation or diminution in value	
Intangible fixed assets, other than goodwill	Current cost (Sch 1.32(1))
Tangible fixed assets	Market value (as at the date of their last valuation) *or* Current cost (Sch 1.32(2))
Investments (fixed assets)	Market value (as at the date of their last valuation) *or* Directors' valuation (or any basis which the directors consider to be appropriate in the circumstances; the method of valuation and the reasons for adopting it must be disclosed) (Sch 1.32(3))

Current assets   (Sch 1.23–24)

Primary method of valuation	Alternative method of valuation ('Alternative accounting rules')
Cost (purchase price or production cost – other than distribution costs) or net realisable value, if lower	
Investments (current assets)	Current cost (Sch 1.32(4))
Stocks	Current cost (Sch 1.32(5))

Chapter 12 Guidelines and definitions

12.5.1 Purchase price

Sch 1.27   Includes any consideration, whether in cash or otherwise, and also any incidental expenses.

12.5.2 Production cost

Sch 1.27   The price of raw materials and consumables together with costs directly attributable to the production of the asset; a reasonable proportion of indirect costs (relating to the period of production); and interest on capital borrowed to finance the production of the asset (to the extent that it is accrued during the period of production).

12.5.3 Revaluation reserve

Sch 1.35   The difference between the amount of any item determined according to one of the alternative accounting rules and the amount at which it would be determined on the historical cost accounting rules should be debited or credited, as applicable, to a 'revaluation reserve'.

12.6 Groups – parent and subsidiary undertakings

The principal definitions for accounting purposes for a parent company and its subsidiaries, which cover 'undertakings' and not just 'bodies corporate', are set out below.

s. 474   *A group comprises a parent undertaking and its subsidiary undertakings.*

A company is a 'subsidiary' of another company, its 'holding company', if that other company:

- holds a majority of the voting rights in it;
- is a member of it and has the right to appoint or remove a majority of its board of directors; or
- is a member of it and controls alone, pursuant to an agreement with other members, a majority of the voting rights in it,

s. 1159(1)   or if it is a 'subsidiary' of a company that is itself a subsidiary of that other company.

A company is a 'wholly-owned subsidiary of another company if:

s. 1159(2)
- it has no members except that other company, and that other's wholly-owned subsidiaries (or persons acting on behalf of that other company or its wholly-owned subsidiaries).

An undertaking is a 'parent undertaking' in relation to another undertaking ('a subsidiary undertaking') if:

- it holds a majority of the voting rights in the undertaking; or
- it is a member of the undertaking and has the right to appoint or remove a majority of its board of directors; or
- it has the right to exercise a dominant influence over the undertaking:
  - by virtue of provisions contained in the undertaking's articles;
  - by virtue of a control contract; or
- it is a member of the undertaking and controls alone, pursuant to an agreement with other shareholders or members, a majority of the voting rights in the undertaking.

s. 1162(2)

An undertaking is treated as a member of another undertaking:

- if any of its subsidiary undertakings is a member of that undertaking, or if any shares in that other undertaking are held by a person acting on behalf of the undertaking or any of its subsidiary undertakings. *s. 1162(3)*

An undertaking is also a parent undertaking in relation to another undertaking (a subsidiary undertaking) if:

- it has the power to exercise, or actually exercises, a dominant influence or control over it, or

it and the subsidiary undertaking are managed on a unified basis.

A participating interest no longer has to exist in order for an undertaking to be a 'subsidiary undertaking'. An undertaking will be a 'parent undertaking' in relation to a 'subsidiary undertaking' if it has the power to exercise, or actually exercises, dominant influence or control over it.

An 'undertaking' means: *s. 1161(1)*

- a body corporate or partnership, or
- an unincorporated association carrying on a trade or business, with or without a view to profit.

'Fellow subsidiary undertakings' are undertakings which are subsidiary undertakings of the same parent undertaking but are not parent undertakings or subsidiary undertakings of each other. *s. 1161(4)*

'Group undertaking' means an undertaking which is: *s. 1161(5)*

- a parent undertaking or subsidiary undertaking of that undertaking, or
- a subsidiary undertaking of any parent undertaking of that undertaking.

A *'participating interest'* basically is an interest in an undertaking (other than one which is a group undertaking) which is held on a long-term basis (generally, an equity interest in excess of 20 per cent) for the purpose of securing a contribution to activities by the exercise of control or influence arising from that interest. *FRS 2*

A holding of 20 per cent or more of the shares of an undertaking is presumed to be a participating interest unless the contrary is shown.

An interest in shares includes:

- an interest which is convertible into an interest in shares, and
- an option to acquire shares or any such interest.

An interest held on behalf of an undertaking shall be treated as held by it.

In the statutory balance sheet and profit and loss formats 'participating interest' does not include an interest in a group undertaking.

An 'associated undertaking' means an undertaking in which an undertaking, included in the consolidation, has a participating interest and over whose operating and financial policy it exercises a significant influence, and which is not:

- a subsidiary undertaking of the parent company, or
- a joint venture.

Where an undertaking holds 20 per cent or more of the voting rights in another undertaking, it is presumed to exercise such 'significant influence' over it unless the contrary is shown. *SI 2008 No. 409 Sch 6.19*

Chapter 12 Guidelines and definitions

A 'joint venture' may be dealt with in group accounts by the method of proportional consolidation. A 'joint venture' is an undertaking, which (not being a body corporate or subsidiary undertaking of the parent company) is managed jointly by two or more undertakings, one of which is included in a consolidation.

SI 2008 No. 409 Sch 6.18

References to 'shares' are references to:

- allotted shares (for an undertaking with a share capital);
- rights to share in the capital of the undertaking (for an undertaking with capital but no share capital); or
- interests:
    (a) conferring any right to share in the profits or liability to contribute to the losses of the undertaking; or
    (b) giving rise to an obligation to contribute to the debts or expenses of the undertaking in the event of a winding-up (undertaking without capital).

s. 1161(2) FRS 2

12.7 Groups – related undertakings disclosure

12.7.1 Disclosures where group accounts not required

The information to be given in notes to a small company's annual accounts in relation to related undertakings, **where group accounts are not required** are provided by Part 1 of Schedule 2 to SI 2008 No. 409 (The Small Companies and Groups (Accounts and Directors' Report) Regulations 2008) 'Information about related undertakings where company not preparing Group accounts (Companies Act or IAS individual accounts)').

Information required to be given in the notes to a small company's annual accounts are as follows.

With certain exceptions, exemption from disclosure may be granted by the Secretary of State in respect of certain foreign undertakings carrying on business outside the UK.

s. 409

Subsidiary undertakings
(a) The name of each subsidiary undertaking.
(b) With respect to each subsidiary undertaking:
    (i) the country in which it is incorporated (if it is incorporated outside UK);
    (ii) the address of its principal place of business (if it is unincorporated).

Holdings in subsidiary undertakings
In relation to shares of each class held by the company in a subsidiary undertaking:

(a) the identity of the class, and
(b) the proportion of the nominal value of the shares of that class represented by those shares.

The shares held by or on behalf of the company itself shall be distinguished from those attributed to the company which are held by or on behalf of a subsidiary undertaking.

Financial information about subsidiary undertakings
With respect to each subsidiary undertaking:

(a) the aggregate amount of its capital and reserves as at the end of its relevant financial year, and
(b) its profit or loss for that year.

This information need not be given if:

Groups – related undertakings disclosure

(a) *the company would be exempt (but for being subject to the small companies regime) by virtue of ss. 400 or 401 CA 2006 from the requirement to prepare group accounts (Parent company included in accounts of larger group);*
(b) *the company's investment in the subsidiary undertaking is included in the company's accounts by way of the equity method of valuation;*
(c) *the subsidiary undertaking is not required to deliver or publish its balance sheet in the UK or elsewhere; and the company's holding is less than 50 per cent of the nominal value of the shares in the undertaking; or*
(d) *the information is not material.*

If this information is given where a subsidiary undertaking's financial year does not end with that of the company, in relation to each undertaking, the date on which its last financial year ended (last before the end of the company's financial year) must be disclosed.

Shares and debentures of company held by subsidiary undertakings
The number, description and amount of the shares in the company held by, or on behalf of, its subsidiary undertakings. *Does not apply in relation to shares held as personal representative or (in certain circumstances) as trustee.*

Significant holdings in undertakings other than subsidiary undertakings
A holding is significant for this purpose if:

(a) *it amounts to 20 per cent or more of the nominal value of any class of shares in the undertaking, or*
(b) *the amount of the holding (as stated or included in the company's accounts) exceeds one-fifth of the amount (as so stated) of the company's assets.*

The following information must be supplied:

(a) The name of the undertaking and:
　(i) the country in which it is incorporated (if the undertaking is incorporated outside the UK);
　(ii) the address of its principal place of business (if it is unincorporated).
(b) (i) The identity of each class of shares in the undertaking held by the company, and
　(ii) the proportion of the nominal value of the shares of that class represented by those shares.
(c) (i) The aggregate amount of the capital and reserves of the undertaking as at the end of its relevant financial year, and
　(ii) its profit or loss for that year.

Need not be given if:
(a) *the company would be exempt (but for being subject to the small companies regime) by virtue of ss. 400 or 401 CA 2006 from the requirement to prepare group accounts (Parent company included in accounts of larger group);*
(b) *the company's investment in the subsidiary undertaking is included in the company's accounts by way of the equity method of valuation;*
(c) *the subsidiary undertaking is not required to deliver or publish its balance sheet in the UK or elsewhere; and the company's holding is less than 50 per cent of the nominal value of the shares in the undertaking; or*
(d) *the information is not material.*

Membership of certain undertakings
Information to be given, if material, where the company is subject to the Partnerships and Unlimited Companies (Accounts) Regulations 1993 (SI 1993 No. 1820).

Unless the notes to the company's accounts disclose that advantage has been taken of exemption conferred by Regulation 7 of SI 1993 No. 1820, where the company is a member of a qualifying partnership (company) it must disclose:

- its name and legal form, and
- the address of its registered or head office.

In addition, the accounts of the qualifying partnership must state:

- that its accounts have been or will be appended to the company's accounts delivered to the Registrar of Companies, and
- the name of the body corporate in whose group accounts the partnership has been or will be consolidated.

Parent undertaking drawing up accounts for larger group (where the company is a subsidiary undertaking)
The following information shall be given with respect to the parent undertakings of:

(a) *the largest group of undertakings for which group accounts are drawn up and of which the company is a member, and*
(b) *the smallest such group of undertakings.*

(a) The name of the parent undertaking and:

(b) (i) the country in which it is incorporated (if the undertaking is incorporated outside the UK);
(ii) the address of its principal place of business (if it is unincorporated);
(c) the addresses from which copies of group accounts can be obtained if available to the public.

Identification of ultimate parent company (where the company is a subsidiary undertaking)

(a) The name of the company (if any) (including any body corporate) regarded by the directors as being the company's ultimate parent company.
(b) The country in which it is incorporated (if incorporated outside the UK).

Schedule 2 to SI 2008 No. 409 (The Small Companies and Groups (Accounts and Directors' Report) Regulations 2008) is set out in full in **Appendix E**.

12.7.2 Disclosures where group accounts required

In many respects the disclosure requirements are identical to those identified above in **12.7.1** and are not repeated here. The detailed requirements are provided by Part 2 of Schedule 6 to SI 2008 No. 409 (The Small Companies and Groups (Accounts and Directors' Report) Regulations 2008) 'Information about related undertakings where company preparing Group accounts (Companies Act or IAS Group accounts)').

In addition to the above disclosure requirements, disclosure is required for:

(a) subsidiary undertakings not included in the consolidation;
(b) joint ventures; and
(c) associated undertakings.

SI 2008 No. 409 Sch 6.17 together with appropriate adjustments for minority interests.

Crown copyright (within 12.7.1 and 12.7.2 above) is reproduced with permission of the Controller of Her Majesty's Stationery Office.

12.8 The substance of transactions

12.8.1 Determining the substance of transactions

FRS 5 *Reporting the substance of transactions* requires that accounts should represent faithfully the commercial effects of the transactions and other events they purport to represent.

The scope of FRS 5 extends to all kinds of transactions, subject only to certain specific exclusions. Where transactions are straightforward and their substance and commercial effect are readily apparent, applying established accounting practices will usually be sufficient to ensure that such transactions are appropriately reported in the accounts. FRS 5 affects mainly those more complex transactions whose substance may not be readily apparent.

Under CA 2006, SI 2008 No. 409 Sch 1.9 specifies that the directors of a company must, in determining how amounts are presented within items in the profit and loss account and balance sheet, have regard to the substance of the reported transaction or arrangement, in accordance with generally accepted accounting principles or practice.

12.8.2 Principle of 'substance over form'

Transactions should be accounted for in accordance with their substance and not merely their legal form, since the latter may not fully indicate the commercial effect of the arrangements entered into. FRS 5 was introduced to address the issue of 'off balance sheet financing' where complex arrangements were developed, the result of which was (invariably deliberately) that the legal form as reported in the accounts was not in accordance with the commercial effect of the arrangement. The most widely recognised effect was the omission of liabilities from the balance sheet.

A reporting entity's accounts should report the substance of the transactions into which it has entered. In determining the substance of a transaction, all its aspects and implications should be identified and greater weight given to those more likely to have a commercial effect in practice. A series of transactions that achieves or is designed to achieve an overall commercial effect should be viewed as a whole.

Some arrangements within groups give as much effective control over another entity as if that entity were a subsidiary. A 'quasi-subsidiary' of a reporting entity is a company, trust, partnership or other vehicle that, although not fulfilling the definition of a subsidiary, is directly or indirectly controlled by the reporting entity and gives rise to benefits for that entity which are in substance no different from those that would arise were the vehicle a subsidiary. Quasi-subsidiaries should therefore be included in statutory group accounts.

Examples of complex transactions are given in the Application Notes included in FRS 5. Those transactions may be summarised as follows.

1. *Consignment stock* – Consignment stock is stock held by one party but legally owned by another, on terms that give the stockholder the right to sell the stock in the normal course of its business or, at its option, to return it unsold to the legal owner.
2. *Sale and repurchase agreements* – Sale and repurchase agreements are arrangements under which assets are sold by one party to another on terms that provide for the seller to repurchase the asset in certain circumstances.
3. *Factoring of debts* – Factoring of debts takes a variety of forms of obtaining finance, sales ledger administration services or protection from bad debts.
4. *Securitised assets* – Securitisation is a means by which providers of finance fund a specific block of assets rather than the general business of a company. Securitised assets have included household mortgages, credit card balances, hire purchase loans and trade debts and such non-monetary assets as property and stocks.

Chapter 12 Guidelines and definitions

5. *Loan transfers* – The transfer of interest-bearing loans to an entity other than a special purpose vehicle.
6. *PFI (Public Finance Initiative) and similar contracts* – under a PFI contract, a service such as the operation of hospital, prison, road or bridge is awarded by a public sector body to a private sector operator.

12.9 Revenue recognition

12.9.1 Basic principles of revenue recognition

Application Note G to FRS 5 provides guidance on the principles of revenue recognition and the treatment of turnover. The Application Note codifies existing practice and sets out a consistent treatment of revenue transactions ('exchange transactions' between seller and customer). The guidance explains how, when and whether to recognise revenue, in a variety of circumstances.

Turnover (or 'sales') is the revenue resulting from exchange transactions under which a seller supplies to customers the goods and services that it is in business to provide, as part of its 'operating activities'. Sales of fixed assets are not normally revenue transactions giving rise to 'turnover'.

In essence, revenue is recognised on the performance of a transaction when a seller:

- fulfils its contractual obligation to a customer through the supply of goods and services, and
- obtains the right to consideration (payment) in exchange for performance of the transaction.

This means that revenue must be accounted for generally at the point of delivery ('fulfilling a contractual obligation') rather than, for example, when an order is taken.

Payments in advance from a customer give rise to a liability (rather than revenue) until such time as the transaction is completed ('performed'), with the seller fulfilling their contractual obligation. In the case of partial performance of an obligation, revenue is recognised to the appropriate extent of such partial performance. Stage payments may, or may not, represent 'partial performance' under a contractual arrangement and will only equate to partial performance where the timing of payments coincide with the extent of partial performance.

Revenue is measured at 'fair value' of the right to consideration (amount receivable), which is normally the price specified in the contractual arrangement net of discounts, value added tax and similar sales taxes. Occasionally, the fair value at the time of the transaction may also reflect the time value of money (for example, an interest free period) or allow for possible debtor default (credit risk), but any such adjustments made subsequently should not be included in revenue but expensed within costs and overheads.

'Fair value' is defined in Application Note G as 'the amount at which goods or services could be exchanged in an arm's length transaction between informed and willing parties, other than in a forced or liquidation sale'.

12.9.2 Revenue recognition: areas of specific guidance

Revenue recognition is generally straightforward. However, for a number of instances where there has been inappropriate or inconsistent accounting treatment Application Note G provides specific guidance. Further, UITF 40 has subsequently endeavoured to clarify the accounting for service contracts (see **12.9.3** below).

Revenue recognition

Areas of specific guidance given in FRS 5 Application Note G, mainly concerning transactions giving rise to turnover, cover:

- long-term contractual performance;
- separation and linking of contractual arrangements;
- bill and hold arrangements;
- sales with rights of return; and
- presentation of turnover as principal or agent.

The requirements for accounting and disclosure of stocks and long-term contracts provided by SSAP 9 are not amended by FRS 5 Application Note G nor by UITF 40 (see **12.9.3** below). Long term contractual performance results in the seller recognising turnover as contract activity progresses, to the extent that the contract can be assessed with reasonable certainty. Recognition is determined by, and in accordance with, the stage of completion of the contractual obligations; proportion of costs incurred should be a determining factor of recognition only where the costs provide evidence of the extent of the seller's performance.

A contract for services should be accounted for as a long- term contract where contract activity falls into different accounting periods and (having regard to the aggregate effect of all such contracts within the accounts) it is concluded that the effect is material.

Separation and linking should reflect the commercial substance of an arrangement. Examples provided by the Application Note include sales of software and related maintenance services, inception (or non-refundable) fees, and vouchers (such as money off or 'points' schemes). The accounting treatment of such arrangements invariably depend upon the contractual detail and whether component parts of the arrangement can be separately and independently identified (for example, the sale of some packaged software and a subsequent support service). A retailer selling on a 'two-for-one' basis, for example, must only account for actual revenue taken (reflecting the discount given) and not the notional value of two items sold. Gift vouchers must only be recorded as revenue when exchanged for goods or services.

In 'bill and hold arrangements' (where goods are supplied and title transferred but physical delivery deferred to a later date), if the seller is determined to have a right to consideration and stock becomes an asset of the customer, then it follows that the seller should recognise turnover together with the related changes in assets or liabilities.

Turnover should exclude the sales value of estimated returns from the total sales value of the goods supplied to customers.

Turnover is generally assumed to be sales on the seller's own account. Where there is no disclosure of acting as 'Agent', there is a rebuttable presumption that the seller is acting as 'Principal'. Turnover should be accordingly reported as follows:

- principal – gross amount received or receivable, and
- agent – commission or such other income (excluding amounts payable to the Principal).

Application Note G 'encourages' a seller acting as agent to disclose (as additional non-statutory information) the gross value of sales throughput, together with a brief explanation of the relationship of turnover as agent to such gross value of sales. Although not statutorily required, such disclosure is therefore established as good practice.

12.9.3 Revenue recognition: contracts for services

UITF 40 *Revenue recognition and service contracts* (http://www.frc.org.uk/asb/uitf/pub0758.html) was issued in March 2005 in order to clarify the accounting for service contracts and in particular service contracts that are not treated as long term contracts under SSAP 9 (see **12.9.2** above).

Revenue on service contracts should be accrued as service activity takes place (to reflect the seller's partial performance of its contractual obligations). Revenue should reflect the accrual of the right to consideration as contract activity progresses by reference to value of the work performed. Distinguishable phases of a single contract may be accounted for as two or more separate transactions, provided the value of each phase can be reliably estimated.

A contract for services should be accounted for as a long-term contract where contract activity falls into different accounting periods and it is concluded that the effect is material, having regard to the aggregate effect of all such contracts on the financial statements.

Contracts for services should not be accounted for as long-term contracts unless they involve the provision of a single service or a number of services that constitute a single project.

Where the substance of a contract is that a right to consideration does not arise until the occurrence of a specified future event or outcome (a 'critical event'), revenue is not recognised until that event occurs. This only applies where:

- the right to consideration is conditional or contingent on the 'critical event': or
- the occurrence of the 'critical event' is outside the control of the seller.

UITF 40 *Revenue recognition and service contracts* applies to all reporting entities, including those adopting the FRSSE (see **10.12** above).

12.10 Dividends

12.10.1 Treatment of dividends

SI 2004 No. 2947 'The Companies Act 1985 (International Accounting Standards and Other Accounting Amendments) Regulations 2004' implemented changes to bring UK accounting into line with EU accounting requirements and best practice, to apply to financial years beginning on or after 1 January 2005.

There is no longer any requirement for companies to show paid and proposed dividends as separate items in the profit and loss account. Companies are now required to state in accounts:

- amounts set aside or withdrawn (or proposed to be set aside or withdrawn) from reserves;
- aggregate of dividends paid in the financial year (other than those for which a liability existed at the immediately preceding balance sheet date);
- aggregate of dividends liable to be paid at the balance sheet date; and
- aggregate of dividends proposed before the date of approval of the accounts and not otherwise disclosed. *(SI 2008 No. 409 Sch 1 para 43)*.

These requirements were subsequently reflected by the ASB within the updated FRSSE 2005 and subsequent versions. The FRSSE (at **FRSSE para 12.6**) requires the following: 'Dividends relating to a financial instrument or a component that is a financial liability shall be recognised as expense in profit or loss. Distributions to holders of an equity instrument shall be debited by the entity directly to equity, net of any related income tax benefit. If an entity declares dividends after the balance sheet date, the dividends shall not be recognised as a liability at the balance sheet date'. The FRSSE says that: 'the notes to the accounts must state' [inter alia] the items bullet-listed above (**FRSSE para 12.7**).

12.10.2 Classification of preference dividends

Classifying capital instruments as either debt or equity under FRS 25 is a difficult issue. The revised 'FRSSE (effective January 2007) (and the subsequent version April 2008) (in Appendix III) has therefore provided some practical illustrative guidance on the features of preference shares to help in their classification for accounting purposes.

The FRSSE appendix explains that in determining whether preference shares are a 'financial liability' or an 'equity instrument', it is necessary to assess the particular rights attached to the shares. For example, preference shares may (a) carry fixed rights to dividends (cumulative or otherwise); (b) have the same voting rights as the ordinary shares; (c) place an obligation or discretion as to redemption on the issuer; and (d) rank above ordinary shares (and receive par value) in a winding up.

In a straightforward case, where the shares provide for redemption on a set date, they would be classified as 'financial liabilities' because under the rights attached to the shares (the set redemption date), the issuer has an obligation to redeem (that is, to transfer financial assets to the holder of the preference shares). The same applies where preference shares carry fixed rights to cumulative dividends (which are not at the discretion of the issuer).

Where the issuer is not obliged to redeem the preference shares, appropriate classification is determined by the other rights attaching to them, by assessing the substance of the contractual arrangements and by reference to the definitions of 'financial liabilities' and 'equity instruments'. Only when the distributions to the holders of the preference shares are at the discretion of the issuer would such shares be classified as 'equity instruments'.

Preference Dividends – as a result of the above, some preference shares will be shown as liabilities in the balance sheet rather than as part of share capital and reserves, where the shares in question would fall to be treated as liabilities (in accordance with FRS 25 (IAS 32) and FRSSE (effective January 2007) and FRSSE (effective April 2008)).

12.10.3 Presentation of dividends

Traditionally, dividends (both paid and proposed/equity or preference) have been charged on the face of the profit and loss account as an item after *'Profit (loss) for the financial year after taxation'* as an appropriation of profit.

With the changes introduced by company legislation in 2004 (and also FRS 25 in respect of full UK GAAP), (a) dividends paid and proposed dividends; and (b) equity dividends and preference dividends are therefore treated differently *depending on the facts*, being either:

- charged as an (interest) expense;
- 'debited directly to equity' as a distribution to equity shareholders; or
- included as narrative within the note as a means of disclosure.

'Debited directly to equity' is a new term within the UK and is currently taken to mean 'charged directly to, or as a movement on, reserves'.

Henceforth, equity dividends may disappear from the face of the profit and loss account and be presented wholly within the notes to the accounts as a movement on reserves ('Profit and loss account reserve') or within the reconciliation of shareholders funds ('Statement of shareholders equity'), with a narrative note dealing with aggregate dividends liable to be paid at the balance sheet date and aggregate dividends proposed before the date of approval of the accounts.

ABCDE# Part IV Example accounts

Chapter 13 Example accounts

The example accounts set out in this chapter are entirely fictional.

The example accounts do not represent a comprehensive checklist of the statutory disclosure requirements nor do they purport to be definitive or exhaustive. The intention is to illustrate the more common situations. Other presentations may be equally acceptable, provided that they adhere to the rules set out in the Companies Act 2006, supporting statutory regulations and relevant financial reporting accounting standards.

Depending on the circumstances, the accounts may contain:

- no accountants' report (in the case of audit exemption);
- an appropriate auditors' report (where an audit is required); or
- an independent accountants' report (for the purpose of assurance).

Alternative reports are illustrated, to be adopted according to the circumstances, in **Chapter 14**.

> In the example accounts, tinted or boxed items indicate the following:
> - **grey tint** – text that may be omitted or is relevant, as the case may be, only in the circumstances where the FRSSE is adopted;
> - **other boxed items** – text that is optional or may be omitted according to the circumstances.
>
> Text in *italics* in the example accounts represents commentary and explanation or alternative presentation.

13.1 Accounts of Small Company Limited

The illustrative example accounts of Small Company Limited illustrate the unaudited accounts of a small company (as defined in **Chapter 5**) producing accounts under the provisions of the **Companies Act 2006** for a financial period beginning on or after **6 April 2008**; the example year end is 30 April 2009.

Pages 1–12 of the example accounts comprise the unaudited 'Companies Act individual accounts' of the company (a small company) prepared in accordance with Companies Act 2006, **and taking full advantage of special provisions with respect to the preparation of annual accounts of small companies in accordance with Schedule 1 of SI 2008 No. 409.**

In practice, a small company is entitled to exceed the basic minimum disclosure as is considered desirable.

The form of both the profit and loss account and the balance sheet are presented in Format 1.

The company has also chosen to adopt the FRSSE (effective April 2008).

The company is audit-exempt.

Pages 13–15 of the example accounts, indicated as 'For management information only', do not

Chapter 13 Example accounts

form part of the statutory accounts but are illustrative of a detailed profit and loss account, together with summaries, that might be prepared for management accounting purposes. In practice, these summaries or schedules may often be print-outs produced from or within software accounting packages.

13.2 Abbreviated accounts of Small Company Limited

Pages 1–4 of the example abbreviated accounts comprise the 'Companies Act abbreviated accounts' of the company prepared for filing with the Registrar of Companies in accordance with Companies Act 2006 s. 444, including a balance sheet complying with Part 1 of Schedule 4 of SI 2008 No. 409.

The accounts are based upon the 'Companies Act individual accounts' above of the small company.

Abbreviated accounts will include as appropriate:

- *Directors' balance sheet statement* under CA 2006 (**SI 2008 No. 409 Schedule 4.1(2)**) – company subject to the small companies regime.
- *Directors' balance sheet statement* under CA 2006 **Section 475** – audit-exempt small company under CA 2006 s. 477.

These are illustrated immediately above the director's signature on abbreviated balance sheet in the example abbreviated accounts below.

- *Independent auditors' report* under CA 2006 **Section 495** (Audited small company) – see examples in **Chapter 14** at **14.4**.

CA 2006 sections 444 and 495 are reproduced in **Appendix B** and **Table 14.1** in **Chapter 14** respectively. SI 2008 No. 409 Schedule 4 paragraph 1(2) is reproduced in **Appendix E**.

13.3 Unaudited accounts of Dormant Small Company Limited

The example dormant company accounts illustrate the unaudited accounts of a dormant small company.

13.4 Auditors' reports

The illustrative example accounts of Small Company Limited illustrate the accounts of an unaudited (audit exempt) small company. The example accounts therefore exclude an illustrative audit report. **Chapter 14** provides examples of audit reports appropriate where a small company is subject to audit.

13.5 FRC guidance: Going concern and the FRSSE

As explained in **10.14** above, the Financial Reporting Council (FRC) has published guidance on the 'going concern basis' entitled *Update for directors of companies that adopt the Financial Reporting Standard for Smaller Entities (FRSSE): Going concern and financial reporting* (March 2009)

This FRC document, containing practical examples of disclosure, is available at: http://www.frc.org.uk/images/uploaded/documents/An%20Update%20-%20Going%20concern%20smaller%20companies.pdf

Small Company Limited annual report and accounts

**Registered number:
02075561200
England and Wales**

**SMALL COMPANY LIMITED
ANNUAL REPORT AND UNAUDITED ACCOUNTS
30 APRIL 2009**

Small company – definition

As a basic rule, a company is treated as a small company under CA 2006 if it does not exceed more than two of the following criteria:

Turnover	*£6.5 million*
Balance sheet total	*£3.26 million*
Average number of employees	*50*

See **Chapter 5** at **5.2** for the detailed definition.

The qualifications for a small company are specified in CA 2006 section 382 and (for a group) section 383.

Annual report and unaudited accounts – *These comprise: (a) the directors' report ('annual report'); and (b) the company's annual accounts ('Companies Act individual accounts') together with notes to the accounts.*

Advantage has been taken of the special provisions available under CA 2006 ss. 381–384 and Schedule 1 of SI 2008 No. 409 as a small company.

Registered number – Any document delivered to the Registrar of Companies must state in a prominent position the registered number of the company to which it relates (CA 2006 s. 1068(3)(c)).

SMALL COMPANY LIMITED

Directors Teresa L Bramshaw – Chairman
James Longslade – Managing director
Charles TG Favell
William D Norley

Secretary *Charles TG Favell*

Registered office 10 Crockford Street
London SW19 7JP

Registered number 02075561200 England and Wales

[*Auditors*] *True & Fairview*
Chartered Accountants
17 Queen's Place
London EC4P 3BC

ANNUAL REPORT AND UNAUDITED ACCOUNTS – 30 APRIL 2009

Pages

1 Report of the directors

[–] *Accountants' report [unaudited accounts, where relevant]*
or
[–] *Auditors' report [audited accounts only]*

Accounts, comprising:
2 Profit and loss account
3 Balance sheet
4 *Statement of total recognised gains and losses*
5–12 Notes to the accounts

The following pages do not form part of the statutory accounts:

13–14 Detailed profit and loss account
15 Profit and loss account summaries

Directors and advisers, etc. – Although it is common practice to give the information on this page, there is no requirement to do so, and the page may be omitted.

Company Secretary – A private company is not required to have a secretary. CA 2006 s.270(1)

Chapter 13   Example accounts

SMALL COMPANY LIMITED
REPORT OF THE DIRECTORS

Page [1]

The directors present their annual report with the unaudited accounts of the company for the year ended 30 April 2009.

Principal activity
The principal activity of the company in the year under review was the manufacture and distribution of office equipment and components.

The company's subsidiary company, Smallsub Limited, provides office design and consultancy services.

Directors
The directors in office in the year were as follows:

　J Longslade
　TL Bramshaw
　CTG Favell (appointed 1 December 2008)
　WD Norley

　DV Bolderwood (retired on 31 May 2008)

Political and charitable contributions
During the year the company made a political contribution of £2,500 to the New Conservative Party and various charitable contributions totalling £3,000.

CA 2006 s. 419(2)   The above report has been prepared in accordance with the special provisions relating to small companies within Part 15 of the Companies Act 2006.

CA 2006 s. 419(1)   Signed on behalf of *[/by order of]* the board of directors

C. Favell
....
CTG FAVELL
Director [*or Secretary*]

Approved by the board: 28 September 2009

Directors' responsibilities statements – *A small company eligible for audit exemption is required to provide a statutory statement in accordance with CA 2006 section 475 to appear in the balance sheet above the director's signature of approval (see statement illustrated on **Example accounts page [3]** below). A small company subject to audit is required (in accordance with international auditing standards) to prepare a more detailed statement appearing generally within the directors' report (See **Example 6.4** in **Chapter 6** at 6.9.3).*

*The APB ISA (UK and Ireland) 700 'The auditors' report on financial statements' requires the financial statements or accompanying information (for example, the directors' report) to include an adequate statement of directors' responsibilities (see **Chapter 14**). Where the accounts omit such a statement of responsibilities, the auditors' report must include one instead. An independent accountants' report on unaudited (audit-exempt) accounts, should, on the same basis, include a statement that the directors are responsible for the preparation of the accounts.*

Auditors or accountants re-appointment – *There is no requirement to disclose the appointment or reappointment of auditors (if relevant) or accountants, although it is common practice to do so. Similarly no reference to 'independent accountants' need be made.*

SMALL COMPANY LIMITED
PROFIT AND LOSS ACCOUNT
FOR THE YEAR ENDED 30 APRIL 2009

	Notes	2009 £	2008 £
Turnover – Continuing operations	2	1,558,080	950,700
Cost of sales		(891,586)	(577,211)
Gross profit		666,494	373,489
Distribution costs		(258,536)	(180,641)
Administrative expenses		(270,243)	(205,193)
Operating profit (loss) – Continuing operations	3	137,715	(12,345)
Income from fixed asset investments		14,276	1,000
Interest payable and similar changes		(20,654)	(9,200)
[Non-equity] preference dividend – paid		(700)	(700)
Profit (loss) on ordinary activities before taxation		130,637	(21,245)
Taxation – UK corporation tax		(34,100)	5,720
Profit (loss) for the financial year after taxation		96,537	(15,525)
Retained profit at 1 May 2008		131,920	147,445
Profit (loss) for the financial year after taxation		96,537	(15,525)
[Equity] dividends paid	4	(16,800)	—
Retained profit at 30 April 2009		£211,657	£131,920

Alternative disclosures (Not required if FRSSE adopted).

Continuing operations
All of the company's activities [operations] in the above two financial years derived from continuing operations. [or:]
Turnover and operating profit derive wholly from continuing operations.

Total recognised gains and losses
The company has no recognised gains or losses other than the profit or loss for the period [above two financial years].

The above statements are only to be used where applicable.

Statement of total recognised gains and losses – *this could be presented on this page beneath the profit and loss account (see* **Example accounts page [4]**).

Taxation – *the full format heading is 'Tax on profit or loss on ordinary activities'. 'Taxation' will include current and deferred tax, the material components of both of which should be disclosed separately in the notes. For a deferred tax charge (or credit), the main components will be timing adjustments (originating and reversing) and tax rate adjustments (increasing or reducing the opening liability).*

Dividends – *see* **12.10** *for comment on the presentation of dividends (both equity and preference [non-equity] dividends).*

Chapter 13 Example accounts

SMALL COMPANY LIMITED
BALANCE SHEET – 30 APRIL 2009

Page [3]

	Notes	2009 £	2008 £
Fixed assets			
Intangible assets	5	22,065	18,846
Tangible assets	6	310,544	282,548
Investments	7	1,000	11,500
		333,609	312,894
Current assets			
Stocks		195,667	156,750
Debtors	8	251,531	146,237
Cash at bank and in hand		2,708	5,463
		449,906	308,450
Creditors: amounts falling due within one year	9	(233,191)	(251,924)
Net current assets		216,715	56,526
Total assets less current liabilities		550,324	369,420
Creditors: amounts falling due after more than one year	10	(76,667)	(20,500)
Net assets		£473,657	£348,920
Capital and reserves			
Called up share capital		65,000	40,000
Share premium account	11	10,000	10,000
Revaluation reserve		187,000	167,000
Profit and loss account	12	211,657	131,920
Shareholders' funds	13	£473,657	£348,920

These accounts have been prepared in accordance with the special provisions relating to small companies within Part 15 of the Companies Act 2006 *[and with the Financial Reporting Standard for Smaller Entities (effective April 2008)]*.

For the financial year ended 30 April 2009 the company was entitled to exemption from audit under section 477 [*small company exemption*] Companies Act 2006; and no notice has been deposited under section 476 [*member or members requesting an audit*].

The directors acknowledge their responsibilities for ensuring that the company keeps accounting records which comply with s. 386 [of the Act] and for preparing accounts which give a true and fair view of the state of affairs of the company as at the end of the financial year and of its profit or loss for the financial year in accordance with the requirements of sections 394 and 395 and which otherwise comply with the requirements of the Companies Act 2006 relating to accounts, so far as applicable to the company.

[*or (alternative)*:

The directors acknowledge their responsibilities for complying with the requirements of the Companies Act 2006 with respect to accounting records and the preparation of accounts. [s. 475(3)]

Signed on behalf of
the board of directors

C. Favell
....
CTG FAVELL
Director

Approved by the board: 28 September 2009

Small Company Limited annual report and accounts

Directors' statements – *The statements above the director's signature represent the statements required by (a) CA 2006 s. 414 (Small company accounts prepared in accordance with the special provisions) applicable to companies subject to the small companies regime), (b) the FRSSE, and (c) CA 2006 ss. 475 and 477 (Small company audit exempt accounts only). See footnote to* **Example accounts Page [1]** *('Directors' responsibilities statements').*

Approval of accounts – *A company's annual accounts must be approved by the board of directors and be signed on behalf of the board by a director of the company (CA 2006 s. 414).*

Chapter 13 Example accounts

SMALL COMPANY LIMITED Page [4]
STATEMENT OF TOTAL RECOGNISED GAINS AND LOSSES
FOR THE YEAR ENDED 30 APRIL 2009

	2009 £	2008 £
Profit (loss) for the financial year after taxation	96,537	(15,525)
Unrealised surplus on revaluation of property	20,000	—
Total recognised gains relating to the year	£117,237	(£14,825)

Note of historical cost profits and losses
The difference between the results as disclosed in the profit and loss account and the result on an unmodified historical cost basis is not material.

Statement of total recognised gains and losses – *This statement, showing the total of recognised gains and losses and its components, should be presented as a primary statement with the same prominence as the other primary statements, ie profit and loss account and balance sheet. The gains and losses are those recognised in the period insofar as they are attributable to shareholders. The statement could be presented in the* **Example accounts page [2]** *beneath the profit and loss account:*

Where the 'profit (loss) for the financial year after taxation' represents the entire total recognised gains or losses relating to the year (where, for example, there are no other unrealised surpluses or losses), a separate 'statement of total recognised gains and losses' is not required. However, unless the company adopts the FRSSE, the profit and loss account on **page [2]** *should include a statement on the following lines, immediately below the profit and loss account:*

'The company has no recognised gains and losses other than the profit and loss for the above two periods.'

Note of historical cost profits and losses – *A note of historical cost profits and losses should be presented immediately following the profit and loss account or the statement of total recognised gains and losses. Where there is a material difference between the result disclosed in the profit and loss account and the result on an unmodified basis (for example where a company charges a significant amount of depreciation on a revalued fixed asset), this should be disclosed in a note.*

Small Company Limited annual report and accounts

SMALL COMPANY LIMITED
NOTES TO THE UNAUDITED ACCOUNTS – 30 APRIL 2009

1 Accounting policies

Basis of accounting
The accounts have been prepared under the historical cost convention as modified by the revaluation of certain fixed assets [and in accordance with the Financial Reporting Standard for Smaller Entities (effective April 2008)].

Consolidation
The company is a parent company subject to the small companies regime. The company and its subsidiary comprise a small group. The company has therefore taken advantage of the option provided by section 398 of the Companies Act 2006 not to prepare group accounts.

Cash flow
The accounts do not include a cash flow statement because the company, as a small reporting entity, is exempt from the requirement to prepare such a statement [under Financial Reporting Standard 1 *Cash flow statements*/Financial Reporting Standard for Smaller Entities (effective April 2008)].

Turnover
Turnover represents net invoiced sales of goods, excluding VAT [*having regard to the fulfilment of contractual obligations*].

Tangible fixed assets
Depreciation is provided, after taking account of any grants receivable, at the following annual rates in order to write off each asset over its estimated useful life:

Freehold buildings	–	2% on cost or revalued amounts
Plant and machinery	–	15% on cost
Fixtures and fittings	–	10% on cost
Motor vehicles	–	25% on cost

No depreciation is provided on freehold land.

Intangible fixed assets
Intangible fixed assets (including purchased goodwill and patents) are amortised at rates calculated to write off the assets on a straight basis over their estimated useful economic lives. Impairment of intangible assets is only reviewed where circumstances indicate that the carrying value of an asset may not be fully recoverable.

Stocks
Stocks and work-in-progress are valued at the lower of cost and net realisable value, after making due allowance for obsolete and slow-moving items. Cost includes all direct expenditure and an appropriate proportion of fixed and variable overheads.

Deferred taxation
Deferred tax arises as a result of including items of income and expenditure in taxation computations in periods different from those in which they are included in the company's accounts. Deferred tax is provided in full on timing differences which result in an obligation to pay more (or less) tax at a future date, at the average tax rates that are expected to apply when the timing differences reverse, based on current tax rates and laws.

Deferred tax is not provided on timing differences arising from the revaluation of fixed assets where there is no commitment to sell the asset.

Deferred tax assets and liabilities are not discounted.

Research and development
Expenditure on research and development is written off in the year in which it is incurred.

Foreign currencies
Monetary assets and liabilities in foreign currencies are translated into sterling at the rates of exchange ruling at the balance sheet date. Transactions in foreign currencies are translated into sterling at the rate of exchange ruling at the date of the transaction. Exchange differences are taken into account in arriving at the operating profit.

Chapter 13   Example accounts

SMALL COMPANY LIMITED
NOTES TO THE UNAUDITED ACCOUNTS – 30 APRIL 2009

Page [6]

Leased assets
Rentals applicable to operating leases where substantially all of the benefits and risks of ownership remain with the lessor are charged against profit on a straight line basis over the lease term.

Assets held under finance leases and hire purchase contracts are capitalised and depreciated over their useful lives. The corresponding lease or hire purchase obligation is treated in the balance sheet as a liability. The interest element of rental obligations is charged to profit and loss account over the period of the lease at a constant proportion of the outstanding balance of capital repayments.

Pension costs
Contributions in respect of the company's defined contribution pension scheme are charged to the profit and loss account for the year in which they are payable to the scheme. Differences between contributions payable and contributions actually paid in the year are shown as either accruals or prepayments at the year end.

Going concern basis of accounting
The accounts have been prepared on the assumption that the company is able to carry on business as a going concern, which the directors consider appropriate having regard to the circumstances outlined in Note 18 to the accounts.

Disclosure of accounting policies – *The FRSSE (effective April 2008) requires the disclosure of each material accounting policy and also any changes in accounting policies or estimation techniques.*

Although not specifically stated within the FRSSE, in the absence of any specifically disclosed statement of accounting policy, the presumption is that the accounting principles set out in the FRSSE have been observed in the preparation of the accounts.

Although the disclosure of certain accounting policies is indicated above (by boxing) as not required by the FRSSE, disclosure will nevertheless be appropriate either to show a true and fair view or because the policies are considered to be 'material' in presenting the accounts.

There is a general presumption that the company is a 'going concern', to be determined for a period of not less than one year from the date of approval of the accounts.

Deferred tax – *The FRSSE (effective April 2008) requires deferred tax where appropriate to be provided on the 'full provision' basis. On the previously adopted 'partial provision' basis, provision was made in respect of material timing differences only when there was a reasonable probability that a liability would arise in the foreseeable future.*

SMALL COMPANY LIMITED
NOTES TO THE UNAUDITED ACCOUNTS – 30 April 2009

2 Turnover

Turnover attributable to geographical markets outside the United Kingdom amounted to 23% (2008 – 19%).

3 Operating profit (loss)

The operating profit (2008 – loss) is stated after charging:

	2009 £	2008 £
Depreciation of tangible fixed assets	44,496	42,178
Amortisation of intangible fixed assets	6,847	5,100
Operating lease charges	4,100	3,600
[Auditors' remuneration]	5,200	5,700
Exceptional development expenditure	62,000	—
Pension costs	18,100	13,200
Directors' remuneration	77,031	62,254

Two directors (2008 – 2) are members of money purchase pension schemes.

4 Dividends

	2009 £	2008 £
[Non-equity] preference dividend – paid	700	700
Dividend on ordinary shares – paid	16,800	—
(25.85p per share)		
	£17,500	£700

Directors' remuneration – A small company's individual accounts must give the overall aggregate total of:

(a) directors' remuneration (for qualifying services as director or management of the company or any subsidiary);
(b) amounts receivable under long-term incentive schemes, and
(c) company contributions to purchase schemes in respect of directors' qualifying services (*SI 2008 No. 409 Sch 3.1*) (see *Chapter 6* at *6.11*). **SI 2008 No. 409 Schedule 3**

Disclosure is also required of the number of directors (if any) to whom retirement benefits are accruing in respect of qualifying services under:

(a) money purchase schemes, and
(b) defined benefit schemes. (*SI 2008 No. 409 Sch 3.2*)

Auditors' remuneration – small companies **(CA 2006 s. 494)**

Not applicable to audit-exempt small companies:

The notes to the annual accounts of a small or medium-sized company (as defined) must disclose the amount of any remuneration receivable by the company's auditors for the auditing of the accounts, including the nature and estimated money-value of benefits in kind.

The provisions are contained in *SI 2008 No. 489 'The Companies (Disclosure of Auditor Remuneration and Liability Limitation Agreements) Regulations 2008' reg 4* and apply to accounts for any financial year beginning on or after 6 April 2008. The non-audit work provisions (as they apply to medium-sized companies for services other than audit) are provided by *SI 2008 No. 489 reg 4.4(4)*.

SMALL COMPANY LIMITED
NOTES TO THE UNAUDITED ACCOUNTS – 30 APRIL 2009

Page [8]

5 Intangible fixed assets

	Goodwill £	Other intangible assets £	Total £
Cost			
At 1 May 2008	15,000	13,127	28,127
Additions	—	10,264	10,264
Disposals	—	(3,000)	(3,000)
At 30 April 2009	15,000	20,391	35,391
Amortisation			
At 1 May 2008	7,500	1,781	9,281
On disposals	—	(2,802)	(2,802)
Charge for the year	2,000	4,847	6,847
At 30 April 2009	9,500	3,826	13,326
Net book values			
At 30 April 2009	£5,500	£16,565	£22,065
At 30 April 2008	£7,500	£11,346	£18,846

6 Tangible fixed assets

	Land and buildings £	Plant and machinery, etc. £	Total £
Cost or valuation			
At 1 May 2008	283,500	266,914	550,414
Additions	—	55,893	55,893
Revaluation	20,000	—	20,000
Disposals	(2,500)	(9,213)	(11,713)
At 30 April 2009	301,000	313,594	614,594
Cost	31,000	313,594	344,594
Valuation – 2009	270,000	—	270,000
	301,000	313,594	614,594
Depreciation			
At 1 May 2008	31,340	236,526	267,866
On disposals	—	(8,312)	(8,312)
Charge for year	3,160	41,336	44,496
At 30 April 2009	34,500	269,550	304,050
Net book values			
At 30 April 2009	£266,500	£44,044	£310,544
At 30 April 2008	£252,160	£30,388	£282,548

Small Company Limited annual report and accounts

SMALL COMPANY LIMITED
NOTES TO THE UNAUDITED ACCOUNTS – 30 APRIL 2009

Page [9]

6 Tangible fixed assets (*continued*)

The net book value of plant and machinery includes £5,000 (2008 – Nil) in respect of assets held under finance leases. The amount of depreciation in respect of such assets amounted to £850 for the year (2008 – Nil).

Land and buildings were revalued during the year by A. Surveyor FRICS on the basis of open market value. The cost or valuation of freehold buildings on which depreciation is charged amounted to £158,000 (2008 – £158,000).

The historical cost of freehold land and buildings included above at a valuation of £270,000 was £83,000 (2008 – £85,500) and the aggregate depreciation thereon would have been £28,200 (2008 – £27,300).

7 Investments

	Subsidary undertaking £	Listed investments £	Total £
Cost			
At 1 May 2008	1,000	10,500	11,500
Disposals	—	(10,500)	(10,500)
At 30 April 2009	£1,000	£ —	£1,000

Subsidiary undertaking
The company's investment in its subsidiary company represents the cost of acquisition of the whole of the ordinary share capital of Smallsub Limited, which provides office design and consultancy services.

At 30 April 2009, the aggregate of the share capital and reserves of Smallsub Limited amounted to £56,300 and the profit for the year to that date was £3,560.

Listed investments
Listed investments comprise investments listed on the London Stock Exchange, the market value of which at 30 April 2009 (the previous year end) amounted to £11,100.

8 Debtors

	2009 £	2008 £
Trade debtors	190,579	111,150
Others	60,952	35,087
	£251,531	£146,237

Other debtors include an amount of £4,000 (2008 – Nil) falling due after more than one year.

Creditors – Taxation and social security (Note 9)

Deferred tax – *The FRSSE (effective April 2008) requires deferred tax where appropriate to be provided on the 'full provision' basis. Where deferred tax is provided, disclosure is required of the deferred tax balance and its material components (for example, accelerated capital allowances and tax losses carried forward) and the amount of tax that would be payable or recoverable if revalued assets were sold at the values shown in the accounts.*

Chapter 13 Example accounts

SMALL COMPANY LIMITED Page [10]
NOTES TO THE UNAUDITED ACCOUNTS – 30 APRIL 2009

9 Creditors: amounts falling due within one year

	2009 £	2008 £
Bank loans and overdrafts (secured)	38,790	74,920
Obligations under finance leases	3,000	—
Debt due within one year	41,790	74,920
Trade creditors	94,506	125,390
Other creditors	57,795	46,164
Taxation and social security	39,100	5,450
	£233,191	£251,924

10 Creditors: amounts falling due after more than one year

	2009 £	2008 £
Bank loans and overdraft	62,500	—
Obligations under finance leases	2,000	—
Debt due after more than one year	64,500	
Other creditors	2,167	10,500
Preference shares – 7% preference shares of £1 each	10,000	10,000
	£76,667	£20,500

Debt due after more than one year		
repayable between one and five years	52,000	—
repayable in five years or more	12,500	—
Preference shares	10,000	10,000
	£74,500	10,000

The bank loan, the aggregate total of which amounts to £75,000, is repayable in annual instalments of £12,500 commencing 31 October 2009.

Preference shares represent non-equity interests stated at par value. Dividends are payable annually at 7% net of tax credit and are cumulative. The shares are redeemable (at par value) on 30 April 2017; have a priority over ordinary shares, in the event of an earlier winding-up (to the extent of their par value and the arrears (if any) of dividends); and have no vote, provided dividends are not in arrears.

Creditors: amounts falling due after more than one year (Note 10)
Preference shares – *Preference shares providing for mandatory redemption at a fixed or determinable future date or for fixed or determinable amounts are classified as 'financial liabilities' in accordance with the revised FRSSE (effective April 2008). 'Financial instruments are 'financial liabilities', 'financial assets' or 'equity instruments' depending on the substance of the underlying contractual arrangement (see **12.4**).*

SMALL COMPANY LIMITED
NOTES TO THE UNAUDITED ACCOUNTS – 30 APRIL 2009

11 Called up share capital

	2009 £	2008 £
Allotted, called up and fully paid		
65,000 (2008 – 40,000) ordinary shares of £1 each	65,000	40,000

During the year 25,000 ordinary shares of £1 each were allotted and fully paid for cash at par.

12 Revaluation reserve

	£
At 1 May 2008	167,000
Surplus on revaluation or property (note 6)	20,000
At 30 April 2009	£187,000

13 Shareholders' funds

Reconciliation of movements on shareholders' funds

	2009 £	2008 £
Profit (loss) for the financial year after taxation	96,537	(15,525)
Dividends	(16,800)	—
	79,737	(15,525)
Other recognised gains relating to the year	20,000	—
New share capital subscribed	25,000	—
Net additions to shareholders' funds	124,737	(15,525)
Opening shareholders' funds at 1 May 2008	348,920	364,445
Closing shareholders' funds at 30 April 2009	£473,657	£348,920

14 Contingent liability

A writ for damages amounting to £120,000 has been served on the company, alleging supply of faulty goods. The directors have obtained legal advice and are contesting the claim, which they consider is without foundation. No provision has been made in these accounts in respect of the claim.

SMALL COMPANY LIMITED Page [12]
NOTES TO THE UNAUDITED ACCOUNTS – 30 APRIL 2009

15 Commitments

At 30 April 2009, capital expenditure commitments were as follows:

	2009	2008
Contracted but not provided for in the accounts	£20,000	£ —

Pension commitments
The company operates a defined contribution pension scheme on behalf of its directors and certain employees. The assets of the scheme are held separately from those of the company in an independently administered fund. The annual pension commitment under this scheme is for contributions of £21,300 (2008 – £18,100).

Lease commitments – operating leases
At 30 April 2009, the company had annual commitments of £4,000 (2008 – £3,400) under non-cancellable operating leases which expire within two to five years.

Other financial commitments
At 30 April 2009, the company had entered into a joint venture agreement to commence in 2009, the initial contribution to which will be £50,000.

16 Related party transactions

Advance to director
During the year James Longslade was granted a short-term loan to facilitate the purchase of a house. Indebtedness on the loan was as follows:

Liability at 1 May 2008 £	Maximum liability during the year £	Liability at 30 April 2009 £
—	15,000	15,000

The loan is repayable on 28 February 2010. Interest, at the rate of 6% per annum, is payable upon repayment and at 30 April 2009 no interest was due and unpaid.

Transactions with related party
During the year the company purchased goods to the value of £312,100 (2008 – £197,000) from Medium Company (London) Limited, a company in which Teresa Bramshaw and James Longslade are materially interested as shareholders. The purchases were made on a normal trading basis.

Controlling party
During the two years ending 30 April 2009, James Longslade, a director, together with members of his close family, controlled the company by virtue of a controlling interest (directly or indirectly) of 61.2% of the issued ordinary share capital.

17 Post balance sheet events

On 5 August 2009 the company acquired the goodwill and net assets of Automated Office Technology Products for a consideration of £50,000 which has been financed by a secured bank loan, repayable over five years.

18 Future trading and the current economic environment

Subsequent to the financial year end, the company has experienced a significant reduction in business activity, resulting in significantly lower sales. However, costs are anticipated to reduce correspondingly and, whilst the company is dependent upon the continuation of existing banking and trading facilities, it should be able to operate within its overdraft. Despite serious doubts about future trading conditions, the directors are not aware of any reason why overdraft or other facilities will not be extended. As a result they have adopted the going concern basis of accounting.

Small Company Limited annual report and accounts

FOR MANAGEMENT INFORMATION ONLY

SMALL COMPANY LIMITED
DETAILED PROFIT AND LOSS ACCOUNT
FOR THE YEAR ENDED 30 APRIL 2009

Page [13]

	2009 £	£	*2008* £	£
Sales		1,558,080		950,700
Cost of sales				
Stocks 1 May 2008	156,750		133,281	
Purchases	519,166		345,210	
	675,916		478,491	
Less: stocks 30 April 2009	195,667		156,750	
	480,249		321,741	
Production wages	266,519		177,500	
Depreciation	38,717		35,270	
Hire of plant and machinery (operating leases)	4,100		3,600	
Other production expenses (including research and development)	102,001		39,100	
	411,337		255,470	
Cost of sales		891,586		577,211
Gross profit (42.8% – 2008: 39.3%)		666,494		373,489
Distribution costs				
Distribution				
Carriage	50,104		29,606	
Motor expenses	30,402		20,204	
Lorry and warehouse	18,702		7,648	
Depreciation	3,508		3,648	
	102,716		61,106	
Selling and marketing				
Salaries	84,588		73,440	
Advertising	18,900		17,225	
Travel and motor expenses	29,111		19,120	
Entertaining	23,221		9,750	
	155,820		119,535	
	258,536		180,641	
Totals carried forward	258,536	666,494	180,641	373,489

This page does not form part of the statutory accounts.

Chapter 13 Example accounts

FOR MANAGEMENT INFORMATION ONLY

SMALL COMPANY LIMITED
DETAILED PROFIT AND LOSS ACCOUNT
FOR THE YEAR ENDED 30 APRIL 2009
(*continued*)

Page [14]

	2009 £	2009 £	2008 £	2008 £
Totals brought forward	258,536	666,494	180,641	373,489
Administrative expenses				
Establishment expenses				
Rent and rates	55,270		41,777	
Light, heat and power	18,100		12,120	
Insurance	15,900		10,091	
Repairs	12,012		6,171	
Depreciation	5,030		4,611	
	106,312		74,770	
Administration costs				
Salaries and payroll	35,457		33,520	
Directors' remuneration	57,031		52,254	
Pension costs	18,100		13,200	
Postage and telephone	8,211		5,100	
Printing and stationery	12,100		8,275	
Depreciation	4,088		3,749	
General administration	9,834		1,200	
Accountancy [and Audit]	5,200		5,700	
Legal and professional	600		—	
Bank charges	500		305	
Bad debts	12,810		7,120	
	163,931		130,423	
	270,243		205,193	
		528,779		385,834
Operating profit (loss)		137,715		(12,345)
Income from investments		14,276		1,000
Interest payable				
Bank loan	(12,100)		—	
Bank overdraft	(8,554)		(9,200)	
		(20,654)		(9,200)
Preference dividend		(700)		(700)
Profit (loss) on ordinary activities before taxation		£130,637		(£21,245)

This page does not form part of the statutory accounts.

176

Small Company Limited annual report and accounts

FOR MANAGEMENT INFORMATION ONLY
Page [15]

SMALL COMPANY LIMITED
PROFIT AND LOSS ACCOUNT SUMMARIES
FOR THE YEAR ENDED 30 APRIL 2009

Summaries of items disclosed in the statutory profit and loss account

	2009 £	2008 £
Depreciation		
Production – cost of sales	31,870	30,170
Amortisation – cost of sales	6,847	5,100
	38,717	35,270
Distribution	3,508	3,648
Establishment expenses	5,030	4,611
Administration costs	4,088	3,749
	£51,343	£47,278
Staff costs*		
Production wages	266,519	177,500
Selling and marketing salaries	64,588	63,440
Administration salaries	35,457	33,520
Directors' remuneration	77,031	62,254
Pension costs	18,100	13,200
	£461,695	£349,914

* Not disclosed in small company annual accounts.

This page does not form part of the statutory accounts.

177

Small Company Limited abbreviated accounts

**Registered number:
0205561200
England and Wales**

SMALL COMPANY LIMITED
ABBREVIATED [UNAUDITED] ACCOUNTS
30 APRIL 2009

Abbreviated accounts and audit exemption

*Audit exemption is available for companies subject to the small companies regime and not exceeding the small company thresholds of £6.5 million (turnover) and £3.26 million (balance sheet total). See **Chapter 5** at **5.2** for the detailed definition. No auditors' report or accountants' report is statutorily required to be attached to the accounts.*

*A company which is entitled to take advantage of audit exemption in preparing Companies Act individual accounts may prepare abbreviated accounts for filing with the Registrar of Companies. This is explained in **Chapter 8** and **Table 8.1**.*

*Abbreviated accounts delivered to the Registrar of Companies (other than those of audit-exempt or dormant companies) must otherwise be accompanied by a special report of the auditors under CA 2006 section 449. See **Chapter 8** at **8.9**.*

Independent auditors' report under CA 2006 Section 449 – Audit exempt small company
No statutory auditors' report under Section 449 is required where a small company is entitled to audit exemption afforded by CA 2006 sections 477 or 480.

Abbreviated accounts (small company) – These comprise: (a) unaudited abbreviated balance sheet (SI 2008 No. 409 Sch 4) (with directors' statements); (b) notes to the abbreviated accounts and (c) special auditors' report – but only where appropriate for audit-exempt accounts.

Registered number – Any document delivered to the Registrar of Companies must state in a prominent position the registered number of the company to which it relates (CA 2006 s. 1068(3)(c)).

Chapter 13 Example accounts

SMALL COMPANY LIMITED
ABBREVIATED BALANCE SHEET – 30 APRIL 2009

Page [1]

	Notes	2009 £	2008 £
Fixed assets	2		
Intangible assets		22,065	18,846
Tangible assets		310,544	282,548
Investments		1,000	11,500
		333,609	312,894
Current assets			
Stocks		195,667	156,750
Debtors	3	251,531	146,237
Cash at bank and in hand		2,708	5,463
		449,906	308,450
Creditors: amounts falling due within one year	4	(233,191)	(251,924)
Net current assets		216,715	56,526
Total assets less current liabilities		550,324	369,420
Creditors: amounts falling due after more than one year	4	(76,667)	(20,500)
Net assets		£473,657	£348,920
Capital and reserves			
Called up share capital	5	65,000	40,000
Share premium account		10,000	10,000
Revaluation reserve		187,000	167,000
Profit and loss account		211,657	131,920
Shareholders' funds		£473,657	£348,920

These abbreviated accounts have been prepared in accordance with the special provisions relating/applicable to companies subject to the small companies regime within Part 15 of Companies Act 2006.

[Audit exemption only – ss. 475 and 477]
For the financial year ended 30 April 2009 the company was entitled to exemption from audit under s. 477 [*small company exemption*] Companies Act 2006 and no notice has been deposited under s. 476 [*member or members requesting an audit*].

The directors acknowledge their responsibilities for ensuring that the company keeps accounting records which comply with s. 386 [of the Act] and for preparing accounts which give a true and fair view of the state of affairs of the company as at the end of the financial year and of its profit or loss for the financial year in accordance with the requirements of sections 394–395 and which otherwise comply with the requirements of the Companies Act 2006 relating to accounts, so far as applicable to the company. *[or (alternative): The directors acknowledge their responsibilities for complying with the requirements of the Companies Act 2006 with respect to accounting records and the preparation of accounts. [s.475 (3)]*

Signed on behalf of the board of directors

C. Favell
....
CTG FAVELL
Director
Approved by the board: 28 September 2009

SMALL COMPANY LIMITED
NOTES TO THE ABBREVIATED ACCOUNTS – 30 APRIL 2009

1 Accounting policies

Basis of accounting
The accounts have been prepared under the historical cost convention as modified by the revaluation of certain fixed assets [and in accordance with the Financial Reporting Standard for Smaller Entities (effective April 2008)].

Consolidation
The company is a parent company subject to the small companies regime. The company and its subsidiary comprise a small group. The company has therefore taken advantage of the option provided by section 398 of the Companies Act 2006 not to prepare group accounts.

Turnover
Turnover represents net invoiced sales of goods, excluding VAT [having regard to the fulfilment of contractural obligations].

Tangible fixed assets
Depreciation is provided, after taking account of any grants receivable, at the following annual rates in order to write off each asset over its estimated useful life:

Freehold buildings –	2% on cost or revalued amounts
Plant and machinery –	15% on cost
Fixtures and fittings –	10% on cost
Motor vehicles –	25% on cost

No depreciation is provided on freehold land.

Intangible fixed assets
Intangible fixed assets (including purchased goodwill and patents) are amortised at rates calculated to write off the assets on a straight basis over their estimated useful economic lives. Impairment of intangible assets is only reviewed where circumstances indicate that the carrying value of an asset may not be fully recoverable

Stocks
Stocks and work-in-progress are valued at the lower of cost and net realisable value, after making due allowance for obsolete and slow-moving items. Cost includes all direct expenditure and an appropriate proportion of fixed and variable overheads.

Deferred taxation
Deferred tax arises as a result of including items of income and expenditure in taxation computations in periods different from those in which they are included in the company's accounts. Deferred tax is provided in full on timing differences which result in an obligation to pay more (or less) tax at a future date, at the average tax rates that are expected to apply when the timing differences reverse, based on current tax rates and laws.

Deferred tax is not provided on timing differences arising from the revaluation of fixed assets where there is no commitment to sell the asset.

Deferred tax assets and liabilities are not discounted.

Research and development
Expenditure on research and development is written off in the year in which it is incurred.

Foreign currencies
Monetary assets and monetary liabilities in foreign currencies are translated into sterling at the rates of exchange ruling at the balance sheet date. Transactions in foreign currencies are translated into sterling at the rate of exchange ruling at the date of the transaction. Exchange differences are taken into account in arriving at the operating profit.

Disclosure of accounting policies – See comment on Small Company Limited Annual Report and Accounts, example accounts page [6]. See also SI 2008 No. 409 Schedule 4.3 (**Appendix E**).

Chapter 13 Example accounts

SMALL COMPANY LIMITED Page [3]
NOTES TO THE ABBREVIATED ACCOUNTS – 30 APRIL 2009

Leased assets
Rentals applicable to operating leases where substantially all of the benefits and risks of ownership remain with the lessor are charged against profit on a straight line basis over the lease term.

Assets held under finance leases and hire purchase contracts are capitalised and depreciated over their useful lives. The corresponding lease or hire purchase obligation is treated in the balance sheet as a liability. The interest element of rental obligations is charged to profit and loss account over the period of the lease at a constant proportion of the outstanding balance of capital repayments.

Pension costs
Contributions in respect of the company's defined contribution pension scheme are charged to the profit and loss account for the year in which they are payable to the scheme. Differences between contributions payable and contributions actually paid in the year are shown as either accruals or prepayments at the year end.

Going concern basis of accounting
The accounts have been prepared on the assumption that the company is able to carry on business as a going concern, which the directors consider appropriate having regard to the circumstances outlined in Note 7 to the abbreviated accounts.

---

2 Fixed assets

	Intangible assets £	Tangible fixed assets £	Investments £	Total £
Cost or valuation				
At 1 May 2008	28,127	550,414	11,500	590,041
Additions	10,264	55,893	—	66,157
Revaluation	—	20,000	—	20,000
Disposals	(3,000)	(11,713)	(10,500)	(25,213)
At 30 April 2009	35,391	614,594	1,000	650,985
Depreciation				
At 1 May 2008	9,281	267,866	—	277,147
On disposals	(2,802)	(8,312)	—	(11,114)
Charge for year	6,847	44,496	—	51,343
At 30 April 2009	13,326	304,050	—	317,376
Net book values				
At 30 April 2009	£22,065	£310,544	£1,000	£333,609
At 30 April 2008	£18,846	£282,548	£11,500	£312,894

Investments
At 30 April 2009 investments comprise an investment in a subsidiary undertaking. The company's investment in its subsidiary company of £1,000 represents the cost of acquisition of the whole of the ordinary share capital of Smallsub Ltd which provides office design and consultancy services. At 30 April 2009, the aggregate amount of the share capital and reserves of Smallsub Limited amounted to £56,300 and the profit for the year to that date was £3,560.

3 Debtors

Debtors include an amount of £4,000 (2008 – Nil) falling due after more than one year.

SMALL COMPANY LIMITED
NOTES TO THE ABBREVIATED ACCOUNTS – 30 APRIL 2009

Page [4]

4 Creditors

Creditors include the following:

	2009 £	2008 £
Bank loan not wholly repayable within five years		
repayable within five years	62,500	—
repayable after five years	12,500	—
	75,000	—
Bank overdraft	26,290	74,920
	£101,290	£74,920

The bank loan and overdraft are secured.

5 Called up share capital

	2009 £	2008 £
Allotted, called up and fully paid		
65,000 (2008 – 40,000) ordinary shares of £1 each	£65,000	£40,000

During the year 25,000 ordinary shares of £1 each were allotted and fully paid for cash at par.

6 Transactions with directors

Advance to director
During the year James Longslade was granted a short-term loan to facilitate the purchase of a house. Indebtedness on the loan was as follows:

Liability at 1 May 2008 £	Maximum liability during the year £	Liability at 30 April 2009 £
—	15,000	15,000

The loan is repayable on 28 February 2010. Interest, at the rate of 6% per annum, is payable upon repayment and at 30 April 2009 no interest was due and unpaid.

Material interests of directors
During the year the company purchased goods to the value of £312,100 (2008 – £197,000) from Medium Company (London) Limited, a company in which TL Bramshaw and CTG Favell are materially interested as shareholders. The purchases were made on a normal trading basis.

7 Future trading and the current economic environment

Subsequent to the financial year end, the company has experienced a significant reduction in business activity, resulting in significantly lower sales. However costs are anticipated to reduce correspondingly and, whilst the company is dependent upon the continuation of existing banking and trading facilities, it should be able to operate within its overdraft. Despite serious doubts about future trading conditions, the directors are not aware of any reason why overdraft or other facilities will not be extended. As a result they have adopted the going concern basis of accounting.

Transactions with directors
*Information about directors' benefits: advances, credit and guarantees CA 2006 s. 413 (see **10.8.3**).*

Dormant Small Company – dormant company accounts

**Registered number:
0205561212
England and Wales**

**DORMANT SMALL COMPANY LIMITED
ANNUAL REPORT AND UNAUDITED ACCOUNTS
YEAR ENDED 30 APRIL 2009**

Dormant company definition – A dormant company is a company which (during any period) has no 'significant accounting transaction' and meets the criteria set out in **Chapter 7** at **7.3** and **7.4** above.

Unaudited dormant company accounts – *These accounts illustrate the accounts of a company which has been dormant (within the meaning of section 1169(1)) of the Companies Act 2006) throughout the financial year and which is exempt from the provisions relating to the audit of accounts (section 480).* See **Chapter 7**.

There is little benefit in preparing abbreviated dormant company accounts other than the omission of the directors' report and the profit and loss account. Abbreviated accounts will omit the boxed text but need to include the directors' statement.

Disclosure: The form and content of small dormant company accounts must have regard to SI 2008 No. 409 Schs 1 and 4 (see **Appendix E**). *See also checklist items 10 and 11 in* **Chapter 8** *at* **8.11**.

DORMANT SMALL COMPANY LIMITED

Report of the directors
Not required in abbreviated accounts

The directors present their annual report with the unaudited accounts of the company for the year ended 30 April 2009. The company is dormant and has not traded during the year. [The company has, however, acted as agent during the year.]

RG Brown and CTG Favell were the directors of the company throughout the year. Their share interests in the ultimate parent company, Small Company Limited, are shown in the report and accounts of that company.

Signed on behalf of the board of directors by

C. Favell
....
CGT FAVELL
Director/Secretary   Approved by the board: 28 September 2009

Profit and loss account for the year ended 30 April 2009
The company has not traded during the year or the preceding financial year. During these years, the company received no income and incurred no expenditure and therefore made neither profit nor loss.

BALANCE SHEET – 30 APRIL 2009

	2009 £	2008 £
CURRENT ASSETS		
Debtors		
Amounts owed by group undertakings – (Ultimate parent company – Small Company Limited)	100	100
TOTAL ASSETS LESS CURRENT LIABILITIES	£100	£100
CAPITAL AND RESERVES		
Called up share capital		
Authorised, allotted and fully paid 100 ordinary shares of £1	100	100
SHAREHOLDERS' FUNDS	£100	£100

For the financial year ended 30 April 2009 the company was entitled to exemption from audit under section 480 Companies Act 2006 (as a dormant company) and no notice requiring an audit has been deposited under section 476 [*member or members requesting an audit*].

The directors acknowledge their responsibilities for complying with the requirements of the Companies Act 2006 with respect to accounting records and the preparation of accounts. [*s. 475(3)*] *[or (alternative): The directors acknowledge their responsibilities for ensuring that the company keeps accounting records which comply with section 386 [of the Act] and for preparing accounts which give a true and fair view of the state of affairs of the company as at the end of the financial year and of its profit or loss for the financial year in accordance with the requirements of sections 394 and 395 and which otherwise comply with the requirements of the Companies Act 2006 relating to accounts, so far as applicable to the company].*

Signed on behalf of the board of directors by

C. Favell
....
CGT FAVELL
Director   Approved by the board: 28 September 2009

Note to the accounts – Agency arrangements – *see next page.*

Chapter 13   Example accounts

DORMANT SMALL COMPANY LIMITED
NOTES TO THE ACCOUNTS – 30 APRIL 2009

Note to the accounts – Agency arrangements
Audit-exempt dormant company

The company was dormant and has not traded during the year. It has, however, acted in certain transactions as agent, for which it received no income.

Chapter 14 Small company audit reports

14.1 Auditors' reports

No statutory report is required where a small company is entitled to (and takes advantage of) audit exemption (CA 2006 s. 477); see **Chapter 11**.

This chapter comments on, and provides examples of, audit reports where a small company is subject to audit – either as required by statute or voluntarily requested by the directors.

14.1.1 Audit – Part 16 of Companies Act 2006

Company law as amended basically restates the previous requirements under Companies Act 1985 for the audit of company accounts. **(CA 2006 s. 475)**

Audit is covered in Part 16 of Companies Act 2006, which contains provisions (sections 475 to 539), concerning, *inter alia*, the requirement for audited accounts and the auditor's report. The statutory sections within Part 16 are identified in **Appendix A**.

14.1.2 Elements of the audit report

The audit report must include an introduction identifying the annual accounts and the financial reporting framework under which they are prepared, together with a description of the scope of the audit identifying the auditing standards adopted.

In essence, under CA 2006 s. 495, the auditor will henceforth be required to report his opinion on four elements:

(1) *True and fair view* – whether the annual accounts show a 'true and fair view' (having regard to the directors' statutory duty under CA 2006 s. 393(1)).
(2) *Relevant reporting framework* – whether the accounts have been prepared in accordance with the relevant financial reporting framework.
(3) *Appropriate legislation* – whether the accounts have been prepared in accordance with CA 2006 (Part 15) or IAS (IAS Regulation Article 4), if applicable.
(4) *Form of report or emphasis* – whether the report is 'unqualified or qualified' or contains reference to any emphasis of any matters without qualifying the report.

14.1.3 Auditor's report – CA 2006 s. 495

The form of report by auditors to be adopted with respect to Companies Act accounts is determined by Companies Act 2006 and by international auditing standards applicable within the UK. Following the adoption of International Standards on Auditing (ISAs), auditors' reports on accounts are required to follow ISA (UK and Ireland) 700 *The Auditor's Report on Financial Statements* – see **Example 14.1** below.

Companies Act 2006 s. 495 (Auditor's report on company's annual accounts) is reproduced in full in **Table 14.1**.

Chapter 14 Small company audit reports

Table 14.1   Auditor's report on annual accounts CA 2006 s. 495

495 Auditor's report on company's annual accounts

(1) A company's auditor must make a report to the company's members on all annual accounts of the company of which copies are, during his tenure of office—
   (a) in the case of a private company, to be sent out to members under section 423; and
   (b) in the case of a public company, to be laid before the company in general meeting under section 437.

(2) The auditor's report must include—
   (a) an introduction identifying the annual accounts that are the subject of the audit and the financial reporting framework that has been applied in their preparation; and
   (b) a description of the scope of the audit identifying the auditing standards in accordance with which the audit was conducted.

(3) The report must state clearly whether, in the auditor's opinion, the annual accounts—
   (a) give a true and fair view—
      (i) in the case of an individual balance sheet, of the state of affairs of the company as at the end of the financial year;
      (ii) in the case of an individual profit and loss account, of the profit or loss of the company for the financial year; and
      (iii) in the case of group accounts, of the state of affairs as at the end of the financial year and of the profit or loss for the financial year of the undertakings included in the consolidation as a whole, so far as concerns members of the company;
   (b) have been properly prepared in accordance with the relevant financial reporting framework; and
   (c) have been prepared in accordance with the requirements of this Act (and, where applicable, Article 4 of the IAS Regulation).

Expressions used in this subsection that are defined for the purposes of Part 15 (see section 474) have the same meaning as in that Part.

(4) The auditor's report—
   (a) must be either unqualified or qualified; and
   (b) must include a reference to any matters to which the auditor wishes to draw attention by way of emphasis without qualifying the report.

Crown copyright is reproduced with the permission of the Controller of Her Majesty's Stationery Office.

14.1.5 Signature of auditor's report

The auditor's report must, as previously required, state the name of the auditor and be signed and dated. However, where the auditor is a firm, the report must now be signed by the 'senior statutory auditor' in his own name, for and on behalf of the auditor. **(CA 2006 s. 504)**

Companies Act 2006 sections 503 and 504 (Signature of auditor's report – senior statutory auditor) are reproduced in full in **Table 14.2**.

Table 14.2   Signature of auditor's report CA 2006 ss. 503–504

503 Signature of auditor's report

(1) The auditor's report must state the name of the auditor and be signed and dated.

(2) Where the auditor is an individual, the report must be signed by him.

(3) Where the auditor is a firm, the report must be signed by the senior statutory auditor in his own name, for and on behalf of the auditor.

> **504 Senior statutory auditor**
>
> (1) The senior statutory auditor means the individual identified by the firm as senior statutory auditor in relation to the audit in accordance with—
>   (a) standards issued by the European Commission; or
>   (b) if there is no applicable standard so issued, any relevant guidance issued by—
>   (i) the Secretary of State; or
>   (ii) a body appointed by order of the Secretary of State.
>
> (2) The person identified as senior statutory auditor must be eligible for appointment as auditor of the company in question (see Chapter 2 of Part 42 of this Act).
>
> (3) The senior statutory auditor is not, by reason of being named or identified as senior statutory auditor or by reason of his having signed the auditor's report, subject to any civil liability to which he would not otherwise be subject.
>
> (4) An order appointing a body for the purpose of subsection (1)(b)(ii) is subject to negative resolution procedure.
>
> *Crown copyright is reproduced with the permission of the Controller of Her Majesty's Stationery Office.*

14.2 ISA (UK and Ireland) 700 The Auditor's Report on Financial Statements

Following the adoption of International Standards on Auditing (ISAs) in 2004, auditors' reports are required to follow ISA (UK and Ireland) 700 *The Auditor's Report on Financial Statements.*

ISA (UK and Ireland) 700 explains that '[the] purpose of [the ISA] is to establish standards and provide guidance on the form and content of the auditor's report issued as result of an audit performed by an independent auditor of financial statements of an entity'.

ISA (UK and Ireland) 700, although generally prescriptive as to the form and content of the auditors' report, does not preclude some flexibility when using the format and wording of the example reports prescribed by the Statement. The use of the term 'accounts', for example, in preference to 'financial statements' accords with the Companies Act 2006 and is essentially a question of personal choice, permissible provided the term is adequately defined (see example accounts in **Chapter 13** on the index page preceding **page 1**).

APB issues from time to time an APB Bulletin *Auditor's Reports on Financial Statements* providing illustrative examples of auditor's reports. (APB Bulletin 2006/6 *Auditor's Reports on Financial Statements in Great Britain and Northern Ireland* was issued in September 2006 superseding APB Bulletin 2005/4.)

It is anticipated that in spring of 2009 APB will issue a revised ISA (UK and Ireland) 700 and also a revision to APB Bulletin 2006/6 (updating the example APB auditor's reports to reflect compliance with the ISA). An international standard ISA 700 (Revised), issued by the IAASB in 2005, is also currently being redrafted as part of the IAASB 'Clarity Project' to clarify the objectives, requirements and presentation of international auditing standards generally.

ISA (UK and Ireland) 700 "The Auditor's Report on Financial Statements" will facilitate, but not mandate, a more concise auditor's report. This may be achieved by permitting the description of the scope of an audit and the auditor's reporting responsibilities to be made either:

- within the auditor's report (as presently); or
- by cross reference to the APB website (where a relevant statement of scope is maintained).

Chapter 14 Small company audit reports

ISA (UK and Ireland) 700 (Revised) will take effect for accounting periods ending on or after 5 April 2009.

In September 2008, APB issued as an interim measure APB Bulletin 2008/8 "Auditor's Reports for short accounting periods in compliance with the United Kingdom Companies Act 2006". The purpose of the Bulletin was to illustrate how the example auditor's reports set out in Appendix 1 to Bulletin 2006/6 could be amended to reflect the requirements of CA 2006 for accounting periods beginning on or after 6 April 2008 and ending before 5 April 2009 (that is, for 'short accounting periods').

14.3 Example Auditor's Report of a small company

Example 14.1 is extracted from APB Bulletin 2006/6 (September 2006) and illustrates an unmodified (that is, 'unqualified') auditor's report of a small company performed in accordance with International Standards on Auditing (UK and Ireland) issued by the APB. The example assumes:

- the company qualifies as a 'small company';
- the company does not prepare group accounts (financial statements);
- the company prepares a directors' report but no other 'surround information' (for example chairman's report, corporate governance statement or other financial commentary);
- the company adopts UK GAAP (that is, the accounts are Companies Act accounts and not IAS accounts);
- where the company adopts the FRSSE, the report includes the text indicated by grey tinting; and
- the auditor does not take advantage of ES–PASE (APB Ethical Standard – *Provisions Available for Small Entities* (April 2005)).

The APB Bulletin 2006/6 example illustrated in **Example 14.1** has been amended to reflect statutory references for Companies Act 2006 and also APB Bulletin 2008/8 on "Auditor's Reports for short accounting periods". The APB is proposing changes to the form and content of the auditor's report. Amendments made (by the author) to reflect Companies Act 2006 are presented in **bold text**.

Example 14.1

INDEPENDENT AUDITOR'S REPORT TO THE [MEMBERS] SHAREHOLDERS OF SMALL COMPANY LIMITED

We have audited the financial statements [*accounts*] of Small Company Limited for the year ended **30 April 2009**, which comprise the Profit and Loss Account, the Balance Sheet, [the Cash Flow Statement], the Statement of Total Recognised Gains and Losses and the related notes. These financial statements [*accounts*] have been prepared under the accounting policies set out therein [and the requirements of the Financial Reporting Standard for Smaller Entities (effective April 2008)].

This report is made solely to the company's members, as a body, in accordance with **Sections 495 and 496 of the Companies Act 2006**. *Our audit work has been undertaken so that we might state to the company's members those matters that we are required to state to them in an auditor's report and for no other purpose. To the fullest extent permitted by law, we do not accept or assume responsibility to anyone other than the company and the company's members as a body, for our audit work, for this report, or for the opinions we have formed.*

(see Authors' note) (3)

Respective responsibilities of directors and auditors
The directors' responsibilities for preparing the financial statements [*accounts*] in accordance with applicable law and United Kingdom Accounting Standards (United Kingdom Generally Accepted Accounting Practice) **and for being satisfied that the financial statements *[accounts]* give a true and fair view** are set out in the Statement of Directors' Responsibilities.

Our responsibility is to audit the financial statements [*accounts*] in accordance with relevant legal and regulatory requirements and International Standards on Auditing (UK and Ireland). **In forming our opinion we are also required to comply with the Auditing Practice Board's Ethical Standards.**

Example Auditor's Report of a small company

We report to you our opinion as to whether the financial statements [*accounts*] have been properly prepared in accordance with United Kingdom Generally Accepted Accounting Practice, **have been prepared in accordance with the Companies Act 2006, and give a true and fair view**. We also report to you whether in our opinion the information given in the Directors' Report is consistent with the financial statements [*accounts*].

In addition we report to you if, in our opinion, the company has not kept **adequate** accounting records, if we have not received all the information and explanations we require for our audit, or if **certain disclosures of directors' remuneration specified by law are not made**.

We read the Directors' Report and consider the implications for our report if we become aware of any apparent misstatements **or material inconsistencies with the audited financial statements** [*accounts*]. *Our responsibilities do not extend to any other information.*

Basis of audit opinion
We conducted our audit in accordance with International Standards on Auditing (UK and Ireland) issued by the Auditing Practices Board. An audit includes examination, on a test basis, of evidence relevant to the amounts and disclosures in the financial statements [*accounts*]. It also includes an assessment of the significant estimates and judgements made by the directors in the preparation of the financial statements [*accounts*], and of whether the accounting policies are appropriate to the company's circumstances, consistently applied and adequately disclosed.

We planned and performed our audit so as to obtain all the information and explanations which we considered necessary in order to provide us with sufficient evidence to give reasonable assurance that the financial statements [*accounts*] are free from material misstatement, whether caused by fraud or other irregularity or error. In forming our opinion we also evaluated the overall adequacy of the presentation of information in the financial statements [*accounts*].

Opinion
In our opinion:

- the financial statements [*accounts*] give a true and fair view, in accordance with United Kingdom Generally Accepted Accounting Practice applicable to Smaller Entities, of the state of the company's affairs as at [30 April 2009] and of its profit [*loss*] for the year then ended;
- **the financial statements *[accounts]* have been properly prepared in accordance with United Kingdom Generally Accepted Accounting Practice**;
- the financial statements [*accounts*] have been prepared in accordance with the **Companies Act 2006**; and
- the information given in the Directors' Report is consistent with the financial statements [*accounts*].

Rupert Tickett

Rupert Tickett (Senior Statutory Auditor)
for and on behalf of
TRUE & FAIRVIEW
[Chartered Accountants and] Statutory Auditors

17 Queens Place,
LONDON EC4P 3BC   3 October 2009

Author's notes and commentary to **Example 14.1**

(1) **Report to the shareholders** – *The statutory auditors' report is made to the members of the company, who are normally the shareholders (CA 2006 s. 495). No statutory report is required where a small company is otherwise entitled to audit exemption (CA 2006 section 477). A non-statutory report for an audit exempt company would be addressed to the directors of the company, in accordance with whose instructions the audit is conducted (See* **Example 14.1** *above).*

(2) **Website publication of accounts** – *Auditors' reports of entities that do not publish their financial statements on a web site or publish them using 'PDF' format may continue to refer to the financial statements by reference to page numbers. The Introductory paragraphs (in a statutory report) would be on the following lines:*

Chapter 14 Small company audit reports

> 'We have audited the financial statements [accounts] of Small Company Limited for the year ended 30 April 2009 set out on pages [4 to 13]. These financial statements [accounts] have been prepared under the accounting policies set out therein [and the requirements of the Financial Reporting Standard for Smaller Entities (effective April 2008)].
>
> This report is made solely to the company's members. . . . . .
>
> **Respective responsibilities of directors and auditors**
> The directors' responsibilities for preparing the financial statements [accounts] in accordance with applicable law and United Kingdom Accounting Standards (United Kingdom Generally Accepted Accounting Practice) **and for being satisfied that the financial statements [accounts] give a true and fair view** are set out in the Statement of Directors' Responsibilities on page [1].
>
> Our responsibility is to . . . . . .'

APB Bulletin 2001/1 *The electronic publication of auditors' reports* and ISA (UK and Ireland) 720 *Other information in documents containing audited financial statements* (Appendix 1) deal with the publication of auditors' reports electronically for example, on a website or otherwise over the internet.

(3) **Duty of care to third parties** – the ICAEW recommends that auditors include additional wording in audit reports in order to clarify auditors' responsibilities to third parties – that is, other than to the shareholders/members (or the directors, as the case may be) as a body. (*Audit 1/03 – The Audit Report and The Auditors' Duty of Care to Third Parties.*) (January 2003 as updated 2008).

(4) **Cash flows** – Where a cash flow statement under FRS 1 (or the FRSSE) is not required, and not presented, in the accounts, the auditors' report is only required to refer explicitly to 'the state of affairs' and 'profit or loss', and no reference is required to 'cash flows'.

(5) **Signature and dating of auditors' report** – CA 2006 s. 414.

(6) **Reappointment of auditors** – Auditors of a private company are reappointed under the Companies Act 2006 s. 485.

Example 14.2

REAPPOINTMENT OF AUDITORS NARRATIVE HEADING (DIRECTORS' REPORT)

'Auditors
The auditors, True & Fairview, will be proposed for reappointment in accordance with section 485 of the Companies Act 2006.'

or:

'The auditors, True & Fairview, are deemed to be reappointed in accordance with section 487 of the Companies Act 2006'.

14.4 Special Auditors' Report – abbreviated accounts

Two examples below illustrate statutory reports on abbreviated accounts relating to a small company that has not taken advantage of audit exemption. The reports below are not appropriate (or required) if the company is exempt from audit (CA 2006 s. 477 or s. 480).

The example special auditors' reports on abbreviated accounts comprise:

Special auditors' report – abbreviated accounts

- **(Example 14.3)** – small company abbreviated accounts (advantage not taken (or available) of audit exemption);
- **(Example 14.4)** – small company abbreviated accounts (qualified full audit opinion – advantage not taken (or available) of audit exemption).

The example auditors' or accountants' reports illustrated within the abbreviated accounts assume that the accounts are not published on a website.

APB Bulletin 2008/4 (April 2008) 'The *special auditor's report on abbreviated accounts in the United Kingdom'* provides guidance for auditors regarding the filing obligations of small (and medium-sized) companies under the Companies Act 2006, and in particular, provides guidance concerning the "Special Auditor's Report on Abbreviated Accounts" (CA 2006 s, 449). **Examples 14.3** and **14.4** reflect the guidance in APB Bulletin 2008/4.

Example 14.3 Page [1]

INDEPENDENT AUDITORS' REPORT TO SMALL COMPANY LIMITED UNDER SECTION 449 OF THE COMPANIES ACT 2006

We have examined the abbreviated accounts set out on pages [2 to 5], together with the [full statutory] accounts of the company for the year ended 30 April 2009 prepared under section 396 of the Companies Act 2006.

> This report is made solely to the company, in accordance with section 449 of the Companies Act 2006. Our work has been undertaken so that we might state to the company those matters we are required to state to it in a special auditors' report and for no other purpose. To the fullest extent permitted by law, we do not accept or assume responsibility to anyone other than the company, for our work, for this report, or for the opinions we have formed.

Respective responsibilities of directors and auditors
The directors are responsible for preparing the abbreviated accounts **in accordance with section 444 of the Companies Act 2006.** It is our responsibility to form an independent opinion as to whether the company is entitled to deliver abbreviated accounts to the Registrar of Companies and whether the abbreviated accounts have been properly prepared in accordance with the regulations made under that section and to report our opinion to you.

We conducted our work in accordance with Bulletin 2008/4 [*'The special auditor's report on abbreviated accounts in the United Kingdom'*] issued by the Auditing Practices Board. In accordance with that Bulletin we have carried out the procedures we consider necessary to confirm, by reference to the financial statements [full statutory accounts], that the company is entitled to deliver abbreviated accounts and that the abbreviated accounts to be delivered are properly prepared. *The scope of our work for the purpose of this report did not include examining or dealing with events after the date of our report on the full statutory accounts.*

Opinion
In our opinion the company is entitled to deliver abbreviated accounts prepared in accordance with section 444(3) of the Companies Act 2006 and the abbreviated accounts [on pages 2 to 5] have been properly prepared in accordance with the regulations made under that section.

Rupert Tickett. s. 503 CA 2006

Rupert Tickett (Senior Statutory Auditor)
for and on behalf of
TRUE & FAIRVIEW
[Chartered Accountants and] Statutory Auditors

17 Queens Place,
LONDON EC4P 3BC 3 October 2009

Chapter 14 Small company audit reports

Audit-exempt accounts – the above report is not required if the company is exempt from audit (CA 2006 ss. 477 or 480).

Duty of care to third parties – *additional wording as recommended by ICAEW (Audit 1/03 – The Audit Report and The Auditors' Duty of Care to Third Parties) (January 2003).*

Events after the date of the report – Text in *italics* in the penultimate paragraph above is only appropriate where the special report is dated **after** the signing of the auditor's report on the full statutory accounts.

Example 14.4 Page [1]

INDEPENDENT AUDITORS' REPORT TO SMALL COMPANY LIMITED UNDER SECTION 449 OF THE COMPANIES ACT 2006 [*QUALIFIED FULL AUDIT OPINION*]

We have examined the abbreviated accounts set out on pages [2 to 5], together with the [full statutory] accounts of the company for the year ended 30 April 2009 prepared under section 396 of the Companies Act 2006.

> This report is made solely to the company, in accordance with section 449 of the Companies Act 2006. Our work has been undertaken so that we might state to the company those matters we are required to state to it in a special auditors' report and for no other purpose. To the fullest extent permitted by law, we do not accept or assume responsibility to anyone other than the company, for our work, for this report, or for the opinions we have formed.

Respective responsibilities of directors and auditors
The directors are responsible for preparing the abbreviated accounts **in accordance with section 444 of the Companies Act 2006.** It is our responsibility to form an independent opinion as to whether the company is entitled to deliver abbreviated accounts to the Registrar of Companies and whether the abbreviated accounts have been properly prepared in accordance with the regulations made under that section and to report our opinion to you.

We conducted our work in accordance with Bulletin 2008/4 ['*The special auditor's report on abbreviated accounts in the United Kingdom*'] issued by the Auditing Practices Board. In accordance with that Bulletin we have carried out the procedures we consider necessary to confirm, by reference to the financial statements [full statutory accounts], that the company is entitled to deliver abbreviated accounts and that the abbreviated accounts to be delivered are properly prepared. *The scope of our work for the purpose of this report did not include examining or dealing with events after the date of our report on the full statutory accounts.*

Opinion
In our opinion the company is entitled to deliver abbreviated accounts prepared in accordance with section 444(3) of the Companies Act 2006, and the abbreviated accounts [on pages 2 to 5] have been properly prepared in accordance with the regulations made under that section.

Other information
On 3 October 2009 we reported as auditors to the shareholders of the company on the full statutory accounts prepared under section 396 of the Companies Act 2006 and our audit report *[under section 495 of the Companies Act 2006]* was as follows [/included the following statement/paragraph]:

[Qualified audit report under section 495 Companies Act 2006 or Statements under section 498(2) [Inadequate accounting records] or section 498(3) [Failure to obtain necessary information] or Explanatory comment contained in Unqualified Audit Report under section 495 Companies Act 2006 concerning fundamental uncertainty to be set out in full]:

Rupert Tickett.
....
Rupert Tickett (Senior Statutory Auditor)
for and on behallf of
TRUE & FAIRVIEW
[Chartered Accountants and] Statutory Auditors

17 Queens Place,
LONDON EC4P 3BC   3 October 2009

s. 503 CA 2006

> Example of other information: explanatory paragraph
> *Going concern.* In forming our opinion, we have considered the adequacy of disclosures made in note 1 of the accounts concerning the uncertainty as to the continuation and renewal of the company's bank overdraft facility. In view of the significance of this uncertainty we consider that it should be drawn to your attention, but our opinion is not qualified in this respect.

Qualified full audit opinion – The special auditors' report (where necessary) in connection with abbreviated accounts is no longer required to reproduce the full text of the auditors' report on the annual accounts, except (as illustrated above) in the circumstances of a qualification or explanatory paragraph regarding a fundamental uncertainty. This is explained further in **8.9**.

Other comments on above example – See comments in **Example 14.3**

14.5 Duty of care to third parties

Example 14.1 reproduces an example auditors' report from APB Bulletin 2006/6 *Auditor's Reports on Financial Statements in Great Britain and Northern Ireland*, supplemented by guidance of January 2003 from the ICAEW concerning the auditors' duty of care to third parties. The ICAEW recommends that additional wording is included in audit reports (on full statutory accounts under s. 495 Companies Act 2006), as a second introductory paragraph, in order to clarify auditors' responsibilities to third parties – that is, other than to the members (normally, the shareholders) as a body. The guidance is contained in Technical Release *Audit 1/03 – The Audit Report and the Auditors' Duty of Care to Third Parties.*

The special auditors' report on abbreviated accounts should also include additional wording based on Technical Release *Audit 1/03* concerning the auditors' duty of care to third parties. In addition, auditors may wish to ensure that the accounts are clearly distinguished as 'abbreviated accounts' (rather than 'full statutory accounts').

14.6 Non-statutory audit and assurance reports

Following the increase in audit exemption threshold many companies with a turnover below £6.5 million, although no longer required to have a statutory audit, may nevertheless choose to have one carried out.

Where a company is entitled to audit exemption, the directors may wish to have some form of independent review of the accounts, being either:

- *an audit* – a non-statutory or 'contractual' audit (voluntarily obtained on terms decided by the directors), or
- *a compilation report* – an accountants' report on the proper compilation of the accounts.

Reports on accounts prepared for unaudited companies are discussed below in **14.7** (and illustrated in **Example 14.6**).

The example accountants' report contained in the Technical Release issued in April 2004 by the Audit and Assurance Faculty of the Institute of Chartered Accountants in England and Wales (Audit 02/04 *Chartered Accountants' Reports on Compilation of Financial Statements of Incorporated Entities*) is reproduced in **Example 14.5**. The special auditors' report under s. 449 (see **Chapter 8** at **8.9**) is reflected within **Examples 14.3** and **14.4**, but is only required in the event of audited accounts.

In August 2006, the Audit and Assurance Faculty of the Institute of Chartered Accountants in England and Wales proposed a further alternative form of independent review of the accounts for audit exempt companies, being:

Chapter 14 Small company audit reports

- *a independent assurance report* – an accountants' report covering both the proper compilation of the accounts and the directors' 'true and fair view' assertion.

This initiative is contained in an Interim Technical Release (Audit and Assurance Faculty) AAF 03/06 *The ICAEW Assurance Service on Unaudited Financial Statements*. The Technical Release contains a number of examples illustrating report situations, depending on the parties to the engagement terms. The objectives of the independent assurance report would be to provide comfort to the directors and to enhance the credibility of the accounts with third parties, including members and the Registrar of Companies.

Example 14.5 below reproduces one of the example Independent Assurance Reports from AAF 03/06. It is the intention of the ICAEW to review the use and effectiveness of the initiative in due course and in the light of the continuing development by IAASB of an international standard on review and compilation engagements. Meanwhile the use of the Independent Assurance Report represents current 'best practice' guidance.

Example 14.5 *Example Independent Assurance Report*
ICAEW Interim Technical Release (Audit and Assurance Faculty) –
AAF 03/06 (August 2006)
Example Reports Appendix E (E.a.i – Reporting to Directors)

CHARTERED ACCOUNTANTS' INDEPENDENT ASSURANCE REPORT ON THE UNAUDITED FINANCIAL STATEMENTS OF [NAME OF ENTITY]

TO THE BOARD OF DIRECTORS OF [NAME OF ENTITY] ('THE COMPANY')

We have performed certain procedures in respect of the Company's unaudited financial statements for the year [/period] ended [date] as set out on pages [ ] to [ ], made enquiries of the Company's directors and assessed accounting policies adopted by the directors, in order to gather sufficient evidence for our conclusion in this report.

This report is made solely to the Company's directors, as a body, in accordance with the terms of our engagement letter dated [date]. It has been released to the directors on the basis that this report shall not be copied, referred to or disclosed in whole (save for the directors' own internal purposes or as may be required by law or by a competent regulator) or in part, without our prior written consent. Our work has been undertaken so that we might state to the directors those matters that we have agreed to state to them in this report and for no other purpose. To the fullest extent permitted by law, we do not accept or assume responsibility to anyone other than the Company and the Company's directors, as a body for our work, for this report or for the conclusions we have formed.

Respective responsibilities

You have confirmed that you have met your duty as set out in the directors' statement on page [ ]. You consider that the company is exempt from the statutory requirement for an audit for the year [/period]. Our responsibility is to form and express an independent conclusion, based on the work carried out, to you on the financial statements.

Scope

We conducted our engagement in accordance with the Institute of Chartered Accountants in England and Wales Interim Technical Release AAF 03/06. Our work was based primarily upon enquiry, analytical procedures and assessing accounting policies in accordance with Generally Accepted Accounting Practice in the UK [/the Financial Reporting Standard for Smaller Entities]. If we considered it to be necessary, we also performed limited examination of evidence relevant to certain balances and disclosures in the financial statements where we became aware of matters that might indicate a risk of material misstatement in the financial statements.

Conclusion

Based on our work, nothing has come to our attention to refute the directors' confirmation that in accordance with the [Companies Act 2006] the financial statements give a true and fair view of the state of the Companies affairs as at [date] and of its profit [/loss] for the year [/period] then ended and have been properly prepared in accordance with Generally Accepted Accounting Practice in the UK [/the Financial Reporting Standard for Smaller Entities].

....

Name of firm
Chartered Accountants [**NOT** *'Statutory Auditors'*]

[Location]

[Date]

14.7 Reports on accounts prepared for unaudited companies

Notwithstanding that a company is able to take advantage of audit exemption in preparing its annual accounts, the company may nevertheless wish to have the comfort of some form of report from independent (but non-statutory) reporting accountants. Any report attached to the accounts of the company where no statutory report is required should be addressed to the directors, since the accountants are acting as agents of the directors.

Example 14.6 provides an example of a non-statutory (or contractual) report.

Where accounts are compiled by a professional accountant and an accountants' report is prepared on the lines of **Example 14.6**, it is important that the terms of engagement, and the mutual responsibilities for the accounts, are agreed by the directors and reporting accountants.

A Technical Release, issued by the Audit and Assurance Faculty of the Institute of Chartered Accountants in England and Wales in April 2004 (Audit 02/04 *Chartered Accountants' Reports on Compilation of Financial Statements of Incorporated Entities*) gives general guidance on the form and content of reports where accountants 'compile' (being the generally acknowledged term for 'prepare') accounts on behalf of client companies.

Technical Release Audit 02/04 is written with particular emphasis on financial statements prepared in accordance with the Companies Act 1985 and remains relevant for Companies Act 2006.

Example 14.6 reproduces the example report set out in Audit 02/04 *Chartered Accountants' Reports on Compilation of Financial Statements of Incorporated Entities*. The example is essentially appropriate in circumstances where the directors wish the accountants to assist them in meeting the directors' statutory obligation under the Companies Act, to prepare annual accounts showing a true and fair view.

Where the accounts compiled by an accountant constitute abbreviated accounts, the form of report in **Example 14.6** may also be used to support the abbreviated accounts.

Reports on accounts prepared for unaudited companies discussed in this section are prepared solely on the basis of terms of engagement agreed between the accountant and the client company. It is important to remember that, for a company which is audit-exempt, no auditors' report is statutorily required, and neither is there a requirement for any form of statutory accountants' report (other than for charitable companies). Technical Release Audit 02/04 stresses the importance of agreeing terms of engagement and provides example terms.

Example 14.6   Example Accountants' Report
ICAEW Technical Release (Audit and Assurance Faculty) – Audit 02/04
Example Reports Appendix B

CHARTERED ACCOUNTANTS'/ACCOUNTANTS' REPORT TO THE BOARD OF DIRECTORS ON THE UNAUDITED ACCOUNTS OF XYZ LIMITED

In accordance with the engagement letter dated [xyz], and in order to assist you to fulfil your duties under the Companies Act **[2006]**, we have compiled the financial statements of the company which comprise [state the primary financial statements such as the Profit and Loss Account, the Balance Sheet, the Cash Flow Statement, the Statement of Total Recognised Gains and Losses] and the related notes from the accounting records and information and explanations you have given to us.

This report is made solely to the Company's Board of Directors, as a body, in accordance with the terms of our engagement. Our work has been undertaken so that we might compile the financial statements that we have been engaged to compile, report to the Company's Board of Directors that we have done so, and state those matters that we have agreed to state to them in this report and for no other purpose. To the fullest extent permitted by law, we do not accept or assume responsibility to anyone other than the Company and the Company's Board of Directors, as a body, for our work or for this report

We have carried out this engagement in accordance with technical guidance issued by the Institute of Chartered Accountants in England and Wales and have complied with the ethical guidance laid down by the Institute relating to members undertaking the compilation of financial statements.

You have acknowledged on the balance sheet as at . . . your duty to ensure that the company has kept **[adequate]** accounting records and to prepare financial statements that give a true and fair view under the Companies Act **[2006]**. You consider that the company is exempt from the statutory requirement for an audit for the year.

We have not been instructed to carry out an audit of the financial statements. For this reason, we have not verified the accuracy or completeness of the accounting records or information and explanations you have given to us and we do not, therefore, express any opinion on the financial statements.

Explanatory paragraph – departure from applicable accounting standards

We draw your attention to note x in the financial statements which discloses and explains a departure from applicable accounting standards. The company has not depreciated its goodwill held in the financial statements in the year and this is a departure from the Financial Reporting Standard for Smaller Entities **(effective [April 2008])** *and from the Companies Act* **[2006]**.

PQR LLP

Chartered Accountants [NOT 'Statutory Auditors']

[Address]

[Date]

AUTHOR'S NOTES

1   The above example is appropriate in circumstances where accountants assist in the compilation of accounts for an audit-exempt company.

2   Explanatory paragraph – departure from applicable accounting standards.

Accounts for the purposes of the Companies Act *[2006] are required to give a 'true and fair view'. The accountants may wish to highlight appropriate disclosures made in the financial statements (for example, covering departures from accounting standards) in an explanatory paragraph, as illustrated above.*

3   References in the above example to 'CA 2006' or the FRSSE have been amended by the author and identified by **bold text**.

Appendices

Appendix A Company accounts sections

Companies Act 2006

This appendix sets out relevant company accounts sections under the Companies Act 2006 within:

- CA 2006 Part 15 'Accounts and reports';
- SI 2008 No. 409 *The Small Companies and Groups (Accounts and Directors' Report) Regulations 2008;* and
- CA 2006 Part 16 'Audit'.

> Section, paragraph or schedule references of particular relevance to small companies and the small companies regime are indicted by boxing.

CA 2006: *www.opsi.gov.uk/acts/acts2006/ukpga_20060046_en_1*

SI 2008 No. 409: *www.opsi.gov.uk/si/si2008/uksi_20080409_en_1*

Companies Act 2006 Part 15 – Accounts and Reports

CA 2006 Section

INTRODUCTION

General

380	Scheme of this Part
Companies subject to the small companies regime	
381	Companies subject to the small companies regime
382	Companies qualifying as small: general
383	Companies qualifying as small: parent companies
384	Companies excluded from the small companies regime

Quoted and unquoted companies

385	Quoted and unquoted companies

ACCOUNTING RECORDS

386   Duty to keep accounting records
387   Duty to keep accounting records: offence
388   Where and for how long records to be kept
389   Where and for how long records to be kept: offences

A COMPANY'S FINANCIAL YEAR

390	A company's financial year
391	Accounting reference periods and accounting reference date
392	Alteration of accounting reference date

Appendix A Company accounts sections

ANNUAL ACCOUNTS

General
393 Accounts to give true and fair view

Individual accounts
394 Duty to prepare individual accounts
395 Individual accounts: applicable accounting framework
396 Companies Act individual accounts
397 IAS individual accounts

Group accounts: small companies
398 Option to prepare group accounts

Group accounts: other companies
399 Duty to prepare group accounts
400 Exemption for company included in EEA group accounts of larger group
401 Exemption for company included in non-EEA group accounts of larger group
402 Exemption if no subsidiary undertakings need be included in the Consolidation

Group accounts: general
403 Group accounts: applicable accounting framework
404 Companies Act group accounts
405 Companies Act group accounts: subsidiary undertakings included in the consolidation
406 IAS group accounts
407 Consistency of financial reporting within group
408 Individual profit and loss account where group accounts prepared

Information to be given in notes to the accounts
409 Information about related undertakings
410 Information about related undertakings: alternative compliance
410A Information about off-balance sheet arrangements *(inserted by SI 2008 No. 393)*
411 Information about employee numbers and costs
412 Information about directors' benefits: remuneration
413 Information about directors' benefits: advances, credit and guarantees

Approval and signing of accounts
414 Approval and signing of accounts

DIRECTORS' REPORT

Directors' report
415 Duty to prepare directors' report
415A Directors' report: small companies exemption *(inserted by SI 2008 No. 393)*
416 Contents of directors' report: general

417 Contents of directors' report: business review

418 Contents of directors' report: statement as to disclosure to auditors
419 Approval and signing of directors' report

QUOTED COMPANIES: DIRECTORS' REMUNERATION REPORT

420 Duty to prepare directors' remuneration report
421 Contents of directors' remuneration report
422 Approval and signing of directors' remuneration report

PUBLICATION OF ACCOUNTS AND REPORTS

Duty to circulate copies of accounts and reports
423 Duty to circulate copies of annual accounts and reports
424 Time allowed for sending out copies of accounts and reports
425 Default in sending out copies of accounts and reports: offences

Option to provide summary financial statement
426 Option to provide summary financial statement
427 Form and contents of summary financial statement: unquoted companies

428 Form and contents of summary financial statement: quoted companies

429 Summary financial statements: offences

Quoted companies: requirements as to website publication
430 Quoted companies: annual accounts and reports to be made available on website

Right of member or debenture holder to demand copies of accounts and reports
431 Right of member or debenture holder to copies of accounts and reports: unquoted companies

432 Right of member or debenture holder to copies of accounts and reports: quoted companies

Requirements in connection with publication of accounts and reports
433 Name of signatory to be stated in published copies of accounts and reports
434 Requirements in connection with publication of statutory accounts
435 Requirements in connection with publication of non-statutory accounts
436 Meaning of 'publication' in relation to accounts and reports

PUBLIC COMPANIES: LAYING OF ACCOUNTS AND REPORTS BEFORE GENERAL MEETING

437 Public companies: laying of accounts and reports before general meeting
438 Public companies: offence of failure to lay accounts and reports

QUOTED COMPANIES: MEMBERS' APPROVAL OF DIRECTORS' REMUNERATION REPORT

439 Quoted companies: members' approval of directors' remuneration report
440 Quoted companies: offences in connection with procedure for approval

FILING OF ACCOUNTS AND REPORTS

Duty to file accounts and reports
441 Duty to file accounts and reports with the registrar
442 Period allowed for filing accounts
443 Calculation of period allowed

Appendix A Company accounts sections

Filing obligations of different descriptions of company
444   Filing obligations of companies subject to small companies regime
444A Filing obligations of companies entitled to small companies exemption in relation to directors' report *(inserted by SI 2008 No. 393)*

445   Filing obligations of medium-sized companies
446   Filing obligations of unquoted companies
447   Filing obligations of quoted companies
448   Unlimited companies exempt from obligation to file accounts

Requirements where abbreviated accounts delivered
449   Special auditor's report where abbreviated accounts delivered
450   Approval and signing of abbreviated accounts

Failure to file accounts and reports
451   Default in filing accounts and reports: offences
452   Default in filing accounts and reports: court order
453   Civil penalty for failure to file accounts and reports

REVISION OF DEFECTIVE ACCOUNTS AND REPORTS

Voluntary revision
454   Voluntary revision of accounts etc.

Secretary of State's notice
455   Secretary of State's notice in respect of accounts or reports

Application to court
456   Application to court in respect of defective accounts or reports
457   Other persons authorised to apply to the court
458   Disclosure of information by tax authorities

Power of authorised person to require documents etc.
459   Power of authorised person to require documents, information and explanations
460   Restrictions on disclosure of information obtained under compulsory powers
461   Permitted disclosure of information obtained under compulsory powers
462   Power to amend categories of permitted disclosure

SUPPLEMENTARY PROVISIONS

Liability for false or misleading statements in reports
463   Liability for false or misleading statements in reports

Accounting and reporting standards
464   Accounting standards

Companies qualifying as medium-sized
465   Companies qualifying as medium-sized: general
466   Companies qualifying as medium-sized: parent companies
467   Companies excluded from being treated as medium-sized

General power to make further provision about accounts and reports
468   General power to make further provision about accounts and reports

The Small Companies and Groups (Accounts and Directors' Report) Regulations 2008

	Other supplementary provisions
469	Preparation and filing of accounts in euros

470	Power to apply provisions to banking partnerships
471	Meaning of 'annual accounts' and related expressions

472	Notes to the accounts
473	Parliamentary procedure for certain regulations under this Part
474	Minor definitions

SI 2008 No. 409 The Small Companies and Groups (Accounts and Directors' Report) Regulations 2008

Part 1 Introduction

Part 2 Form and content of individual accounts

Part 3 Directors' report

Part 4 Form and content of group accounts

Part 5 Interpretation

Schedule 1 Companies Act individual accounts

- *general rules and formats*
- *accounting principles and rules*
- *notes to the accounts*

Schedule 2 Information about related undertakings where company not preparing group accounts (Companies Act or IAS individual accounts)

- *required disclosures*
- *interpretation of references to 'beneficial interest'*

Schedule 3 Information about directors' benefits: remuneration (Companies Act or IAS accounts)

- *information required to be disclosed*
- *supplementary provisions*

Schedule 4 Companies Act abbreviated accounts for delivery to registrar of companies

- *required balance sheet formats*
- *notes to the accounts*

Schedule 5 Matters to be dealt with in directors' report

Schedule 6 Group accounts

- form and content of Companies Act group accounts
- information about related undertakings where company preparing group accounts (Companies Act or IAS group accounts)

Schedule 7 Interpretation of term 'provisions'

Schedule 8 General interpretation

Appendix A Company accounts sections

Companies Act 2006 Part 16 – Audit

REQUIREMENT FOR AUDITED ACCOUNTS

Requirement for audited accounts
475   Requirement for audited accounts
476   Right of members to require audit

Exemption from audit: small companies
477   Small companies: conditions for exemption from audit
478   Companies excluded from small companies exemption
479   Availability of small companies exemption in case of group company

Exemption from audit: dormant companies
480   Dormant companies: conditions for exemption from audit
481   Companies excluded from dormant companies exemption

Companies subject to public sector audit
482   Non-profit-making companies subject to public sector audit
483   Scottish public sector companies: audit by Auditor General for Scotland

General power of amendment by regulations
484   General power of amendment by regulations

APPOINTMENT OF AUDITORS

Private companies
485   Appointment of auditors of private company: general
486   Appointment of auditors of private company: default power of Secretary of State
487   Term of office of auditors of private company
488   Prevention by members of deemed re-appointment of auditor

Public companies
489   Appointment of auditors of public company: general
490   Appointment of auditors of public company: default power of Secretary of State
491   Term of office of auditors of public company

General provisions
492   Fixing of auditor's remuneration
493   Disclosure of terms of audit appointment
494   Disclosure of services provided by auditor or associates and related remuneration

FUNCTIONS OF AUDITOR

Auditor's report
495   Auditor's report on company's annual accounts
496   Auditor's report on directors' report

497   Auditor's report on auditable part of directors' remuneration report

Duties and rights of auditors
498   Duties of auditor
499   Auditor's general right to information
500   Auditor's right to information from overseas subsidiaries
501   Auditor's rights to information: offences
502   Auditor's rights in relation to resolutions and meetings

Signature of auditor's report
503   Signature of auditor's report
504   Senior statutory auditor
505   Names to be stated in published copies of auditor's report
506   Circumstances in which names may be omitted

Offences in connection with auditor's report
507   Offences in connection with auditor's report
508   Guidance for regulatory and prosecuting authorities: England, Wales and Northern Ireland
509   Guidance for regulatory authorities: Scotland

REMOVAL, RESIGNATION, ETC OF AUDITORS

Removal of auditor
510   Resolution removing auditor from office
511   Special notice required for resolution removing auditor from office
512   Notice to registrar of resolution removing auditor from office
513   Rights of auditor who has been removed from office

Failure to re-appoint auditor
514   Failure to re-appoint auditor: special procedure required for written resolution
515   Failure to re-appoint auditor: special notice required for resolution at general Meeting

Resignation of auditor
516   Resignation of auditor
517   Notice to registrar of resignation of auditor
518   Rights of resigning auditor

Statement by auditor on ceasing to hold office
519   Statement by auditor to be deposited with company
520   Company's duties in relation to statement
521   Copy of statement to be sent to registrar
522   Duty of auditor to notify appropriate audit authority
523   Duty of company to notify appropriate audit authority
524   Information to be given to accounting authorities
525   Meaning of 'appropriate audit authority' and 'major audit'

Supplementary
526   Effect of casual vacancies

Appendix A Company accounts sections

QUOTED COMPANIES: RIGHT OF MEMBERS TO RAISE AUDIT CONCERNS AT ACCOUNTS MEETING

527 Members' power to require website publication of audit concerns
528 Requirements as to website availability
529 Website publication: company's supplementary duties
530 Website publication: offences
531 Meaning of 'quoted company'

AUDITORS' LIABILITY

Voidness of provisions protecting auditors from liability
532 Voidness of provisions protecting auditors from liability

Indemnity for costs of defending proceedings
533 Indemnity for costs of successfully defending proceedings

Liability limitation agreements
534 Liability limitation agreements
535 Terms of liability limitation agreement
536 Authorisation of agreement by members of the company
537 Effect of liability limitation agreement
538 Disclosure of agreement by company

SUPPLEMENTARY PROVISIONS
539 Minor definitions

© *Crown copyright is reproduced with the permission of the Controller of Her Majesty's Stationery Office.*

Appendix B Companies Act 2006 Part 15 – Accounts and reports (Sections 380–474)

This appendix reproduces Part 15 of the Companies Act 2006 (Accounts and reports) – sections 380 to 474.

The text of the legislation has been reproduced in full, enhanced or amended only as follows:

> Text boxed: of particular interest to small companies (other than of general application).

Text in **bold/italics**: CA 2006 as amended by SI 2008 No. 393 *The Companies Act 2006 (Amendment) (Accounts and Reports) Regulations 2008*.

Text in *italics (sections 444–449)*: CA 2006 as adapted transitionally by SI 2007 No. 3495 The Companies Act 2006 (Commencement No. 5, Transitional Provisions and Savings) Order. Transitional adaptations to sections 446 to 449 will be revoked (repealed) on 1 October 2009 by SI 2008 No.2860 article 6(1)(d) – such revoked adaptations are indicated within sections 446 and 447.

Text highlighted in grey tinting: Not applicable to Small companies.

Material specific to medium-sized companies is contained throughout Part 15 (including section 445 (abbreviated accounts and filing obligations) and sections 465–467 (qualifying criteria of medium sized companies) together with SI 2008 No. 410 *'The Large and Medium-sized Companies and Groups (Accounts and Reports) Regulations 2008'*.

COMPANIES ACT 2006 PART 15 ACCOUNTS AND REPORTS REPRODUCED

PART 15

ACCOUNTS AND REPORTS

CHAPTER 1

INTRODUCTION

General

380 Scheme of this Part

(1) The requirements of this Part as to accounts and reports apply in relation to each financial year of a company.

(2) In certain respects different provisions apply to different kinds of company.

(3) The main distinctions for this purpose are:
  (a) between companies subject to the small companies regime (see section 381) and companies that are not subject to that regime; and
  (b) between quoted companies (see section 385) and companies that are not quoted.

Appendix B Companies Act 2006

(4) In this Part, where provisions do not apply to all kinds of company:
  (a) provisions applying to companies subject to the small companies regime appear before the provisions applying to other companies;
  (b) provisions applying to private companies appear before the provisions applying to public companies; and
  (c) provisions applying to quoted companies appear after the provisions applying to other companies.

Companies subject to the small companies regime

381 Companies subject to the small companies regime

The small companies regime *[..........]* applies to a company for a financial year in relation to which the company:

(a) qualifies as small (see sections 382 and 383); and
(b) is not excluded from the regime (see section 384).

382 Companies qualifying as small: general

(1) A company qualifies as small in relation to its first financial year if the qualifying conditions are met in that year.

(2) A company qualifies as small in relation to a subsequent financial year:
  (a) if the qualifying conditions are met in that year and the preceding financial year;
  (b) if the qualifying conditions are met in that year and the company qualified as small in relation to the preceding financial year; and
  (c) if the qualifying conditions were met in the preceding financial year and the company qualified as small in relation to that year.

(3) The qualifying conditions are met by a company in a year in which it satisfies two or more of the following requirements:

  1. Turnover   Not more than **£6.5 million**
  2. Balance sheet total Not more than **£3.26 million**
  3. Number of employees Not more than 50

(4) For a period that is a company's financial year but not in fact a year the maximum figures for turnover must be proportionately adjusted.

(5) The balance sheet total means the aggregate of the amounts shown as assets in the company's balance sheet.

(6) The number of employees means the average number of persons employed by the company in the year, determined as follows:
  (a) find for each month in the financial year the number of persons employed under contracts of service by the company in that month (whether throughout the month or not);
  (b) add together the monthly totals; and
  (c) divide by the number of months in the financial year.

(7) This section is subject to section 383 (companies qualifying as small: parent companies).

383 Companies qualifying as small: parent companies

(1) A parent company qualifies as a small company in relation to a financial year only if the group headed by it qualifies as a small group.

(2) A group qualifies as small in relation to the parent company's first financial year if the qualifying conditions are met in that year.

(3) A group qualifies as small in relation to a subsequent financial year of the parent company:

(a) if the qualifying conditions are met in that year and the preceding financial year;
(b) if the qualifying conditions are met in that year and the group qualified as small in relation to the preceding financial year; and
(c) if the qualifying conditions were met in the preceding financial year and the group qualified as small in relation to that year.

(4) The qualifying conditions are met by a group in a year in which it satisfies two or more of the following requirements:

1. Aggregate turnover	Not more than **£6.5 million net (or £7.8 million gross)**
2. Aggregate balance sheet total	Not more than **£3.26 million net (or £3.9 million gross)**
3. Aggregate number of employees	Not more than 50

(5) The aggregate figures are ascertained by aggregating the relevant figures determined in accordance with section 382 for each member of the group.

(6) In relation to the aggregate figures for turnover and balance sheet total:
'net' means after any set-offs and other adjustments made to eliminate group transactions:
(a) in the case of Companies Act accounts, in accordance with regulations under section 404;
(b) in the case of IAS accounts, in accordance with international accounting standards; and
'gross' means without those set-offs and other adjustments.
A company may satisfy any relevant requirement on the basis of either the net or the gross figure.

(7) The figures for each subsidiary undertaking shall be those included in its individual accounts for the relevant financial year, that is:
(a) if its financial year ends with that of the parent company, that financial year; and
(b) if not, its financial year ending last before the end of the financial year of the parent company.
If those figures cannot be obtained without disproportionate expense or undue delay, the latest available figures shall be taken.

384 Companies excluded from the small companies regime

(1) The small companies regime does not apply to a company that is, or was at any time within the financial year to which the accounts relate:
(a) a public company;
(b) a company that:
(i) is an authorised insurance company, a banking company, an e-money issuer, [a MiFID] investment firm or a UCITS management company;
(ii) carries on insurance market activity; or
(c) a member of an ineligible group.

(2) A group is ineligible if any of its members is:
(a) a public company;
(b) a body corporate (other than a company) whose shares are admitted to trading on a regulated market in an EEA State;
(c) a person (other than a small company) who has permission under Part 4 of the Financial Services and Markets Act 2000 (c. 8) to carry on a regulated activity;
(d) a small company that is an authorised insurance company, a banking company, an e-money issuer, [a MiFID] investment firm or a UCITS management company; or
(e) a person who carries on insurance market activity.

(3) A company is a small company for the purposes of subsection (2) if it qualified as small in relation to its last financial year ending on or before the end of the financial year to which the accounts relate.

Quoted and unquoted companies

385 Quoted and unquoted companies

(1) For the purposes of this Part a company is a quoted company in relation to a financial year if it is a quoted company immediately before the end of the accounting reference period by reference to which that financial year was determined.

(2) A 'quoted company' means a company whose equity share capital:
 (a) has been included in the official list in accordance with the provisions of Part 6 of the Financial Services and Markets Act 2000 (c. 8);
 (b) is officially listed in an EEA State; or
 (c) is admitted to dealing on either the New York Stock Exchange or the exchange known as Nasdaq.
In paragraph (a) 'the official list' has the meaning given by section 103(1) of the Financial Services and Markets Act 2000.

(3) An 'unquoted company' means a company that is not a quoted company.

(4) The Secretary of State may by regulations amend or replace the provisions of subsections (1) to (2) so as to limit or extend the application of some or all of the provisions of this Part that are expressed to apply to quoted companies.

(5) Regulations under this section extending the application of any such provision of this Part are subject to affirmative resolution procedure.

(6) Any other regulations under this section are subject to negative resolution procedure.

CHAPTER 2

ACCOUNTING RECORDS

386 Duty to keep accounting records

(1) Every company must keep adequate accounting records.

(2) Adequate accounting records means records that are sufficient:
 (a) to show and explain the company's transactions;
 (b) to disclose with reasonable accuracy, at any time, the financial position of the company at that time; and
 (c) to enable the directors to ensure that any accounts required to be prepared comply with the requirements of this Act (and, where applicable, of Article 4 of the IAS Regulation).

(3) Accounting records must, in particular, contain:
 (a) entries from day to day of all sums of money received and expended by the company and the matters in respect of which the receipt and expenditure takes place; and
 (b) a record of the assets and liabilities of the company.

(4) If the company's business involves dealing in goods, the accounting records must contain:
 (a) statements of stock held by the company at the end of each financial year of the company;
 (b) all statements of stocktakings from which any statement of stock as is mentioned in paragraph (a) has been or is to be prepared; and
 (c) except in the case of goods sold by way of ordinary retail trade, statements of all goods sold and purchased, showing the goods and the buyers and sellers in sufficient detail to enable all these to be identified.

(5) A parent company that has a subsidiary undertaking in relation to which the above

requirements do not apply must take reasonable steps to secure that the undertaking keeps such accounting records as to enable the directors of the parent company to ensure that any accounts required to be prepared under this Part comply with the requirements of this Act (and, where applicable, of Article 4 of the IAS Regulation).

387 Duty to keep accounting records: offence

(1) If a company fails to comply with any provision of section 386 (duty to keep accounting records), an offence is committed by every officer of the company who is in default.

(2) It is a defence for a person charged with such an offence to show that he acted honestly and that in the circumstances in which the company's business was carried on the default was excusable.

(3) A person guilty of an offence under this section is liable:
   (a) on conviction on indictment, to imprisonment for a term not exceeding two years or a fine (or both);
   (b) on summary conviction:
      (i) in England and Wales, to imprisonment for a term not exceeding twelve months or to a fine not exceeding the statutory maximum (or both); and
      (ii) in Scotland or Northern Ireland, to imprisonment for a term not exceeding six months, or to a fine not exceeding the statutory maximum (or both).

388 Where and for how long records to be kept

(1) A company's accounting records:
   (a) must be kept at its registered office or such other place as the directors think fit; and
   (b) must at all times be open to inspection by the company's officers.

(2) If accounting records are kept at a place outside the United Kingdom, accounts and returns with respect to the business dealt with in the accounting records so kept must be sent to, and kept at, a place in the United Kingdom, and must at all times be open to such inspection.

(3) The accounts and returns to be sent to the United Kingdom must be such as to:
   (a) disclose with reasonable accuracy the financial position of the business in question at intervals of not more than six months; and
   (b) enable the directors to ensure that the accounts required to be prepared under this Part comply with the requirements of this Act (and, where applicable, of Article 4 of the IAS Regulation).

(4) Accounting records that a company is required by section 386 to keep must be preserved by it:
   (a) in the case of a private company, for three years from the date on which they are made; and
   (b) in the case of a public company, for six years from the date on which they are made.

(5) Subsection (4) is subject to any provision contained in rules made under section 411 of the Insolvency Act 1986 (c. 45) (company insolvency rules) or Article 359 of the Insolvency (Northern Ireland) Order 1989 (S.I. 1989/2405 (N.I. 19)).

389 Where and for how long records to be kept: offences

(1) If a company fails to comply with any provision of subsections (1) to (3) of section 388 (requirements as to keeping of accounting records), an offence is committed by every officer of the company who is in default.

(2) It is a defence for a person charged with such an offence to show that he acted honestly and that in the circumstances in which the company's business was carried on the default was excusable.

Appendix B Companies Act 2006

(3) An officer of a company commits an offence if he:
  (a) fails to take all reasonable steps for securing compliance by the company with subsection (4) of that section (period for which records to be preserved); or
  (b) intentionally causes any default by the company under that subsection.

(4) A person guilty of an offence under this section is liable:
  (a) on conviction on indictment, to imprisonment for a term not exceeding two years or a fine (or both); and
  (b) on summary conviction:
    (i) in England and Wales, to imprisonment for a term not exceeding twelve months or to a fine not exceeding the statutory maximum (or both); and
    (ii) in Scotland or Northern Ireland, to imprisonment for a term not exceeding six months, or to a fine not exceeding the statutory maximum (or both).

CHAPTER 3

A COMPANY'S FINANCIAL YEAR

390 A company's financial year

(1) A company's financial year is determined as follows.

(2) Its first financial year:
  (a) begins with the first day of its first accounting reference period; and
  (b) ends with the last day of that period or such other date, not more than seven days before or after the end of that period, as the directors may determine.

(3) Subsequent financial years:
  (a) begin with the day immediately following the end of the company's previous financial year; and
  (b) end with the last day of its next accounting reference period or such other date, not more than seven days before or after the end of that period, as the directors may determine.

(4) In relation to an undertaking that is not a company, references in this Act to its financial year are to any period in respect of which a profit and loss account of the undertaking is required to be made up (by its constitution or by the law under which it is established), whether that period is a year or not.

(5) The directors of a parent company must secure that, except where in their opinion there are good reasons against it, the financial year of each of its subsidiary undertakings coincides with the company's own financial year.

391 Accounting reference periods and accounting reference date

(1) A company's accounting reference periods are determined according to its accounting reference date in each calendar year.

(2) The accounting reference date of a company incorporated in Great Britain before 1st April 1996 is:
  (a) the date specified by notice to the registrar in accordance with section 224(2) of the Companies Act 1985 (c. 6) (notice specifying accounting reference date given within nine months of incorporation); or
  (b) failing such notice:
    (i) in the case of a company incorporated before 1 April 1990, 31 March; and
    (ii) in the case of a company incorporated on or after 1 April 1990, the last day of the month in which the anniversary of its incorporation falls.

(3) The accounting reference date of a company incorporated in Northern Ireland before 22nd August 1997 is:

(a) the date specified by notice to the registrar in accordance with article 232(2) of the Companies (Northern Ireland) Order 1986 (S.I. 1986/1032 (N.I. 6)) (notice specifying accounting reference date given within nine months of incorporation); or
(b) failing such notice;
  (i) in the case of a company incorporated before the coming into operation of Article 5 of the Companies (Northern Ireland) Order 1990 (S.I. 1990/593 (N.I. 5)), 31st March; and
  (ii) in the case of a company incorporated after the coming into operation of that Article, the last day of the month in which the anniversary of its incorporation falls.

(4) The accounting reference date of a company incorporated;
(a) in Great Britain on or after 1st April 1996 and before the commencement of this Act;
(b) in Northern Ireland on or after 22nd August 1997 and before the commencement of this Act; or
(c) after the commencement of this Act,
is the last day of the month in which the anniversary of its incorporation falls.

(5) A company's first accounting reference period is the period of more than six months, but not more than 18 months, beginning with the date of its incorporation and ending with its accounting reference date.

(6) Its subsequent accounting reference periods are successive periods of twelve months beginning immediately after the end of the previous accounting reference period and ending with its accounting reference date.

(7) This section has effect subject to the provisions of section 392 (alteration of accounting reference date).

392 Alteration of accounting reference date

(1) A company may by notice given to the registrar specify a new accounting reference date having effect in relation to:
(a) the company's current accounting reference period and subsequent periods; or
(b) the company's previous accounting reference period and subsequent periods.
A company's 'previous accounting reference period' means the one immediately preceding its current accounting reference period.

(2) The notice must state whether the current or previous accounting reference period:
(a) is to be shortened, so as to come to an end on the first occasion on which the new accounting reference date falls or fell after the beginning of the period; or
(b) is to be extended, so as to come to an end on the second occasion on which that date falls or fell after the beginning of the period.

(3) A notice extending a company's current or previous accounting reference period is not effective if given less than five years after the end of an earlier accounting reference period of the company that was extended under this section.

This does not apply:
(a) to a notice given by a company that is a subsidiary undertaking or parent undertaking of another EEA undertaking if the new accounting reference date coincides with that of the other EEA undertaking or, where that undertaking is not a company, with the last day of its financial year; or
(b) where the company is in administration under Part 2 of the Insolvency Act 1986 (c. 45) or Part 3 of the Insolvency (Northern Ireland) Order 1989 (S.I. 1989/2405 (N.I. 19)); or
(c) where the Secretary of State directs that it should not apply, which he may do with respect to a notice that has been given or that may be given.

(4) A notice under this section may not be given in respect of a previous accounting reference period if the period for filing accounts and reports for the financial year determined by reference to that accounting reference period has already expired.

(5) An accounting reference period may not be extended so as to exceed 18 months and a notice under this section is ineffective if the current or previous accounting reference period as extended in accordance with the notice would exceed that limit.

This does not apply where the company is in administration under Part 2 of the Insolvency Act 1986 (c. 45) or Part 3 of the Insolvency (Northern Ireland) Order 1989 (S.I. 1989/2405 (N.I. 19)).

(6) In this section 'EEA undertaking' means an undertaking established under the law of any part of the United Kingdom or the law of any other EEA State.

CHAPTER 4

ANNUAL ACCOUNTS

General

393 Accounts to give true and fair view

(1) The directors of a company must not approve accounts for the purposes of this chapter unless they are satisfied that they give a true and fair view of the assets, liabilities, financial position and profit or loss:
  (a) in the case of the company's individual accounts, of the company; and
  (b) in the case of the company's group accounts, of the undertakings included in the consolidation as a whole, so far as concerns members of the company.

(2) The auditor of a company in carrying out his functions under this Act in relation to the company's annual accounts must have regard to the directors' duty under subsection (1).

Individual accounts

394 Duty to prepare individual accounts

The directors of every company must prepare accounts for the company for each of its financial years.

Those accounts are referred to as the company's 'individual accounts'.

395 Individual accounts: applicable accounting framework

(1) A company's individual accounts may be prepared:
  (a) in accordance with section 396 ('Companies Act individual accounts'); or
  (b) in accordance with international accounting standards ('IAS individual accounts').

This is subject to the following provisions of this section and to section 407 (consistency of financial reporting within group).

(2) The individual accounts of a company that is a charity must be Companies Act individual accounts.

(3) After the first financial year in which the directors of a company prepare IAS individual accounts ('the first IAS year'), all subsequent individual accounts of the company must be prepared in accordance with international accounting standards unless there is a relevant change of circumstance.

Part 15 Accounts and reports (Sections 380–474)

(4) There is a relevant change of circumstance if, at any time during or after the first IAS year:
  (a) the company becomes a subsidiary undertaking of another undertaking that does not prepare IAS individual accounts;
  (aa) the company ceases to be a subsidiary undertaking,
  (b) the company ceases to be a company with securities admitted to trading on a regulated market in an EEA State; or
  (c) a parent undertaking of the company ceases to be an undertaking with securities admitted to trading on a regulated market in an EEA State.

(5) If, having changed to preparing Companies Act individual accounts following a relevant change of circumstance, the directors again prepare IAS individual accounts for the company, subsections (3) and (4) apply again as if the first financial year for which such accounts are again prepared were the first IAS year.

396 Companies Act individual accounts

(1) Companies Act individual accounts must comprise:
  (a) a balance sheet as at the last day of the financial year; and
  (b) a profit and loss account.

(2) The accounts must:
  (a) in the case of the balance sheet, give a true and fair view of the state of affairs of the company as at the end of the financial year; and
  (b) in the case of the profit and loss account, give a true and fair view of the profit or loss of the company for the financial year.

(3) The accounts must comply with provision made by the Secretary of State by regulations as to:
  (a) the form and content of the balance sheet and profit and loss account; and
  (b) additional information to be provided by way of notes to the accounts.

(4) If compliance with the regulations, and any other provision made by or under this Act as to the matters to be included in a company's individual accounts or in notes to those accounts, would not be sufficient to give a true and fair view, the necessary additional information must be given in the accounts or in a note to them.

(5) If in special circumstances compliance with any of those provisions is inconsistent with the requirement to give a true and fair view, the directors must depart from that provision to the extent necessary to give a true and fair view.

Particulars of any such departure, the reasons for it and its effect must be given in a note to the accounts.

397 IAS individual accounts

Where the directors of a company prepare IAS individual accounts, they must state in the notes to the accounts that the accounts have been prepared in accordance with international accounting standards.

Group accounts: small companies

398 Option to prepare group accounts

If at the end of a financial year a company subject to the small companies regime is a parent company the directors, as well as preparing individual accounts for the year, may prepare group accounts for the year.

221

Appendix B Companies Act 2006

Group accounts: other companies

399 Duty to prepare group accounts

(1) This section applies to companies that are not subject to the small companies regime.

(2) If at the end of a financial year the company is a parent company the directors, as well as preparing individual accounts for the year, must prepare group accounts for the year unless the company is exempt from that requirement.

(3) There are exemptions under:
section 400 (company included in EEA accounts of larger group);
section 401 (company included in non-EEA accounts of larger group); and
section 402 (company none of whose subsidiary undertakings need be included in the consolidation).

(4) A company to which this section applies but which is exempt from the requirement to prepare group accounts, may do so.

400 Exemption for company included in EEA group accounts of larger group

(1) A company is exempt from the requirement to prepare group accounts if it is itself a subsidiary undertaking and its immediate parent undertaking is established under the law of an EEA State, in the following cases:
   (a) where the company is a wholly-owned subsidiary of that parent undertaking;
   (b) where that parent undertaking holds more than 50% of the allotted shares in the company and notice requesting the preparation of group accounts has not been served on the company by shareholders holding in aggregate:
      (i) more than half of the remaining allotted shares in the company; or
      (ii) Five per cent of the total allotted shares in the company.
   Such notice must be served not later than six months after the end of the financial year before that to which it relates.

(2) Exemption is conditional upon compliance with all of the following conditions:
   (a) the company must be included in consolidated accounts for a larger group drawn up to the same date, or to an earlier date in the same financial year, by a parent undertaking established under the law of an EEA State;
   (b) those accounts must be drawn up and audited, and that parent undertaking's annual report must be drawn up, according to that law:
      (i) in accordance with the provisions of the Seventh Directive (83/ 349/EEC) (as modified, where relevant, by the provisions of the Bank Accounts Directive (86/635/EEC) or the Insurance Accounts Directive (91/674/EEC)); or
      (ii) in accordance with international accounting standards;
   (c) the company must disclose in its individual accounts that it is exempt from the obligation to prepare and deliver group accounts;
   (d) the company must state in its individual accounts the name of the parent undertaking that draws up the group accounts referred to above and:
      (i) if it is incorporated outside the United Kingdom, the country in which it is incorporated; or
      (ii) if it is unincorporated, the address of its principal place of business;
   (e) the company must deliver to the registrar, within the period for filing its accounts and reports for the financial year in question, copies of:
      (i) those group accounts; and
      (ii) the parent undertaking's annual report, together with the auditor's report on them;
   (f) any requirement of Part 35 of this Act as to the delivery to the registrar of a certified translation into English must be met in relation to any document comprised in the accounts and reports delivered in accordance with paragraph (e).

(3) For the purposes of subsection (1)(b) shares held by a wholly-owned subsidiary of the parent undertaking, or held on behalf of the parent undertaking or a wholly-owned subsidiary, shall be attributed to the parent undertaking.

(4) The exemption does not apply to a company any of whose securities are admitted to trading on a regulated market in an EEA State.

(5) Shares held by directors of a company for the purpose of complying with any share qualification requirement shall be disregarded in determining for the purposes of this section whether the company is a wholly-owned subsidiary.

(6) In subsection (4) "securities" includes:
(a) shares and stock;
(b) debentures, including debenture stock, loan stock, bonds, certificates of deposit and other instruments creating or acknowledging indebtedness;
(c) warrants or other instruments entitling the holder to subscribe for securities falling within paragraph (a) or (b); and
(d) certificates or other instruments that confer:
  (i) property rights in respect of a security falling within paragraph (a), (b) or (c),
  (ii) any right to acquire, dispose of, underwrite or convert a security, being a right to which the holder would be entitled if he held any such security to which the certificate or other instrument relates; or
  (iii) a contractual right (other than an option) to acquire any such security otherwise than by subscription.

401 Exemption for company included in non-EEA group accounts of larger group

(1) A company is exempt from the requirement to prepare group accounts if it is itself a subsidiary undertaking and its parent undertaking is not established under the law of an EEA State, in the following cases:
(a) where the company is a wholly-owned subsidiary of that parent undertaking;
(b) where that parent undertaking holds more than 50% of the allotted shares in the company and notice requesting the preparation of group accounts has not been served on the company by shareholders holding in aggregate:
  (i) more than half of the remaining allotted shares in the company; or
  (ii) Five per cent of the total allotted shares in the company.
Such notice must be served not later than six months after the end of the financial year before that to which it relates.

(2) Exemption is conditional upon compliance with all of the following conditions:
(a) the company and all of its subsidiary undertakings must be included in consolidated accounts for a larger group drawn up to the same date, or to an earlier date in the same financial year, by a parent undertaking;
(b) those accounts and, where appropriate, the group's annual report, must be drawn up:
  (i) in accordance with the provisions of the Seventh Directive (83/349/EEC) (as modified, where relevant, by the provisions of the Bank Accounts Directive (86/635/EEC) or the Insurance Accounts Directive (91/674/EEC)); or
  (ii) in a manner equivalent to consolidated accounts and consolidated annual reports so drawn up;
(c) the group accounts must be audited by one or more persons authorised to audit accounts under the law under which the parent undertaking which draws them up is established;
(d) the company must disclose in its individual accounts that it is exempt from the obligation to prepare and deliver group accounts;
(e) the company must state in its individual accounts the name of the parent undertaking which draws up the group accounts referred to above and:
  (i) if it is incorporated outside the United Kingdom, the country in which it is incorporated; or
  (ii) if it is unincorporated, the address of its principal place of business;

Appendix B Companies Act 2006

(f) the company must deliver to the registrar, within the period for filing its accounts and reports for the financial year in question, copies of:
    (i) the group accounts; and
    (ii) where appropriate, the consolidated annual report, together with the auditor's report on them;

(g) any requirement of Part 35 of this Act as to the delivery to the registrar of a certified translation into English must be met in relation to any document comprised in the accounts and reports delivered in accordance with paragraph (f).

(3) For the purposes of subsection (1) (b), shares held by a wholly-owned subsidiary of the parent undertaking, or held on behalf of the parent undertaking or a wholly-owned subsidiary, are attributed to the parent undertaking.

(4) The exemption does not apply to a company any of whose securities are admitted to trading on a regulated market in an EEA State.

(5) Shares held by directors of a company for the purpose of complying with any share qualification requirement shall be disregarded in determining for the purposes of this section whether the company is a wholly-owned subsidiary.

(6) In subsection (4) "securities" includes:
  (a) shares and stock;
  (b) debentures, including debenture stock, loan stock, bonds, certificates of deposit and other instruments creating or acknowledging indebtedness;
  (c) warrants or other instruments entitling the holder to subscribe for securities falling within paragraph (a) or (b); and
  (d) certificates or other instruments that confer:
    (i) property rights in respect of a security falling within paragraph (a), (b) or (c);
    (ii) any right to acquire, dispose of, underwrite or convert a security, being a right to which the holder would be entitled if he held any such security to which the certificate or other instrument relates; or
    (iii) a contractual right (other than an option) to acquire any such security otherwise than by subscription.

402 Exemption if no subsidiary undertakings need be included in the consolidation

A parent company is exempt from the requirement to prepare group accounts if under section 405 all of its subsidiary undertakings could be excluded from consolidation in Companies Act group accounts.

Group accounts: general

403 Group accounts: applicable accounting framework

(1) The group accounts of certain parent companies are required by Article 4 of the IAS Regulation to be prepared in accordance with international accounting standards ('IAS group accounts').

(2) The group accounts of other companies may be prepared:
  (a) in accordance with section 404 ('Companies Act group accounts'); or
  (b) in accordance with international accounting standards ('IAS group accounts').
This is subject to the following provisions of this section.

(3) The group accounts of a parent company that is a charity must be Companies Act group accounts.

(4) After the first financial year in which the directors of a parent company prepare IAS group accounts ('the first IAS year'), all subsequent group accounts of the company must be prepared in accordance with international accounting standards unless there is a relevant change of circumstance.

(5) There is a relevant change of circumstance if, at any time during or after the first IAS year:
   (a) the company becomes a subsidiary undertaking of another undertaking that does not prepare IAS group accounts;
   (b) the company ceases to be a company with securities admitted to trading on a regulated market in an EEA State; or
   (c) a parent undertaking of the company ceases to be an undertaking with securities admitted to trading on a regulated market in an EEA State.

(6) If, having changed to preparing Companies Act group accounts following a relevant change of circumstance, the directors again prepare IAS group accounts for the company, subsections (4) and (5) apply again as if the first financial year for which such accounts are again prepared were the first IAS year.

404 Companies Act group accounts

(1) Companies Act group accounts must comprise:
   (a) a consolidated balance sheet dealing with the state of affairs of the parent company and its subsidiary undertakings; and
   (b) a consolidated profit and loss account dealing with the profit or loss of the parent company and its subsidiary undertakings.

(2) The accounts must give a true and fair view of the state of affairs as at the end of the financial year, and the profit or loss for the financial year, of the undertakings included in the consolidation as a whole, so far as concerns members of the company.

(3) The accounts must comply with provision made by the Secretary of State by regulations as to:
   (a) the form and content of the consolidated balance sheet and consolidated profit and loss account; and
   (b) additional information to be provided by way of notes to the accounts.

(4) If compliance with the regulations, and any other provision made by or under this Act as to the matters to be included in a company's group accounts or in notes to those accounts, would not be sufficient to give a true and fair view, the necessary additional information must be given in the accounts or in a note to them.

(5) If in special circumstances compliance with any of those provisions is inconsistent with the requirement to give a true and fair view, the directors must depart from that provision to the extent necessary to give a true and fair view.

Particulars of any such departure, the reasons for it and its effect must be given in a note to the accounts.

405 Companies Act group accounts: subsidiary undertakings included in the consolidation

(1) Where a parent company prepares Companies Act group accounts, all the subsidiary undertakings of the company must be included in the consolidation, subject to the following exceptions.

(2) A subsidiary undertaking may be excluded from consolidation if its inclusion is not material for the purpose of giving a true and fair view (but two or more undertakings may be excluded only if they are not material taken together).

(3) A subsidiary undertaking may be excluded from consolidation where:
   (a) severe long-term restrictions substantially hinder the exercise of the rights of the parent company over the assets or management of that undertaking;
   (b) the information necessary for the preparation of group accounts cannot be obtained without disproportionate expense or undue delay; or
   (c) the interest of the parent company is held exclusively with a view to subsequent resale.

(4) The reference in subsection (3)(a) to the rights of the parent company and the reference in subsection (3)(c) to the interest of the parent company are, respectively, to rights and interests held by or attributed to the company for the purposes of the definition of 'parent undertaking' (see section 1162) in the absence of which it would not be the parent company.

406 IAS group accounts

Where the directors of a company prepare IAS group accounts, they must state in the notes to those accounts that the accounts have been prepared in accordance with international accounting standards.

407 Consistency of financial reporting within group

(1) The directors of a parent company must secure that the individual accounts of:
 (a) the parent company; and
 (b) each of its subsidiary undertakings, are all prepared using the same financial reporting framework, except to the extent that in their opinion there are good reasons for not doing so.

(2) Subsection (1) does not apply if the directors do not prepare group accounts for the parent company.

(3) Subsection (1) only applies to accounts of subsidiary undertakings that are required to be prepared under this Part.

(4) Subsection (1) does not require accounts of undertakings that are charities to be prepared using the same financial reporting framework as accounts of undertakings which are not charities.

(5) Subsection (1)(a) does not apply where the directors of a parent company prepare IAS group accounts and IAS individual accounts.

408 Individual profit and loss account where group accounts prepared

(1) This section applies where:
 (a) a company prepares group accounts in accordance with this Act; and
 (b) the notes to the company's individual balance sheet show the company's profit or loss for the financial year determined in accordance with this Act.

(2) *The company's individual profit and loss account* need not contain the information specified in section 411 (information about employee numbers and costs).

(3) The company's individual profit and loss account must be approved in accordance with section 414(1) (approval by directors) but may be omitted from the company's annual accounts for the purposes of the other provisions of the Companies Acts.

(4) The exemption conferred by this section is conditional upon its being disclosed in the company's annual accounts that the exemption applies.

Information to be given in notes to the accounts

409 Information about related undertakings

(1) The Secretary of State may make provision by regulations requiring information about related undertakings to be given in notes to a company's annual accounts.

(2) The regulations:
 (a) may make different provision according to whether or not the company prepares group accounts; and
 (b) may specify the descriptions of undertaking in relation to which they apply, and make different provision in relation to different descriptions of related undertaking.

(3) The regulations may provide that information need not be disclosed with respect to an undertaking that:
(a) is established under the law of a country outside the United Kingdom; or
(b) carries on business outside the United Kingdom, if the following conditions are met.

(4) The conditions are:
(a) that in the opinion of the directors of the company the disclosure would be seriously prejudicial to the business of:
  (i) that undertaking;
  (ii) the company;
  (iii) any of the company's subsidiary undertakings; or
  (iv) any other undertaking which is included in the consolidation;
(b) that the Secretary of State agrees that the information need not be disclosed.

(5) Where advantage is taken of any such exemption, that fact must be stated in a note to the company's annual accounts.

410 Information about related undertakings: alternative compliance

(1) This section applies where the directors of a company are of the opinion that the number of undertakings in respect of which the company is required to disclose information under any provision of regulations under section 409 (related undertakings) is such that compliance with that provision would result in information of excessive length being given in notes to the company's annual accounts.

(2) The information need only be given in respect of:
(a) the undertakings whose results or financial position, in the opinion of the directors, principally affected the figures shown in the company's annual accounts; and
(b) where the company prepares group accounts, undertakings excluded from consolidation under section 405(3) (undertakings excluded on grounds other than materiality).

(3) If advantage is taken of subsection (2):
(a) there must be included in the notes to the company's annual accounts a statement that the information is given only with respect to such undertakings as are mentioned in that subsection; and
(b) the full information (both that which is disclosed in the notes to the accounts and that which is not) must be annexed to the company's next annual return.
For this purpose the 'next annual return' means that next delivered to the registrar after the accounts in question have been approved under section 414.

(4) If a company fails to comply with subsection (3)(b), an offence is committed by:
(a) the company; and
(b) every officer of the company who is in default.

(5) A person guilty of an offence under subsection (4) is liable on summary conviction to a fine not exceeding level 3 on the standard scale and, for continued contravention, a daily default fine not exceeding one-tenth of level 3 on the standard scale.

410A *Information about off-balance sheet arrangements*

(1) In the case of a company that is not subject to the small companies regime, if in any financial year:
(a) the company is or has been party to arrangements that are not reflected in its balance sheet; and
(b) at the balance sheet date the risks or benefits arising from those arrangements are material,
The information required by this section must be given in notes to the company's annual accounts.

Appendix B Companies Act 2006

(2) *The information required is:*
   (a) *the nature and business purpose of the arrangements; and*
   (b) *the financial impact of the arrangements on the company.*

(3) *The information need only be given to the extent necessary for enabling the financial position of the company to be assessed.*

(4) *If the company qualifies as medium-sized in relation to the financial year (see sections 465 to 467) it need not comply with subsection (2)(b).*

(5) *This section applies in relation to group accounts as if the undertakings included in the consolidation were a single company.*

411 Information about employee numbers and costs

(1) In the case of a company not subject to the small companies regime, the following information with respect to the employees of the company must be given in notes to the company's annual accounts:
   (a) the average number of persons employed by the company in the financial year; and
   (b) the average number of persons so employed within each category of persons employed by the company.

(2) The categories by reference to which the number required to be disclosed by subsection (1)(b) is to be determined must be such as the directors may select having regard to the manner in which the company's activities are organised.

(3) The average number required by subsection (1)(a) or (b) is determined by dividing the relevant annual number by the number of months in the financial year.

(4) The relevant annual number is determined by ascertaining for each month in the financial year:
   (a) for the purposes of subsection (1)(a), the number of persons employed under contracts of service by the company in that month (whether throughout the month or not); and
   (b) for the purposes of subsection (1)(b), the number of persons in the category in question of persons so employed; and adding together all the monthly numbers.

(5) In respect of all persons employed by the company during the financial year who are taken into account in determining the relevant annual number for the purposes of subsection (1)(a) there must also be stated the aggregate amounts respectively of:
   (a) wages and salaries paid or payable in respect of that year to those persons;
   (b) social security costs incurred by the company on their behalf; and
   (c) other pension costs so incurred.
   This does not apply in so far as those amounts, or any of them, are stated elsewhere in the company's accounts.

(6) In subsection (5):

   'pension costs' includes any costs incurred by the company in respect of:
   (a) any pension scheme established for the purpose of providing pensions for persons currently or formerly employed by the company;
   (b) any sums set aside for the future payment of pensions directly by the company to current or former employees; and
   (c) any pensions paid directly to such persons without having first been set aside;
   'social security costs' means any contributions by the company to any state social security or pension scheme, fund or arrangement.

(7) *This section applies in relation to group accounts as if the undertakings included in the consolidation were a single company.*

412 Information about directors' benefits: remuneration

(1) The Secretary of State may make provision by regulations requiring information to be given in notes to a company's annual accounts about directors' remuneration.

(2) The matters about which information may be required include:
   (a) gains made by directors on the exercise of share options;
   (b) benefits received or receivable by directors under long-term incentive schemes;
   (c) payments for loss of office (as defined in section 215);
   (d) benefits receivable, and contributions for the purpose of providing benefits, in respect of past services of a person as director or in any other capacity while director; and
   (e) consideration paid to or receivable by third parties for making available the services of a person as director or in any other capacity while director.

(3) Without prejudice to the generality of subsection (1), regulations under this section may make any such provision as was made immediately before the commencement of this Part by Part 1 of Schedule 6 to the Companies Act 1985 (c. 6).

(4) For the purposes of this section, and regulations made under it, amounts paid to or receivable by:
   (a) a person connected with a director; or
   (b) a body corporate controlled by a director, are treated as paid to or receivable by the director.
   The expressions 'connected with' and 'controlled by' in this subsection have the same meaning as in Part 10 (company directors).

(5) It is the duty of:
   (a) any director of a company; and
   (b) any person who is or has at any time in the preceding five years been a director of the company, to give notice to the company of such matters relating to himself as may be necessary for the purposes of regulations under this section.

(6) A person who makes default in complying with subsection (5) commits an offence and is liable on summary conviction to a fine not exceeding level 3 on the standard scale.

413 Information about directors' benefits: advances, credit and guarantees

(1) In the case of a company that does not prepare group accounts, details of:
   (a) advances and credits granted by the company to its directors; and
   (b) guarantees of any kind entered into by the company on behalf of its directors, must be shown in the notes to its individual accounts.

(2) In the case of a parent company that prepares group accounts, details of:
   (a) advances and credits granted to the directors of the parent company, by that company or by any of its subsidiary undertakings; and
   (b) guarantees of any kind entered into on behalf of the directors of the parent company, by that company or by any of its subsidiary undertakings, must be shown in the notes to the group accounts.

(3) The details required of an advance or credit are:
   (a) its amount;
   (b) an indication of the interest rate;
   (c) its main conditions; and
   (d) any amounts repaid.

(4) The details required of a guarantee are:
   (a) its main terms;
   (b) the amount of the maximum liability that may be incurred by the company (or its subsidiary); and
   (c) any amount paid and any liability incurred by the company (or its subsidiary) for the purpose of fulfilling the guarantee (including any loss incurred by reason of enforcement of the guarantee).

Appendix B Companies Act 2006

(5) There must also be stated in the notes to the accounts the totals:
 (a) of amounts stated under subsection (3)(a);
 (b) of amounts stated under subsection (3)(d);
 (c) of amounts stated under subsection (4)(b); and
 (d) of amounts stated under subsection (4)(c).

(6) References in this section to the directors of a company are to the persons who were a director at any time in the financial year to which the accounts relate.

(7) The requirements of this section apply in relation to every advance, credit or guarantee subsisting at any time in the financial year to which the accounts relate:
 (a) whenever it was entered into;
 (b) whether or not the person concerned was a director of the company in question at the time it was entered into; and
 (c) in the case of an advance, credit or guarantee involving a subsidiary undertaking of that company, whether or not that undertaking was such a subsidiary undertaking at the time it was entered into.

(8) Banking companies and the holding companies of credit institutions need only state the details required by subsections (5)(a) and (5)(c).

Approval and signing of accounts

414 Approval and signing of accounts

(1) A company's annual accounts must be approved by the board of directors and signed on behalf of the board by a director of the company.

(2) The signature must be on the company's balance sheet.

(3) If the accounts are prepared in accordance with the provisions applicable to companies subject to the small companies regime, the balance sheet must contain a statement to that effect in a prominent position above the signature.

(4) If annual accounts are approved that do not comply with the requirements of this Act (and, where applicable, of Article 4 of the IAS Regulation), every director of the company who:
 (a) knew that they did not comply, or was reckless as to whether they complied; and
 (b) failed to take reasonable steps to secure compliance with those requirements or, as the case may be, to prevent the accounts from being approved, commits an offence.

(5) A person guilty of an offence under this section is liable:
 (a) on conviction on indictment, to a fine; and
 (b) on summary conviction, to a fine not exceeding the statutory maximum.

CHAPTER 5

DIRECTORS' REPORT

Directors' report

415 Duty to prepare directors' report

(1) The directors of a company must prepare a directors' report for each financial year of the company.

Part 15 Accounts and reports (Sections 380–474)

(2) For a financial year in which:
   (a) the company is a parent company; and
   (b) the directors of the company prepare group accounts, the directors' report must be a consolidated report (a 'group directors' report') relating to the undertakings included in the consolidation.

(3) A group directors' report may, where appropriate, give greater emphasis to the matters that are significant to the undertakings included in the consolidation, taken as a whole.

(4) In the case of failure to comply with the requirement to prepare a directors' report, an offence is committed by every person who:
   (a) was a director of the company immediately before the end of the period for filing accounts and reports for the financial year in question; and
   (b) failed to take all reasonable steps for securing compliance with that requirement.

(5) A person guilty of an offence under this section is liable:
   (a) on conviction on indictment, to a fine; and
   (b) on summary conviction, to a fine not exceeding the statutory maximum.

Directors' report: small companies exemption

415A. *Directors' report: small companies exemption*

(1) A company is entitled to small companies exemption in relation to the directors' report for a financial year if:
   (a) it is entitled to prepare accounts for the year in accordance with the small companies regime; or
   (b) it would be so entitled but for being or having been a member of an ineligible group.

(2) The exemption is relevant to:
   - *section 416(3) (contents of report: statement of amount recommended by way of dividend),*
   - *section 417 (contents of report: business review), and*
   - *sections 444 to 446 (filing obligations of different descriptions of company).*

---

416 Contents of directors' report: general

(1) The directors' report for a financial year must state:
   (a) the names of the persons who, at any time during the financial year, were directors of the company; and
   (b) the principal activities of the company in the course of the year.

(2) In relation to a group directors' report subsection (1)(b) has effect as if the reference to the company was to the undertakings included in the consolidation.

(3) Except in the case of a company **entitled to the small companies exemption**, the report must state the amount (if any) that the directors recommend should be paid by way of dividend.

(4) The Secretary of State may make provision by regulations as to other matters that must be disclosed in a directors' report.
Without prejudice to the generality of this power, the regulations may make any such provision as was formerly made by Schedule 7 to the Companies Act 1985.

417 Contents of directors' report: business review

(1) Unless the company is **entitled to the small companies exemption**, the directors' report must contain a business review.

231

Appendix B Companies Act 2006

(2) The purpose of the business review is to inform members of the company and help them assess how the directors have performed their duty under section 172 (duty to promote the success of the company).

(3) The business review must contain:
 (a) a fair review of the company's business; and
 (b) a description of the principal risks and uncertainties facing the company.

(4) The review required is a balanced and comprehensive analysis of:
 (a) the development and performance of the company's business during the financial year; and
 (b) the position of the company's business at the end of that year, consistent with the size and complexity of the business.

(5) In the case of a quoted company the business review must, to the extent necessary for an understanding of the development, performance or position of the company's business, include:
 (a) the main trends and factors likely to affect the future development, performance and position of the company's business; and
 (b) information about:
  (i) environmental matters (including the impact of the company's business on the environment);
  (ii) the company's employees; and
  (iii) social and community issues, including information about any policies of the company in relation to those matters and the effectiveness of those policies; and
 (c) subject to subsection (11), information about persons with whom the company has contractual or other arrangements which are essential to the business of the company.
 If the review does not contain information of each kind mentioned in paragraphs (b)(i), (ii) and (iii) and (c), it must state which of those kinds of information it does not contain.

(6) The review must, to the extent necessary for an understanding of the development, performance or position of the company's business, include:
 (a) analysis using financial key performance indicators; and
 (b) where appropriate, analysis using other key performance indicators, including information relating to environmental matters and employee matters.
 'Key performance indicators' means factors by reference to which the development, performance or position of the company's business can be measured effectively.

(7) Where a company qualifies as medium-sized in relation to a financial year (see sections 465 to 467), the directors' report for the year need not comply with the requirements of subsection (6) so far as they relate to non-financial information.

(8) The review must, where appropriate, include references to, and additional explanations of, amounts included in the company's annual accounts.

(9) In relation to a group directors' report this section has effect as if the references to the company were references to the undertakings included in the consolidation.

(10) Nothing in this section requires the disclosure of information about impending developments or matters in the course of negotiation if the disclosure would, in the opinion of the directors, be seriously prejudicial to the interests of the company.

(11) Nothing in subsection (5)(c) requires the disclosure of information about a person if the disclosure would, in the opinion of the directors, be seriously prejudicial to that person and contrary to the public interest.

Part 15 Accounts and reports (Sections 380–474)

418 Contents of directors' report: statement as to disclosure to auditors

(1) This section applies to a company unless:
   (a) it is exempt for the financial year in question from the requirements of Part 16 as to audit of accounts; and
   (b) the directors take advantage of that exemption.

(2) The directors' report must contain a statement to the effect that, in the case of each of the persons who are directors at the time the report is approved:
   (a) so far as the director is aware, there is no relevant audit information of which the company's auditor is unaware; and
   (b) he has taken all the steps that he ought to have taken as a director in order to make himself aware of any relevant audit information and to establish that the company's auditor is aware of that information.

(3) 'Relevant audit information' means information needed by the company's auditor in connection with preparing his report.

(4) A director is regarded as having taken all the steps that he ought to have taken as a director in order to do the things mentioned in subsection (2)(b) if he has:
   (a) made such enquiries of his fellow directors and of the company's auditors for that purpose; and
   (b) taken such other steps (if any) for that purpose, as are required by his duty as a director of the company to exercise reasonable care, skill and diligence.

(5) Where a directors' report containing the statement required by this section is approved but the statement is false, every director of the company who:
   (a) knew that the statement was false, or was reckless as to whether it was false; and
   (b) failed to take reasonable steps to prevent the report from being approved,

   commits an offence.

(6) A person guilty of an offence under subsection (5) is liable:
   (a) on conviction on indictment, to imprisonment for a term not exceeding two years or a fine (or both); and
   (b) on summary conviction:
      (i) in England and Wales, to imprisonment for a term not exceeding twelve months or to a fine not exceeding the statutory maximum (or both); and
      (ii) in Scotland or Northern Ireland, to imprisonment for a term not exceeding six months, or to a fine not exceeding the statutory maximum (or both).

419 Approval and signing of directors' report

(1) The directors' report must be approved by the board of directors and signed on behalf of the board by a director or the secretary of the company.

(2) *If in preparing the report advantage is taken of the small companies exemption*, it must contain a statement to that effect in a prominent position above the signature.

(3) If a directors' report is approved that does not comply with the requirements of this Act, every director of the company who:
   (a) knew that it did not comply, or was reckless as to whether it complied; and
   (b) failed to take reasonable steps to secure compliance with those requirements or, as the case may be, to prevent the report from being approved, commits an offence.

(4) A person guilty of an offence under this section is liable:
   (a) on conviction on indictment, to a fine; and
   (b) on summary conviction, to a fine not exceeding the statutory maximum.

CHAPTER 6

QUOTED COMPANIES: DIRECTORS' REMUNERATION REPORT

420 Duty to prepare directors' remuneration report

(1) The directors of a quoted company must prepare a directors' remuneration report for each financial year of the company.

(2) In the case of failure to comply with the requirement to prepare a directors' remuneration report, every person who:
   (a) was a director of the company immediately before the end of the period for filing accounts and reports for the financial year in question; and
   (b) failed to take all reasonable steps for securing compliance with that requirement, commits an offence.

(3) A person guilty of an offence under this section is liable:
   (a) on conviction on indictment, to a fine; and
   (b) on summary conviction, to a fine not exceeding the statutory maximum.

421 Contents of directors' remuneration report

(1) The Secretary of State may make provision by regulations as to:
   (a) the information that must be contained in a directors' remuneration report;
   (b) how information is to be set out in the report; and
   (c) what is to be the auditable part of the report.

(2) Without prejudice to the generality of this power, the regulations may make any such provision as was made, immediately before the commencement of this Part, by Schedule 7A to the Companies Act 1985 (c. 6).

(3) It is the duty of:
   (a) any director of a company; and
   (b) any person who is or has at any time in the preceding five years been a director of the company, to give notice to the company of such matters relating to himself as may be necessary for the purposes of regulations under this section.

(4) A person who makes default in complying with subsection (3) commits an offence and is liable on summary conviction to a fine not exceeding level 3 on the standard scale.

422 Approval and signing of directors' remuneration report

(1) The directors' remuneration report must be approved by the board of directors and signed on behalf of the board by a director or the secretary of the company.

(2) If a directors' remuneration report is approved that does not comply with the requirements of this Act, every director of the company who:
   (a) knew that it did not comply, or was reckless as to whether it complied; and
   (b) failed to take reasonable steps to secure compliance with those requirements or, as the case may be, to prevent the report from being approved, commits an offence.

(3) A person guilty of an offence under this section is liable:
   (a) on conviction on indictment, to a fine; and
   (b) on summary conviction, to a fine not exceeding the statutory maximum.

Part 15 Accounts and reports (Sections 380–474)

CHAPTER 7

PUBLICATION OF ACCOUNTS AND REPORTS

Duty to circulate copies of accounts and reports

423 Duty to circulate copies of annual accounts and reports

(1) Every company must send a copy of its annual accounts and reports for each financial year to:
 (a) every member of the company;
 (b) every holder of the company's debentures; and
 (c) every person who is entitled to receive notice of general meetings.

(2) Copies need not be sent to a person for whom the company does not have a current address.

(3) A company has a 'current address' for a person if:
 (a) an address has been notified to the company by the person as one at which documents may be sent to him; and
 (b) the company has no reason to believe that documents sent to him at that address will not reach him.

(4) In the case of a company not having a share capital, copies need not be sent to anyone who is not entitled to receive notices of general meetings of the company.

(5) Where copies are sent out over a period of days, references in the Companies Acts to the day on which copies are sent out shall be read as references to the last day of that period.

(6) This section has effect subject to section 426 (option to provide summary financial statement).

424 Time allowed for sending out copies of accounts and reports

(1) The time allowed for sending out copies of the company's annual accounts and reports is as follows.

(2) A private company must comply with section 423 not later than:
 (a) the end of the period for filing accounts and reports; or
 (b) if earlier, the date on which it actually delivers its accounts and reports to the registrar.

(3) A public company must comply with section 423 at least 21 days before the date of the relevant accounts meeting.

(4) If in the case of a public company copies are sent out later than is required by subsection (3), they shall, despite that, be deemed to have been duly sent if it is so agreed by all the members entitled to attend and vote at the relevant accounts meeting.

(5) Whether the time allowed is that for a private company or a public company is determined by reference to the company's status immediately before the end of the accounting reference period by reference to which the financial year for the accounts in question was determined.

(6) In this section the 'relevant accounts meeting' means the accounts meeting of the company at which the accounts and reports in question are to be laid.

425 Default in sending out copies of accounts and reports: offences

(1) If default is made in complying with section 423 or 424, an offence is committed by:
   (a) the company; and
   (b) every officer of the company who is in default.

(2) A person guilty of an offence under this section is liable:
   (a) on conviction on indictment, to a fine; and
   (b) on summary conviction, to a fine not exceeding the statutory maximum.

Option to provide summary financial statement

426 Option to provide summary financial statement

(1) A company may:
   (a) in such cases as may be specified by regulations made by the Secretary of State; and
   (b) provided any conditions so specified are complied with, provide a summary financial statement instead of copies of the accounts and reports required to be sent out in accordance with section 423.

(2) Copies of those accounts and reports must, however, be sent to any person entitled to be sent them in accordance with that section and who wishes to receive them.

(3) The Secretary of State may make provision by regulations as to the manner in which it is to be ascertained, whether before or after a person becomes entitled to be sent a copy of those accounts and reports, whether he wishes to receive them.

(4) A summary financial statement must comply with the requirements of:
   section 427 (form and contents of summary financial statement: unquoted companies); or
   section 428 (form and contents of summary financial statement: quoted companies).

(5) This section applies to copies of accounts and reports required to be sent out by virtue of section 146 to a person nominated to enjoy information rights as it applies to copies of accounts and reports required to be sent out in accordance with section 423 to a member of the company.

(6) Regulations under this section are subject to negative resolution procedure.

427 Form and contents of summary financial statement: unquoted companies

(1) A summary financial statement by a company that is not a quoted company must:
   (a) be derived from the company's annual accounts; and
   (b) be prepared in accordance with this section and regulations made under it.

(2) The summary financial statement must be in such form, and contain such information, as the Secretary of State may specify by regulations.

The regulations may require the statement to include information derived from the directors' report.

(3) Nothing in this section or regulations made under it prevents a company from including in a summary financial statement additional information derived from the company's annual accounts or the directors' report.

(4) The summary financial statement must:
   (a) state that it is only a summary of information derived from the company's annual accounts;
   (b) state whether it contains additional information derived from the directors' report and, if so, that it does not contain the full text of that report;
   (c) state how a person entitled to them can obtain a full copy of the company's annual accounts and the directors' report;
   (d) contain a statement by the company's auditor of his opinion as to whether the summary financial statement:

Part 15 Accounts and reports (Sections 380–474)

        (i)   is consistent with the company's annual accounts and, where information derived from the directors' report is included in the statement, with that report; and

        (ii)   complies with the requirements of this section and regulations made under it;

   (e)   state whether the auditor's report on the annual accounts was unqualified or qualified and, if it was qualified, set out the report in full together with any further material needed to understand the qualification;

   (f)   state whether, in that report, the auditor's statement under section 496 (whether directors' report consistent with accounts) was qualified or unqualified and, if it was qualified, set out the qualified statement in full together with any further material needed to understand the qualification;

   (g)   state whether that auditor's report contained a statement under:

        (i)   section 498(2)(a) or (b) (accounting records or returns inadequate or accounts not agreeing with records and returns); or

        (ii)   section 498(3) (failure to obtain necessary information and explanations),

        and if so, set out the statement in full.

(5)   Regulations under this section may provide that any specified material may, instead of being included in the summary financial statement, be sent separately at the same time as the statement.

(6)   Regulations under this section are subject to negative resolution procedure.

428   Form and contents of summary financial statement: quoted companies

(1)   A summary financial statement by a quoted company must:
   (a)   be derived from the company's annual accounts and the directors' remuneration report; and
   (b)   be prepared in accordance with this section and regulations made under it.

(2)   The summary financial statement must be in such form, and contain such information, as the Secretary of State may specify by regulations.

The regulations may require the statement to include information derived from the directors' report.

(3)   Nothing in this section or regulations made under it prevents a company from including in a summary financial statement additional information derived from the company's annual accounts, the directors' remuneration report or the directors' report.

(4)   The summary financial statement must:
   (a)   state that it is only a summary of information derived from the company's annual accounts and the directors' remuneration report;
   (b)   state whether it contains additional information derived from the directors' report and, if so, that it does not contain the full text of that report;
   (c)   state how a person entitled to them can obtain a full copy of the company's annual accounts, the directors' remuneration report or the directors' report;
   (d)   contain a statement by the company's auditor of his opinion as to whether the summary financial statement:
        (i)   is consistent with the company's annual accounts and the directors' remuneration report and, where information derived from the directors' report is included in the statement, with that report; and
        (ii)   complies with the requirements of this section and regulations made under it;
   (e)   state whether the auditor's report on the annual accounts and the auditable part of the directors' remuneration report was unqualified or qualified and, if it was qualified, set out the report in full together with any further material needed to understand the qualification;

(f) state whether that auditor's report contained a statement under:
  (i) section 498(2) (accounting records or returns inadequate or accounts or directors' remuneration report not agreeing with records and returns), or
  (ii) section 498(3) (failure to obtain necessary information and explanations),
  and if so, set out the statement in full;
(g) state whether, in that report, the auditor's statement under section 496 (whether directors' report consistent with accounts) was qualified or unqualified and, if it was qualified, set out the qualified statement in full together with any further material needed to understand the qualification.

(5) Regulations under this section may provide that any specified material may, instead of being included in the summary financial statement, be sent separately at the same time as the statement.

(6) Regulations under this section are subject to negative resolution procedure.

429 Summary financial statements: offences

(1) If default is made in complying with any provision of section 426, 427 or 428, or of regulations under any of those sections, an offence is committed by:
(a) the company; and
(b) every officer of the company who is in default.

(2) A person guilty of an offence under this section is liable on summary conviction to a fine not exceeding level 3 on the standard scale.

Quoted companies: requirements as to website publication

430 Quoted companies: annual accounts and reports to be made available on website

(1) A quoted company must ensure that its annual accounts and reports:
(a) are made available on a website; and
(b) remain so available until the annual accounts and reports for the company's next financial year are made available in accordance with this section.

(2) The annual accounts and reports must be made available on a website that:
(a) is maintained by or on behalf of the company; and
(b) identifies the company in question.

(3) Access to the annual accounts and reports on the website, and the ability to obtain a hard copy of the annual accounts and reports from the website, must not be:
(a) conditional on the payment of a fee; or
(b) otherwise restricted, except so far as necessary to comply with any enactment or regulatory requirement (in the United Kingdom or elsewhere).

(4) The annual accounts and reports:
(a) must be made available as soon as reasonably practicable; and
(b) must be kept available throughout the period specified in subsection (1)(b).

(5) A failure to make the annual accounts and reports available on a website throughout that period is disregarded if:
(a) the annual accounts and reports are made available on the website for part of that period; and
(b) the failure is wholly attributable to circumstances that it would not be reasonable to have expected the company to prevent or avoid.

(6) In the event of default in complying with this section, an offence is committed by every officer of the company who is in default.

(7) A person guilty of an offence under subsection (6) is liable on summary conviction to a fine not exceeding level 3 on the standard scale.

Part 15 Accounts and reports (Sections 380–474)

Right of member or debenture holder to demand copies of accounts and reports

431 Right of member or debenture holder to copies of accounts and reports: unquoted companies

(1) A member of, or holder of debentures of, an unquoted company is entitled to be provided, on demand and without charge, with a copy of:
 (a) the company's last annual accounts;
 (b) the last directors' report; and
 (c) the auditor's report on those accounts (including the statement on that report).

(2) The entitlement under this section is to a single copy of those documents, but that is in addition to any copy to which a person may be entitled under section 423.

(3) If a demand made under this section is not complied with within seven days of receipt by the company, an offence is committed by:
 (a) the company; and
 (b) every officer of the company who is in default.

(4) A person guilty of an offence under this section is liable on summary conviction to a fine not exceeding level 3 on the standard scale and, for continued contravention, a daily default fine not exceeding one-tenth of level 3 on the standard scale.

432 Right of member or debenture holder to copies of accounts and reports: quoted companies

(1) A member of, or holder of debentures of, a quoted company is entitled to be provided, on demand and without charge, with a copy of:
 (a) the company's last annual accounts;
 (b) the last directors' remuneration report;
 (c) the last directors' report; and
 (d) the auditor's report on those accounts (including the report on the directors' remuneration report and on the directors' report).

(2) The entitlement under this section is to a single copy of those documents, but that is in addition to any copy to which a person may be entitled under section 423.

(3) If a demand made under this section is not complied with within seven days of receipt by the company, an offence is committed by:
 (a) the company; and
 (b) every officer of the company who is in default.

(4) A person guilty of an offence under this section is liable on summary conviction to a fine not exceeding level 3 on the standard scale and, for continued contravention, a daily default fine not exceeding one-tenth of level 3 on the standard scale.

Requirements in connection with publication of accounts and reports

433 Name of signatory to be stated in published copies of accounts and reports

(1) Every copy of a document to which this section applies that is published by or on behalf of the company must state the name of the person who signed it on behalf of the board.

(2) In the case of an unquoted company, this section applies to copies of:
 (a) the company's balance sheet; and
 (b) the directors' report.

(3) In the case of a quoted company, this section applies to copies of:
 (a) the company's balance sheet;

Appendix B Companies Act 2006

> (b) the directors' remuneration report; and
> (c) the directors' report.

(4) If a copy is published without the required statement of the signatory's name, an offence is committed by:
   (a) the company; and
   (b) every officer of the company who is in default.

(5) A person guilty of an offence under this section is liable on summary conviction to a fine not exceeding level 3 on the standard scale.

434 Requirements in connection with publication of statutory accounts

(1) If a company publishes any of its statutory accounts, they must be accompanied by the auditor's report on those accounts (unless the company is exempt from audit and the directors have taken advantage of that exemption).

(2) A company that prepares statutory group accounts for a financial year must not publish its statutory individual accounts for that year without also publishing with them its statutory group accounts.

(3) A company's 'statutory accounts' are its accounts for a financial year as required to be delivered to the registrar under section 441.

(4) If a company contravenes any provision of this section, an offence is committed by:
   (a) the company; and
   (b) every officer of the company who is in default.

(5) A person guilty of an offence under this section is liable on summary conviction to a fine not exceeding level 3 on the standard scale.

(6) This section does not apply in relation to the provision by a company of a summary financial statement (see section 426).

435 Requirements in connection with publication of non-statutory accounts

(1) If a company publishes non-statutory accounts, it must publish with them a statement indicating:
   (a) that they are not the company's statutory accounts;
   (b) whether statutory accounts dealing with any financial year with which the non-statutory accounts purport to deal have been delivered to the registrar; and
   (c) whether an auditor's report has been made on the company's statutory accounts for any such financial year, and if so whether the report:
      (i) was qualified or unqualified, or included a reference to any matters to which the auditor drew attention by way of emphasis without qualifying the report; or
      (ii) contained a statement under section 498(2) (accounting records or returns inadequate or accounts or directors' remuneration report not agreeing with records and returns), or section 498(3) (failure to obtain necessary information and explanations).

(2) The company must not publish with non-statutory accounts the auditor's report on the company's statutory accounts.

(3) References in this section to the publication by a company of 'non-statutory accounts' are to the publication of:
   (a) any balance sheet or profit and loss account relating to, or purporting to deal with, a financial year of the company, or
   (b) an account in any form purporting to be a balance sheet or profit and loss account for a group headed by the company relating to, or purporting to deal with, a financial year of the company, otherwise than as part of the company's statutory accounts.

(4) In subsection (3)(b) 'a group headed by the company' means a group consisting of the company and any other undertaking (regardless of whether it is a subsidiary undertaking of the company) other than a parent undertaking of the company.

(5) If a company contravenes any provision of this section, an offence is committed by:
(a) the company; and
(b) every officer of the company who is in default.

(6) A person guilty of an offence under this section is liable on summary conviction to a fine not exceeding level 3 on the standard scale.

(7) This section does not apply in relation to the provision by a company of a summary financial statement (see section 426).

436 Meaning of 'publication' in relation to accounts and reports

(1) This section has effect for the purposes of:
section 433 (name of signatory to be stated in published copies of accounts and reports);
section 434 (requirements in connection with publication of statutory accounts); and
section 435 (requirements in connection with publication of non-statutory accounts).

(2) For the purposes of those sections a company is regarded as publishing a document if it publishes, issues or circulates it or otherwise makes it available for public inspection in a manner calculated to invite members of the public generally, or any class of members of the public, to read it.

CHAPTER 8

PUBLIC COMPANIES: LAYING OF ACCOUNTS AND REPORTS BEFORE GENERAL MEETING

437 Public companies: laying of accounts and reports before general meeting

(1) The directors of a public company must lay before the company in general meeting copies of its annual accounts and reports.

(2) This section must be complied with not later than the end of the period for filing the accounts and reports in question.

(3) In the Companies Acts 'accounts meeting', in relation to a public company, means a general meeting of the company at which the company's annual accounts and reports are (or are to be) laid in accordance with this section.

438 Public companies: offence of failure to lay accounts and reports

(1) If the requirements of section 437 (public companies: laying of accounts and reports before general meeting) are not complied with before the end of the period allowed, every person who immediately before the end of that period was a director of the company commits an offence.

(2) It is a defence for a person charged with such an offence to prove that he took all reasonable steps for securing that those requirements would be complied with before the end of that period.

(3) It is not a defence to prove that the documents in question were not in fact prepared as required by this Part.

(4) A person guilty of an offence under this section is liable on summary conviction to a fine not exceeding level 5 on the standard scale and, for continued contravention, a daily default fine not exceeding one-tenth of level 5 on the standard scale.

Appendix B Companies Act 2006

CHAPTER 9

QUOTED COMPANIES: MEMBERS' APPROVAL OF DIRECTORS' REMUNERATION REPORT

439 Quoted companies: members' approval of directors' remuneration report

(1) A quoted company must, prior to the accounts meeting, give to the members of the company entitled to be sent notice of the meeting notice of the intention to move at the meeting, as an ordinary resolution, a resolution approving the directors' remuneration report for the financial year.

(2) The notice may be given in any manner permitted for the service on the member of notice of the meeting.

(3) The business that may be dealt with at the accounts meeting includes the resolution.

This is so notwithstanding any default in complying with subsection (1) or (2).

(4) The existing directors must ensure that the resolution is put to the vote of the meeting.

(5) No entitlement of a person to remuneration is made conditional on the resolution being passed by reason only of the provision made by this section.

(6) In this section:

'the accounts meeting' means the general meeting of the company before which the company's annual accounts for the financial year are to be laid; and
'existing director' means a person who is a director of the company immediately before that meeting.

440 Quoted companies: offences in connection with procedure for approval

(1) In the event of default in complying with section 439(1) (notice to be given of resolution for approval of directors' remuneration report), an offence is committed by every officer of the company who is in default.

(2) If the resolution is not put to the vote of the accounts meeting, an offence is committed by each existing director.

(3) It is a defence for a person charged with an offence under subsection (2) to prove that he took all reasonable steps for securing that the resolution was put to the vote of the meeting.

(4) A person guilty of an offence under this section is liable on summary conviction to a fine not exceeding level 3 on the standard scale.

(5) In this section:

'the accounts meeting' means the general meeting of the company before which the company's annual accounts for the financial year are to be laid; and
'existing director' means a person who is a director of the company immediately before that meeting.

CHAPTER 10

FILING OF ACCOUNTS AND REPORTS

Duty to file accounts and reports

441 Duty to file accounts and reports with the registrar

(1) The directors of a company must deliver to the registrar for each financial year the accounts and reports required by:

section 444 (filing obligations of companies subject to small companies regime);

section 444A (filing obligations of companies entitled to small companies exemption in relation to directors' report);

section 445 (filing obligations of medium-sized companies);
section 446 (filing obligations of unquoted companies); or
section 447 (filing obligations of quoted companies).

(2) This is subject to section 448 (unlimited companies exempt from filing obligations).

442 Period allowed for filing accounts

(1) This section specifies the period allowed for the directors of a company to comply with their obligation under section 441 to deliver accounts and reports for a financial year to the registrar.
This is referred to in the Companies Acts as the 'period for filing' those accounts and reports.

(2) The period is:
  (a) for a private company, nine months after the end of the relevant accounting reference period; and
  (b) for a public company, six months after the end of that period.
This is subject to the following provisions of this section.

(3) If the relevant accounting reference period is the company's first and is a period of more than twelve months, the period is:
  (a) nine months or six months, as the case may be, from the first anniversary of the incorporation of the company; or
  (b) three months after the end of the accounting reference period, whichever last expires.

(4) If the relevant accounting reference period is treated as shortened by virtue of a notice given by the company under section 392 (alteration of accounting reference date), the period is:
  (a) that applicable in accordance with the above provisions; or
  (b) three months from the date of the notice under that section, whichever last expires.

(5) If for any special reason the Secretary of State thinks fit he may, on an application made before the expiry of the period otherwise allowed, by notice in writing to a company extend that period by such further period as may be specified in the notice.

(6) Whether the period allowed is that for a private company or a public company is determined by reference to the company's status immediately before the end of the relevant accounting reference period.

(7) In this section 'the relevant accounting reference period' means the accounting reference period by reference to which the financial year for the accounts in question was determined.

443 Calculation of period allowed

(1) This section applies for the purposes of calculating the period for filing a company's accounts and reports which is expressed as a specified number of months from a specified date or after the end of a specified previous period.

(2) Subject to the following provisions, the period ends with the date in the appropriate month corresponding to the specified date or the last day of the specified previous period.

(3) If the specified date, or the last day of the specified previous period, is the last day of a

Appendix B Companies Act 2006

month, the period ends with the last day of the appropriate month (whether or not that is the corresponding date).

(4) If:
  (a) the specified date, or the last day of the specified previous period, is not the last day of a month but is the 29th or 30th; and
  (b) the appropriate month is February,
  the period ends with the last day of February.

(5) 'The appropriate month' means the month that is the specified number of months after the month in which the specified date, or the end of the specified previous period, falls.

Filing obligations of different descriptions of company

---

444 Filing obligations of companies subject to small companies regime

(1) The directors of a company subject to the small companies regime:
  (a) must deliver to the registrar for each financial year a copy of a balance sheet drawn up as at the last day of that year; and
  (b) may also deliver to the registrar:
    (i) a copy of the company's profit and loss account for that year; and
    (ii) a copy of the directors' report for that year.

(2) The directors must also deliver to the registrar a copy of the auditor's report on *the accounts (and any directors' report) that it delivers*.

This does not apply if the company is exempt from audit and the directors have taken advantage of that exemption.

(3) The copies of accounts and reports delivered to the registrar must be copies of the company's annual accounts and reports, except that where the company prepares Companies Act accounts:
  (a) the directors may deliver to the registrar a copy of a balance sheet drawn up in accordance with regulations made by the Secretary of State; and
  (b) there may be omitted from the copy profit and loss account delivered to the registrar such items as may be specified by the regulations.
  These are referred to in this Part as 'abbreviated accounts'.

(4) If abbreviated accounts are delivered to the registrar the obligation to deliver a copy of the auditor's report on the accounts is to deliver a copy of the special auditor's report required by section 449.

(5) Where the directors of a company subject to the small companies regime deliver to the registrar IAS accounts, or Companies Act accounts that are not abbreviated accounts, and in accordance with this section:
  (a) do not deliver to the registrar a copy of the company's profit and loss account; or
  (b) do not deliver to the registrar a copy of the directors' report,
  the copy of the balance sheet delivered to the registrar must contain in a prominent position a statement that the company's annual accounts and reports have been delivered in accordance with the provisions applicable to companies subject to the small companies regime.

Sub-sections (6) and (7) below are adapted transitionally by SI 2007 No.3495 (article 6 and paragraph 6 of Schedule 1) as set out below (transitional sections 6,6A and 7):

(6) The copies of the balance sheet and any directors' report delivered to the registrar under this section must state the name of the person who signed it on behalf of the board.

(7) The copy of the auditor's report delivered to the registrar under this section must—
  (a) state the name of the auditor and (where the auditor is a firm) the name of the person who signed it as senior statutory auditor, or

Part 15 Accounts and reports (Sections 380–474)

>   (b) if the conditions in section 506 (circumstances in which names may be omitted) are met, state that a resolution has been passed and notified to the Secretary of State in accordance with that section.
>
> **Transitional adaptations (transitional sections 6,6A and 7) – (SI 2007 No.3495) (article 6 and paragraphs 6 to 10 of Schedule 1). These transitional sections are revoked (repealed) on 1 October 2009 in accordance with SI 2008 No. 2860.**
>
> *(6) The copy of the balance sheet delivered to the registrar under this section must:*
>   *(a) state the name of the person who signed it on behalf of the board under section 414; and*
>   *(b) be signed on behalf of the board by a director of the company.*
>
> *(6A) The copy of the directors' report delivered to the registrar under this section must:*
>   *(a) state the name of the person who signed it on behalf of the board under section 419; and*
>   *(b) be signed on behalf of the board by a director or the secretary of the company.*
>
> *(7) The copy of the auditor's report delivered to the registrar under this section must:*
>   *(a) state the name of the auditor and (where the auditor is a firm) the name of the person who signed it as senior statutory auditor; and*
>   *(b) be signed by the auditor or (where the auditor is a firm) in the name of the firm by a person authorised to sign on its behalf,*
>
> *or, if the conditions in section 506 (circumstances in which names may be omitted) are met, state that a resolution has been passed and notified to the Secretary of State in accordance with that section.*

> **444A Filing obligations of companies entitled to small companies exemption in relation to directors' report.**
> *(1) The directors of a company that is entitled to small companies exemption in relation to the directors' report for a financial year:*
>   *(a) must deliver to the registrar a copy of the company's annual accounts for that year; and*
>   *(b) may also deliver to the registrar a copy of the directors' report.*
>
> *(2) The directors must also deliver to the registrar a copy of the auditor's report on the accounts (and any directors' report) that it delivers.*
> *This does not apply if the company is exempt from audit and the directors have taken advantage of that exception.*
>
> *(3) The copies of the balance sheet and directors' report delivered to the registrar under this section must state the name of the person who signed it on behalf of the board.*
>
> *(4) The copy of the auditor's report delivered to the registrar under this section must:*
>   *(a) state the name of the auditor and (where the auditor is a firm) the name of the person who signed it as senior statutory auditor; and*
>   *(b) be signed by the auditor or (where the auditor is a firm) in the name of the firm by a person authorised to sign on its behalf, or, if the conditions in section 506 (circumstances in which names may be omitted) are met, state that a resolution has been passed and notified to the Secretary of State in accordance with that section.*
>
> *(5) This section does not apply to companies within section 444 (filing obligations of companies subject to the small companies regime).*

Appendix B Companies Act 2006

445 Filing obligations of medium-sized companies

(1) The directors of a company that qualifies as a medium-sized company in relation to a financial year (see sections 465 to 467) must deliver to the registrar a copy of:
   (a) the company's annual accounts; and
   (b) the directors' report.

(2) They must also deliver to the registrar a copy of the auditor's report on those accounts (and on the directors' report).

This does not apply if the company is exempt from audit and the directors have taken advantage of that exemption.

(3) Where the company prepares Companies Act accounts, the directors may deliver to the registrar a copy of the company's annual accounts for the financial year:
   (a) that includes a profit and loss account in which items are combined in accordance with regulations made by the Secretary of State; and
   (b) that does not contain items whose omission is authorised by the regulations.
These are referred to in this Part as 'abbreviated accounts'.

(4) If abbreviated accounts are delivered to the registrar the obligation to deliver a copy of the auditor's report on the accounts is to deliver a copy of the special auditor's report required by section 449.

Sub-sections (5) and (6) below are adapted transitionally by SI 2007 No.3495 (article 6 and paragraph 7 of Schedule 1) as set out below:

(5) The copies of the balance sheet and directors' report delivered to the registrar under this section must state the name of the person who signed it on behalf of the board.

(6) The copy of the auditor's report delivered to the registrar under this section must—
   (a) state the name of the auditor and (where the auditor is a firm) the name of the person who signed it as senior statutory auditor, or
   (b) if the conditions in section 506 (circumstances in which names may be omitted) are met, state that a resolution has been passed and notified to the Secretary of State in accordance with that section.

Transitional adaptations (transitional sections 5,5A and 6) – (SI 2007 No.3495) (article 6 and paragraphs 6 to 10 of Schedule 1). These transitional sections are revoked (repealed) on 1 October 2009 in accordance with SI 2008 No. 2860.

(5) The copy of the balance sheet delivered to the registrar under this section must:
   (a) state the name of the person who signed it on behalf of the board under section 414, and
   (b) be signed on behalf of the board by a director of the company.

(5A) The copy of the directors' report delivered to the registrar under this section must:
   (a) state the name of the person who signed it on behalf of the board under section 419, and
   (b) be signed on behalf of the board by a director or the secretary of the company.

(6) The copy of the auditor's report delivered to the registrar under this section must:
   (a) state the name of the auditor and (where the auditor is a firm) the name of the person who signed it as senior statutory auditor; and
   (b) be signed by the auditor or (where the auditor is a firm) in the name of the firm by a person authorised to sign on its behalf,

or, if the conditions in section 506 (circumstances in which names may be omitted) are met, state that a resolution has been passed and notified to the Secretary of State in accordance with that section.

(7) This section does not apply to companies within:
   (a) section 444 (filing obligations of companies subject to the small companies regime); or
   (b) section 444A (filing obligations of companies entitled to small companies exemption in relation to directors' report).

446 Filing obligations of unquoted companies

(1) The directors of an unquoted company must deliver to the registrar for each financial year of the company a copy of:
   (a) the company's annual accounts;
   (b) the directors' report.

(2) The directors must also deliver to the registrar a copy of the auditor's report on those accounts (and the directors' report).
This does not apply if the company is exempt from audit and the directors have taken advantage of that exemption.

Sub-sections (3) and (4) below are adapted transitionally by SI 2007 No.3495 (article 6 and paragraph 8 of Schedule 1) as set out below:

(3) The copies of the balance sheet and directors' report delivered to the registrar under this section must state the name of the person who signed it on behalf of the board.

(4) The copy of the auditor's report delivered to the registrar under this section must—
   (a) state the name of the auditor and (where the auditor is a firm) the name of the person who signed it as senior statutory auditor, or
   (b) if the conditions in section 506 (circumstances in which names may be omitted) are met, state that a resolution has been passed and notified to the Secretary of State in accordance with that section.

Transitional adaptations (transitional sections 3, 3A, 3B and 4) – (SI 2007 No.3495) (article 6 and paragraphs 6 to 10 of Schedule 1). These transitional sections are revoked (repealed) on 1 October 2009 in accordance with SI 2008 No. 2860

(3) The copies of the balance sheet and directors' report delivered to the registrar under this section must:
   (a) state the name of the person who signed it on behalf of the board under section 414, and
   (b) be signed on behalf of the board by a director of the company.

(3A) The copy of the directors' report delivered to the registrar under this section must—
   (a) state the name of the person who signed it on behalf of the board under section 419, and
   (b) be signed on behalf of the board by a director or the secretary of the company.

(4) The copy of the auditor's report delivered to the registrar under this section must:
   (a) state the name of the auditor and (where the auditor is a firm) the name of the person who signed it as senior statutory auditor; and
   (b) be signed by the auditor or (where the auditor is a firm) in the name of the firm by a person authorised to sign on its behalf,

or, if the conditions in section 506 (circumstances in which names may be omitted) are met, state that a resolution has been passed and notified to the Secretary of State in accordance with that section.

[Author's note: Paragraph (4) will cease to have effect when this transitional adaptation ceases to have effect on 1 October 2009].

Appendix B Companies Act 2006

(5) This section does not apply to companies within:
  (a) section 444 (filing obligations of companies subject to the small companies regime), [. . .];
  (aa) *section 444A (filing obligations of companies entitled to small companies exemption in relation to directors' report); or*
  (b) section 445 (filing obligations of medium-sized companies).

447 Filing obligations of quoted companies

(1) The directors of a quoted company must deliver to the registrar for each financial year of the company a copy of:
  (a) the company's annual accounts;
  (b) the directors' remuneration report;
  (c) the directors' report.

(2) They must also deliver a copy of the auditor's report on those accounts (and on the directors' remuneration report and the directors' report).

Sub-sections (3) and (4) below are adapted transitionally by SI 2007 No.3495 (article 6 and paragraph 9 of Schedule 1) as set out below:

(3) The copies of the balance sheet, the directors' remuneration report and directors' report delivered to the registrar under this section must state the name of the person who signed it on behalf of the board.

(4) The copy of the auditor's report delivered to the registrar under this section must—
  (a) state the name of the auditor and (where the auditor is a firm) the name of the person who signed it as senior statutory auditor, or
  (b) if the conditions in section 506 (circumstances in which names may be omitted) are met, state that a resolution has been passed and notified to the Secretary of State in accordance with that section.

Transitional adaptations (transitional sections 3, 3A, 3B, 3C and 4) – (SI 2007 No.3495) (article 6 and paragraphs 6 to 10 of Schedule 1). These transitional sections are revoked (repealed) on 1 October 2009 in accordance with SI 2008 No. 2860.

(3) The copy of the balance sheet delivered to the registrar under this section must:
  (a) state the name of the person who signed it on behalf of the board under section 414, and
  (b) be signed on behalf of the board by a director of the company.

(3A) The copy of the directors' remuneration report delivered to the registrar under this section must:
  (a) state the name of the person who signed it on behalf of the board under section 422, and
  (b) be signed on behalf of the board by a director or the secretary of the company.

(3B) The copy of the directors' report delivered to the registrar under this section must:
  (a) state the name of the person who signed it on behalf of the board under section 419;and
  (b) be signed on behalf of the board by a director or the secretary of the company.

(4) The copy of the auditor's report delivered to the registrar under this section must:
   (a) state the name of the auditor and (where the auditor is a firm) the name of the person who signed it as senior statutory auditor, and
   (b) be signed by the auditor or (where the auditor is a firm) in the name of the firm by a person authorised to sign on its behalf,

or, if the conditions in section 506 (circumstances in which names may be omitted) are met, state that a resolution has been passed and notified to the Secretary of State in accordance with that section.

[Author's note: Paragraph (4) will cease to have effect when this transitional adaptation ceases to have effect on 1 October 2009]

448 Unlimited companies exempt from obligation to file accounts

(1) The directors of an unlimited company are not required to deliver accounts and reports to the registrar in respect of a financial year if the following conditions are met.

(2) The conditions are that at no time during the relevant accounting reference period:
   (a) has the company been, to its knowledge, a subsidiary undertaking of an undertaking which was then limited; or
   (b) have there been, to its knowledge, exercisable by or on behalf of two or more undertakings which were then limited, rights which if exercisable by one of them would have made the company a subsidiary undertaking of it; or
   (c) has the company been a parent company of an undertaking which was then limited.

The references above to an undertaking being limited at a particular time are to an undertaking (under whatever law established) the liability of whose members is at that time limited.

(3) The exemption conferred by this section does not apply if:
   (a) the company is a banking or insurance company or the parent company of a banking or insurance group; or
   (b) *each of the members of the company is:*
      (i) *a limited company;*
      (ii) *another unlimited company each of whose members is a limited company; or*
      (iii) *a Scottish partnership each of whose members is a limited company.*

The references in paragraph (b) to a limited company, another unlimited company or a Scottish partnership include a comparable undertaking incorporated in or formed under the law of a country or territory outside the United Kingdom.

(4) Where a company is exempt by virtue of this section from the obligation to deliver accounts:
   (a) section 434(3) (requirements in connection with publication of statutory accounts: meaning of 'statutory accounts') has effect with the substitution for the words 'as required to be delivered to the registrar under section 441' of the words 'as prepared in accordance with this Part and approved by the board of directors'; and
   (b) section 435(1)(b) (requirements in connection with publication of non-statutory accounts: statement whether statutory accounts delivered) has effect with the substitution for the words from 'whether statutory accounts' to 'have been delivered to the registrar' of the words 'that the company is exempt from the requirement to deliver statutory accounts'.

(5) In this section the 'relevant accounting reference period', in relation to a financial year, means the accounting reference period by reference to which that financial year was determined.

Requirements where abbreviated accounts delivered

449 Special auditor's report where abbreviated accounts delivered

(1) This section applies where:
   (a) the directors of a company deliver abbreviated accounts to the registrar; and
   (b) the company is not exempt from audit (or the directors have not taken advantage of any such exemption).

(2) The directors must also deliver to the registrar a copy of a special report of the company's auditor stating that in his opinion:
   (a) the company is entitled to deliver abbreviated accounts in accordance with the section in question; and
   (b) the abbreviated accounts to be delivered are properly prepared in accordance with regulations under that section.

(3) The auditor's report on the company's annual accounts need not be delivered, but:
   (a) if that report was qualified, the special report must set out that report in full together with any further material necessary to understand the qualification; and
   (b) if that report contained a statement under:
      (i) section 498(2)(a) or (b) (accounts, records or returns inadequate or accounts not agreeing with records and returns); or
      (ii) section 498(3) (failure to obtain necessary information and explanations),
      the special report must set out that statement in full.

(4) The provisions of:
   sections 503 to 506 (signature of auditor's report); and
   sections 507 to 509 (offences in connection with auditor's report),
   apply to a special report under this section as they apply to an auditor's report on the company's annual accounts prepared under Part 16.

Sub-section (4A) below is adapted transitionally by SI 2007 No.3495 (article 6 and paragraph 10 of Schedule 1) as set out below:

This transitional adaptation is revoked (repealed) on 1 October 2009 in accordance with SI 2008 No. 2860

(4A) The copy of the special report delivered to the registrar under this section must:
   (a) be signed by the auditor or (where the auditor is a firm) in the name of the firm by a person authorised to sign on its behalf, or
   (b) if the conditions in section 506 (circumstances in which names may be omitted) are met, state that a resolution has been passed and notified to the Secretary of State in accordance with that section.

(5) If abbreviated accounts are delivered to the registrar, the references in section 434 or 435 (requirements in connection with publication of accounts) to the auditor's report on the company's annual accounts shall be read as references to the special auditor's report required by this section.

450 Approval and signing of abbreviated accounts

(1) Abbreviated accounts must be approved by the board of directors and signed on behalf of the board by a director of the company.

(2) The signature must be on the balance sheet.

(3) The balance sheet must contain in a prominent position above the signature a statement to the effect that it is prepared in accordance with the special provisions of this Act relating (as the case may be) to companies subject to the small companies regime or to medium-sized companies.

(4) If abbreviated accounts are approved that do not comply with the requirements of regulations under the relevant section, every director of the company who:
   (a) knew that they did not comply, or was reckless as to whether they complied; and
   (b) failed to take reasonable steps to prevent them from being approved, commits an offence.

(5) A person guilty of an offence under subsection (4) is liable:
   (a) on conviction on indictment, to a fine; and
   (b) on summary conviction, to a fine not exceeding the statutory maximum.

Failure to file accounts and reports

451 Default in filing accounts and reports: offences

(1) If the requirements of section 441 (duty to file accounts and reports) are not complied with in relation to a company's accounts and reports for a financial year before the end of the period for filing those accounts and reports, every person who immediately before the end of that period was a director of the company commits an offence.

(2) It is a defence for a person charged with such an offence to prove that he took all reasonable steps for securing that those requirements would be complied with before the end of that period.

(3) It is not a defence to prove that the documents in question were not in fact prepared as required by this Part.

(4) A person guilty of an offence under this section is liable on summary conviction to a fine not exceeding level 5 on the standard scale and, for continued contravention, a daily default fine not exceeding one-tenth of level 5 on the standard scale.

452 Default in filing accounts and reports: court order

(1) If:
   (a) the requirements of section 441 (duty to file accounts and reports) are not complied with in relation to a company's accounts and reports for a financial year before the end of the period for filing those accounts and reports; and
   (b) the directors of the company fail to make good the default within 14 days after the service of a notice on them requiring compliance, the court may, on the application of any member or creditor of the company or of the registrar, make an order directing the directors (or any of them) to make good the default within such time as may be specified in the order.

(2) The court's order may provide that all costs (in Scotland, expenses) of and incidental to the application are to be borne by the directors.

453 Civil penalty for failure to file accounts and reports

(1) Where the requirements of section 441 are not complied with in relation to a company's accounts and reports for a financial year before the end of the period for filing those accounts and reports, the company is liable to a civil penalty.

This is in addition to any liability of the directors under section 451.

(2) The amount of the penalty shall be determined in accordance with regulations made by the Secretary of State by reference to:
   (a) the length of the period between the end of the period for filing the accounts and reports in question and the day on which the requirements are complied with; and
   (b) whether the company is a private or public company.

(3) The penalty may be recovered by the registrar and is to be paid into the Consolidated Fund.

Appendix B Companies Act 2006

(4) It is not a defence in proceedings under this section to prove that the documents in question were not in fact prepared as required by this Part.

(5) Regulations under this section having the effect of increasing the penalty payable in any case are subject to affirmative resolution procedure.

Otherwise, the regulations are subject to negative resolution procedure.

CHAPTER 11

REVISION OF DEFECTIVE ACCOUNTS AND REPORTS

Voluntary revision

454 Voluntary revision of accounts etc.

(1) If it appears to the directors of a company that:
   (a) the company's annual accounts;
   (b) the directors' remuneration report or the directors' report; or
   (c) a summary financial statement of the company,
   did not comply with the requirements of this Act (or, where applicable, of Article 4 of the IAS Regulation), they may prepare revised accounts or a revised report or statement.

(2) Where copies of the previous accounts or report have been sent out to members, delivered to the registrar or (in the case of a public company) laid before the company in general meeting, the revisions must be confined to:
   (a) the correction of those respects in which the previous accounts or report did not comply with the requirements of this Act (or, where applicable, of Article 4 of the IAS Regulation); and
   (b) the making of any necessary consequential alterations.

(3) The Secretary of State may make provision by regulations as to the application of the provisions of this Act in relation to:
   (a) revised annual accounts;
   (b) a revised directors' remuneration report or directors' report; or
   (c) a revised summary financial statement.

(4) The regulations may, in particular:
   (a) make different provision according to whether the previous accounts, report or statement are replaced or are supplemented by a document indicating the corrections to be made;
   (b) make provision with respect to the functions of the company's auditor in relation to the revised accounts, report or statement;
   (c) require the directors to take such steps as may be specified in the regulations where the previous accounts or report have been:
      (i) sent out to members and others under section 423;
      (ii) laid before the company in general meeting; or
      (iii) delivered to the registrar,
      or where a summary financial statement containing information derived from the previous accounts or report has been sent to members under section 426;
   (d) apply the provisions of this Act (including those creating criminal offences) subject to such additions, exceptions and modifications as are specified in the regulations.

(5) Regulations under this section are subject to negative resolution procedure.

Secretary of State's notice

455 Secretary of State's notice in respect of accounts or reports

(1) This section applies where:

(a) copies of a company's annual accounts or directors' report have been sent out under section 423; or
(b) a copy of a company's annual accounts or directors' report has been delivered to the registrar or (in the case of a public company) laid before the company in general meeting,

and it appears to the Secretary of State that there is, or may be, a question whether the accounts or report comply with the requirements of this Act (or, where applicable, of Article 4 of the IAS Regulation).

(2) The Secretary of State may give notice to the directors of the company indicating the respects in which it appears that such a question arises or may arise.

(3) The notice must specify a period of not less than one month for the directors to give an explanation of the accounts or report or prepare revised accounts or a revised report.

(4) If at the end of the specified period, or such longer period as the Secretary of State may allow, it appears to the Secretary of State that the directors have not:
(a) given a satisfactory explanation of the accounts or report; or
(b) revised the accounts or report so as to comply with the requirements of this Act (or, where applicable, of Article 4 of the IAS Regulation),
the Secretary of State may apply to the court.

(5) The provisions of this section apply equally to revised annual accounts and revised directors' reports, in which case they have effect as if the references to revised accounts or reports were references to further revised accounts or reports.

Application to court

456 Application to court in respect of defective accounts or reports

(1) An application may be made to the court:
(a) by the Secretary of State, after having complied with section 455; or
(b) by a person authorised by the Secretary of State for the purposes of this section,
for a declaration (in Scotland, a declarator) that the annual accounts of a company do not comply, or a directors' report does not comply, with the requirements of this Act (or, where applicable, of Article 4 of the IAS Regulation) and for an order requiring the directors of the company to prepare revised accounts or a revised report.

(2) Notice of the application, together with a general statement of the matters at issue in the proceedings, shall be given by the applicant to the registrar for registration.

(3) If the court orders the preparation of revised accounts, it may give directions as to:
(a) the auditing of the accounts;
(b) the revision of any directors' remuneration report, directors' report or summary financial statement; and
(c) the taking of steps by the directors to bring the making of the order to the notice of persons likely to rely on the previous accounts, and such other matters as the court thinks fit.

(4) If the court orders the preparation of a revised directors' report it may give directions as to:
(a) the review of the report by the auditors;
(b) the revision of any summary financial statement;
(c) the taking of steps by the directors to bring the making of the order to the notice of persons likely to rely on the previous report; and
(d) such other matters as the court thinks fit.

(5) If the court finds that the accounts or report did not comply with the requirements of this Act (or, where applicable, of Article 4 of the IAS Regulation) it may order that all or part of:

(a) the costs (in Scotland, expenses) of and incidental to the application; and
(b) any reasonable expenses incurred by the company in connection with or in consequence of the preparation of revised accounts or a revised report, are to be borne by such of the directors as were party to the approval of the defective accounts or report.

For this purpose every director of the company at the time of the approval of the accounts or report shall be taken to have been a party to the approval unless he shows that he took all reasonable steps to prevent that approval.

(6) Where the court makes an order under subsection (5) it shall have regard to whether the directors party to the approval of the defective accounts or report knew or ought to have known that the accounts or report did not comply with the requirements of this Act (or, where applicable, of Article 4 of the IAS Regulation), and it may exclude one or more directors from the order or order the payment of different amounts by different directors.

(7) On the conclusion of proceedings on an application under this section, the applicant must send to the registrar for registration a copy of the court order or, as the case may be, give notice to the registrar that the application has failed or been withdrawn.

(8) The provisions of this section apply equally to revised annual accounts and revised directors' reports, in which case they have effect as if the references to revised accounts or reports were references to further revised accounts or reports.

457 Other persons authorised to apply to the court

(1) The Secretary of State may by order (an 'authorisation order') authorise for the purposes of section 456 any person appearing to him:
   (a) to have an interest in, and to have satisfactory procedures directed to securing, compliance by companies with the requirements of this Act (or, where applicable, of Article 4 of the IAS Regulation) relating to accounts and directors' reports;
   (b) to have satisfactory procedures for receiving and investigating complaints about companies' annual accounts and directors' reports; and
   (c) otherwise to be a fit and proper person to be authorised.

(2) A person may be authorised generally or in respect of particular classes of case, and different persons may be authorised in respect of different classes of case.

(3) The Secretary of State may refuse to authorise a person if he considers that his authorisation is unnecessary having regard to the fact that there are one or more other persons who have been or are likely to be authorised.

(4) If the authorised person is an unincorporated association, proceedings brought in, or in connection with, the exercise of any function by the association as an authorised person may be brought by or against the association in the name of a body corporate whose constitution provides for the establishment of the association.

(5) An authorisation order may contain such requirements or other provisions relating to the exercise of functions by the authorised person as appear to the Secretary of State to be appropriate.

No such order is to be made unless it appears to the Secretary of State that the person would, if authorised, exercise his functions as an authorised person in accordance with the provisions proposed.

(6) Where authorisation is revoked, the revoking order may make such provision as the Secretary of State thinks fit with respect to pending proceedings.

(7) An order under this section is subject to negative resolution procedure.

458 Disclosure of information by tax authorities

(1) The Commissioners for Her Majesty's Revenue and Customs may disclose information to a person authorised under section 457 for the purpose of facilitating:

(a) the taking of steps by that person to discover whether there are grounds for an application to the court under section 456 (application in respect of defective accounts etc.); or
(b) a decision by the authorised person whether to make such an application.

(2) This section applies despite any statutory or other restriction on the disclosure of information.

Provided that, in the case of personal data within the meaning of the Data Protection Act 1998 (c. 29), information is not to be disclosed in contravention of that Act.

(3) Information disclosed to an authorised person under this section:
  (a) may not be used except in or in connection with:
    (i) taking steps to discover whether there are grounds for an application to the court under section 456; or
    (ii) deciding whether or not to make such an application, or in, or in connection with, proceedings on such an application; and
  (b) must not be further disclosed except:
    (i) to the person to whom the information relates; or
    (ii) in, or in connection with, proceedings on any such application to the court.

(4) A person who contravenes subsection (3) commits an offence unless:
  (a) he did not know, and had no reason to suspect, that the information had been disclosed under this section; or
  (b) he took all reasonable steps and exercised all due diligence to avoid the commission of the offence.

(5) A person guilty of an offence under subsection (4) is liable:
  (a) on conviction on indictment, to imprisonment for a term not exceeding two years or a fine (or both);
  (b) on summary conviction:
    (i) in England and Wales, to imprisonment for a term not exceeding twelve months or to a fine not exceeding the statutory maximum (or both); and
    (ii) in Scotland or Northern Ireland, to imprisonment for a term not exceeding six months, or to a fine not exceeding the statutory maximum (or both).

Power of authorised person to require documents etc.

459 Power of authorised person to require documents, information and explanations

(1) This section applies where it appears to a person who is authorised under section 457 that there is, or may be, a question whether a company's annual accounts or directors' report comply with the requirements of this Act (or, where applicable, of Article 4 of the IAS Regulation).

(2) The authorised person may require any of the persons mentioned in subsection (3) to produce any document, or to provide him with any information or explanations, that he may reasonably require for the purpose of:
  (a) discovering whether there are grounds for an application to the court under section 456; or
  (b) deciding whether to make such an application.

(3) Those persons are:
  (a) the company;
  (b) any officer, employee, or auditor of the company; and
  (c) any persons who fell within paragraph (b) at a time to which the document or information required by the authorised person relates.

(4) If a person fails to comply with such a requirement, the authorised person may apply to the court.

(5) If it appears to the court that the person has failed to comply with a requirement under subsection (2), it may order the person to take such steps as it directs for

Appendix B Companies Act 2006

securing that the documents are produced or the information or explanations are provided.

(6) A statement made by a person in response to a requirement under subsection (2) or an order under subsection (5) may not be used in evidence against him in any criminal proceedings.

(7) Nothing in this section compels any person to disclose documents or information in respect of which a claim to legal professional privilege (in Scotland, to confidentiality of communications) could be maintained in legal proceedings.

(8) In this section 'document' includes information recorded in any form.

460 Restrictions on disclosure of information obtained under compulsory powers

(1) This section applies to information (in whatever form) obtained in pursuance of a requirement or order under section 459 (power of authorised person to require documents etc.) that relates to the private affairs of an individual or to any particular business.

(2) No such information may, during the lifetime of that individual or so long as that business continues to be carried on, be disclosed without the consent of that individual or the person for the time being carrying on that business.

(3) This does not apply:
    (a) to disclosure permitted by section 461 (permitted disclosure of information obtained under compulsory powers); or
    (b) to the disclosure of information that is or has been available to the public from another source.

(4) A person who discloses information in contravention of this section commits an offence, unless:
    (a) he did not know, and had no reason to suspect, that the information had been disclosed under section 459; or
    (b) he took all reasonable steps and exercised all due diligence to avoid the commission of the offence.

(5) A person guilty of an offence under this section is liable:
    (a) on conviction on indictment, to imprisonment for a term not exceeding two years or a fine (or both);
    (b) on summary conviction:
        (i) in England and Wales, to imprisonment for a term not exceeding twelve months or to a fine not exceeding the statutory maximum (or both); and
        (ii) in Scotland or Northern Ireland, to imprisonment for a term not exceeding six months, or to a fine not exceeding the statutory maximum (or both).

461 Permitted disclosure of information obtained under compulsory powers

(1) The prohibition in section 460 of the disclosure of information obtained in pursuance of a requirement or order under section 459 (power of authorised person to require documents etc.) that relates to the private affairs of an individual or to any particular business has effect subject to the following exceptions.

(2) It does not apply to the disclosure of information for the purpose of facilitating the carrying out by the authorised person of his functions under section 456.

(3) It does not apply to disclosure to:
    (a) the Secretary of State;
    (b) the Department of Enterprise, Trade and Investment for Northern Ireland;
    (c) the Treasury;
    (d) the Bank of England;
    (e) the Financial Services Authority; or
    (f) the Commissioners for Her Majesty's Revenue and Customs.

(4) It does not apply to disclosure:
 (a) for the purpose of assisting a body designated by an order under section 1252 (delegation of functions of the Secretary of State) to exercise its functions under Part 42;
 (b) with a view to the institution of, or otherwise for the purposes of, disciplinary proceedings relating to the performance by an accountant or auditor of his professional duties;
 (c) for the purpose of enabling or assisting the Secretary of State or the Treasury to exercise any of their functions under any of the following:
  (i) the Companies Acts;
  (ii) Part 5 of the Criminal Justice Act 1993 (c. 36) (insider dealing);
  (iii) the Insolvency Act 1986 (c. 45) or the Insolvency (Northern Ireland) Order 1989 (S.I. 1989/2405 (N.I. 19));
  (iv) the Company Directors Disqualification Act 1986 (c. 46) or the Company Directors Disqualification (Northern Ireland) Order 2002 (S.I. 2002/3150 (N.I. 4));
  (v) the Financial Services and Markets Act 2000 (c. 8);
 (d) for the purpose of enabling or assisting the Department of Enterprise, Trade and Investment for Northern Ireland to exercise any powers conferred on it by the enactments relating to companies, directors' disqualification or insolvency;
 (e) for the purpose of enabling or assisting the Bank of England to exercise its functions;
 (f) for the purpose of enabling or assisting the Commissioners for Her Majesty's Revenue and Customs to exercise their functions;
 (g) for the purpose of enabling or assisting the Financial Services Authority to exercise its functions under any of the following:
  (i) the legislation relating to friendly societies or to industrial and provident societies;
  (ii) the Building Societies Act 1986 (c. 53);
  (iii) Part 7 of the Companies Act 1989 (c. 40);
  (iv) the Financial Services and Markets Act 2000; or
 (h) in pursuance of any Community obligation.

(5) It does not apply to disclosure to a body exercising functions of a public nature under legislation in any country or territory outside the United Kingdom that appear to the authorised person to be similar to his functions under section 456 for the purpose of enabling or assisting that body to exercise those functions.

(6) In determining whether to disclose information to a body in accordance with subsection (5), the authorised person must have regard to the following considerations:
 (a) whether the use which the body is likely to make of the information is sufficiently important to justify making the disclosure;
 (b) whether the body has adequate arrangements to prevent the information from being used or further disclosed other than:
  (i) for the purposes of carrying out the functions mentioned in that subsection; or
  (ii) for other purposes substantially similar to those for which information disclosed to the authorised person could be used or further disclosed.

(7) Nothing in this section authorises the making of a disclosure in contravention of the Data Protection Act 1998 (c. 29).

462 Power to amend categories of permitted disclosure

(1) The Secretary of State may by order amend section 461(3), (4) and (5).

(2) An order under this section must not:
 (a) amend subsection (3) of that section (UK public authorities) by specifying a person unless the person exercises functions of a public nature (whether or not he exercises any other function);

(b) amend subsection (4) of that section (purposes for which disclosure permitted) by adding or modifying a description of disclosure unless the purpose for which the disclosure is permitted is likely to facilitate the exercise of a function of a public nature; or

(c) amend subsection (5) of that section (overseas regulatory authorities) so as to have the effect of permitting disclosures to be made to a body other than one that exercises functions of a public nature in a country or territory outside the United Kingdom.

(3) An order under this section is subject to negative resolution procedure.

CHAPTER 12

SUPPLEMENTARY PROVISIONS

Liability for false or misleading statements in reports

463 Liability for false or misleading statements in reports

(1) The reports to which this section applies are:
(a) the directors' report;
(b) the directors' remuneration report; and
(c) a summary financial statement so far as it is derived from either of those reports.

(2) A director of a company is liable to compensate the company for any loss suffered by it as a result of:
(a) any untrue or misleading statement in a report to which this section applies; or
(b) the omission from a report to which this section applies of anything required to be included in it.

(3) He is so liable only if:
(a) he knew the statement to be untrue or misleading or was reckless as to whether it was untrue or misleading; or
(b) he knew the omission to be dishonest concealment of a material fact.

(4) No person shall be subject to any liability to a person other than the company resulting from reliance, by that person or another, on information in a report to which this section applies.

(5) The reference in subsection (4) to a person being subject to a liability includes a reference to another person being entitled as against him to be granted any civil remedy or to rescind or repudiate an agreement.

(6) This section does not affect:
(a) liability for a civil penalty; or
(b) liability for a criminal offence.

Accounting and reporting standards

464 Accounting standards

(1) In this Part 'accounting standards' means statements of standard accounting practice issued by such body or bodies as may be prescribed by regulations.

(2) References in this Part to accounting standards applicable to a company's annual accounts are to such standards as are, in accordance with their terms, relevant to the company's circumstances and to the accounts.

(3) Regulations under this section may contain such transitional and other supplementary and incidental provisions as appear to the Secretary of State to be appropriate.

Part 15 Accounts and reports (Sections 380–474)

Companies qualifying as medium-sized

465 Companies qualifying as medium-sized: general

(1) A company qualifies as medium-sized in relation to its first financial year if the qualifying conditions are met in that year.

(2) A company qualifies as medium-sized in relation to a subsequent financial year:
  (a) if the qualifying conditions are met in that year and the preceding financial year;
  (b) if the qualifying conditions are met in that year and the company qualified as medium-sized in relation to the preceding financial year; and
  (c) if the qualifying conditions were met in the preceding financial year and the company qualified as medium-sized in relation to that year.

(3) The qualifying conditions are met by a company in a year in which it satisfies two or more of the following requirements:

1.	Turnover	Not more than *£25.9 million*
2.	Balance sheet total	Not more than *£12.9 million*
3.	Number of employees	Not more than 250

(4) For a period that is a company's financial year but not in fact a year the maximum figures for turnover must be proportionately adjusted.

(5) The balance sheet total means the aggregate of the amounts shown as assets in the company's balance sheet.

(6) The number of employees means the average number of persons employed by the company in the year, determined as follows:
  (a) find for each month in the financial year the number of persons employed under contracts of service by the company in that month (whether throughout the month or not);
  (b) add together the monthly totals; and
  (c) divide by the number of months in the financial year.

(7) This section is subject to section 466 (companies qualifying as medium-sized: parent companies).

466 Companies qualifying as medium-sized: parent companies

(1) A parent company qualifies as a medium-sized company in relation to a financial year only if the group headed by it qualifies as a medium-sized group.

(2) A group qualifies as medium-sized in relation to the parent company's first financial year if the qualifying conditions are met in that year.

(3) A group qualifies as medium-sized in relation to a subsequent financial year of the parent company:
  (a) if the qualifying conditions are met in that year and the preceding financial year;
  (b) if the qualifying conditions are met in that year and the group qualified as medium-sized in relation to the preceding financial year; and
  (c) if the qualifying conditions were met in the preceding financial year and the group qualified as medium-sized in relation to that year.

(4) The qualifying conditions are met by a group in a year in which it satisfies two or more of the following requirements:

1.	Aggregate turnover	Not more than *£25.9 million net (or £31.1 million gross)*
2.	Aggregate balance sheet total	Not more than *£12.9 million net (or £15.5 million gross)*
3.	Aggregate number of employees	Not more than 250

(5) The aggregate figures are ascertained by aggregating the relevant figures determined in accordance with section 465 for each member of the group.

(6) In relation to the aggregate figures for turnover and balance sheet total:

'net' means after any set-offs and other adjustments made to eliminate group transactions:
   (a) in the case of Companies Act accounts, in accordance with regulations under section 404;
   (b) in the case of IAS accounts, in accordance with international accounting standards; and

'gross' means without those set-offs and other adjustments.

A company may satisfy any relevant requirement on the basis of either the net or the gross figure.

(7) The figures for each subsidiary undertaking shall be those included in its individual accounts for the relevant financial year, that is:
   (a) if its financial year ends with that of the parent company, that financial year; and
   (b) if not, its financial year ending last before the end of the financial year of the parent company.

If those figures cannot be obtained without disproportionate expense or undue delay, the latest available figures shall be taken.

467 Companies excluded from being treated as medium-sized

(1) A company is not entitled to take advantage of any of the provisions of this Part relating to companies qualifying as medium-sized if it was at any time within the financial year in question:
   (a) a public company;
   (b) a company that:
      (i) has permission under Part 4 of the Financial Services and Markets Act 2000 (c. 8) to carry on a regulated activity; or
      (ii) carries on insurance market activity, or
   (c) a member of an ineligible group.

(2) A group is ineligible if any of its members is:
   (a) a public company;
   (b) a body corporate (other than a company) whose shares are admitted to trading on a regulated market;
   (c) a person (other than a small company) who has permission under Part 4 of the Financial Services and Markets Act 2000 to carry on a regulated activity;
   (d) a small company that is an authorised insurance company, a banking company, an e-money issuer, or a UCITS management company, or [a MiFID investment firm]. *[SI 2007 No.2932]*
   (e) a person who carries on insurance market activity.

(3) A company is a small company for the purposes of subsection (2) if it qualified as small in relation to its last financial year ending on or before the end of the financial year in question.

(4) This section does not prevent a company from taking advantage of section 417(7) (business review: non-financial information) by reason only of its having been a member of an ineligible group at any time within the financial year in question.

General power to make further provision about accounts and reports

468 General power to make further provision about accounts and reports

(1) The Secretary of State may make provision by regulations about:
   (a) the accounts and reports that companies are required to prepare;
   (b) the categories of companies required to prepare accounts and reports of any description;

(c) the form and content of the accounts and reports that companies are required to prepare;
(d) the obligations of companies and others as regards:
  (i) the approval of accounts and reports;
  (ii) the sending of accounts and reports to members and others;
  (iii) the laying of accounts and reports before the company in general meeting;
  (iv) the delivery of copies of accounts and reports to the registrar; and
  (v) the publication of accounts and reports.

(2) The regulations may amend this Part by adding, altering or repealing provisions.

(3) But they must not amend (other than consequentially):
  (a) section 393 (accounts to give true and fair view); or
  (b) the provisions of Chapter 11 (revision of defective accounts and reports).

(4) The regulations may create criminal offences in cases corresponding to those in which an offence is created by an existing provision of this Part.
The maximum penalty for any such offence may not be greater than is provided in relation to an offence under the existing provision.

(5) The regulations may provide for civil penalties in circumstances corresponding to those within section 453(1) (civil penalty for failure to file accounts and reports).
The provisions of section 453(2) to (5) apply in relation to any such penalty.

Other supplementary provisions

469 Preparation and filing of accounts in euros

(1) The amounts set out in the annual accounts of a company may also be shown in the same accounts translated into euros.

(2) When complying with section 441 (duty to file accounts and reports), the directors of a company may deliver to the registrar an additional copy of the company's annual accounts in which the amounts have been translated into euros.

(3) In both cases:
  (a) the amounts must have been translated at the exchange rate prevailing on the date to which the balance sheet is made up; and
  (b) that rate must be disclosed in the notes to the accounts.

(4) For the purposes of sections 434 and 435 (requirements in connection with published accounts) any additional copy of the company's annual accounts delivered to the registrar under subsection (2) above shall be treated as statutory accounts of the company.

In the case of such a copy, references in those sections to the auditor's report on the company's annual accounts shall be read as references to the auditor's report on the annual accounts of which it is a copy.

470 Power to apply provisions to banking partnerships

(1) The Secretary of State may by regulations apply to banking partnerships, subject to such exceptions, adaptations and modifications as he considers appropriate, the provisions of this Part (and of regulations made under this Part) applying to banking companies.

(2) A 'banking partnership' means a partnership which has permission under Part 4 of the Financial Services and Markets Act 2000 (c. 8).

But a partnership is not a banking partnership if it has permission to accept deposits only for the purpose of carrying on another regulated activity in accordance with that permission.

Appendix B Companies Act 2006

(3) Expressions used in this section that are also used in the provisions regulating activities under the Financial Services and Markets Act 2000 have the same meaning here as they do in those provisions.

See section 22 of that Act, orders made under that section and Schedule 2 to that Act.

(4) Regulations under this section are subject to affirmative resolution procedure.

471 Meaning of 'annual accounts' and related expressions

(1) In this Part a company's 'annual accounts', in relation to a financial year, means:
   (a) the company's individual accounts for that year (see section 394); and
   (b) any group accounts prepared by the company for that year (see sections 398 and 399).
   This is subject to section 408 (option to omit individual profit and loss account from annual accounts where information given in group accounts).

(2) In the case of an unquoted company, its "annual accounts and reports" for a financial year are:
   (a) its annual accounts;
   (b) the directors' report; and
   (c) the auditor's report on those accounts and the directors' report (unless the company is exempt from audit).

(3) In the case of a quoted company, its 'annual accounts and reports' for a financial year are:
   (a) its annual accounts;
   (b) the directors' remuneration report;
   (c) the directors' report; and
   (d) the auditor's report on those accounts, on the auditable part of the directors' remuneration report and on the directors' report.

472 Notes to the accounts

(1) Information required by this Part to be given in notes to a company's annual accounts may be contained in the accounts or in a separate document annexed to the accounts.

(2) References in this Part to a company's annual accounts, or to a balance sheet or profit and loss account, include notes to the accounts giving information which is required by any provision of this Act or international accounting standards, and required or allowed by any such provision to be given in a note to company accounts.

472A Meaning of "corporate governance statement" etc.

(1) In this Part "corporate governance statement" means the statement required by rules 7.2.1 to 7.2.11 in the Disclosure Rules and Transparency Rules sourcebook issued by the Financial Services Authority.

(2) Those rules were inserted by Annex C of the Disclosure Rules and Transparency Rules Sourcebook (Corporate Governance Rules) Instrument 2008 made by the Authority on 26th June 2008 (FSA 2008/32).

(3) A "separate" corporate governance statement means one that is not included in the directors' report.

473 Parliamentary procedure for certain regulations under this Part

(1) This section applies to regulations under the following provisions of this Part:
   section 396 (Companies Act individual accounts);
   section 404 (Companies Act group accounts);
   section 409 (information about related undertakings);

section 412 (information about directors' benefits: remuneration, pensions and compensation for loss of office);
section 416 (contents of directors' report: general);
section 421 (contents of directors' remuneration report);
section 444 (filing obligations of companies subject to small companies regime);
section 445 (filing obligations of medium-sized companies); and
section 468 (general power to make further provision about accounts and reports).

(2) Any such regulations may make consequential amendments or repeals in other provisions of this Act, or in other enactments.

(3) Regulations that:
   (a) restrict the classes of company which have the benefit of any exemption, exception or special provision;
   (b) require additional matter to be included in a document of any class; or
   (c) otherwise render the requirements of this Part more onerous, **are subject to affirmative resolution procedure.**

(4) Otherwise, the regulations are subject to **negative resolution procedure**.

474 Minor definitions

(1) In this Part:

'e-money issuer' means a person who has permission under Part 4 of the Financial Services and Markets Act 2000 (c. 8) to carry on the activity of issuing electronic money within the meaning of article 9B of the Financial Services and Markets Act 2000 (Regulated Activities) Order 2001 (S.I. 2001/544);

'group' means a parent undertaking and its subsidiary undertakings;

'IAS Regulation' means EC Regulation No. 1606/2002 of the European Parliament and of the Council of 19 July 2002 on the application of international accounting standards;

'included in the consolidation', in relation to group accounts, or 'included in consolidated group accounts', means that the undertaking is included in the accounts by the method of full (and not proportional) consolidation, and references to an undertaking excluded from consolidation shall be construed accordingly;

'international accounting standards' means the international accounting standards, within the meaning of the IAS Regulation, adopted from time to time by the European Commission in accordance with that Regulation;

[...........] *[SI 2007 No. 2932]*

'MiFID investment firm' means an investment firm within the meaning of Article 4.1.1 of Directive 2004/39/EC of the European Parliament and of the Council of 21 April 2004 on markets in financial instruments, other than:
   (a) a company to which that Directive does not apply by virtue of Article 2 of that Directive;
   (b) a company which is an exempt investment firm within the meaning of regulation 4A(3) of the Financial Services and Markets Act 2000 (Markets in Financial Instruments) Regulations 2007; and
   (c) any other company which fulfils all the requirements set out in regulation 4C(3) of those Regulations.

'profit and loss account', in relation to a company that prepares IAS accounts, includes an income statement or other equivalent financial statement required to be prepared by international accounting standards;

'regulated activity' has the meaning given in section 22 of the Financial Services and Markets Act 2000, except that it does not include activities of the kind specified in any of the following provisions of the Financial Services and Markets Act 2000 Regulated Activities) Order 2001 (S.I. 2001/544):
   (a) article 25A (arranging regulated mortgage contracts);
   (b) article 25B (arranging regulated home reversion plans);
   (c) article 25C (arranging regulated home purchase plans);

(d) article 39A (assisting administration and performance of a contract of insurance);
(e) article 53A (advising on regulated mortgage contracts);
(f) article 53B (advising on regulated home reversion plans);
(g) article 53C (advising on regulated home purchase plans);
(h) article 21 (dealing as agent), article 25 (arranging deals in investments) or article 53 (advising on investments) where the activity concerns relevant investments that are not contractually based investments (within the meaning of article 3 of that Order); or
(i) article 64 (agreeing to carry on a regulated activity of the kind mentioned in paragraphs (a) to (h)).

'turnover', in relation to a company, means the amounts derived from the provision of goods and services falling within the company's ordinary activities, after deduction of:
(a) trade discounts;
(b) value added tax; and
(c) any other taxes based on the amounts so derived.

'UCITS management company' has the meaning given by the Glossary forming part of the Handbook made by the Financial Services Authority under the Financial Services and Markets Act 2000 (c. 8).

(2) In the case of an undertaking not trading for profit, any reference in this Part to a profit and loss account is to an income and expenditure account.

References to profit and loss and, in relation to group accounts, to a consolidated profit and loss account shall be construed accordingly.

Appendix C Statutory formats of accounts – SI 2008 No. 409 Schedule 1

This appendix reproduces the formats contained in SI 2008 No. 409 *The Small Companies and Groups (Accounts and Directors' Report) Regulations 2008* Schedule 1 ('The required formats for accounts').

For ease of reference, the 'notes following the formats' (SI 2008 No. 409 Schedule 1) have been summarised and annotated against the format headings.

The formats for group accounts are as for individual companies in Schedule 1 amended for group circumstances by Schedule 6 (Sch 6. 1(2)–(3)).

Refer to **Chapters 3** and **6** for use of the formats and **Chapter 10 Table 10.7** at **10.9.2** ('Balance sheet format presentation') (for presentational considerations of a defined benefit pension scheme asset or liability within the FRSSE).

The formats are as follows:

Balance sheet formats (small companies) – SI 2008 No. 409 Schedule 1
Balance sheet – Format 1
                Format 2

Profit and loss account formats (small companies) – SI 2008 No. 409 Schedule 1
Profit and loss account – Format 1
                            Format 2
                            Format 3
                            Format 4

Abbreviated accounts (small companies)
The formats may be further abbreviated in abbreviated accounts *(SI 2008 No. 409 Schedule 4)* – see also **Chapter 8**.

Appendix C Statutory formats of accounts

Small company balance sheet Format 1 (*SI 2008 No. 409 Schedule 1*)

The balance sheet format of a small company which adopts balance sheet Format 1 in accordance with *SI 2008 No. 409 Schedule 1* is as follows:

A Called up share capital not paid *Alternative position under C II 3 below*

B Fixed assets
    I Intangible assets
        1 Goodwill   *Must only be included to the extent acquired for valuable consideration*
        2 Other intangible assets   *Assets must have been acquired for valuable consideration or created by company itself (See Note 1 below)*
    II Tangible assets
        1 Land and buildings
        2 Plant and machinery, etc.
    III Investments (See *Note 2 below*)
        1 Shares in group undertakings and participating interests
        2 Loans to group undertakings and undertakings in which the company has a participating interest
        3 Other investments other than loans
        4 Other investments   *Show the nominal value of own shares separately*

C Current assets
    I Stocks
        1 Stocks
        2 Payments on account
    II Debtors (See *Note 3 below*)
        1 Trade debtors
        2 Amounts owed by group undertakings and undertakings in which the company has a participating interest
        3 Other debtors   *Alternative position of A or D*
    III Investments
        1 Shares in group undertakings
        2 Other investments   *Show the nominal value of own shares held separately*
    IV Cash at bank and in hand

D Prepayments and accrued income   *Alternative position under C II 3 above*

E Creditors: amounts falling due within one year
        1 Bank loans and overdrafts
        2 Trade creditors
        3 Amounts owed to group undertakings and undertakings in which the company has a participating interest
        4 Other creditors   *Show taxation and social security, and convertible loans separately*
                            Include payments received on account of orders if not shown as deductions from stocks
                            Accruals and deferred income may be shown under J or H4

Small company balance sheet Format 1 (SI 2008 No. 409 Schedule 1)

Small company balance sheet Format 1 (*SI 2008 No. 409 Schedule 1*) (*continued*)

F Net current assets (liabilities) *Take into account any prepayments and accrued income*

G Total assets less current liabilities

H Creditors: amounts falling due after more than one year
    1 Bank loans and overdrafts
    2 Trade creditors
    3 Amounts owed to group undertakings and undertakings in which the company has a participating interest
    4 Other creditors   *Show taxation and social security and convertible loans separately*
    Include payments received on account of orders if not shown as deductions from stocks
    Accruals and deferred income may be shown under J or E4

I Provisions for liabilities

J Accruals and deferred income *Alternative position E4 or H4 as appropriate*

---
* Minority interests *Group accounts – Alternative position below K*

K Capital and reserves
    I   Called up share capital   *Show (a) allotted and (b) called up and paid up share capital separately*
    II Share premium account
    III Revaluation reserve
    IV Other reserves
    V Profit and loss account

---
* Minority interests *Group accounts – Alternative position below J*

Notes
The italicised notes in the above formats are extracted from the notes on the balance sheet formats contained in SI 2008 No. 409 Schedule 1. The following comments support the notes:

(1) Such assets comprise (a) concessions, patents, licences, trade marks and similar rights and assets, and (b) goodwill not otherwise required to be shown at B1.

(2) In a consolidated balance sheet the format for BIII 'Investments' (where a small company prepares small group accounts) is: SI 2008 No. 409 Schedule 6.1(2)

    1 Shares in group undertakings
    2 Interests in associated undertakings
    3 Other participating interests
    4 Loans to group undertakings and undertakings in which a participating interest is held
    5 Other investments other than loans
    6 Others.

(3) A small company must disclose the amount of 'debtors falling due after more than one year' for each item unless the aggregate amount of such debtors is disclosed in the notes to the accounts rather than in the balance sheet. Except for entities applying the FRSSE, ASB UITF abstract No. 4 requires disclosure in the balance sheet if it is material in the context of total net current assets.

* *Ascribed a letter in balance sheet formats*

Appendix C Statutory formats of accounts

Small company balance sheet Format 2 (*SI 2008 No. 409 Schedule 1*)

ASSETS

A Called up share capital not paid *Alternative position under C II 3 below*

B Fixed assets
    I   Intangible assets
        1 Goodwill   *Must only be included to the extent acquired for valuable consideration*
        2 Other intangible assets   *Concessions, patents, licences, trade marks and similar rights and assets must have been acquired for valuable consideration or created by company itself*
    II Tangible assets
        1 Land and buildings
        2 Plant and machinery, etc.
    III Investments
        1 Shares in group undertakings and participating interests
        2 Loans to group undertakings and undertakings in which the company has a participating interest
        3 Other investments other than loans
        4 Other investments   *Show the nominal value of own shares held separately*

C Current assets
    I   Stocks
        1 Stocks
        2 Payments on accounts
    II Debtors   *For each item show amounts falling due after more than one year unless aggregate is disclosed in the notes*
        1 Trade debtors
        2 Amounts owed by group undertakings and undertakings in which the company has a participating interest
        3 Other debtors   *Alternative position of A or D*
    III Investments
        1 Shares in group undertakings
        2 Other investments   *Show the nominal value of own shares held separately*
    IV Cash at bank and in hand

D Prepayments and accrued income   *Alternative position under C II 3 above*

Small company balance sheet Format 2 (SI 2008 No. 409 Schedule 1)

Small company balance sheet Format 2 (*SI 2008 No. 409 Schedule 1*) (*continued*)

LIABILITIES

Notes

A *Capital and reserves*
    I   Called up share capital   *Show (a) allotted and (b) called up and paid up share capital separately*

    II   Share premium account
    III Revaluation reserve
    IV Other reserves
    V   Profit and loss account

---

* *Minority interests*   *Group accounts*

B *Provisions for liabilities*

C *Creditors*   *Amounts falling due: 'within one year' and 'after one year' should be shown separately in aggregate and separately for each item of 'Creditors' unless the separate aggregate amounts are disclosed in the notes*

    1 Bank loans and overdrafts
    2 Trade creditors
    3 Amounts owed to group undertakings and undertakings in which the company has a participating interest
    4 Other creditors   *Show taxation and social security and convertible loans separately from other creditors
Include payments received on account of orders if not shown as deductions from stocks
Accruals and deferred income–alternative position D below*
    5 Accruals and deferred income   *Alternative position D below*

D *Accruals and deferred income*   *Alternative position within C4 above*

* *Ascribed a letter in balance sheet formats*

Appendix C Statutory formats of accounts

Profit and loss account   Format 1

Notes

1. Turnover
2. Cost of sales — *Take into account any provision for depreciation or diminution of assets*
3. Gross profit or loss
4. Distribution costs — *Take into account any provision for depreciation or diminution of assets*
5. Administrative expenses — *Take into account any provision for depreciation or diminution of assets*
6. Other operating income
7. Income from shares in group undertakings
8. Income from participating interests

> Or
> (Group accounts):
> 8. (a) Income from interests in associated undertakings — *Include interests held by all group companies*
>   (b) Income from other participating interests — *Sch. 6.1(3)*

9. Income from other fixed asset investments — *Show group income separately*
10. Other interest receivable and similar income — *Show group income separately*
11. Amounts written off investments
12. Interest payable and similar charges — *Show group interest separately*
13. Tax on profit or loss on ordinary activities
14. Profit or loss on ordinary activities after taxation

> * Minority interests — *Group accounts*
> 15. Extraordinary income
> 16. Extraordinary charges
> 17. Extraordinary profit or loss
> 18. Tax on extraordinary profit or loss
> * Minority interests — *Group accounts – Minority interests share in extraordinary items*

19. Other taxes not shown under the above items
20. Profit or loss for the financial year

Depreciation and other amounts written off tangible and intangible fixed assets must be disclosed in a note

Every profit and loss account must show the amount of a company's profit or loss on ordinary activities before taxation. (SI 2008 No. 409 Sch. 1.6)

---

* *Ascribed an Arabic number in profit and loss account formats*

Profit and loss account   Format 2

Notes

1. Turnover
2. Change in stocks of finished goods and in work-in-progress
3. Own work capitalised
4. Other operating income
5. (a) Raw materials and consumables
   (b) Other external charges
6. Staff costs:
   (a) wages and salaries
   (b) social security costs
   (c) other pension costs
7. (a) Depreciation and other amounts written off tangible and intangible fixed assets
   (b) Exceptional amounts written off current assets
8. Other operating charges
9. Income from shares in group undertakings
10. Income from participating interests

or (Group accounts):	
10 (a) Income from interests in associated undertakings	*Include interests held by all group companies*
(b) Income from other participating interests	**Sch. 6.1(3)**

11. Income from other fixed asset investments — *Show group income separately*
12. Other interest receivable and similar income — *Show group income separately*
13. Amounts written off investments
14. Interest payable and similar charges — *Show group interest separately*
15. Tax on profit or loss on ordinary activities
16. Profit or loss on ordinary activities after taxation

* Minority interests	*Group accounts*
17 Extraordinary income	
18 Extraordinary charges	
19 Extraordinary profit or loss	
20 Tax on extraordinary profit or loss	
* Minority interests	*Group accounts – Minority interests share in extraordinary items*

21. Other taxes not shown under the above items
22. Profit or loss for the financial year

Every profit and loss account must show the amount of a company's profit or loss on ordinary activities before taxation. (SI 2008 No. 409 Sch. 1.6)

---

* *Ascribed an Arabic number in profit and loss account formats*

Appendix C Statutory formats of accounts

Profit and loss account   Format 3

A Charges

		Notes
1	Cost of sales	*Take into account any provision for depreciation or diminution of assets*
2	Distribution costs	*Take into account any provison for depreciation or diminution of assets*
3	Administrative expenses	*Take into account any provision for depreciation or diminution of assets*
4	Amounts written off investments	
5	Interest payable and similar charges	*Show group interest separately*
6	Tax on profit or loss on ordinary activities	
7	Profit or loss on ordinary activities after taxation	

*	Minority interests	*Group accounts – Where minority interests share in loss*
8	Extraordinary charges	
9	Tax on extraordinary profit or loss	
*	Minority interests	*Group accounts – Minority interests share in extraordinary items*

10	Other taxes not shown under the above items	
11	Profit or loss for the financial year	

B Income

1. Turnover
2. Other operating income
3. Income from shares in group undertakings
4. Income from participating interests

	or (Group accounts):	*Include interests held by all group companies*
4	(a) Income from interests in associated undertakings	
	(b) Income from other participating interests	Sch. 6.1(3)

5	Income from other fixed asset investments	*Show group income separately*
6	Other interest receivable and similar income	*Show group income separately*
7	Profit or loss on ordinary activities after taxation	

*	Minority interests	*Group accounts – Where minority interests share in loss*
8	Extraordinary income	
*	Minority interests	*Group accounts – Minority interests share in extraordinary items*

Profit and loss account Format 3 (*continued*)

9 Profit or loss for the financial year

Depreciation and other amounts written off tangible and intangible fixed assets must be disclosed in a note

Every profit and loss account must show the amount of a company's profit or loss on ordinary activities before taxation. (SI 2008 No. 409 Sch. 1.6)

Profit and loss account formats 3 and 4 are not recognised under the FRSSE.

* *Ascribed an Arabic number in profit and loss account formats*

Appendix C Statutory formats of accounts

Profit and loss account Format 4

Notes

A Charges
1. Reduction in stocks of finished goods and in work-in-progress
2. (a) Raw materials and consumables
   (b) Other external charges
3. Staff costs:
   (a) wages and salaries
   (b) social security costs
   (c) other pension costs
4. (a) Depreciation and other amounts written off tangible and intangible fixed assets
   (b) Exceptional amounts written off current assets
5. Other operating charges
6. Amounts written off investments
7. Interest payable and similar charges *Show group interest separately*
8. Tax on profit or loss on ordinary activities
9. Profit or loss on ordinary activities after taxation

---
* Minority interests *Group accounts – Where minority interests share in loss*

10. Extraordinary charges
11. Tax on extraordinary profit or loss
* Minority interests *Group accounts – Minority interests share in extraordinary items*

---

12. Other taxes not shown under the above items
13. Profit or loss for the financial year

B Income
1. Turnover
2. Increase in stocks of finished goods and in work-in-progress
3. Own work capitalised
4. Other operating income
5. Income from shares in group undertakings
6. Income from participating interests

---
or (Group accounts): *Include interests held by all group companies*
6. (a) Income from interests in associated undertakings
   (b) Income from other participating interests Sch. 6.1(3)

---

7. Income from other fixed asset investments *Show group income separately*
8. Other interest receivable and similar income *Show group income separately*
9. Profit or loss on ordinary activities after taxation

---
* Minority interests *Where minority interests share in profit*
10. Extraordinary income
* Minority interests *Minority interests share in extraordinary items*

---

11. Profit or loss for the financial year

Every profit and loss account must show the amount of a company's profit or loss on ordinary activities before taxation. (SI 2008 No. 409 Sch. 1.6)

Profit and loss account formats 3 and 4 are not recognised under the FRSSE.

* *Ascribed an Arabic number in profit and loss account formats*

Companies Act abbreviated accounts – company abbreviated balance sheets

Formats 1 and 2 (*SI 2008 No. 409 Schedule 4*)

A small company may deliver to the registrar a copy of the balance sheet showing the items listed in either of the balance sheet formats set out below, in the order and under the headings and sub-headings given in the format adopted, but in other respects corresponding to the full balance sheet.

The required balance sheet formats are as follows:

[Abbreviated] Balance sheet formats (*SI 2008 No. 409 Schedule 4*)

Format 1

A. Called up share capital not paid
B. Fixed assets
   I Intangible assets
   II Tangible assets
   III Investments
C. Current assets
   I Stocks
   II Debtors *(1)*
   III Investments
   IV Cash at bank and in hand
D. Prepayments and accrued income
E. Creditors: amounts falling due within one year
F. Net current assets (liabilities)
G. Total assets less current liabilities
H. Creditors: amounts falling due after more than one year
I. Provisions for liabilities
J. Accruals and deferred income
K. Capital and reserves
   I Called up share capital
   II Share premium account
   III Revaluation reserve
   IV Other reserves
   V Profit and loss account

Format 2

ASSETS

A. Called up share capital not paid
B. Fixed assets
   I Intangible assets
   II Tangible assets
   III Investments
C. Current assets
   I Stocks
   II Debtors *(1)*
   III Investments
   IV Cash at bank and in hand
D. Prepayments and accrued income

LIABILITIES

A. Capital and reserves
   I Called up share capital
   II Share premium account
   III Revaluation reserve
   IV Other reserves
   V Profit and loss account
B. Provisions for liabilities
C. Creditors *(2)*
D. Accruals and deferred income

Note 1 Debtors (Formats 1 and 2) – The aggregate amount of debtors falling due after more than one year must be shown separately, unless it is disclosed in the notes to the accounts.

Note 2 Creditors (Format 2) – The aggregate amount of creditors falling due within one year and of creditors falling due after more than one year must be shown separately, unless it is disclosed in the notes to the accounts.

© *Crown copyright is reproduced with the permission of the Controller of Her Majesty's Stationery Office.*

Appendix D Form and content of abbreviated accounts of small companies delivered to Registrar – Companies Act 2006 (SI 2008 No. 409 Schedule 4)

This appendix reproduces Schedule 4 to SI 2008 No. 409 ('Companies Act abbreviated accounts for delivery to Registrar of Companies').

SI 2008 No. 409 *The Small Companies and Groups (Accounts and Directors' Report) Regulations 2008* are reproduced in full in **Appendix E**.

PART 1

THE REQUIRED BALANCE SHEET FORMATS

1.—(1) A small company may deliver to the registrar a copy of the balance sheet showing the items listed in either of the balance sheet formats set out in 2 below in the order and under the headings and sub-headings given in the format adopted, but in other respects corresponding to the full balance sheet.

(2) The copy balance sheet must contain in a prominent position a statement that it has been prepared in accordance with the provisions applicable to companies subject to the small companies regime.

Balance sheet formats

Format 1

A. Called up share capital not paid
B. Fixed assets
   I Intangible assets
   II Tangible assets
   III Investments
C. Current assets
   I Stocks
   II Debtors *(1)*
   III Investments
   IV Cash at bank and in hand
D. Prepayments and accrued income
E. Creditors: amounts falling due within one year
F. Net current assets (liabilities)
G. Total assets less current liabilities
H. Creditors: amounts falling due after more than one year
I. Provisions for liabilities
J. Accruals and deferred income
K. Capital and reserves
   I Called up share capital
   II Share premium account
   III Revaluation reserve
   IV Other reserves
   V Profit and loss account

Format 2

ASSETS
A. Called up share capital not paid
B. Fixed assets
   I Intangible assets
   II Tangible assets
   III Investments
C. Current assets
   I Stocks
   II Debtors *(1)*
   III Investments
   IV Cash at bank and in hand
D. Prepayments and accrued income

LIABILITIES
A. Capital and reserves
   I Called up share capital
   II Share premium account
   III Revaluation reserve
   IV Other reserves
   V Profit and loss account
B. Provisions for liabilities
C. Creditors *(2)*
D. Accruals and deferred income

Appendix D Form and content of abbreviated accounts of small companies

Notes on the balance sheet formats

(1) Debtors
(Formats 1 and 2, item C.II.)

The aggregate amount of debtors falling due after more than one year must be shown separately, unless it is disclosed in the notes to the accounts.

(2) Creditors
(Format 2, Liabilities item C.)

The aggregate amount of creditors falling due within one year and of creditors falling due after more than one year must be shown separately, unless it is disclosed in the notes to the accounts.

PART 2

NOTES TO THE ACCOUNTS

Preliminary

2. Any information required in the case of any small company by the following provisions of this Part of this Schedule must (if not given in the company's accounts) be given by way of a note to those accounts.

Disclosure of accounting policies

3. The accounting policies adopted by the company in determining the amounts to be included in respect of items shown in the balance sheet and in determining the profit or loss of the company must be stated (including such policies with respect to the depreciation and diminution in value of assets).

Information supplementing the balance sheet

Share capital and debentures
4.—(1) Where shares of more than one class have been allotted, the number and aggregate nominal value of shares of each class allotted must be given.

(2) In the case of any part of the allotted share capital that consists of redeemable shares, the following information must be given—
    (a) the earliest and latest dates on which the company has power to redeem those shares;
    (b) whether those shares must be redeemed in any event or are liable to be redeemed at the option of the company or of the shareholder; and
    (c) whether any (and, if so, what) premium is payable on redemption.

5. If the company has allotted any shares during the financial year, the following information must be given—
    (a) the classes of shares allotted, and
    (b) as respects each class of shares, the number allotted, their aggregate nominal value, and the consideration received by the company for the allotment.

Fixed assets
6.—(1) In respect of each item to which a letter or Roman number is assigned under the general item 'fixed assets' in the company's balance sheet the following information must be given—
    (a) the appropriate amounts in respect of that item as at the date of the beginning of the financial year and as at the balance sheet date respectively;

(b) the effect on any amount shown in the balance sheet in respect of that item of—
  (i) any revision of the amount in respect of any assets included under that item made during that year on any basis mentioned in paragraph 32 of Schedule 1 of these Regulations,
  (ii) acquisitions during that year of any assets,
  (iii) disposals during that year of any assets, and
  (iv) any transfers of assets of the company to and from that item during that year.

(2) The reference in sub-paragraph (1)(a) to the appropriate amounts in respect of any item as at any date there mentioned is a reference to amounts representing the aggregate amounts determined, as at that date, in respect of assets falling to be included under that item on either of the following bases, that is to say—
  (a) on the basis of purchase price or production cost (determined in accordance with paragraphs 27 and 28 of Schedule 1 of these Regulations, or
  (b) on any basis mentioned in paragraph 32 of that Schedule,

(leaving out of account in either case any provisions for depreciation or diminution in value).

(3) In respect of each item within sub-paragraph (1) there must also be stated—
  (a) the cumulative amount of provisions for depreciation or diminution in value of assets included under that item as at each date mentioned in sub-paragraph (1)(a),
  (b) the amount of any such provisions made in respect of the financial year,
  (c) the amount of any adjustments made in respect of any such provisions during that year in consequence of the disposal of any assets, and
  (d) the amount of any other adjustments made in respect of any such provisions during that year.

Financial fixed assets
7—(1) This paragraph applies if—
  (a) the company has financial fixed assets that could be included at fair value by virtue of paragraph 36 of Schedule 1 of these Regulations;
  (b) the amount at which those assets are included under any item in the company's accounts is in excess of their fair value; and
  (c) the company has not made provision for diminution in value of those assets in accordance with paragraph 19(1) of that Schedule.

(2) There must be stated—
  (a) the amount at which either the individual assets or appropriate groupings of those individual assets are included in the company's accounts;
  (b) the fair value of those assets or groupings; and
  (c) the reasons for not making a provision for diminution in value of those assets, including the nature of the evidence that provides the basis for the belief that the amount at which they are stated in the accounts will be recovered.

Details of indebtedness
8.—(1) For the aggregate of all items shown under 'creditors' in the company's balance sheet there must be stated the aggregate of the following amounts, that is to say—
  (a) the amount of any debts included under 'creditors' which are payable or repayable otherwise than by instalments and fall due for payment or repayment after the end of the period of five years beginning with the day next following the end of the financial year; and
  (b) in the case of any debts so included which are payable or repayable by instalments, the amount of any instalments which fall due for payment after the end of that period.

(2) In respect of each item shown under 'creditors' in the company's balance sheet there must be stated the aggregate amount of any debts included under that item, in respect of which any security has been given by the company.

Appendix D Form and content of abbreviated accounts of small companies

General

9. Where sums originally denominated in foreign currencies have been brought into account under any items shown in the balance sheet or profit and loss account, the basis on which those sums have been translated into sterling must be stated.

Dormant companies acting as agents

10. Where the directors of a company take advantage of the exemption conferred by section 480 of the Companies Act 2006 (dormant companies: exemption from audit), and the company has during the financial year in question acted as an agent for any person, the fact that it has so acted must be stated.

© *Crown copyright is reproduced with the permission of the Controller of Her Majesty's Stationery Office.*

Appendix E SI 2008 No. 409 – The Small Companies and Groups (Accounts and Directors' Report) Regulations 2008

This appendix reproduces in full SI 2008 No. 409 *The Small Companies and Groups (Accounts and Directors' Report) Regulations 2008*. It is also available at *http://www.opsi.gov.uk/si/si2008/pdf/uksi_20080409_en.pdf*

In summary, a set out in the Contents below, the statutory instrument comprises:

Part 1   Introduction

Part 2   Form and content of individual accounts

Part 3   Directors' report

Part 4   Form and content of group accounts

Part 5   Interpretation

Schedule 1 – Companies Act individual accounts

Schedule 2 – Information about related undertakings where company not preparing group accounts (companies act or IAS individual accounts)

Schedule 3 – Information about directors' benefits: remuneration (Companies Act or IAS accounts)

Schedule 4 – Companies Act abbreviated accounts for delivery to registrar of companies

Schedule 5 – Matters to be dealt with in directors' report

Schedule 6 – Group accounts

Schedule 7 – Interpretation of term 'provisions'

Schedule 8 – General interpretation

Appendix E SI 2008 No. 409

STATUTORY INSTRUMENTS

2008 No. 409

COMPANIES

The Small Companies and Groups (Accounts and Directors' Report) Regulations 2008

Made - - - -	*19th February 2008*
Coming into force - -	*6th April 2008*

CONTENTS

PART 1
INTRODUCTION

1. Citation and interpretation
2. Commencement and application

PART 2
FORM AND CONTENT OF INDIVIDUAL ACCOUNTS

3. Companies Act individual accounts
4. Information about related undertakings (Companies Act or IAS individual accounts)
5. Information about directors' benefits: remuneration (Companies Act or IAS individual accounts)
6. Accounts for delivery to registrar of companies (Companies Act individual accounts)

PART 3
DIRECTORS' REPORT

7. Directors' report

PART 4
FORM AND CONTENT OF GROUP ACCOUNTS

8. Companies Act group accounts
9. Information about directors' benefits: remuneration (Companies Act or IAS group accounts)
10. Information about related undertakings (Companies Act or IAS group accounts)
11. Accounts for delivery to registrar of companies (Companies Act group accounts)

The Small Companies and Groups (Accounts and Directors' Report) Regulations 2008

PART 5
INTERPRETATION

12. Definition of "provisions"
13. General interpretation

SCHEDULE 1 — COMPANIES ACT INDIVIDUAL ACCOUNTS
    PART 1 — GENERAL RULES AND FORMATS
    PART 2 — ACCOUNTING PRINCIPLES AND RULES
    PART 3 — NOTES TO THE ACCOUNTS
SCHEDULE 2 — INFORMATION ABOUT RELATED UNDERTAKINGS WHERE COMPANY NOT PREPARING GROUP ACCOUNTS (COMPANIES ACT OR IAS INDIVIDUAL ACCOUNTS)
    PART 1 — REQUIRED DISCLOSURES
    PART 2 — INTERPRETATION OF REFERENCES TO "BENEFICIAL INTEREST"
SCHEDULE 3 — INFORMATION ABOUT DIRECTORS' BENEFITS: REMUNERATION (COMPANIES ACT OR IAS ACCOUNTS)
    PART 1 — INFORMATION REQUIRED TO BE DISCLOSED
    PART 2 — SUPPLEMENTARY PROVISIONS
SCHEDULE 4 — COMPANIES ACT ABBREVIATED ACCOUNTS FOR DELIVERY TO REGISTRAR OF COMPANIES
    PART 1 — THE REQUIRED BALANCE SHEET FORMATS
    PART 2 — NOTES TO THE ACCOUNTS
SCHEDULE 5 — MATTERS TO BE DEALT WITH IN DIRECTORS' REPORT
SCHEDULE 6 — GROUP ACCOUNTS
    PART 1 — FORM AND CONTENT OF COMPANIES ACT GROUP ACCOUNTS
    PART 2 — INFORMATION ABOUT RELATED UNDERTAKINGS WHERE COMPANY PREPARING GROUP ACCOUNTS (COMPANIES ACT OR IAS GROUP ACCOUNTS)
SCHEDULE 7 — INTERPRETATION OF TERM "PROVISIONS"
    PART 1 — MEANING FOR PURPOSES OF THESE REGULATIONS
    PART 2 — MEANING FOR PURPOSES OF PARTS 18 AND 23 OF THE 2006 ACT
SCHEDULE 8 — GENERAL INTERPRETATION

The Secretary of State makes the following Regulations in exercise of the powers conferred by sections 396(3), 404(3), 409(1) to (3), 412(1) to (3), 416(4), 444(3)(a) and (b), 677(3)(a), 712(2)(b)(i), 836(1)(b)(i) and 1292(1)(a) and (c) of the Companies Act 2006(**a**).

In accordance with sections 473(3) and 1290 of the Companies Act 2006 a draft of this instrument was laid before Parliament and approved by a resolution of each House of Parliament.

(**a**) 2006 c.46.

Appendix E SI 2008 No. 409

PART 1
INTRODUCTION

Citation and interpretation

1.—(1) These Regulations may be cited as the Small Companies and Groups (Accounts and Directors' Report) Regulations 2008.

(2) In these Regulations "the 2006 Act" means the Companies Act 2006.

Commencement and application

2.—(1) These Regulations come into force on 6th April 2008.

(2) They apply in relation to financial years beginning on or after 6th April 2008.

(3) They apply to companies which are subject to the small companies regime under Part 15 of the 2006 Act (see section 381 of that Act(**a**)).

PART 2
FORM AND CONTENT OF INDIVIDUAL ACCOUNTS

Companies Act individual accounts

3.—(1) Companies Act individual accounts under section 396 of the 2006 Act (Companies Act: individual accounts) must comply with the provisions of Schedule 1 to these Regulations as to the form and content of the balance sheet and profit and loss account, and additional information to be provided by way of notes to the accounts.

(2) The profit and loss account of a company that falls within section 408 of the 2006 Act (individual profit and loss account where group accounts prepared)(**b**) need not contain the information specified in paragraphs 59 to 61 of Schedule 1 to these Regulations (information supplementing the profit and loss account).

(3) Accounts are treated as having complied with any provision of Schedule 1 to these Regulations if they comply instead with the corresponding provision of Schedule 1 to the Large and Medium-Sized Companies and Groups (Accounts and Reports) Regulations 2008(**c**).

Information about related undertakings (Companies Act or IAS individual accounts)

4.—(1) Companies Act or IAS individual accounts must comply with the provisions of Schedule 2 to these Regulations as to information about related undertakings to be given in notes to the company's accounts.

(2) Information otherwise required to be given by Schedule 2 to these Regulations need not be disclosed with respect to an undertaking that—

(a) is established under the law of a country outside the United Kingdom, or

(b) carries on business outside the United Kingdom,

if the conditions specified in section 409(4) of the 2006 Act are met (see section 409(5) of the 2006 Act for disclosure required where advantage taken of this exemption).

This paragraph does not apply in relation to the information required by paragraphs 4 and 8 of Schedule 2 to these Regulations.

(**a**) Section 381 is amended by regulation 6(1) of S.I. 2008/393.
(**b**) Section 408 is amended by regulation 10 of S.I. 2008/393.
(**c**) S.I. 2008/410.

The Small Companies and Groups (Accounts and Directors' Report) Regulations 2008

Information about directors' benefits: remuneration (Companies Act or IAS individual accounts)

5. Companies Act or IAS individual accounts must comply with the provisions of Schedule 3 to these Regulations as to information about directors' remuneration to be given in notes to the company's accounts.

Accounts for delivery to registrar of companies (Companies Act individual accounts)

6.—(1) The directors of a company for which they are preparing Companies Act individual accounts may deliver to the registrar of companies under section 444 of the 2006 Act (filing obligations of companies subject to small companies regime) a copy of a balance sheet which complies with Schedule 4 to these Regulations rather than Schedule 1.

(2) Companies Act individual accounts delivered to the registrar need not give the information required by—
  (a) paragraph 4 of Schedule 2 to these Regulations (shares of company held by subsidiary undertakings), or
  (b) Schedule 3 to these Regulations (directors' benefits).

PART 3
DIRECTORS' REPORT

Directors' report

7. The report which the directors of a company are required to prepare under section 415 of the 2006 Act (duty to prepare directors' report) must disclose the matters specified in Schedule 5 to these Regulations.

PART 4
FORM AND CONTENT OF GROUP ACCOUNTS

Companies Act group accounts

8.—(1) Where the directors of a parent company which—
  (a) is subject to the small companies regime, and
  (b) has prepared Companies Act individual accounts in accordance with regulation 3,

prepare Companies Act group accounts under section 398 of the 2006 Act (option to prepare group accounts), those accounts must comply with the provisions of Part 1 of Schedule 6 to these Regulations as to the form and content of the consolidated balance sheet and consolidated profit and loss account, and additional information to be provided by way of notes to the accounts.

(2) Accounts are treated as having complied with any provision of Part 1 of Schedule 6 if they comply instead with the corresponding provision of Schedule 6 to the Large and Medium-Sized Companies and Groups (Accounts and Reports) Regulations 2008.

Information about directors' benefits: remuneration (Companies Act or IAS group accounts)

9. Companies Act or IAS group accounts must comply with the provisions of Schedule 3 to these Regulations as to information about directors' remuneration to be given in notes to the company's accounts.

Information about related undertakings (Companies Act or IAS group accounts)

10.—(1) Companies Act or IAS group accounts must comply with the provisions of Part 2 of Schedule 6 to these Regulations as to information about related undertakings to be given in notes to the company's accounts.

(2) Information otherwise required to be given by Part 2 of Schedule 6 need not be disclosed with respect to an undertaking that—

(a) is established under the law of a country outside the United Kingdom, or

(b) carries on business outside the United Kingdom,

if the conditions specified in section 409(4) of the 2006 Act are met (see section 409(5) of the 2006 Act for disclosure required where advantage taken of this exemption).

This paragraph does not apply in relation to the information required by paragraphs 26 and 35 of Schedule 6 to these Regulations.

Accounts for delivery to registrar of companies (Companies Act group accounts)

11. Companies Act group accounts delivered to the registrar of companies under section 444 of the 2006 Act need not give the information required by—

(a) Schedule 3 to these Regulations (directors' benefits), or

(b) paragraph 25 of Schedule 6 to these Regulations (shares of company held by subsidiary undertakings).

PART 5
INTERPRETATION

Definition of "provisions"

12. Schedule 7 to these Regulations defines "provisions" for the purpose of these Regulations and for the purposes of—

(a) section 677(3)(a) (Companies Act accounts: relevant provisions for purposes of financial assistance) in Part 18 of the 2006 Act,

(b) section 712(2)(b)(i) (Companies Act accounts: relevant provisions to determine available profits for redemption or purchase by private company out of capital) in that Part,

(c) section 836(1)(b)(i) (Companies Act accounts: relevant provisions for distribution purposes) in Part 23 of that Act; and

General interpretation

13. Schedule 8 to these Regulations contains general definitions for the purposes of these Regulations.

Gareth Thomas
Parliamentary Under Secretary of State for Trade and Consumer Affairs,
19th February 2008   Department for Business, Enterprise and Regulatory Reform

The Small Companies and Groups (Accounts and Directors' Report) Regulations 2008

SCHEDULE 1

Regulation 3(1)

COMPANIES ACT INDIVIDUAL ACCOUNTS

PART 1

GENERAL RULES AND FORMATS

SECTION A

GENERAL RULES

1.—(1) Subject to the following provisions of this Schedule—

(a) every balance sheet of a company must show the items listed in either of the balance sheet formats in Section B of this Part, and

(b) every profit and loss account must show the items listed in any one of the profit and loss account formats in Section B.

(2) References in this Schedule to the items listed in any of the formats in Section B are to those items read together with any of the notes following the formats which apply to those items.

(3) The items must be shown in the order and under the headings and sub-headings given in the particular format used, but—

(a) the notes to the formats may permit alternative positions for any particular items, and

(b) the heading or sub-heading for any item does not have to be distinguished by any letter or number assigned to that item in the format used.

2.—(1) Where in accordance with paragraph 1 a company's balance sheet or profit and loss account for any financial year has been prepared by reference to one of the formats in Section B, the company's directors must use the same format in preparing Companies Act individual accounts for subsequent financial years, unless in their opinion there are special reasons for a change.

(2) Particulars of any such change must be given in a note to the accounts in which the new format is first used, and the reasons for the change must be explained.

3.—(1) Any item required to be shown in a company's balance sheet or profit and loss account may be shown in greater detail than required by the particular format used.

(2) The balance sheet or profit and loss account may include an item representing or covering the amount of any asset or liability, income or expenditure not otherwise covered by any of the items listed in the format used, save that none of the following may be treated as assets in any balance sheet—

(a) preliminary expenses,

(b) expenses of, and commission on, any issue of shares or debentures,

(c) costs of research.

4.—(1) Where the special nature of the company's business requires it, the company's directors must adapt the arrangement, headings and sub-headings otherwise required in respect of items given an Arabic number in the balance sheet or profit and loss account format used.

(2) The directors may combine items to which Arabic numbers are given in any of the formats set out in Section B if—

(a) their individual amounts are not material to assessing the state of affairs or profit or loss of the company for the financial year in question, or

(b) the combination facilitates that assessment.

(3) Where sub-paragraph (2)(b) applies, the individual amounts of any items which have been combined must be disclosed in a note to the accounts.

5.—(1) Subject to sub-paragraph (2), the directors must not include a heading or sub-heading corresponding to an item in the balance sheet or profit and loss account format used if there is no amount to be shown for that item for the financial year to which the balance sheet or profit and loss account relates.

(2) Where an amount can be shown for the item in question for the immediately preceding financial year that amount must be shown under the heading or sub-heading required by the format for that item.

6. Every profit and loss account must show the amount of a company's profit or loss on ordinary activities before taxation.

7.—(1) For every item shown in the balance sheet or profit and loss account the corresponding amount for the immediately preceding financial year must also be shown.

(2) Where that corresponding amount is not comparable with the amount to be shown for the item in question in respect of the financial year to which the balance sheet or profit and loss account relates, the former amount may be adjusted, and particulars of the non-comparability and of any adjustment must be disclosed in a note to the accounts.

8. Amounts in respect of items representing assets or income may not be set off against amounts in respect of items representing liabilities or expenditure (as the case may be), or vice versa.

9. The company's directors must, in determining how amounts are presented within items in the profit and loss account and balance sheet, have regard to the substance of the reported transaction or arrangement, in accordance with generally accepted accounting principles or practice.

SECTION B

THE REQUIRED FORMATS FOR ACCOUNTS(a)

Balance sheet formats

Format 1

A. Called up share capital not paid *(1)*

B. Fixed assets
    I. Intangible assets
        1. Goodwill *(2)*
        2. Other intangible assets *(3)*
    II. Tangible assets
        1. Land and buildings
        2. Plant and machinery etc.
    III. Investments
        1. Shares in group undertakings and participating interests
        2. Loans to group undertakings and undertakings in which the company has a participating interest
        3. Other investments other than loans
        4. Other investments *(4)*

C. Current assets
    I. Stocks

(a) A number in brackets following any item is a reference to the note of that number in the notes following the formats.

The Small Companies and Groups (Accounts and Directors' Report) Regulations 2008

        1. Stocks
        2. Payments on account
    II. Debtors *(5)*
        1. Trade debtors
        2. Amounts owed by group undertakings and undertakings in which the company has a participating interest
        3. Other debtors *(1)*
    III. Investments
        1. Shares in group undertakings
        2. Other investments *(4)*
    IV. Cash at bank and in hand

D. Prepayments and accrued income *(6)*

E. Creditors: amounts falling due within one year
        1. Bank loans and overdrafts
        2. Trade creditors
        3. Amounts owed to group undertakings and undertakings in which the company has a participating interest
        4. Other creditors *(7)*

F. Net current assets (liabilities) *(8)*

G. Total assets less current liabilities

H. Creditors: amounts falling due after more than one year
        1. Bank loans and overdrafts
        2. Trade creditors
        3. Amounts owed to group undertakings and undertakings in which the company has a participating interest
        4. Other creditors *(7)*

I. Provisions for liabilities

J. Accruals and deferred income *(7)*

K. Capital and reserves
    I. Called up share capital *(9)*
    II. Share premium account
    III. Revaluation reserve
    IV. Other reserves
    V. Profit and loss account

Balance sheet formats

Format 2

ASSETS

A. Called up share capital not paid *(1)*

B. Fixed assets
    I. Intangible assets

1. Goodwill *(2)*
2. Other intangible assets *(3)*

II. Tangible assets
1. Land and buildings
2. Plant and machinery etc.

III. Investments
1. Shares in group undertakings and participating interests
2. Loans to group undertakings and undertakings in which the company has a participating interest
3. Other investments other than loans
4. Other investments *(4)*

C. Current assets
I. Stocks
1. Stocks
2. Payments on account

II. Debtors *(5)*
1. Trade debtors
2. Amounts owed by group undertakings and undertakings in which the company has a participating interest
3. Other debtors *(1)*

III. Investments
1. Shares in group undertakings
2. Other investments *(4)*

IV. Cash at bank and in hand

D. Prepayments and accrued income *(6)*

LIABILITIES

A. Capital and reserves
I. Called up share capital *(9)*
II. Share premium account
III. Revaluation reserve
IV. Other reserves
V. Profit and loss account

B. Provisions for liabilities

C. Creditors *(10)*
1. Bank loans and overdrafts
2. Trade creditors
3. Amounts owed to group undertakings and undertakings in which the company has a participating interest
4. Other creditors *(7)*

D. Accruals and deferred income *(7)*

Notes on the balance sheet formats

(1) *Called up share capital not paid*

(Formats 1 and 2, items A and C.II.3.)

This item may either be shown at item A or included under item C.II.3 in Format 1 or 2.

(2) Goodwill

(Formats 1 and 2, item B.I.1.)

Amounts representing goodwill must only be included to the extent that the goodwill was acquired for valuable consideration.

(3) Other intangible assets

(Formats 1 and 2, item B.I.2.)

Amounts in respect of concessions, patents, licences, trade marks and similar rights and assets must only be included in a company's balance sheet under this item if either—
  (a) the assets were acquired for valuable consideration and are not required to be shown under goodwill, or
  (b) the assets in question were created by the company itself.

(4) Others: Other investments

(Formats 1 and 2, items B.III.4 and C.III.2.)

Where amounts in respect of own shares held are included under either of these items, the nominal value of such shares must be shown separately.

(5) Debtors

(Formats 1 and 2, items C.II.1 to 3.)

The amount falling due after more than one year must be shown separately for each item included under debtors unless the aggregate amount of debtors falling due after more than one year is disclosed in the notes to the accounts.

(6) Prepayments and accrued income

(Formats 1 and 2, item D.)

This item may alternatively be included under item C.II.3 in Format 1 or 2.

(7) Other creditors

(Format 1, items E.4, H.4 and J and Format 2, items C.4 and D.)

There must be shown separately—
  (a) the amount of any convertible loans, and
  (b) the amount for creditors in respect of taxation and social security.

Payments received on account of orders must be included in so far as they are not shown as deductions from stocks.

In Format 1, accruals and deferred income may be shown under item J or included under item E.4 or H.4, or both (as the case may require). In Format 2, accruals and deferred income may be shown under item D or within item C.4 under Liabilities.

(8) Net current assets (liabilities)

(Format 1, item F.)

In determining the amount to be shown under this item any prepayments and accrued income must be taken into account wherever shown.

Appendix E SI 2008 No. 409

(9)   Called up share capital

(Format 1, item K.I and Format 2, Liabilities item A.I.)

The amount of allotted share capital and the amount of called up share capital which has been paid up must be shown separately.

(10)   Creditors

(Format 2, Liabilities items C.1 to 4.)

Amounts falling due within one year and after one year must be shown separately for each of these items and for the aggregate of all of these items unless the aggregate amount of creditors falling due within one year and the aggregate amount of creditors falling due after more than one year is disclosed in the notes to the accounts.

Profit and loss account formats

Format 1
(see note (14) below)

1. Turnover

2. Cost of sales *(11)*

3. Gross profit or loss

4. Distribution costs *(11)*

5. Administrative expenses *(11)*

6. Other operating income

7. Income from shares in group undertakings

8. Income from participating interests

9. Income from other fixed asset investments *(12)*

10. Other interest receivable and similar income *(12)*

11. Amounts written off investments

12. Interest payable and similar charges *(13)*

13. Tax on profit or loss on ordinary activities

14. Profit or loss on ordinary activities after taxation

15. Extraordinary income

16. Extraordinary charges

17. Extraordinary profit or loss

The Small Companies and Groups (Accounts and Directors' Report) Regulations 2008

18. Tax on extraordinary profit or loss

19. Other taxes not shown under the above items

20. Profit or loss for the financial year

Profit and loss account formats

Format 2

1. Turnover

2. Change in stocks of finished goods and in work in progress

3. Own work capitalised

4. Other operating income

5. (a) Raw materials and consumables
   (b) Other external charges

6. Staff costs
   (a) wages and salaries
   (b) social security costs
   (c) other pension costs

7. (a) Depreciation and other amounts written off tangible and intangible fixed assets
   (b) Exceptional amounts written off current assets

8. Other operating charges

9. Income from shares in group undertakings

10. Income from participating interests

11. Income from other fixed asset investments *(12)*

12. Other interest receivable and similar income *(12)*

13. Amounts written off investments

14. Interest payable and similar charges *(13)*

15. Tax on profit or loss on ordinary activities

16. Profit or loss on ordinary activities after taxation

17. Extraordinary income

18. Extraordinary charges

19. Extraordinary profit or loss

Appendix E SI 2008 No. 409

20. Tax on extraordinary profit or loss

21. Other taxes not shown under the above items

22. Profit or loss for the financial year

Profit and loss account formats

Format 3
(see note (14) below)

A. Charges

1. Cost of sales *(11)*

2. Distribution costs *(11)*

3. Administrative expenses *(11)*

4. Amounts written off investments

5. Interest payable and similar charges *(13)*

6. Tax on profit or loss on ordinary activities

7. Profit or loss on ordinary activities after taxation

8. Extraordinary charges

9. Tax on extraordinary profit or loss

10. Other taxes not shown under the above items

11. Profit or loss for the financial year

B. Income

1. Turnover

2. Other operating income

3. Income from shares in group undertakings

4. Income from participating interests

5. Income from other fixed asset investments *(12)*

6. Other interest receivable and similar income *(12)*

7. Profit or loss on ordinary activities after taxation

8. Extraordinary income

The Small Companies and Groups (Accounts and Directors' Report) Regulations 2008

    9. Profit or loss for the financial year

Profit and loss account formats

Format 4

A. Charges

    1. Reduction in stocks of finished goods and in work in progress

    2. (a) Raw materials and consumables
       (b) Other external charges

    3. Staff costs
       (a) wages and salaries
       (b) social security costs
       (c) other pension costs

    4. (a) Depreciation and other amounts written off tangible and intangible fixed assets
       (b) Exceptional amounts written off current assets

    5. Other operating charges

    6. Amounts written off investments

    7. Interest payable and similar charges *(13)*

    8. Tax on profit or loss on ordinary activities

    9. Profit or loss on ordinary activities after taxation

    10. Extraordinary charges

    11. Tax on extraordinary profit or loss

    12. Other taxes not shown under the above items

    13. Profit or loss for the financial year

B. Income

    1. Turnover

    2. Increase in stocks of finished goods and in work in progress

    3. Own work capitalised

    4. Other operating income

    5. Income from shares in group undertakings

    6. Income from participating interests

7. Income from other fixed asset investments *(12)*

8. Other interest receivable and similar income *(12)*

9. Profit or loss on ordinary activities after taxation

10. Extraordinary income

11. Profit or loss for the financial year

Notes on the profit and loss account formats

(11) Cost of sales: distribution costs: administrative expenses

(Format 1, items 2, 4 and 5 and Format 3, items A.1, 2 and 3.)

These items must be stated after taking into account any necessary provisions for depreciation or diminution in value of assets.

(12) Income from other fixed asset investments: other interest receivable and similar income

(Format 1, items 9 and 10; Format 2, items 11 and 12; Format 3, items B.5 and 6 and Format 4, items B.7 and 8.)

Income and interest derived from group undertakings must be shown separately from income and interest derived from other sources.

(13) Interest payable and similar charges

(Format 1, item 12; Format 2, item 14; Format 3, item A.5 and Format 4, item A.7.)

The amount payable to group undertakings must be shown separately.

(14) Formats 1 and 3

The amount of any provisions for depreciation and diminution in value of tangible and intangible fixed assets falling to be shown under items 7(a) and A.4(a) respectively in Formats 2 and 4 must be disclosed in a note to the accounts in any case where the profit and loss account is prepared using Format 1 or Format 3.

PART 2

ACCOUNTING PRINCIPLES AND RULES

SECTION A
ACCOUNTING PRINCIPLES

Preliminary

10.—(1) The amounts to be included in respect of all items shown in a company's accounts must be determined in accordance with the principles set out in this Section.

(2) But if it appears to the company's directors that there are special reasons for departing from any of those principles in preparing the company's accounts in respect of any financial year they may do so, in which case particulars of the departure, the reasons for it and its effect must be given in a note to the accounts.

The Small Companies and Groups (Accounts and Directors' Report) Regulations 2008

Accounting principles

11. The company is presumed to be carrying on business as a going concern.

12. Accounting policies must be applied consistently within the same accounts and from one financial year to the next.

13. The amount of any item must be determined on a prudent basis, and in particular—
    (a) only profits realised at the balance sheet date must be included in the profit and loss account, and
    (b) all liabilities which have arisen in respect of the financial year to which the accounts relate or a previous financial year must be taken into account, including those which only become apparent between the balance sheet date and the date on which it is signed on behalf of the board of directors in accordance with section 414 of the 2006 Act (approval and signing of accounts).

14. All income and charges relating to the financial year to which the accounts relate must be taken into account, without regard to the date of receipt or payment.

15. In determining the aggregate amount of any item, the amount of each individual asset or liability that falls to be taken into account must be determined separately.

SECTION B

HISTORICAL COST ACCOUNTING RULES

Preliminary

16. Subject to Sections C and D of this Part of this Schedule, the amounts to be included in respect of all items shown in a company's accounts must be determined in accordance with the rules set out in this Section.

Fixed assets

General rules

17.—(1) The amount to be included in respect of any fixed asset must be its purchase price or production cost.

(2) This is subject to any provision for depreciation or diminution in value made in accordance with paragraphs 18 to 20.

Rules for depreciation and diminution in value

18. In the case of any fixed asset which has a limited useful economic life, the amount of—
    (a) its purchase price or production cost, or
    (b) where it is estimated that any such asset will have a residual value at the end of the period of its useful economic life, its purchase price or production cost less that estimated residual value,

must be reduced by provisions for depreciation calculated to write off that amount systematically over the period of the asset's useful economic life.

19.—(1) Where a fixed asset investment of a description falling to be included under item B.III of either of the balance sheet formats set out in Part 1 of this Schedule has diminished in value, provisions for diminution in value may be made in respect of it and the amount to be included in respect of it may be reduced accordingly.

(2) Provisions for diminution in value must be made in respect of any fixed asset which has diminished in value if the reduction in its value is expected to be permanent (whether its useful

economic life is limited or not), and the amount to be included in respect of it must be reduced accordingly.

(3) Any provisions made under sub-paragraph (1) or (2) which are not shown in the profit and loss account must be disclosed (either separately or in aggregate) in a note to the accounts.

20.—(1) Where the reasons for which any provision was made in accordance with paragraph 19 have ceased to apply to any extent, that provision must be written back to the extent that it is no longer necessary.

(2) Any amounts written back in accordance with sub-paragraph (1) which are not shown in the profit and loss account must be disclosed (either separately or in aggregate) in a note to the accounts.

Development costs

21.—(1) Notwithstanding that an item in respect of "development costs" is included under "fixed assets" in the balance sheet formats set out in Part 1 of this Schedule, an amount may only be included in a company's balance sheet in respect of development costs in special circumstances.

(2) If any amount is included in a company's balance sheet in respect of development costs the following information must be given in a note to the accounts—

(a) the period over which the amount of those costs originally capitalised is being or is to be written off, and

(b) the reasons for capitalising the development costs in question.

Goodwill

22.—(1) The application of paragraphs 17 to 20 in relation to goodwill (in any case where goodwill is treated as an asset) is subject to the following.

(2) Subject to sub-paragraph (3), the amount of the consideration for any goodwill acquired by a company must be reduced by provisions for depreciation calculated to write off that amount systematically over a period chosen by the directors of the company.

(3) The period chosen must not exceed the useful economic life of the goodwill in question.

(4) In any case where any goodwill acquired by a company is shown or included as an asset in the company's balance sheet there must be disclosed in a note to the accounts—

(a) the period chosen for writing off the consideration for that goodwill, and

(b) the reasons for choosing that period.

Current assets

23. Subject to paragraph 24, the amount to be included in respect of any current asset must be its purchase price or production cost.

24.—(1) If the net realisable value of any current asset is lower than its purchase price or production cost, the amount to be included in respect of that asset must be the net realisable value.

(2) Where the reasons for which any provision for diminution in value was made in accordance with sub-paragraph (1) have ceased to apply to any extent, that provision must be written back to the extent that it is no longer necessary.

The Small Companies and Groups (Accounts and Directors' Report) Regulations 2008

Miscellaneous and supplementary provisions

Excess of money owed over value received as an asset item

25.—(1) Where the amount repayable on any debt owed by a company is greater than the value of the consideration received in the transaction giving rise to the debt, the amount of the difference may be treated as an asset.

(2) Where any such amount is so treated—

(a) it must be written off by reasonable amounts each year and must be completely written off before repayment of the debt, and

(b) if the current amount is not shown as a separate item in the company's balance sheet, it must be disclosed in a note to the accounts.

Assets included at a fixed amount

26.—(1) Subject to sub-paragraph (2), assets which fall to be included—

(a) amongst the fixed assets of a company under the item "tangible assets", or

(b) amongst the current assets of a company under the item "raw materials and consumables",

may be included at a fixed quantity and value.

(2) Sub-paragraph (1) applies to assets of a kind which are constantly being replaced where—

(a) their overall value is not material to assessing the company's state of affairs, and

(b) their quantity, value and composition are not subject to material variation.

Determination of purchase price or production cost

27.—(1) The purchase price of an asset is to be determined by adding to the actual price paid any expenses incidental to its acquisition.

(2) The production cost of an asset is to be determined by adding to the purchase price of the raw materials and consumables used the amount of the costs incurred by the company which are directly attributable to the production of that asset.

(3) In addition, there may be included in the production cost of an asset—

(a) a reasonable proportion of the costs incurred by the company which are only indirectly attributable to the production of that asset, but only to the extent that they relate to the period of production, and

(b) interest on capital borrowed to finance the production of that asset, to the extent that it accrues in respect of the period of production,

provided, however, in a case within paragraph (b), that the inclusion of the interest in determining the cost of that asset and the amount of the interest so included is disclosed in a note to the accounts.

(4) In the case of current assets distribution costs may not be included in production costs.

28.—(1) The purchase price or production cost of—

(a) any assets which fall to be included under any item shown in a company's balance sheet under the general item "stocks", and

(b) any assets which are fungible assets (including investments),

may be determined by the application of any of the methods mentioned in sub-paragraph (2) in relation to any such assets of the same class, provided that the method chosen is one which appears to the directors to be appropriate in the circumstances of the company.

(2) Those methods are—

(a) the method known as "first in, first out" (FIFO),

(b) the method known as "last in, first out" (LIFO),

(c) a weighted average price, and

(d) any other method similar to any of the methods mentioned above.

(3) For the purposes of this paragraph, assets of any description must be regarded as fungible if assets of that description are substantially indistinguishable one from another.

Substitution of original stated amount where price or cost unknown

29.—(1) This paragraph applies where—

(a) there is no record of the purchase price or production cost of any asset of a company or of any price, expenses or costs relevant for determining its purchase price or production cost in accordance with paragraph 27, or

(b) any such record cannot be obtained without unreasonable expense or delay.

(2) In such a case, the purchase price or production cost of the asset must be taken, for the purposes of paragraphs 17 to 24, to be the value ascribed to it in the earliest available record of its value made on or after its acquisition or production by the company.

SECTION C
ALTERNATIVE ACCOUNTING RULES

Preliminary

30.—(1) The rules set out in Section B are referred to below in this Schedule as the historical cost accounting rules.

(2) Those rules, with the omission of paragraphs 16, 22 and 26 to 29, are referred to below in this Part of this Schedule as the depreciation rules; and references below in this Schedule to the historical cost accounting rules do not include the depreciation rules as they apply by virtue of paragraph 33.

31. Subject to paragraphs 33 to 35, the amounts to be included in respect of assets of any description mentioned in paragraph 32 may be determined on any basis so mentioned.

Alternative accounting rules

32.—(1) Intangible fixed assets, other than goodwill, may be included at their current cost.

(2) Tangible fixed assets may be included at a market value determined as at the date of their last valuation or at their current cost.

(3) Investments of any description falling to be included under item B III of either of the balance sheet formats set out Part 1 of this Schedule may be included either—

(a) at a market value determined as at the date of their last valuation, or

(b) at a value determined on any basis which appears to the directors to be appropriate in the circumstances of the company.

But in the latter case particulars of the method of valuation adopted and of the reasons for adopting it must be disclosed in a note to the accounts.

(4) Investments of any description falling to be included under item C III of either of the balance sheet formats set out in Part 1 of this Schedule may be included at their current cost.

(5) Stocks may be included at their current cost.

Application of the depreciation rules

33.—(1) Where the value of any asset of a company is determined on any basis mentioned in paragraph 32, that value must be, or (as the case may require) be the starting point for determining, the amount to be included in respect of that asset in the company's accounts, instead of its purchase price or production cost or any value previously so determined for that asset.

The depreciation rules apply accordingly in relation to any such asset with the substitution for any reference to its purchase price or production cost of a reference to the value most recently determined for that asset on any basis mentioned in paragraph 32.

(2) The amount of any provision for depreciation required in the case of any fixed asset by paragraphs 18 to 20 as they apply by virtue of sub-paragraph (1) is referred to below in this paragraph as the adjusted amount, and the amount of any provision which would be required by any of those paragraphs in the case of that asset according to the historical cost accounting rules is referred to as the historical cost amount.

(3) Where sub-paragraph (1) applies in the case of any fixed asset the amount of any provision for depreciation in respect of that asset—

   (a) included in any item shown in the profit and loss account in respect of amounts written off assets of the description in question, or

   (b) taken into account in stating any item so shown which is required by note (11) of the notes on the profit and loss account formats set out in Part 1 of this Schedule to be stated after taking into account any necessary provision for depreciation or diminution in value of assets included under it,

may be the historical cost amount instead of the adjusted amount, provided that the amount of any difference between the two is shown separately in the profit and loss account or in a note to the accounts.

Additional information to be provided in case of departure from historical cost accounting rules

34.—(1) This paragraph applies where the amounts to be included in respect of assets covered by any items shown in a company's accounts have been determined on any basis mentioned in paragraph 32.

(2) The items affected and the basis of valuation adopted in determining the amounts of the assets in question in the case of each such item must be disclosed in a note to the accounts.

(3) In the case of each balance sheet item affected (except stocks) either—

   (a) the comparable amounts determined according to the historical cost accounting rules, or

   (b) the differences between those amounts and the corresponding amounts actually shown in the balance sheet in respect of that item,

must be shown separately in the balance sheet or in a note to the accounts.

(4) In sub-paragraph (3), references in relation to any item to the comparable amounts determined as there mentioned are references to—

   (a) the aggregate amount which would be required to be shown in respect of that item if the amounts to be included in respect of all the assets covered by that item were determined according to the historical cost accounting rules, and

   (b) the aggregate amount of the cumulative provisions for depreciation or diminution in value which would be permitted or required in determining those amounts according to those rules.

Revaluation reserve

35.—(1) With respect to any determination of the value of an asset of a company on any basis mentioned in paragraph 32, the amount of any profit or loss arising from that determination (after allowing, where appropriate, for any provisions for depreciation or diminution in value made otherwise than by reference to the value so determined and any adjustments of any such provisions made in the light of that determination) must be credited or (as the case may be) debited to a separate reserve ("the revaluation reserve").

(2) The amount of the revaluation reserve must be shown in the company's balance sheet under a separate sub-heading in the position given for the item "revaluation reserve" in Format 1 or 2 of the balance sheet formats set out in Part 1 of this Schedule, but need not be shown under that name.

(3) An amount may be transferred—

   (a) from the revaluation reserve—

      (i) to the profit and loss account, if the amount was previously charged to that account or represents realised profit, or

      (ii) on capitalisation,

   (b) to or from the revaluation reserve in respect of the taxation relating to any profit or loss credited or debited to the reserve.

The revaluation reserve must be reduced to the extent that the amounts transferred to it are no longer necessary for the purposes of the valuation method used.

(4) In sub-paragraph (3)(a)(ii) "capitalisation", in relation to an amount standing to the credit of the revaluation reserve, means applying it in wholly or partly paying up unissued shares in the company to be allotted to members of the company as fully or partly paid shares.

(5) The revaluation reserve must not be reduced except as mentioned in this paragraph.

(6) The treatment for taxation purposes of amounts credited or debited to the revaluation reserve must be disclosed in a note to the accounts.

SECTION D
FAIR VALUE ACCOUNTING

Inclusion of financial instruments at fair value

36.—(1) Subject to sub-paragraphs (2) to (5), financial instruments (including derivatives) may be included at fair value.

(2) Sub-paragraph (1) does not apply to financial instruments that constitute liabilities unless—

   (a) they are held as part of a trading portfolio,

   (b) they are derivatives, or

   (c) they are financial instruments falling within sub-paragraph (4).

(3) Unless they are financial instruments falling within sub-paragraph (4), sub-paragraph (1) does not apply to—

   (a) financial instruments (other than derivatives) held to maturity,

   (b) loans and receivables originated by the company and not held for trading purposes,

   (c) interests in subsidiary undertakings, associated undertakings and joint ventures,

   (d) equity instruments issued by the company,

   (e) contracts for contingent consideration in a business combination, or

   (f) other financial instruments with such special characteristics that the instruments, according to generally accepted accounting principles or practice, should be accounted for differently from other financial instruments.

(4) Financial instruments that, under international accounting standards adopted by the European Commission on or before 5th September 2006 in accordance with the IAS Regulation, may be included in accounts at fair value, may be so included, provided that the disclosures required by such accounting standards are made.

(5) If the fair value of a financial instrument cannot be determined reliably in accordance with paragraph 37, sub-paragraph (1) does not apply to that financial instrument.

(6) In this paragraph—

"associated undertaking" has the meaning given by paragraph 19 of Schedule 6 to these Regulations;

"joint venture" has the meaning given by paragraph 18 of that Schedule.

Determination of fair value

37.—(1) The fair value of a financial instrument is its value determined in accordance with this paragraph.

(2) If a reliable market can readily be identified for the financial instrument, its fair value is to be determined by reference to its market value.

(3) If a reliable market cannot readily be identified for the financial instrument but can be identified for its components or for a similar instrument, its fair value is determined by reference to the market value of its components or of the similar instrument.

(4) If neither sub-paragraph (2) nor (3) applies, the fair value of the financial instrument is a value resulting from generally accepted valuation models and techniques.

(5) Any valuation models and techniques used for the purposes of sub-paragraph (4) must ensure a reasonable approximation of the market value.

Hedged items

38. A company may include any assets and liabilities, or identified portions of such assets or liabilities, that qualify as hedged items under a fair value hedge accounting system at the amount required under that system.

Other assets that may be included at fair value

39.—(1) This paragraph applies to—
  (a) investment property, and
  (b) living animals and plants,
that, under international accounting standards, may be included in accounts at fair value.

(2) Such investment property and such living animals and plants may be included at fair value, provided that all such investment property or, as the case may be, all such living animals and plants are so included where their fair value can reliably be determined.

(3) In this paragraph, "fair value" means fair value determined in accordance with relevant international accounting standards.

Accounting for changes in value

40.—(1) This paragraph applies where a financial instrument is valued in accordance with paragraph 36 or 38 or an asset is valued in accordance with paragraph 39.

(2) Notwithstanding paragraph 13 in this Part of this Schedule, and subject to sub-paragraphs (3) and (4), a change in the value of the financial instrument or of the investment property or living animal or plant must be included in the profit and loss account.

(3) Where—
  (a) the financial instrument accounted for is a hedging instrument under a hedge accounting system that allows some or all of the change in value not to be shown in the profit and loss account, or
  (b) the change in value relates to an exchange difference arising on a monetary item that forms part of a company's net investment in a foreign entity,
the amount of the change in value must be credited to or (as the case may be) debited from a separate reserve ("the fair value reserve").

(4) Where the instrument accounted for—

Appendix E SI 2008 No. 409

(a) is an available for sale financial asset, and

(b) is not a derivative,

the change in value may be credited to or (as the case may be) debited from the fair value reserve.

The fair value reserve

41.—(1) The fair value reserve must be adjusted to the extent that the amounts shown in it are no longer necessary for the purposes of paragraph 40(3) or (4).

(2) The treatment for taxation purposes of amounts credited or debited to the fair value reserve must be disclosed in a note to the accounts.

PART 3
NOTES TO THE ACCOUNTS

Preliminary

42. Any information required in the case of any company by the following provisions of this Part of this Schedule must (if not given in the company's accounts) be given by way of a note to those accounts.

Reserves and dividends

43. There must be stated—

(a) any amount set aside or proposed to be set aside to, or withdrawn or proposed to be withdrawn from, reserves,

(b) the aggregate amount of dividends paid in the financial year (other than those for which a liability existed at the immediately preceding balance sheet date),

(c) the aggregate amount of dividends that the company is liable to pay at the balance sheet date, and

(d) the aggregate amount of dividends that are proposed before the date of approval of the accounts, and not otherwise disclosed under paragraph (b) or (c).

Disclosure of accounting policies

44. The accounting policies adopted by the company in determining the amounts to be included in respect of items shown in the balance sheet and in determining the profit or loss of the company must be stated (including such policies with respect to the depreciation and diminution in value of assets).

Information supplementing the balance sheet

45. Paragraphs 46 to 58 require information which either supplements the information given with respect to any particular items shown in the balance sheet or is otherwise relevant to assessing the company's state of affairs in the light of the information so given.

Share capital

46.—(1) Where shares of more than one class have been allotted, the number and aggregate nominal value of shares of each class allotted must be given.

(2) In the case of any part of the allotted share capital that consists of redeemable shares, the following information must be given—

(a) the earliest and latest dates on which the company has power to redeem those shares,

(b) whether those shares must be redeemed in any event or are liable to be redeemed at the option of the company or of the shareholder, and

(c) whether any (and, if so, what) premium is payable on redemption.

47. If the company has allotted any shares during the financial year, the following information must be given—

(a) the classes of shares allotted, and

(b) as respects each class of shares, the number allotted, their aggregate nominal value, and the consideration received by the company for the allotment.

Fixed assets

48.—(1) In respect of each item which is or would but for paragraph 4(2)(b) be shown under the general item "fixed assets" in the company's balance sheet the following information must be given—

(a) the appropriate amounts in respect of that item as at the date of the beginning of the financial year and as at the balance sheet date respectively,

(b) the effect on any amount shown in the balance sheet in respect of that item of—

  (i) any revision of the amount in respect of any assets included under that item made during that year on any basis mentioned in paragraph 32,

  (ii) acquisitions during that year of any assets,

  (iii) disposals during that year of any assets, and

  (iv) any transfers of assets of the company to and from that item during that year.

(2) The reference in sub-paragraph (1)(a) to the appropriate amounts in respect of any item as at any date there mentioned is a reference to amounts representing the aggregate amounts determined, as at that date, in respect of assets falling to be included under that item on either of the following bases, that is to say—

(a) on the basis of purchase price or production cost (determined in accordance with paragraphs 27 and 28), or

(b) on any basis mentioned in paragraph 32,

(leaving out of account in either case any provisions for depreciation or diminution in value).

(3) In respect of each item within sub-paragraph (1) there must also be stated—

(a) the cumulative amount of provisions for depreciation or diminution in value of assets included under that item as at each date mentioned in sub-paragraph (1)(a),

(b) the amount of any such provisions made in respect of the financial year,

(c) the amount of any adjustments made in respect of any such provisions during that year in consequence of the disposal of any assets, and

(d) the amount of any other adjustments made in respect of any such provisions during that year.

49. Where any fixed assets of the company (other than listed investments) are included under any item shown in the company's balance sheet at an amount determined on any basis mentioned in paragraph 32, the following information must be given—

(a) the years (so far as they are known to the directors) in which the assets were severally valued and the several values, and

(b) in the case of assets that have been valued during the financial year, the names of the persons who valued them or particulars of their qualifications for doing so and (whichever is stated) the bases of valuation used by them.

Investments

50.—(1) In respect of the amount of each item which is or would but for paragraph 4(2)(b) be shown in the company's balance sheet under the general item "investments" (whether as fixed assets or as current assets) there must be stated how much of that amount is ascribable to listed investments.

(2) Where the amount of any listed investments is stated for any item in accordance with sub-paragraph (1), the following amounts must also be stated—

(a) the aggregate market value of those investments where it differs from the amount so stated, and

(b) both the market value and the stock exchange value of any investments of which the former value is, for the purposes of the accounts, taken as being higher than the latter.

Information about fair value of assets and liabilities

51.—(1) This paragraph applies where financial instruments have been valued in accordance with paragraph 36 or 38.

(2) There must be stated—

(a) the significant assumptions underlying the valuation models and techniques used where the fair value of the instruments has been determined in accordance with paragraph 37(4),

(b) for each category of financial instrument, the fair value of the instruments in that category and the changes in value—

(i) included in the profit and loss account, or

(ii) credited to or (as the case may be) debited from the fair value reserve,

in respect of those instruments, and

(c) for each class of derivatives, the extent and nature of the instruments, including significant terms and conditions that may affect the amount, timing and certainty of future cash flows.

(3) Where any amount is transferred to or from the fair value reserve during the financial year, there must be stated in tabular form—

(a) the amount of the reserve as at the date of the beginning of the financial year and as at the balance sheet date respectively,

(b) the amount transferred to or from the reserve during that year, and

(c) the source and application respectively of the amounts so transferred.

52.—(1) This paragraph applies if—

(a) the company has financial fixed assets that could be included at fair value by virtue of paragraph 36,

(b) the amount at which those items are included under any item in the company's accounts is in excess of their fair value, and

(c) the company has not made provision for diminution in value of those assets in accordance with paragraph 19(1) of this Schedule.

(2) There must be stated—

(a) the amount at which either the individual assets or appropriate groupings of those individual assets are included in the company's accounts,

(b) the fair value of those assets or groupings, and

(c) the reasons for not making a provision for diminution in value of those assets, including the nature of the evidence that provides the basis for the belief that the amount at which they are stated in the accounts will be recovered.

Information where investment property and living animals and plants included at fair value

53.—(1) This paragraph applies where the amounts to be included in a company's accounts in respect of investment property or living animals and plants have been determined in accordance with paragraph 39.

(2) The balance sheet items affected and the basis of valuation adopted in determining the amounts of the assets in question in the case of each such item must be disclosed in a note to the accounts.

(3) In the case of investment property, for each balance sheet item affected there must be shown, either separately in the balance sheet or in a note to the accounts—

   (a) the comparable amounts determined according to the historical cost accounting rules, or

   (b) the differences between those amounts and the corresponding amounts actually shown in the balance sheet in respect of that item.

(4) In sub-paragraph (3), references in relation to any item to the comparable amounts determined in accordance with that sub-paragraph are to—

   (a) the aggregate amount which would be required to be shown in respect of that item if the amounts to be included in respect of all the assets covered by that item were determined according to the historical cost accounting rules, and

   (b) the aggregate amount of the cumulative provisions for depreciation or diminution in value which would be permitted or required in determining those amounts according to those rules.

Reserves and provisions

54.—(1) This paragraph applies where any amount is transferred—

   (a) to or from any reserves, or

   (b) to any provisions for liabilities, or

   (c) from any provision for liabilities otherwise than for the purpose for which the provision was established,

and the reserves or provisions are or would but for paragraph 4(2)(b) be shown as separate items in the company's balance sheet.

(2) The following information must be given in respect of the aggregate of reserves or provisions included in the same item—

   (a) the amount of the reserves or provisions as at the date of the beginning of the financial year and as at the balance sheet date respectively,

   (b) any amounts transferred to or from the reserves or provisions during that year, and

   (c) the source and application respectively of any amounts so transferred.

(3) Particulars must be given of each provision included in the item "other provisions" in the company's balance sheet in any case where the amount of that provision is material.

Details of indebtedness

55.—(1) For the aggregate of all items shown under "creditors" in the company's balance sheet there must be stated the aggregate of the following amounts—

   (a) the amount of any debts included under "creditors" which are payable or repayable otherwise than by instalments and fall due for payment or repayment after the end of the period of five years beginning with the day next following the end of the financial year, and

   (b) in the case of any debts so included which are payable or repayable by instalments, the amount of any instalments which fall due for payment after the end of that period.

(2) In respect of each item shown under "creditors" in the company's balance sheet there must be stated the aggregate amount of any debts included under that item in respect of which any security has been given by the company.

(3) References above in this paragraph to an item shown under "creditors" in the company's balance sheet include references, where amounts falling due to creditors within one year and after more than one year are distinguished in the balance sheet—

(a) in a case within sub-paragraph (1), to an item shown under the latter of those categories,

(b) in a case within sub-paragraph (2), to an item shown under either of those categories.

References to items shown under "creditors" include references to items which would but for paragraph 4(2)(b) be shown under that heading.

56. If any fixed cumulative dividends on the company's shares are in arrear, there must be stated—

(a) the amount of the arrears, and

(b) the period for which the dividends or, if there is more than one class, each class of them are in arrear.

Guarantees and other financial commitments

57.—(1) Particulars must be given of any charge on the assets of the company to secure the liabilities of any other person, including, where practicable, the amount secured.

(2) The following information must be given with respect to any other contingent liability not provided for—

(a) the amount or estimated amount of that liability,

(b) its legal nature, and

(c) whether any valuable security has been provided by the company in connection with that liability and if so, what.

(3) There must be stated, where practicable, the aggregate amount or estimated amount of contracts for capital expenditure, so far as not provided for.

(4) Particulars must be given of—

(a) any pension commitments included under any provision shown in the company's balance sheet, and

(b) any such commitments for which no provision has been made,

and where any such commitment relates wholly or partly to pensions payable to past directors of the company separate particulars must be given of that commitment so far as it relates to such pensions.

(5) Particulars must also be given of any other financial commitments that—

(a) have not been provided for, and

(b) are relevant to assessing the company's state of affairs.

(6) Commitments within any of sub-paragraphs (1) to (5) which are undertaken on behalf of or for the benefit of—

(a) any parent undertaking or fellow subsidiary undertaking, or

(b) any subsidiary undertaking of the company,

must be stated separately from the other commitments within that sub-paragraph, and commitments within paragraph (a) must also be stated separately from those within paragraph (b).

Miscellaneous matters

58. Particulars must be given of any case where the purchase price or production cost of any asset is for the first time determined under paragraph 29.

Information supplementing the profit and loss account

59. Paragraphs 60 and 61 require information which either supplements the information given with respect to any particular items shown in the profit and loss account or otherwise provides particulars of income or expenditure of the company or of circumstances affecting the items shown in the profit and loss account (see regulation 3(2) for exemption for companies falling within section 408 of the 2006 Act).

Particulars of turnover

60.—(1) If the company has supplied geographical markets outside the United Kingdom during the financial year in question, there must be stated the percentage of its turnover that, in the opinion of the directors, is attributable to those markets.

(2) In analysing for the purposes of this paragraph the source of turnover, the directors of the company must have regard to the manner in which the company's activities are organised.

Miscellaneous matters

61.—(1) Where any amount relating to any preceding financial year is included in any item in the profit and loss account, the effect must be stated.

(2) Particulars must be given of any extraordinary income or charges arising in the financial year.

(3) The effect must be stated of any transactions that are exceptional by virtue of size or incidence though they fall within the ordinary activities of the company.

Sums denominated in foreign currencies

62. Where sums originally denominated in foreign currencies have been brought into account under any items shown in the balance sheet or profit and loss account, the basis on which those sums have been translated into sterling (or the currency in which the accounts are drawn up) must be stated.

Dormant companies acting as agents

63. Where the directors of a company take advantage of the exemption conferred by section 480 of the 2006 Act (dormant companies: exemption from audit), and the company has during the financial year in question acted as an agent for any person, the fact that it has so acted must be stated.

SCHEDULE 2

Regulation 4

INFORMATION ABOUT RELATED UNDERTAKINGS WHERE COMPANY NOT PREPARING GROUP ACCOUNTS (COMPANIES ACT OR IAS INDIVIDUAL ACCOUNTS)

PART 1
REQUIRED DISCLOSURES

Subsidiary undertakings

1.—(1) The following information must be given where at the end of the financial year the company has subsidiary undertakings.

(2) The name of each subsidiary undertaking must be stated.

(3) There must be stated with respect to each subsidiary undertaking—

 (a) if it is incorporated outside the United Kingdom, the country in which it is incorporated,

 (b) if it is unincorporated, the address of its principal place of business.

Holdings in subsidiary undertakings

2.—(1) There must be stated in relation to shares of each class held by the company in a subsidiary undertaking—

 (a) the identity of the class, and

 (b) the proportion of the nominal value of the shares of that class represented by those shares.

(2) The shares held by or on behalf of the company itself must be distinguished from those attributed to the company which are held by or on behalf of a subsidiary undertaking.

Financial information about subsidiary undertakings

3.—(1) There must be disclosed with respect to each subsidiary undertaking—

 (a) the aggregate amount of its capital and reserves as at the end of its relevant financial year, and

 (b) its profit or loss for that year.

(2) That information need not be given if the company would (if it were not subject to the small companies regime) be exempt by virtue of section 400 or 401 of the 2006 Act (parent company included in accounts of larger group) from the requirement to prepare group accounts.

(3) That information need not be given if the company's investment in the subsidiary undertaking is included in the company's accounts by way of the equity method of valuation.

(4) That information need not be given if—

 (a) the subsidiary undertaking is not required by any provision of the 2006 Act to deliver a copy of its balance sheet for its relevant financial year and does not otherwise publish that balance sheet in the United Kingdom or elsewhere, and

 (b) the company's holding is less than 50% of the nominal value of the shares in the undertaking.

(5) Information otherwise required by this paragraph need not be given if it is not material.

The Small Companies and Groups (Accounts and Directors' Report) Regulations 2008

(6) For the purposes of this paragraph the "relevant financial year" of a subsidiary undertaking is—

(a) if its financial year ends with that of the company, that year, and

(b) if not, its financial year ending last before the end of the company's financial year.

Shares of company held by subsidiary undertakings

4.—(1) The number, description and amount of the shares in the company held by or on behalf of its subsidiary undertakings must be disclosed.

(2) Sub-paragraph (1) does not apply in relation to shares in the case of which the subsidiary undertaking is concerned as personal representative or, subject as follows, as trustee.

(3) The exception for shares in relation to which the subsidiary undertaking is concerned as trustee does not apply if the company, or any subsidiary undertaking of the company, is beneficially interested under the trust, otherwise than by way of security only for the purposes of a transaction entered into by it in the ordinary course of a business which includes the lending of money.

(4) Part 2 of this Schedule has effect for the interpretation of the reference in sub-paragraph (3) to a beneficial interest under a trust.

Significant holdings in undertakings other than subsidiary undertakings

5.—(1) The information required by paragraphs 6 and 7 must be given where at the end of the financial year the company has a significant holding in an undertaking which is not a subsidiary undertaking of the company.

(2) A holding is significant for this purpose if—

(a) it amounts to 20% or more of the nominal value of any class of shares in the undertaking, or

(b) the amount of the holding (as stated or included in the company's accounts) exceeds 20% of the amount (as so stated) of the company's assets.

6.—(1) The name of the undertaking must be stated.

(2) There must be stated—

(a) if the undertaking is incorporated outside the United Kingdom, the country in which it is incorporated,

(b) if it is unincorporated, the address of its principal place of business.

(3) There must also be stated—

(a) the identity of each class of shares in the undertaking held by the company, and

(b) the proportion of the nominal value of the shares of that class represented by those shares.

7.—(1) There must also be stated—

(a) the aggregate amount of the capital and reserves of the undertaking as at the end of its relevant financial year, and

(b) its profit or loss for that year.

(2) That information need not be given if—

(a) the company would (if it were not subject to the small companies regime) be exempt by virtue of section 400 or 401 of the 2006 Act (parent company included in accounts of larger group) from the requirement to prepare group accounts, and

(b) the investment of the company in all undertakings in which it has such a holding as is mentioned in sub-paragraph (1) is shown, in aggregate, in the notes to the accounts by way of the equity method of valuation.

(3) That information need not be given in respect of an undertaking if—

(a) the undertaking is not required by any provision of the 2006 Act to deliver to the registrar a copy of its balance sheet for its relevant financial year and does not otherwise publish that balance sheet in the United Kingdom or elsewhere, and

(b) the company's holding is less than 50% of the nominal value of the shares in the undertaking.

(4) Information otherwise required by this paragraph need not be given if it is not material.

(5) For the purposes of this paragraph the "relevant financial year" of an undertaking is—

(a) if its financial year ends with that of the company, that year, and

(b) if not, its financial year ending last before the end of the company's financial year.

Membership of certain undertakings

8.—(1) The information required by this paragraph must be given where at the end of the financial year the company is a member of a qualifying undertaking.

(2) There must be stated—

(a) the name and legal form of the undertaking, and

(b) the address of the undertaking's registered office (whether in or outside the United Kingdom) or, if it does not have such an office, its head office (whether in or outside the United Kingdom).

(3) Where the undertaking is a qualifying partnership there must also be stated either—

(a) that a copy of the latest accounts of the undertaking has been or is to be appended to the copy of the company's accounts sent to the registrar under section 444 of the 2006 Act, or

(b) the name of at least one body corporate (which may be the company) in whose group accounts the undertaking has been or is to be dealt with on a consolidated basis.

(4) Information otherwise required by sub-paragraph (2) need not be given if it is not material.

(5) Information otherwise required by sub-paragraph (3)(b) need not be given if the notes to the company's accounts disclose that advantage has been taken of the exemption conferred by regulation 7 of the Partnerships and Unlimited Companies (Accounts) Regulations 1993(**a**).

(6) In this paragraph—

"dealt with on a consolidated basis", "member" and "qualifying partnership" have the same meanings as in the Partnerships and Unlimited Companies (Accounts) Regulations 1993;

"qualifying undertaking" means—

(a) a qualifying partnership, or

(b) an unlimited company each of whose members is—

  (i) a limited company,

  (ii) another unlimited company each of whose members is a limited company, or

  (iii) a Scottish partnership each of whose members is a limited company,

and references in this paragraph to a limited company, another unlimited company or a Scottish partnership include a comparable undertaking incorporated in or formed under the law of a country or territory outside the United Kingdom.

Parent undertaking drawing up accounts for larger group

9.—(1) Where the company is a subsidiary undertaking, the following information must be given with respect to the parent undertaking of—

(a) the largest group of undertakings for which group accounts are drawn up and of which the company is a member, and

---

(**a**) S.I. 1993/1820.

(b) the smallest such group of undertakings.

(2) The name of the parent undertaking must be stated.

(3) There must be stated—

(a) if the undertaking is incorporated outside the United Kingdom, the country in which it is incorporated,

(b) if it is unincorporated, the address of its principal place of business.

(4) If copies of the group accounts referred to in sub-paragraph (1) are available to the public, there must also be stated the addresses from which copies of the accounts can be obtained.

Identification of ultimate parent company

10.—(1) Where the company is a subsidiary undertaking, the following information must be given with respect to the company (if any) regarded by the directors as being the company's ultimate parent company.

(2) The name of that company must be stated.

(3) If that company is incorporated outside the United Kingdom, the country in which it is incorporated must be stated (if known to the directors).

(4) In this paragraph "company" includes any body corporate.

Construction of references to shares held by company

11.—(1) References in this Part of this Schedule to shares held by a company are to be construed as follows.

(2) For the purposes of paragraphs 2 and 3 (information about subsidiary undertakings)—

(a) there must be attributed to the company any shares held by a subsidiary undertaking, or by a person acting on behalf of the company or a subsidiary undertaking; but

(b) there must be treated as not held by the company any shares held on behalf of a person other than the company or a subsidiary undertaking.

(3) For the purposes of paragraphs 5 to 7 (information about undertakings other than subsidiary undertakings)—

(a) there must be attributed to the company shares held on its behalf by any person; but

(b) there must be treated as not held by a company shares held on behalf of a person other than the company.

(4) For the purposes of any of those provisions, shares held by way of security must be treated as held by the person providing the security—

(a) where apart from the right to exercise them for the purpose of preserving the value of the security, or of realising it, the rights attached to the shares are exercisable only in accordance with his instructions, and

(b) where the shares are held in connection with the granting of loans as part of normal business activities and apart from the right to exercise them for the purpose of preserving the value of the security, or of realising it, the rights attached to the shares are exercisable only in his interests.

PART 2
INTERPRETATION OF REFERENCES TO "BENEFICIAL INTEREST"

Introduction

12.—(1) References in this Schedule to a beneficial interest are to be interpreted in accordance with the following provisions.

(2) This Part of this Schedule applies in relation to debentures as it applies in relation to shares.

Residual interests under pension and employees' share schemes

13.—(1) Where shares in an undertaking are held on trust for the purposes of a pension scheme or an employees' share scheme, there must be disregarded any residual interest of the undertaking or any of its subsidiary undertakings (the "residual beneficiary") that has not vested in possession.

(2) A "residual interest" means a right to receive any of the trust property in the event of—

  (a) all the liabilities arising under the scheme having been satisfied or provided for, or

  (b) the residual beneficiary ceasing to participate in the scheme, or

  (c) the trust property at any time exceeding what is necessary for satisfying the liabilities arising or expected to arise under the scheme.

(3) In sub-paragraph (2)—

  (a) references to a right include a right dependent on the exercise of a discretion vested by the scheme in the trustee or any other person, and

  (b) references to liabilities arising under a scheme include liabilities that have resulted or may result from the exercise of any such discretion.

(4) For the purposes of this paragraph a residual interest vests in possession—

  (a) in a case within sub-paragraph (2)(a), on the occurrence of the event there mentioned, whether or not the amount of the property receivable pursuant to the right mentioned in that sub-paragraph is then ascertained,

  (b) in a case within sub-paragraph (2)(b) or (c), when the residual beneficiary becomes entitled to require the trustee to transfer to it any of the property receivable pursuant to that right.

Employer's charges and other rights of recovery

14.—(1) Where shares in an undertaking are held on trust there must be disregarded—

  (a) if the trust is for the purposes of a pension scheme, any such rights as are mentioned in sub-paragraph (2),

  (b) if the trust is for the purposes of an employees' share scheme, any such rights as are mentioned in paragraph (a) of that sub-paragraph,

being rights of the undertaking or any of its subsidiary undertakings.

(2) The rights referred to are—

  (a) any charge or lien on, or set-off against, any benefit or other right or interest under the scheme for the purpose of enabling the employer or former employer of a member of the scheme to obtain the discharge of a monetary obligation due to him from the member,

  (b) any right to receive from the trustee of the scheme, or as trustee of the scheme to retain, an amount that can be recovered or retained under section 61 of the Pension Schemes Act 1993(**a**) or section 57 of the Pension Schemes (Northern Ireland) Act 1993(**b**) (deduction of contributions equivalent premium from refund of scheme contributions) or otherwise, as reimbursement or partial reimbursement for any contributions equivalent premium paid in connection with the scheme under Chapter 3 of Part 3 of that Act.

Trustee's right to expenses, remuneration, indemnity etc.

15.—(1) Where an undertaking is a trustee, there must be disregarded any rights which the undertaking has in its capacity as trustee.

(**a**) 1993 c.48.
(**b**) 1993 c.49.

(2) This includes in particular—
 (a) any right to recover its expenses or be remunerated out of the trust property, and
 (b) any right to be indemnified out of that property for any liability incurred by reason of any act or omission of the undertaking in the performance of its duties as trustee.

Meaning of "pension scheme"

16.—(1) In this Part of this Schedule "pension scheme" means any scheme for the provision of benefits consisting of or including relevant benefits for or in respect of employees or former employees.

(2) For this purpose "relevant benefits" means any pension, lump sum, gratuity or other like benefit given or to be given on retirement or on death or in anticipation of retirement or, in connection with past service, after retirement or death.

Application of provisions to directors

17. In paragraphs 14(2) and 16, "employee" and "employer" are to be read as if a director of an undertaking were employed by it.

Appendix E SI 2008 No. 409

SCHEDULE 3   Regulations 5 and 9

INFORMATION ABOUT DIRECTORS' BENEFITS: REMUNERATION (COMPANIES ACT OR IAS ACCOUNTS)

PART 1

INFORMATION REQUIRED TO BE DISCLOSED

Total amount of directors' remuneration etc.

1.—(1) There must be shown the overall total of the following amounts—
   (a) the amount of remuneration paid to or receivable by directors in respect of qualifying services;
   (b) the amount of money paid to or receivable by directors, and the net value of assets (other than money, share options or shares) received or receivable by directors, under long term incentive schemes in respect of qualifying services; and
   (c) the value of any company contributions—
      (i) paid, or treated as paid, to a pension scheme in respect of directors' qualifying services, and
      (ii) by reference to which the rate or amount of any money purchase benefits that may become payable will be calculated.

(2) There must be shown the number of directors (if any) to whom retirement benefits are accruing in respect of qualifying services—
   (a) under money purchase schemes, and
   (b) under defined benefit schemes.

Compensation to directors for loss of office

2.—(1) There must be shown the aggregate amount of any payments made to directors or past directors for loss of office.

(2) "Payment for loss of office" has the same meaning as in section 215 of the 2006 Act.

Sums paid to third parties in respect of directors' services

3.—(1) There must be shown the aggregate amount of any consideration paid to or receivable by third parties for making available the services of any person—
   (a) as a director of the company, or
   (b) while director of the company—
      (i) as director of any of its subsidiary undertakings, or
      (ii) otherwise in connection with the management of the affairs of the company or any of its subsidiary undertakings.

(2) In sub-paragraph (1)—
   (a) the reference to consideration includes benefits otherwise than in cash, and
   (b) in relation to such consideration the reference to its amount is to the estimated money value of the benefit.

The nature of any such consideration must be disclosed.

The Small Companies and Groups (Accounts and Directors' Report) Regulations 2008

(3) For the purposes of this paragraph a "third party" means a person other than—

(a) the director himself or a person connected with him or body corporate controlled by him, or

(b) the company or any of its subsidiary undertakings.

PART 2

SUPPLEMENTARY PROVISIONS

General nature of obligations

4.—(1) This Schedule requires information to be given only so far as it is contained in the company's books and papers or the company has the right to obtain it from the persons concerned.

(2) For the purposes of this Schedule any information is treated as shown if it is capable of being readily ascertained from other information which is shown.

Provisions as to amounts to be shown

5.—(1) The following provisions apply with respect to the amounts to be shown under this Schedule.

(2) The amount in each case includes all relevant sums, whether paid by or receivable from the company, any of the company's subsidiary undertakings or any other person.

(3) References to amounts paid to or receivable by a person include amounts paid to or receivable by a person connected with him or a body corporate controlled by him (but not so as to require an amount to be counted twice).

(4) Except as otherwise provided, the amounts to be shown for any financial year are—

(a) the sums receivable in respect of that year (whenever paid) or,

(b) in the case of sums not receivable in respect of a period, the sums paid during that year.

(5) Sums paid by way of expenses allowance that are charged to United Kingdom income tax after the end of the relevant financial year must be shown in a note to the first accounts in which it is practicable to show them and must be distinguished from the amounts to be shown apart from this provision.

(6) Where it is necessary to do so for the purpose of making any distinction required in complying with this Schedule, the directors may apportion payments between the matters in respect of which they have been paid or are receivable in such manner as they think appropriate.

Exclusion of sums liable to be accounted for to company etc.

6.—(1) The amounts to be shown under this Schedule do not include any sums that are to be accounted for—

(a) to the company or any of its subsidiary undertakings, or

(b) by virtue of sections 219 and 222(3) of the 2006 Act (payments in connection with share transfers: duty to account), to persons who sold their shares as a result of the offer made.

(2) Where—

(a) any such sums are not shown in a note to the accounts for the relevant financial year on the ground that the person receiving them is liable to account for them, and

(b) the liability is afterwards wholly or partly released or is not enforced within a period of two years,

those sums, to the extent to which the liability is released or not enforced, must be shown in a note to the first accounts in which it is practicable to show them and must be distinguished from the amounts to be shown apart from this provision.

Appendix E SI 2008 No. 409

Meaning of "remuneration"

7.—(1) In this Schedule "remuneration" of a director includes—
  (a) salary, fees and bonuses, sums paid by way of expenses allowance (so far as they are chargeable to United Kingdom income tax), and
  (b) subject to sub-paragraph (2), the estimated money value of any other benefits received by him otherwise than in cash.

(2) The expression does not include—
  (a) the value of any share options granted to a director or the amount of any gains made on the exercise of any such options,
  (b) any company contributions paid, or treated as paid, in respect of him under any pension scheme or any benefits to which he is entitled under any such scheme, or
  (c) any money or other assets paid to or received or receivable by him under any long term incentive scheme.

Meaning of "long term incentive scheme"

8.—(1) In this Schedule "long term incentive scheme" means an agreement or arrangement—
  (a) under which money or other assets may become receivable by a director, and
  (b) which includes one or more qualifying conditions with respect to service or performance which cannot be fulfilled within a single financial year.

(2) For this purpose the following must be disregarded—
  (a) bonuses the amount of which falls to be determined by reference to service or performance within a single financial year;
  (b) compensation for loss of office, payments for breach of contract and other termination payments; and
  (c) retirement benefits.

Meaning of "shares" and "share option" and related expressions

9. In this Schedule—
  (a) "shares" means shares (whether allotted or not) in the company, or any undertaking which is a group undertaking in relation to the company, and includes a share warrant as defined by section 779(1) of the 2006 Act; and
  (b) "share option" means a right to acquire shares.

Meaning of "pension scheme" and related expressions

10.—(1) In this Schedule—

"pension scheme" means a retirement benefits scheme as defined by section 611 of the Income and Corporation Taxes Act 1988(**a**); and

"retirement benefits" has the meaning given by section 612(1) of that Act.

(2) In this Schedule, "company contributions", in relation to a pension scheme and a director, means any payments (including insurance premiums) made, or treated as made, to the scheme in respect of the director by a person other than the director.

(3) In this Schedule, in relation to a director—

"defined benefits" means retirement benefits payable under a pension scheme that are not money purchase benefits;

(**a**) 1988 c.1.

"defined benefit scheme" means a pension scheme that is not a money purchase scheme;

"money purchase benefits" means retirement benefits payable under a pension scheme the rate or amount of which is calculated by reference to payments made, or treated as made, by the director or by any other person in respect of the director and which are not average salary benefits; and

"money purchase scheme" means a pension scheme under which all of the benefits that may become payable to or in respect of the director are money purchase benefits.

(4) Where a pension scheme provides for any benefits that may become payable to or in respect of any director to be whichever are the greater of—

(a) money purchase benefits as determined by or under the scheme; and

(b) defined benefits as so determined,

the company may assume for the purposes of this paragraph that those benefits will be money purchase benefits, or defined benefits, according to whichever appears more likely at the end of the financial year.

(5) For the purpose of determining whether a pension scheme is a money purchase or defined benefit scheme, any death in service benefits provided for by the scheme are to be disregarded.

References to subsidiary undertakings

11.—(1) Any reference in this Schedule to a subsidiary undertaking of the company, in relation to a person who is or was, while a director of the company, a director also, by virtue of the company's nomination (direct or indirect) of any other undertaking, includes that undertaking, whether or not it is or was in fact a subsidiary undertaking of the company.

(2) Any reference to a subsidiary undertaking of the company—

(a) for the purposes of paragraph 1 (remuneration etc.) is to an undertaking which is a subsidiary undertaking at the time the services were rendered, and

(b) for the purposes of paragraph 2 (compensation for loss of office) is to a subsidiary undertaking immediately before the loss of office as director.

Other minor definitions

12.—(1) In this Schedule—

"net value", in relation to any assets received or receivable by a director, means value after deducting any money paid or other value given by the director in respect of those assets;

"qualifying services", in relation to any person, means his services as a director of the company, and his services while director of the company—

(a) as director of any of its subsidiary undertakings; or

(b) otherwise in connection with the management of the affairs of the company or any of its subsidiary undertakings.

(2) For the purposes of this Schedule, remuneration paid or receivable or share options granted in respect of a person's accepting office as a director are treated as emoluments paid or receivable or share options granted in respect of his services as a director.

Appendix E SI 2008 No. 409

SCHEDULE 4 — Regulation 6(1)

COMPANIES ACT ABBREVIATED ACCOUNTS FOR DELIVERY TO REGISTRAR OF COMPANIES

PART 1

THE REQUIRED BALANCE SHEET FORMATS

1.—(1) A company may deliver to the registrar a copy of the balance sheet showing the items listed in either of the balance sheet formats set out below, in the order and under the headings and sub-headings given in the format adopted, but in other respects corresponding to the full balance sheet.

(2) The copy balance sheet must contain in a prominent position a statement that it has been prepared in accordance with the provisions applicable to companies subject to the small companies regime.

Balance sheet formats

Format 1

A. Called up share capital not paid

B. Fixed assets
    I. Intangible assets
    II. Tangible assets
    III. Investments

C. Current assets
    I. Stocks
    II. Debtors *(1)*
    III. Investments
    IV. Cash at bank and in hand

D. Prepayments and accrued income

E. Creditors: amounts falling due within one year

F. Net current assets (liabilities)

G. Total assets less current liabilities

H. Creditors: amounts falling due after more than one year

I. Provisions for liabilities

J. Accruals and deferred income

K. Capital and reserves
    I. Called up share capital

The Small Companies and Groups (Accounts and Directors' Report) Regulations 2008

    II.   Share premium account
    III. Revaluation reserve
    IV. Other reserves
    V.   Profit and loss account

Balance sheet formats

Format 2

ASSETS

A.   Called up share capital not paid

B.   Fixed assets
    I.   Intangible assets
    II.   Tangible assets
    III. Investments

C.   Current assets
    I.   Stocks
    II.   Debtors *(1)*
    III. Investments
    IV. Cash at bank and in hand

D.   Prepayments and accrued income

LIABILITIES

A.   Capital and reserves
    I.   Called up share capital
    II.   Share premium account
    III. Revaluation reserve
    IV. Other reserves
    V.   Profit and loss account

B.   Provisions for liabilities

C.   Creditors *(2)*

D.   Accruals and deferred income

Notes on the balance sheet formats

(1) Debtors

(Formats 1 and 2, items C.II.)

The aggregate amount of debtors falling due after more than one year must be shown separately, unless it is disclosed in the notes to the accounts.

(2) Creditors

(Format 2, Liabilities item C.)

The aggregate amount of creditors falling due within one year and of creditors falling due after more than one year must be shown separately, unless it is disclosed in the notes to the accounts.

PART 2

NOTES TO THE ACCOUNTS

Preliminary

2. Any information required in the case of any company by the following provisions of this Part of this Schedule must (if not given in the company's accounts) be given by way of a note to those accounts.

Disclosure of accounting policies

3. The accounting policies adopted by the company in determining the amounts to be included in respect of items shown in the balance sheet and in determining the profit or loss of the company must be stated (including such policies with respect to the depreciation and diminution in value of assets).

Information supplementing the balance sheet

Share capital and debentures

4.—(1) Where shares of more than one class have been allotted, the number and aggregate nominal value of shares of each class allotted must be given.

(2) In the case of any part of the allotted share capital that consists of redeemable shares, the following information must be given—

 (a) the earliest and latest dates on which the company has power to redeem those shares,

 (b) whether those shares must be redeemed in any event or are liable to be redeemed at the option of the company or of the shareholder, and

 (c) whether any (and, if so, what) premium is payable on redemption.

5. If the company has allotted any shares during the financial year, the following information must be given—

 (a) the classes of shares allotted, and

 (b) as respects each class of shares, the number allotted, their aggregate nominal value, and the consideration received by the company for the allotment.

Fixed assets

6.—(1) In respect of each item to which a letter or Roman number is assigned under the general item "fixed assets" in the company's balance sheet the following information must be given—

 (a) the appropriate amounts in respect of that item as at the date of the beginning of the financial year and as at the balance sheet date respectively,

 (b) the effect on any amount shown in the balance sheet in respect of that item of—

  (i) any revision of the amount in respect of any assets included under that item made during that year on any basis mentioned in paragraph 32 of Schedule 1 to these Regulations,

  (ii) acquisitions during that year of any assets,

  (iii) disposals during that year of any assets, and

  (iv) any transfers of assets of the company to and from that item during that year.

(2) The reference in sub-paragraph (1)(a) to the appropriate amounts in respect of any item as at any date there mentioned is a reference to amounts representing the aggregate amounts determined, as at that date, in respect of assets falling to be included under that item on either of the following bases, that is to say—

- (a) on the basis of purchase price or production cost (determined in accordance with paragraphs 27 and 28 of Schedule 1 to these Regulations), or
- (b) on any basis mentioned in paragraph 32 of that Schedule,

(leaving out of account in either case any provisions for depreciation or diminution in value).

(3) In respect of each item within sub-paragraph (1) there must also be stated—

- (a) the cumulative amount of provisions for depreciation or diminution in value of assets included under that item as at each date mentioned in sub-paragraph (1)(a),
- (b) the amount of any such provisions made in respect of the financial year,
- (c) the amount of any adjustments made in respect of any such provisions during that year in consequence of the disposal of any assets, and
- (d) the amount of any other adjustments made in respect of any such provisions during that year.

Financial fixed assets

7.—(1) This paragraph applies if—

- (a) the company has financial fixed assets that could be included at fair value by virtue of paragraph 36 of Schedule 1 to these Regulations,
- (b) the amount at which those items are included under any item in the company's accounts is in excess of their fair value, and
- (c) the company has not made provision for diminution in value of those assets in accordance with paragraph 19(1) of that Schedule.

(2) There must be stated—

- (a) the amount at which either the individual assets or appropriate groupings of those individual assets are included in the company's accounts,
- (b) the fair value of those assets or groupings, and
- (c) the reasons for not making a provision for diminution in value of those assets, including the nature of the evidence that provides the basis for the belief that the amount at which they are stated in the accounts will be recovered.

Details of indebtedness

8.—(1) For the aggregate of all items shown under "creditors" in the company's balance sheet there must be stated the aggregate of the following amounts—

- (a) the amount of any debts included under "creditors" which are payable or repayable otherwise than by instalments and fall due for payment or repayment after the end of the period of five years beginning with the day next following the end of the financial year, and
- (b) in the case of any debts so included which are payable or repayable by instalments, the amount of any instalments which fall due for payment after the end of that period.

(2) In respect of each item shown under "creditors" in the company's balance sheet there must be stated the aggregate amount of any debts included under that item in respect of which any security has been given by the company.

Sums denominated in foreign currencies

9. Where sums originally denominated in foreign currencies have been brought into account under any items shown in the balance sheet or profit and loss account, the basis on which those sums have been translated into sterling (or the currency in which the accounts are drawn up) must be stated.

Dormant companies acting as agents

10. Where the directors of a company take advantage of the exemption conferred by section 480 of the 2006 Act (dormant companies: exemption from audit), and the company has during the financial year in question acted as an agent for any person, the fact that it has so acted must be stated.

SCHEDULE 5 Regulation 7

MATTERS TO BE DEALT WITH IN DIRECTORS' REPORT

Introduction

1. In addition to the information required by section 416 of the 2006 Act, the directors' report must contain the following information.

Political donations and expenditure

2.—(1) If—
  (a) the company (not being the wholly-owned subsidiary of a company incorporated in the United Kingdom) has in the financial year—
    (i) made any political donation to any political party or other political organisation,
    (ii) made any political donation to any independent election candidate, or
    (iii) incurred any political expenditure, and
  (b) the amount of the donation or expenditure, or (as the case may be) the aggregate amount of all donations and expenditure falling within paragraph (a), exceeded £2000,
the directors' report for the year must contain the following particulars.

(2) Those particulars are—
  (a) as respects donations falling within sub-paragraph (1)(a)(i) or (ii)—
    (i) the name of each political party, other political organisation or independent election candidate to whom any such donation has been made, and
    (ii) the total amount given to that party, organisation or candidate by way of such donations in the financial year; and
  (b) as respects expenditure falling within sub-paragraph (1)(a)(iii), the total amount incurred by way of such expenditure in the financial year.

(3) If—
  (a) at the end of the financial year the company has subsidiaries which have, in that year, made any donations or incurred any such expenditure as is mentioned in sub-paragraph (1)(a), and
  (b) it is not itself the wholly-owned subsidiary of a company incorporated in the United Kingdom,
the directors' report for the year is not, by virtue of sub-paragraph (1), required to contain the particulars specified in sub-paragraph (2).

But, if the total amount of any such donations or expenditure (or both) made or incurred in that year by the company and the subsidiaries between them exceeds £2000, the directors' report for the year must contain those particulars in relation to each body by whom any such donation or expenditure has been made or incurred.

(4) Any expression used in this paragraph which is also used in Part 14 of the 2006 Act (control of political donations and expenditure) has the same meaning as in that Part.

3.—(1) If the company (not being the wholly-owned subsidiary of a company incorporated in the United Kingdom) has in the financial year made any contribution to a non-EU political party, the directors' report for the year must contain—
  (a) a statement of the amount of the contribution, or

(b) (if it has made two or more such contributions in the year) a statement of the total amount of the contributions.

(2) If—

(a) at the end of the financial year the company has subsidiaries which have, in that year, made any such contributions as are mentioned in sub-paragraph (1), and

(b) it is not itself the wholly-owned subsidiary of a company incorporated in the United Kingdom,

the directors' report for the year is not, by virtue of sub-paragraph (1), required to contain any such statement as is there mentioned, but it must instead contain a statement of the total amount of the contributions made in the year by the company and the subsidiaries between them.

(3) In this paragraph, "contribution", in relation to an organisation, means—

(a) any gift of money to the organisation (whether made directly or indirectly);

(b) any subscription or other fee paid for affiliation to, or membership of, the organisation; or

(c) any money spent (otherwise than by the organisation or a person acting on its behalf) in paying any expenses incurred directly or indirectly by the organisation.

(4) In this paragraph, "non-EU political party" means any political party which carries on, or proposes to carry on, its activities wholly outside the member States.

Charitable donations

4.—(1) If—

(a) the company (not being the wholly-owned subsidiary of a company incorporated in the United Kingdom) has in the financial year given money for charitable purposes, and

(b) the money given exceeded £2000 in amount,

the directors' report for the year must contain, in the case of each of the purposes for which money has been given, a statement of the amount of money given for that purpose.

(2) If—

(a) at the end of the financial year the company has subsidiaries which have, in that year, given money for charitable purposes, and

(b) it is not itself the wholly owned subsidiary of a company incorporated in the United Kingdom,

sub-paragraph (1) does not apply to the company.

But, if the amount given in that year for charitable purposes by the company and the subsidiaries between them exceeds £2000, the directors' report for the year must contain, in the case of each of the purposes for which money has been given by the company and the subsidiaries between them, a statement of the amount of money given for that purpose.

(3) Money given for charitable purposes to a person who, when it was given, was ordinarily resident outside the United Kingdom is to be left out of account for the purposes of this paragraph.

(4) For the purposes of this paragraph, "charitable purposes" means purposes which are exclusively charitable, and as respects Scotland a purpose is charitable if it is listed in section 7(2) of the Charities and Trustee Investment (Scotland) Act 2005(**a**).

Disclosure concerning employment etc. of disabled persons

5.—(1) This paragraph applies to the directors' report where the average number of persons employed by the company in each week during the financial year exceeded 250.

(2) That average number is the quotient derived by dividing, by the number of weeks in the financial year, the number derived by ascertaining, in relation to each of those weeks, the number

---

(**a**) 2005 asp 10.

of persons who, under contracts of service, were employed in the week (whether throughout it or not) by the company, and adding up the numbers ascertained.

(3) The directors' report must in that case contain a statement describing such policy as the company has applied during the financial year—

    (a) for giving full and fair consideration to applications for employment by the company made by disabled persons, having regard to their particular aptitudes and abilities,

    (b) for continuing the employment of, and for arranging appropriate training for, employees of the company who have become disabled persons during the period when they were employed by the company, and

    (c) otherwise for the training, career development and promotion of disabled persons employed by the company.

(4) In this paragraph—

    (a) "employment" means employment other than employment to work wholly or mainly outside the United Kingdom, and "employed" and "employee" are to be construed accordingly; and

    (b) "disabled person" means the same as in the Disability Discrimination Act 1995(**a**).

Disclosure required by company acquiring its own shares etc.

6.—(1) This paragraph applies where shares in a company—

    (a) are purchased by the company or are acquired by it by forfeiture or surrender in lieu of forfeiture, or in pursuance of any of the following provisions (acquisition of own shares by company limited by shares)—

        (i) section 143(3) of the Companies Act 1985(**b**),

        (ii) Article 153(3) of the Companies (Northern Ireland) Order 1986(**c**), or

        (iii) section 659 of the 2006 Act, or

    (b) are acquired by another person in circumstances where paragraph (c) or (d) of any of the following provisions applies (acquisition by company's nominee, or by another with company financial assistance, the company having a beneficial interest)—

        (i) section 146(1) of the Companies Act 1985(**d**),

        (ii) Article 156(1) of the Companies (Northern Ireland) Order 1986(**e**), or

        (iii) section 662(1) of the 2006 Act, or

    (c) are made subject to a lien or other charge taken (whether expressly or otherwise) by the company and permitted by any of the following provisions (exceptions from general rule against a company having a lien or charge on its own shares)—

        (i) section 150(2) or (4) of the Companies Act 1985(**f**),

        (ii) Article 160(2) or (4) of the Companies (Northern Ireland) Order 1986(**g**), or

        (iii) section 670(2) or (4) of the 2006 Act.

(2) The directors' report for a financial year must state—

    (a) the number and nominal value of the shares so purchased, the aggregate amount of the consideration paid by the company for such shares and the reasons for their purchase;

(**a**) 1995 c.50.
(**b**) Section 143 is prospectively repealed by the 2006 Act.
(**c**) Article 153 is prospectively repealed by the 2006 Act.
(**d**) Section 146(1)(aa) was inserted by section 102C(5) of 1986 c.53, as inserted by section 1(1) of 1997 c.41. Section 146 is prospectively repealed by the 2006 Act.
(**e**) Article 156(1)(aa) was inserted by section 102C(6) of 1986 c.53, as inserted by section 1(1) of 1997 c.41. Article 156 is prospectively repealed by the 2006 Act.
(**f**) Section 150 is prospectively repealed by the 2006 Act.
(**g**) Article 160 is prospectively repealed by the 2006 Act.

(b) the number and nominal value of the shares so acquired by the company, acquired by another person in such circumstances and so charged respectively during the financial year;

(c) the maximum number and nominal value of shares which, having been so acquired by the company, acquired by another person in such circumstances or so charged (whether or not during that year) are held at any time by the company or that other person during that year;

(d) the number and nominal value of the shares so acquired by the company, acquired by another person in such circumstances or so charged (whether or not during that year) which are disposed of by the company or that other person or cancelled by the company during that year;

(e) where the number and nominal value of the shares of any particular description are stated in pursuance of any of the preceding sub-paragraphs, the percentage of the called-up share capital which shares of that description represent;

(f) where any of the shares have been so charged the amount of the charge in each case; and

(g) where any of the shares have been disposed of by the company or the person who acquired them in such circumstances for money or money's worth the amount or value of the consideration in each case.

The Small Companies and Groups (Accounts and Directors' Report) Regulations 2008

SCHEDULE 6   Regulations 8(1) and 10

GROUP ACCOUNTS

PART 1

FORM AND CONTENT OF COMPANIES ACT GROUP ACCOUNTS

General rules

1.—(1) Subject to sub-paragraphs (1) and (2), group accounts must comply so far as practicable with the provisions of Schedule 1 to these Regulations (Companies Act individual accounts) as if the undertakings included in the consolidation ("the group") were a single company.

(2) For item B.III in each balance sheet format set out in that Schedule substitute—

"B. III. Investments
1. Shares in group undertakings
2. Interests in associated undertakings
3. Other participating interests
4. Loans to group undertakings and undertakings in which a participating interest is held
5. Other investments other than loans
6. Others".

(3) In the profit and loss account formats replace the items headed "Income from participating interests", that is—

(a) in Format 1, item 8,

(b) in Format 2, item 10,

(c) in Format 3, item B.4, and

(d) in Format 4, item B.6,

by two items: "Income from interests in associated undertakings" and "Income from other participating interests".

2.—(1) The consolidated balance sheet and profit and loss account must incorporate in full the information contained in the individual accounts of the undertakings included in the consolidation, subject to the adjustments authorised or required by the following provisions of this Schedule and to such other adjustments (if any) as may be appropriate in accordance with generally accepted accounting principles or practice.

(2) If the financial year of a subsidiary undertaking included in the consolidation does not end with that of the parent company, the group accounts must be made up—

(a) from the accounts of the subsidiary undertaking for its financial year last ending before the end of the parent company's financial year, provided that year ended no more than three months before that of the parent company, or

(b) from interim accounts prepared by the subsidiary undertaking as at the end of the parent company's financial year.

3.—(1) Where assets and liabilities to be included in the group accounts have been valued or otherwise determined by undertakings according to accounting rules differing from those used for the group accounts, the values or amounts must be adjusted so as to accord with the rules used for the group accounts.

(2) If it appears to the directors of the parent company that there are special reasons for departing from sub-paragraph (1) they may do so, but particulars of any such departure, the reasons for it and its effect must be given in a note to the accounts.

(3) The adjustments referred to in this paragraph need not be made if they are not material for the purpose of giving a true and fair view.

4. Any differences of accounting rules as between a parent company's individual accounts for a financial year and its group accounts must be disclosed in a note to the latter accounts and the reasons for the difference given.

5. Amounts that in the particular context of any provision of this Schedule are not material may be disregarded for the purposes of that provision.

Elimination of group transactions

6.—(1) Debts and claims between undertakings included in the consolidation, and income and expenditure relating to transactions between such undertakings, must be eliminated in preparing the group accounts.

(2) Where profits and losses resulting from transactions between undertakings included in the consolidation are included in the book value of assets, they must be eliminated in preparing the group accounts.

(3) The elimination required by sub-paragraph (2) may be effected in proportion to the group's interest in the shares of the undertakings.

(4) Sub-paragraphs (1) and (2) need not be complied with if the amounts concerned are not material for the purpose of giving a true and fair view.

Acquisition and merger accounting

7.—(1) The following provisions apply where an undertaking becomes a subsidiary undertaking of the parent company.

(2) That event is referred to in those provisions as an "acquisition", and references to the "undertaking acquired" are to be construed accordingly.

8. An acquisition must be accounted for by the acquisition method of accounting unless the conditions for accounting for it as a merger are met and the merger method of accounting is adopted.

9.—(1) The acquisition method of accounting is as follows.

(2) The identifiable assets and liabilities of the undertaking acquired must be included in the consolidated balance sheet at their fair values as at the date of acquisition.

(3) The income and expenditure of the undertaking acquired must be brought into the group accounts only as from the date of the acquisition.

(4) There must be set off against the acquisition cost of the interest in the shares of the undertaking held by the parent company and its subsidiary undertakings the interest of the parent company and its subsidiary undertakings in the adjusted capital and reserves of the undertaking acquired.

(5) The resulting amount if positive must be treated as goodwill, and if negative as a negative consolidation difference.

10.—(1) The conditions for accounting for an acquisition as a merger are—

   (a) that at least 90% of the nominal value of the relevant shares in the undertaking acquired (excluding any shares in the undertaking held as treasury shares) is held by or on behalf of the parent company and its subsidiary undertakings,

(b) that the proportion referred to in paragraph (a) was attained pursuant to an arrangement providing for the issue of equity shares by the parent company or one or more of its subsidiary undertakings,

(c) that the fair value of any consideration other than the issue of equity shares given pursuant to the arrangement by the parent company and its subsidiary undertakings did not exceed 10% of the nominal value of the equity shares issued, and

(d) that adoption of the merger method of accounting accords with generally accepted accounting principles or practice.

(2) The reference in sub-paragraph (1)(a) to the "relevant shares" in an undertaking acquired is to those carrying unrestricted rights to participate both in distributions and in the assets of the undertaking upon liquidation.

11.—(1) The merger method of accounting is as follows.

(2) The assets and liabilities of the undertaking acquired must be brought into the group accounts at the figures at which they stand in the undertaking's accounts, subject to any adjustment authorised or required by this Schedule.

(3) The income and expenditure of the undertaking acquired must be included in the group accounts for the entire financial year, including the period before the acquisition.

(4) The group accounts must show corresponding amounts relating to the previous financial year as if the undertaking acquired had been included in the consolidation throughout that year.

(5) There must be set off against the aggregate of—

(a) the appropriate amount in respect of qualifying shares issued by the parent company or its subsidiary undertakings in consideration for the acquisition of shares in the undertaking acquired, and

(b) the fair value of any other consideration for the acquisition of shares in the undertaking acquired, determined as at the date when those shares were acquired,

the nominal value of the issued share capital of the undertaking acquired held by the parent company and its subsidiary undertakings.

(6) The resulting amount must be shown as an adjustment to the consolidated reserves.

(7) In sub-paragraph (5)(a) "qualifying shares" means—

(a) shares in relation to which any of the following provisions applies (merger relief), and in respect of which the appropriate amount is the nominal value—

(i) section 131 of the Companies Act 1985(a),

(ii) Article 141 of the Companies (Northern Ireland) Order 1986(b), or

(iii) section 612 of the 2006 Act, or

(b) shares in relation to which any of the following provisions applies (group reconstruction relief), and in respect of which the appropriate amount is the nominal value together with any minimum premium value within the meaning of that section—

(i) section 132 of the Companies Act 1985(c),

(ii) Article 142 of the Companies (Northern Ireland) Order 1986(d), or

(iii) section 611 of the 2006 Act.

12.—(1) Where a group is acquired, paragraphs 9 to 11 apply with the following adaptations.

(2) References to shares of the undertaking acquired are to be construed as references to shares of the parent undertaking of the group.

(a) Section 131 is prospectively repealed by the 2006 Act.
(b) Article 141 is prospectively repealed by the 2006 Act.
(c) Section 132 is prospectively repealed by the 2006 Act.
(d) Article 142 is prospectively repealed by the 2006 Act.

(3) Other references to the undertaking acquired are to be construed as references to the group; and references to the assets and liabilities, income and expenditure and capital and reserves of the undertaking acquired must be construed as references to the assets and liabilities, income and expenditure and capital and reserves of the group after making the set-offs and other adjustments required by this Schedule in the case of group accounts.

13.—(1) The following information with respect to acquisitions taking place in the financial year must be given in a note to the accounts.

(2) There must be stated—

(a) the name of the undertaking acquired or, where a group was acquired, the name of the parent undertaking of that group, and

(b) whether the acquisition has been accounted for by the acquisition or the merger method of accounting;

and in relation to an acquisition which significantly affects the figures shown in the group accounts, the following further information must be given.

(3) The composition and fair value of the consideration for the acquisition given by the parent company and its subsidiary undertakings must be stated.

(4) Where the acquisition method of accounting has been adopted, the book values immediately prior to the acquisition, and the fair values at the date of acquisition, of each class of assets and liabilities of the undertaking or group acquired must be stated in tabular form, including a statement of the amount of any goodwill or negative consolidation difference arising on the acquisition, together with an explanation of any significant adjustments made.

(5) In ascertaining for the purposes of sub-paragraph (4) the profit or loss of a group, the book values and fair values of assets and liabilities of a group or the amount of the assets and liabilities of a group, the set-offs and other adjustments required by this Schedule in the case of group accounts must be made.

14.—(1) There must also be stated in a note to the accounts the cumulative amount of goodwill resulting from acquisitions in that and earlier financial years which has been written off otherwise than in the consolidated profit and loss account for that or any earlier financial year.

(2) That figure must be shown net of any goodwill attributable to subsidiary undertakings or businesses disposed of prior to the balance sheet date.

15. Where during the financial year there has been a disposal of an undertaking or group which significantly affects the figure shown in the group accounts, there must be stated in a note to the accounts—

(a) the name of that undertaking or, as the case may be, of the parent undertaking of that group, and

(b) the extent to which the profit or loss shown in the group accounts is attributable to profit or loss of that undertaking or group.

16. The information required by paragraph 13, 14 or 15 need not be disclosed with respect to an undertaking which—

(a) is established under the law of a country outside the United Kingdom, or

(b) carries on business outside the United Kingdom,

if in the opinion of the directors of the parent company the disclosure would be seriously prejudicial to the business of that undertaking or to the business of the parent company or any of its subsidiary undertakings and the Secretary of State agrees that the information should not be disclosed.

Minority interests

17.—(1) The formats set out in Schedule 1 to these Regulations have effect in relation to group accounts with the following additions.

(2) In the Balance Sheet Formats there must be shown, as a separate item and under an appropriate heading, the amount of capital and reserves attributable to shares in subsidiary undertakings included in the consolidation held by or on behalf of persons other than the parent company and its subsidiary undertakings.

(3) In the Profit and Loss Account Formats there must be shown, as a separate item and under an appropriate heading—

    (a) the amount of any profit or loss on ordinary activities, and

    (b) the amount of any profit or loss on extraordinary activities,

attributable to shares in subsidiary undertakings included in the consolidation held by or on behalf of persons other than the parent company and its subsidiary undertakings.

(4) For the purposes of paragraph 4 of Schedule 1 (power to adapt or combine items)—

    (a) the additional item required by sub-paragraph (2) is treated as one to which a letter is assigned, and

    (b) the additional items required by sub-paragraph (3)(a) and (b) are treated as ones to which an Arabic number is assigned.

Joint ventures

18.—(1) Where an undertaking included in the consolidation manages another undertaking jointly with one or more undertakings not included in the consolidation, that other undertaking ("the joint venture") may, if it is not—

    (a) a body corporate, or

    (b) a subsidiary undertaking of the parent company,

be dealt with in the group accounts by the method of proportional consolidation.

(2) The provisions of this Schedule relating to the preparation of consolidated accounts apply, with any necessary modifications, to proportional consolidation under this paragraph.

Associated undertakings

19.—(1) An "associated undertaking" means an undertaking in which an undertaking included in the consolidation has a participating interest and over whose operating and financial policy it exercises a significant influence, and which is not—

    (a) a subsidiary undertaking of the parent company, or

    (b) a joint venture dealt with in accordance with paragraph 18.

(2) Where an undertaking holds 20% or more of the voting rights in another undertaking, it is presumed to exercise such an influence over it unless the contrary is shown.

(3) The voting rights in an undertaking means the rights conferred on shareholders in respect of their shares or, in the case of an undertaking not having a share capital, on members, to vote at general meetings of the undertaking on all, or substantially all, matters.

(4) The provisions of paragraphs 5 to 11 of Schedule 7 to the 2006 Act (parent and subsidiary undertakings: rights to be taken into account and attribution of rights) apply in determining for the purposes of this paragraph whether an undertaking holds 20% or more of the voting rights in another undertaking.

20.—(1) The interest of an undertaking in an associated undertaking, and the amount of profit or loss attributable to such an interest, must be shown by the equity method of accounting (including dealing with any goodwill arising in accordance with paragraphs 17 to 20 and 22 of Schedule 1 to these Regulations).

(2) Where the associated undertaking is itself a parent undertaking, the net assets and profits or losses to be taken into account are those of the parent and its subsidiary undertakings (after making any consolidation adjustments).

(3) The equity method of accounting need not be applied if the amounts in question are not material for the purpose of giving a true and fair view.

PART 2

INFORMATION ABOUT RELATED UNDERTAKINGS WHERE COMPANY PREPARING GROUP ACCOUNTS (COMPANIES ACT OR IAS GROUP ACCOUNTS)

Introduction and interpretation

21. In this Part of this Schedule "the group" means the group consisting of the parent company and its subsidiary undertakings.

Subsidiary undertakings

22.—(1) The following information must be given with respect to the undertakings that are subsidiary undertakings of the parent company at the end of the financial year.

(2) The name of each undertaking must be stated.

(3) There must be stated—

   (a) if the undertaking is incorporated outside the United Kingdom, the country in which it is incorporated,

   (b) if it is unincorporated, the address of its principal place of business.

(4) It must also be stated whether the subsidiary undertaking is included in the consolidation and, if it is not, the reasons for excluding it from consolidation must be given.

(5) It must be stated with respect to each subsidiary undertaking by virtue of which of the conditions specified in section 1162(2) or (4) of the 2006 Act it is a subsidiary undertaking of its immediate parent undertaking.

That information need not be given if the relevant condition is that specified in subsection (2)(a) of that section (holding of a majority of the voting rights) and the immediate parent undertaking holds the same proportion of the shares in the undertaking as it holds voting rights.

Holdings in subsidiary undertakings

23.—(1) The following information must be given with respect to the shares of a subsidiary undertaking held—

   (a) by the parent company, and

   (b) by the group,

and the information under paragraphs (a) and (b) must (if different) be shown separately.

(2) There must be stated—

   (a) the identity of each class of shares held, and

   (b) the proportion of the nominal value of the shares of that class represented by those shares.

Financial information about subsidiary undertakings not included in the consolidation

24.—(1) There must be shown with respect to each subsidiary undertaking not included in the consolidation—

   (a) the aggregate amount of its capital and reserves as at the end of its relevant financial year, and

   (b) its profit or loss for that year.

(2) That information need not be given if the group's investment in the undertaking is included in the accounts by way of the equity method of valuation or if—

(a) the undertaking is not required by any provision of the 2006 Act to deliver a copy of its balance sheet for its relevant financial year and does not otherwise publish that balance sheet in the United Kingdom or elsewhere, and

(b) the holding of the group is less than 50% of the nominal value of the shares in the undertaking.

(3) Information otherwise required by this paragraph need not be given if it is not material.

(4) For the purposes of this paragraph the "relevant financial year" of a subsidiary undertaking is—

(a) if its financial year ends with that of the company, that year, and

(b) if not, its financial year ending last before the end of the company's financial year.

Shares of company held by subsidiary undertakings

25.—(1) The number, description and amount of the shares in the company held by or on behalf of its subsidiary undertakings must be disclosed.

(2) Sub-paragraph (1) does not apply in relation to shares in the case of which the subsidiary undertaking is concerned as personal representative or, subject as follows, as trustee.

(3) The exception for shares in relation to which the subsidiary undertaking is concerned as trustee does not apply if the company or any of its subsidiary undertakings is beneficially interested under the trust, otherwise than by way of security only for the purposes of a transaction entered into by it in the ordinary course of a business which includes the lending of money.

(4) Part 2 of Schedule 2 to these Regulations has effect for the interpretation of the reference in sub-paragraph (3) to a beneficial interest under a trust.

Joint ventures

26.—(1) The following information must be given where an undertaking is dealt with in the consolidated accounts by the method of proportional consolidation in accordance with paragraph 18 of this Schedule (joint ventures)—

(a) the name of the undertaking,

(b) the address of the principal place of business of the undertaking,

(c) the factors on which joint management of the undertaking is based, and

(d) the proportion of the capital of the undertaking held by undertakings included in the consolidation.

(2) Where the financial year of the undertaking did not end with that of the company, there must be stated the date on which a financial year of the undertaking last ended before that date.

Associated undertakings

27.—(1) The following information must be given where an undertaking included in the consolidation has an interest in an associated undertaking.

(2) The name of the associated undertaking must be stated.

(3) There must be stated—

(a) if the undertaking is incorporated outside the United Kingdom, the country in which it is incorporated,

(b) if it is unincorporated, the address of its principal place of business.

(4) The following information must be given with respect to the shares of the undertaking held—

(a) by the parent company, and

(b) by the group,

and the information under paragraphs (a) and (b) must be shown separately.

(5) There must be stated—

(a) the identity of each class of shares held, and

(b) the proportion of the nominal value of the shares of that class represented by those shares.

(6) In this paragraph "associated undertaking" has the meaning given by paragraph 19 of this Schedule; and the information required by this paragraph must be given notwithstanding that paragraph 20(3) of this Schedule (materiality) applies in relation to the accounts themselves.

Other significant holdings of parent company or group

28.—(1) The information required by paragraphs 29 and 30 must be given where at the end of the financial year the parent company has a significant holding in an undertaking which is not one of its subsidiary undertakings and does not fall within paragraph 26 (joint ventures) or paragraph 27 (associated undertakings).

(2) A holding is significant for this purpose if—

(a) it amounts to 20% or more of the nominal value of any class of shares in the undertaking, or

(b) the amount of the holding (as stated or included in the company's individual accounts) exceeds 20% of the amount of its assets (as so stated).

29.—(1) The name of the undertaking must be stated.

(2) There must be stated—

(a) if the undertaking is incorporated outside the United Kingdom, the country in which it is incorporated,

(b) if it is unincorporated, the address of its principal place of business.

(3) The following information must be given with respect to the shares of the undertaking held by the parent company.

(4) There must be stated—

(a) the identity of each class of shares held, and

(b) the proportion of the nominal value of the shares of that class represented by those shares.

30.—(1) There must also be stated—

(a) the aggregate amount of the capital and reserves of the undertaking as at the end of its relevant financial year, and

(b) its profit or loss for that year.

(2) That information need not be given in respect of an undertaking if—

(a) the undertaking is not required by any provision of the 2006 Act to deliver a copy of its balance sheet for its relevant financial year and does not otherwise publish that balance sheet in the United Kingdom or elsewhere, and

(b) the company's holding is less than 50% of the nominal value of the shares in the undertaking.

(3) Information otherwise required by this paragraph need not be given if it is not material.

(4) For the purposes of this paragraph the "relevant financial year" of an undertaking is—

(a) if its financial year ends with that of the company, that year, and

(b) if not, its financial year ending last before the end of the company's financial year.

31.—(1) The information required by paragraphs 32 and 33 must be given where at the end of the financial year the group has a significant holding in an undertaking which is not a subsidiary undertaking of the parent company and does not fall within paragraph 26 (joint ventures) or paragraph 27 (associated undertakings).

(2) A holding is significant for this purpose if—

(a) it amounts to 20% or more of the nominal value of any class of shares in the undertaking, or

(b) the amount of the holding (as stated or included in the group accounts) exceeds 20% of the amount of the group's assets (as so stated).

32.—(1) The name of the undertaking must be stated.

(2) There must be stated—

(a) if the undertaking is incorporated outside the United Kingdom, the country in which it is incorporated,

(b) if it is unincorporated, the address of its principal place of business.

(3) The following information must be given with respect to the shares of the undertaking held by the group.

(4) There must be stated—

(a) the identity of each class of shares held, and

(b) the proportion of the nominal value of the shares of that class represented by those shares.

33.—(1) There must also be stated—

(a) the aggregate amount of the capital and reserves of the undertaking as at the end of its relevant financial year, and

(b) its profit or loss for that year.

(2) That information need not be given if—

(a) the undertaking is not required by any provision of the 2006 Act to deliver a copy of its balance sheet for its relevant financial year and does not otherwise publish that balance sheet in the United Kingdom or elsewhere, and

(b) the holding of the group is less than 50% of the nominal value of the shares in the undertaking.

(3) Information otherwise required by this paragraph need not be given if it is not material.

(4) For the purposes of this paragraph the "relevant financial year" of an outside undertaking is—

(a) if its financial year ends with that of the parent company, that year, and

(b) if not, its financial year ending last before the end of the parent company's financial year.

Parent company's or group's membership of certain undertakings

34.—(1) The information required by this paragraph must be given where at the end of the financial year the parent company or group is a member of a qualifying undertaking.

(2) There must be stated—

(a) the name and legal form of the undertaking, and

(b) the address of the undertaking's registered office (whether in or outside the United Kingdom) or, if it does not have such an office, its head office (whether in or outside the United Kingdom).

(3) Where the undertaking is a qualifying partnership there must also be stated either—

(a) that a copy of the latest accounts of the undertaking has been or is to be appended to the copy of the company's accounts sent to the registrar under section 444 of the 2006 Act, or

(b) the name of at least one body corporate (which may be the company) in whose group accounts the undertaking has been or is to be dealt with on a consolidated basis.

(4) Information otherwise required by sub-paragraph (2) need not be given if it is not material.

(5) Information otherwise required by sub-paragraph (3)(b) need not be given if the notes to the company's accounts disclose that advantage has been taken of the exemption conferred by regulation 7 of the Partnerships and Unlimited Companies (Accounts) Regulations 1993(a).

(6) In this paragraph—

"dealt with on a consolidated basis", "member" and "qualifying partnership" have the same meanings as in the Partnerships and Unlimited Companies (Accounts) Regulations 1993;

"qualifying undertaking" means—

(a) a qualifying partnership, or

(b) an unlimited company each of whose members is—

   (i) a limited company,

   (ii) another unlimited company each of whose members is a limited company, or

   (iii) a Scottish partnership each of whose members is a limited company,

and references in this paragraph to a limited company, another unlimited company or a Scottish partnership include a comparable undertaking incorporated in or formed under the law of a country or territory outside the United Kingdom.

Parent undertaking drawing up accounts for larger group

35.—(1) Where the parent company is itself a subsidiary undertaking, the following information must be given with respect to that parent undertaking of the company which heads—

(a) the largest group of undertakings for which group accounts are drawn up and of which that company is a member, and

(b) the smallest such group of undertakings.

(2) The name of the parent undertaking must be stated.

(3) There must be stated—

(a) if the undertaking is incorporated outside the United Kingdom, the country in which it is incorporated,

(b) if it is unincorporated, the address of its principal place of business.

(4) If copies of the group accounts referred to in sub-paragraph (1) are available to the public, there must also be stated the addresses from which copies of the accounts can be obtained.

Identification of ultimate parent company

36.—(1) Where the parent company is itself a subsidiary undertaking, the following information must be given with respect to the company (if any) regarded by the directors as being that company's ultimate parent company.

(2) The name of that company must be stated.

(3) If that company is incorporated outside the United Kingdom, the country in which it is incorporated must be stated (if known to the directors).

(4) In this paragraph "company" includes any body corporate.

Construction of references to shares held by parent company or group

37.—(1) References in this Part of this Schedule to shares held by the parent company or the group are to be construed as follows.

(2) For the purposes of paragraphs 23, 27(4) and (5) and 28 to 30 (information about holdings in subsidiary and other undertakings)—

(a) S.I. 1993/1820.

(a) there must be attributed to the parent company shares held on its behalf by any person; but

(b) there must be treated as not held by the parent company shares held on behalf of a person other than the company.

(3) References to shares held by the group are to any shares held by or on behalf of the parent company or any of its subsidiary undertakings; but any shares held on behalf of a person other than the parent company or any of its subsidiary undertakings are not to be treated as held by the group.

(4) Shares held by way of security must be treated as held by the person providing the security—

(a) where apart from the right to exercise them for the purpose of preserving the value of the security, or of realising it, the rights attached to the shares are exercisable only in accordance with his instructions, and

(b) where the shares are held in connection with the granting of loans as part of normal business activities and apart from the right to exercise them for the purpose of preserving the value of the security, or of realising it, the rights attached to the shares are exercisable only in his interests.

Appendix E SI 2008 No. 409

SCHEDULE 7

Regulation 12

INTERPRETATION OF TERM "PROVISIONS"

PART 1

MEANING FOR PURPOSES OF THESE REGULATIONS

Definition of "Provisions"

1.—(1) In these Regulations, references to provisions for depreciation or diminution in value of assets are to any amount written off by way of providing for depreciation or diminution in value of assets.

(2) Any reference in the profit and loss account formats set out in Part 1 of Schedule 1 to these Regulations to the depreciation of, or amounts written off, assets of any description is to any provision for depreciation or diminution in value of assets of that description.

2. References in these Regulations to provisions for liabilities are to any amount retained as reasonably necessary for the purpose of providing for any liability the nature of which is clearly defined and which is either likely to be incurred, or certain to be incurred but uncertain as to amount or as to the date on which it will arise.

PART 2

MEANING FOR PURPOSES OF PARTS 18 AND 23 OF THE 2006 ACT

Financial assistance for purchase of own shares

3. The specified provisions for the purposes of section 677(3)(a) of the 2006 Act (Companies Act accounts: relevant provisions for purposes of financial assistance) are provisions for liabilities within paragraph 2 of this Schedule.

Redemption or purchase by private company out of capital

4. The specified provisions for the purposes of section 712(2)(b)(i) of the 2006 Act (Companies Act accounts: relevant provisions to determine available profits for redemption or purchase out of capital) are provisions of any of the kinds mentioned in paragraphs 1 and 2 of this Schedule.

Justification of distribution by references to accounts

5. The specified provisions for the purposes of section 836(1)(b)(i) of the 2006 Act (Companies Act accounts: relevant provisions for distribution purposes) are provisions of any of the kinds mentioned in paragraphs 1 and 2 of this Schedule.

The Small Companies and Groups (Accounts and Directors' Report) Regulations 2008

SCHEDULE 8 Regulation 13

GENERAL INTERPRETATION

Financial instruments

1. References to "derivatives" include commodity-based contracts that give either contracting party the right to settle in cash or in some other financial instrument, except where such contracts—

(a) were entered into for the purpose of, and continue to meet, the company's expected purchase, sale or usage requirements,

(b) were designated for such purpose at their inception, and

(c) are expected to be settled by delivery of the commodity.

2.—(1) The expressions listed in sub-paragraph (2) have the same meaning as they have in Council Directive 78/660/EEC on the annual accounts of certain types of companies(a).

(2) Those expressions are "available for sale financial asset", "business combination", "commodity-based contracts", "derivative", "equity instrument", "exchange difference", "fair value hedge accounting system", "financial fixed asset", "financial instrument", "foreign entity", "hedge accounting", "hedge accounting system", "hedged items", "hedging instrument", "held for trading purposes", "held to maturity", "monetary item", "receivables", "reliable market" and "trading portfolio".

Fixed and current assets

3. "Fixed assets" means assets of a company which are intended for use on a continuing basis in the company's activities, and "current assets" means assets not intended for such use.

Historical cost accounting rules

4. References to the historical cost accounting rules are to be read in accordance with paragraph 30 of Schedule 1 to these Regulations.

Listed investments

5.—(1) "Listed investment" means an investment as respects which there has been granted a listing on—

(a) a recognised investment exchange other than an overseas investment exchange, or

(b) a stock exchange of repute outside the United Kingdom.

(2) "Recognised investment exchange" and "overseas investment exchange" have the meaning given in Part 18 of the Financial Services and Markets Act 2000(b).

Loans

6. A loan is treated as falling due for repayment, and an instalment of a loan is treated as falling due for payment, on the earliest date on which the lender could require repayment or (as the case may be) payment, if he exercised all options and rights available to him.

(a) O.J. L222 of 14.8.1978, page 11, as amended in particular by Directives 2001/65/EEC, 2003/51/EEC and 2006/46/EEC of the European Parliament and of the Council (O.J. L238 of 27.12.2001, page 28, O.J. L178 of 17.7.2003, page 16 and O.J. L224 of 16.8.2006, page 1).
(b) 2000 c.8.

Materiality

7. Amounts which in the particular context of any provision of Schedule 1 to these Regulations are not material may be disregarded for the purposes of that provision.

Participating interests

8.—(1) A "participating interest" means an interest held by an undertaking in the shares of another undertaking which it holds on a long-term basis for the purpose of securing a contribution to its activities by the exercise of control or influence arising from or related to that interest.

(2) A holding of 20% or more of the shares of the undertaking is to be presumed to be a participating interest unless the contrary is shown.

(3) The reference in sub-paragraph (1) to an interest in shares includes—

(a) an interest which is convertible into an interest in shares, and

(b) an option to acquire shares or any such interest,

and an interest or option falls within paragraph (a) or (b) notwithstanding that the shares to which it relates are, until the conversion or the exercise of the option, unissued.

(4) For the purposes of this paragraph an interest held on behalf of an undertaking is to be treated as held by it.

(5) In the balance sheet and profit and loss formats set out in Part 1 of Schedule 1 and Part 1 of Schedule 4 to these Regulations, "participating interest" does not include an interest in a group undertaking.

(6) For the purpose of this paragraph as it applies in relation to the expression "participating interest"—

(a) in those formats as they apply in relation to group accounts, and

(b) in paragraph 19 of Schedule 6 (group accounts: undertakings to be accounted for as associated undertakings),

the references in sub-paragraphs (1) to (4) to the interest held by, and the purposes and activities of, the undertaking concerned are to be construed as references to the interest held by, and the purposes and activities of, the group (within the meaning of paragraph 1 of that Schedule).

Purchase price

9. "Purchase price", in relation to an asset of a company or any raw materials or consumables used in the production of such an asset, includes any consideration (whether in cash or otherwise) given by the company in respect of that asset or those materials or consumables, as the case may be.

Realised profits and losses

10. "Realised profits" and "realised losses" have the same meaning as in section 853(4) and (5) of the 2006 Act.

Staff costs

11.—(1) "Social security costs" means any contributions by the company to any state social security or pension scheme, fund or arrangement.

(2) "Pension costs" includes—

(a) any costs incurred by the company in respect of any pension scheme established for the purpose of providing pensions for persons currently or formerly employed by the company,

(b) any sums set aside for the future payment of pensions directly by the company to current or former employees, and

(c) any pensions paid directly to such persons without having first been set aside.

(3) Any amount stated in respect of the item "social security costs" or in respect of the item "wages and salaries" in the company's profit and loss account must be determined by reference to payments made or costs incurred in respect of all persons employed by the company during the financial year under contracts of service.

Appendix E SI 2008 No. 409

EXPLANATORY NOTE

(This note is not part of the Regulations)

These Regulations specify the form and content of the accounts and directors' report of companies subject to the small companies regime under Part 15 of the Companies Act 2006 (c.46) ("the 2006 Act"). Section 381 of the 2006 Act defines what is meant by "small companies regime". The Regulations replace provisions previously contained in the Schedules to Part 7 of the Companies Act 1985 (c.6) ("the 1985 Act") and in the Schedules to Part 8 of the Companies (Northern Ireland) Order 1986 (S.I. 1986/1032 (N.I. 6)) ("the 1986 Order"). They extend to the whole of the United Kingdom, reflecting the extent of the 2006 Act.

The Regulations come into force on 6th April 2008, and apply in relation to financial years beginning on or after that date (regulation 2). The corresponding provisions of the 1985 Act or the 1986 Order continue to apply to accounts and directors' reports for financial years beginning before that date.

The Regulations continue the implementation of the following Directives-

Council Directive 78/660/EEC on the annual accounts of certain types of companies ("the Fourth Directive") (O.J.L222 of 14.8.1978, page 1), and

Council Directive 83/349/EEC on consolidated accounts ("the Seventh Directive") (O.J. L193 of 18.7.1983, page 1).

Regulation 3(1) of, and Schedule 1 to, the Regulations specify the form and content of the individual accounts of a company which is subject to the small companies regime and which is preparing Companies Act individual accounts. Schedule 1 re-enacts Schedule 8 to the 1985 Act and Schedule 8 to the 1986 Order, with one substantive modification.

Paragraph 36(4) of Schedule 1 implements article 1.5 of Directive 2006/46 of the European Parliament and the Council of 14th June 2006 amending the Fourth and Seventh Directives and Council Directives 86/635/EEC on the annual accounts and consolidated accounts of banks and other financial institutions and 91/674/EEC on the annual accounts and consolidated accounts of insurance undertakings (O.J. L224 of 16th August 2006, pages 1 to 7). The Directive is also to be implemented by the Large and Medium-sized Companies and Groups (Accounts and Reports) Regulations 2008, the Companies Act 2006 (Amendment) (Accounts and Reports) Regulations 2008, and by the Financial Services Authority using powers under the Financial Services and Markets Act 2000 (c.8).

Paragraph 36(4) of Schedule 1 gives companies the option of including financial instruments in the accounts at a fair value provided that they may be so included under international accounting standards adopted under the IAS Regulation (as defined in section 474(1) of the 2006 Act) on or before 5th September 2006, and provided that the disclosures required by such standards are made.

Regulation 4 of, and Schedule 2 to, the Regulations re-enact the requirements of Part 1 of Schedule 5 to the 1985 Act and Part 1 of Schedule 5 to the 1986 Order for small companies. They concern information about related undertakings which must be provided in the notes to a company's individual accounts, whether they are Companies Act accounts or IAS accounts.

Regulation 5 of, and Schedule 3 to, the Regulations re-enact the requirements of Part 1 of Schedule 6 to the 1985 Act and Part 1 of Schedule 6 to the 1986 Order as they apply to small companies. They concern information about directors' remuneration which must be provided in the notes to a company's individual accounts, whether they are Companies Act accounts or IAS accounts.

Regulation 6 of, and Schedule 4 to, the Regulations make provision about Companies Act individual accounts which may be delivered to the registrar of companies for a small company under section 444 of the 2006 Act. Schedule 4 re-enacts Schedule 8A to the 1985 Act and Schedule 8A to the 1986 Order.

The Small Companies and Groups (Accounts and Directors' Report) Regulations 2008

Regulation 7 of, and Schedule 5 to, the Regulations specify information to be included in the directors' report which a company's directors are required to prepare under section 415 of the 2006 Act. Schedule 5 re-enacts the provisions in Schedule 7 to the 1985 Act and Schedule 7 to the 1986 Order as they apply to small companies, with two modifications – the thresholds for disclosure of political donations and expenditure and charitable donations have been raised from £200 to £2000 (paragraphs 2 and 4), and provision is now made for disclosure of donations to independent election candidates (paragraph 2).

Regulation 8 of, and Part 1 of Schedule 6 to, the Regulations specify the form and content of Companies Act group accounts which a parent company subject to the small companies regime may choose to prepare, although not required to do so (see section 398 of the 2006 Act). The Schedule re-enacts Schedule 4A to the 1985 Act and Schedule 4A to the 1986 Order as they apply to small companies, save that paragraphs 9, 13 and 17 have been simplified to facilitate convergence with international accounting standards.

Regulations 9 and 10 apply the provisions of Schedule 3 (information in notes to accounts about directors' benefits) and Part 2 of Schedule 6 (information in notes about related undertakings) to Companies Act or IAS group accounts which the directors of a small parent company choose to prepare. Part 2 of Schedule 6 re-enacts Part 2 of Schedule 5 to the 1985 Act and Part 2 of Schedule 5 to the 1986 Order.

Regulation 11 makes provision for exemptions from Companies Act group accounts which may be delivered to the registrar of companies for a small parent company under section 444 of the 2006 Act.

Regulation 12 of, and Schedule 7 to, the Regulations define the term "provisions" for the purposes of the Regulations and for the purposes of sections 677(3)(a) (Companies Act accounts: relevant provisions for purposes of financial assistance), 712(2)(b)(i) (Companies Act accounts: relevant provisions to determine available profits for redemption or purchase out of capital) and 836(1)(b)(i) (Companies Act accounts: relevant provisions for distribution purposes) of the 2006 Act.

Regulation 13 of, and Schedule 8 to, the Regulations contain general interpretation provisions.

A transposition note has been prepared which sets out how Directive 2006/46 is to be transposed into UK law. An Impact Assessment of the effect that the implementation of Directive 2006/46 will have on the costs of business, charities or voluntary bodies has also been prepared. Both are available from the Department for Business, Enterprise and Regulatory Reform, Corporate Law and Governance Directorate, 1 Victoria Street, London SW1. They are also available electronically at www.berr.gov.uk. Copies have also been placed in the libraries of both Houses of Parliament. Otherwise, an Impact Assessment has not been produced for these Regulations as they have only a negligible impact on the costs of business, charities or voluntary bodies.

© Crown copyright 2008

Printed and published in the UK by The Stationery Office Limited
under the authority and superintendence of Carol Tullo, Controller of Her Majesty's
Stationery Office and Queen's Printer of Acts of Parliament.

E1969   2/2008   181969T   19585

Appendix F Selected reading and reference

This appendix provides a selection of the literature to which this book might form a companion.

Legislation and regulation

Companies Act 2006		TSO (The Stationery Office)
Companies Act 2006 – Explanatory notes		TSO
Companies Act 2006 – Tables of origins and destinations		TSO
Butterworths Company Law Handbook (22nd Edition 2008)	K Walmsley (Editor)	Butterworths

(Text contains full (amended and up-to-date) company law statutes (including Companies Act 2006), statutory instruments and European legislation.)

Accounting and Auditing Standards

Accounting Standards 2009/2010		Wolters Kluwer (UK) Limited
Auditing Standards 2009/2010		Wolters Kluwer (UK) Limited
Financial Reporting Standard for Smaller Entities (effective April 2008)	Accounting Standards Board	FRC Publications
International Accounting Standards		
Bound volume of International Financial Reporting Standards (Complete text) 2008		IASB
Exposure Draft of Proposed IFRS for Small and Medium-sized Entities (Feb 2007)		IASB

Commentary and guidance

Manual of Accounting UK GAAP	PWC	Wolters Kluwer (UK) Limited
GAAP Xtra (CD-ROM)		Wolters Kluwer (UK) Limited

Appendix F Selected reading and reference

Checklists

Company Accounts Disclosure Checklist	SWAT UK Ltd	Wolters Kluwer (UK) Limited
Companies Accounts UK GAAP Checklist (Accountants' Digest 529, December 2008)	S Hastie	Wolters Kluwer (UK) Limited

Auditing Practices Board

The Electronic Publication of Auditors' Reports	APB Bulletin 2001/1 (January 2001)
The Auditors' Consideration of FRS 17 'Retirement Benefits' – Defined Benefit schemes	APB Practice Note 22 (April 2002)
Auditor's Reports on Financial Statements in Great Britain and Northern Ireland	APB Bulletin 2006/6 (September 2006)
The Auditor's Statement on the Summary Financial Statement in the United Kingdom	APB Bulletin 2008/3 (April 2008)
The Special Auditor's Report on Abbreviated Accounts in the United Kingdom	APB Bulletin 2008/4 (April 2008)
Auditor's Reports on Revised Accounts and Reports, in the United Kingdom	APB Bulletin 2008/5 (April 2008)
The "Senior statutory auditor" under the United Kingdom Companies Act 2006	APB Bulletin 2008/6 (April 2008)
Auditor's Reports for Short Accounting Periods in Compliance with the United Kingdom Companies Act 2006	APB Bulletin 2008/8 (September 2008)
Miscellaneous Reports by Auditors Required by the United Kingdom Companies Act 2006	APB Bulletin 2008/9 (October 2008)

Useful websites

	http://
Accounting Standards Board	www.frc.org.uk/asb
International Accounting Standard Board	www.iasb.org.uk
Financial Reporting Council • APB • ASB	www.frc.org.uk
International Auditing and Assurance Standards Board	www.ifac.org/IAASB
Auditing Practices Board	www.frc.org.uk/apb

Appendix F Selected reading and reference

EU Directive 1606/2002 on the application of IAS	www.ec.europa.eu./internal_market/ accounting/ias_/en.htm#regulation
EU Single Market – Accounting	www.ec.europa.eu./internal_market/ accounting/ias_/en.htm#regulation
HM Treasury	www.hm-treasury.gov.uk.
BERR (Department for Business Enterprise and regulatory reform) – formerly DTI (Department of Trade and Industry) – Companies Act 2006 Guidance	www.berr.gov.uk/ http://www.berr.gov.uk/whatwedo/ businesslaw/co-act-2006/index.html http://www.berr.gov.uk/files/file46791.pdf
Companies House – *Registrar of Companies*	www.companieshouse.gov.uk
Legislation and statutory instruments	**www.opsi.gov.uk**
Institute of Chartered Accountants – in England and Wales – of Scotland	www.icaew.com www.icas.org.uk
Accountancy Research	www.cch.co.uk/ *(Online research)*
Accountancy Magazine	www.accountancymagazine.com

Index

abbreviated accounts, 1.1.1, 1.1.2, *Table 2.6*, 3.2, 6.2, 8.1, 9.1, 11.1
  accounting policies, *Table 8.1*
  approval and signing, *Table 8.1*, 8.7
  audit exemption, *Table 11.1*, *Table 11.2*
  auditors' report, 3.9, *Table 8.1*, *Table 11.2*
    special report, *Table 8.1*, *Table 8.2*, 8.9, *Table 11.2*, 12.1.3, 14.4
  balance sheet, *Table 8.1*, 8.2, *Table 8.2*, 8.3, 8.4, 8.7, 12.1.4, *Appendix D*, *Appendix E*
    formats, *Table 8.3*
  cash flow statement, *Table 8.2*
  checklist, *Table 8.6*, 8.11
  contents, 8.2, *Table 8.2*
  creditors, *Appendix D*
  debtors, *Appendix D*
  definition, 12.1.4
  directors' report, 6.8.3, *Table 8.1*, *Table 8.2*
  directors' statements, 8.5
  dormant companies, 6.10
  electronic filing, 1.5.1, 1.5.3
  eligibility, 5.4, 5.4.1
  example, 13.2
  filing
    electronic filing, 1.5.1, 1.5.3
    options, *Table 8.1*
    requirements, 2.3, 8.3
  financial fixed assets, *Appendix D*
  formats, *Table 8.3*, *Appendix D*
  FRSSE, 10.1.1
  GAAP, *Table 8.1*
  gross profit or loss, *Table 8.5*
  group accounts, 8.3, 8.8, 9.4
  IAS accounts, 8.3
  investments, *Appendix D*
  liabilities, *Table 8.3*
  medium-sized company, 3.2, 6.2, 8.1, 8.10.2, 9.1, 11.1, 12.1.4
    contents of accounts, 8.2, *Table 8.2*
    filing requirements, 8.3
    profit and loss account, *Table 8.2*, *Table 8.5*, 8.10.3
    transitional determination of qualification, 8.11
  notes to the accounts, *Table 8.2*, *Table 8.4*, 8.6, *Appendix D*, *Appendix E*
  parent companies, 8.8
  period for filing, 2.3
  primary statements, *Table 8.2*, 8.3
  profit and loss account, *Table 8.1*, *Table 8.2*, *Table 8.4*, *Table 8.5*, 8.10.3
  qualifying as a small company, 8.11
  reserves, *Appendix D*
  share capital, *Appendix D*
  shares, *Table 8.4*
  SI 2008 No. 409, 8.1, 8.9, 9.4, 12.1.4, 13.2, *Appendix D*
    balance sheet, *Table 8.2*, 8.4
    form and content, 8.2, *Table 8.3*
    notes, *Table 8.4*
  SI 2008 No. 410, 8.1, 8.2, *Table 8.2*, *Table 8.5*, 8.9, 8.10.2, 12.1.4
  special auditors' report, *Table 8.1*, 8.9, *Table 11.2*, 14.4
  as statutory accounts, 12.1.3
  transitional determination of qualification, 8.11
  'true and fair' view, 8.2
  turnover, *Appendix C*
abridged accounts
  publication, 3.12
accountancy regulation
  framework, 2.1.3
  structure, *Table 2.1*
accountants' report
  approval and signature, 3.11
  audit exemption, *Table 11.2*
  compilation report, 14.6
  independent assurance report, 14.6
  unaudited companies, 14.7
accounting policies
  abbreviated accounts, *Table 8.1*
  accounting standards and, 3.5
  disclosure, 6.7, *Appendix D*
  FRS, 18 3.3, 3.5, *Table 4.2*
  FRSSE, *Table 10.2*, *Table 10.3*
accounting principles and rules, 3.5, 4.5, *Table 6.1*, *Appendix E*
  accruals, 3.5
  alternatives *see* alternative accounting rules
  consistency, 3.5
  departing from, 3.5
  fixed assets, 3.5
  FRSSE and, 3.5, *Table 10.3*
  going concern, 3.5
  historical cost principles, 3.5
  individual determination, 3.5
  netting, 3.5
  prudence, 3.5
  SI 2008 No. 409, 3.5, 6.4.3
  SI 2008 No. 410, 3.5
  statutory formats, 6.4.3
  substance of transactions, 3.5
  see also accounting standards

Index

accounting records, *Appendix B*
  adequate accounting records, 3.2, *Table 3.2*, 3.10, 6.1
  duty to keep, *Appendix B*
  retention period, 3.10, *Appendix B*
accounting reference date, 11.1, *Appendix B*
accounting reference period, 2.3, 11.1, *Appendix B*
accounting standards, 4.4.3, *Appendix B*
  accounting policies and, 3.5
  application, 4.5
  ASB, 4.4.3, 4.6.3
  cash flow statements, *Table 4.2*, 4.3, *Table 10.4*
  Companies Act 2006, *Table 4.1*, 4.4.3, *Appendix A*
  definition, 4.4.3
  exemptions, 4.4.3, 4.5
  FRSSE and, 10.2.3
  'true and fair' view, 4.4.1, 4.4.3
  United States, 4.6.3
  see also accounting principles and rules; Financial Reporting Standard; Financial Reporting Standard for Smaller Entities; international accounting standards; International Financial Reporting Standards; Statements of Standard Accounting Practice; Urgent Issues Task Force Abstracts
Accounting Standards Board (ASB), 1.3, 2.1.2
  accounting standards, 4.4.3, 4.6.3
  FRS issued by *see* Financial Reporting Standard
  Statement of Principles for financial reporting, 4.1
  status, 4.4.3
  'true and fair' view, 4.4.1
  UITF Abstracts *see* Urgent Issue Task Force abstracts
  voluntary disclosures and, 10.4
accruals
  accounting principle, 3.5
  balance sheet format, *Table 6.4*, 12.3.10, *Appendix D*
  as creditors, 12.3.10
  definition, 12.3.10
  FRSSE, *Table 10.3*
acquisitions
  FRSSE, *Table 10.2*
  profit and loss account, 12.2.17
adequate accounting records, 3.2, *Table 3.2*, 3.10, 6.1
administrative expenses
  profit and loss account, 12.2.4
advances
  directors' benefits, 2.3
alternative accounting rules, 3.5, *Table 6.1*, *Table 12.1*, 12.5, *Appendix E*
  current assets, *Table 12.1*
  current cost, 3.5, *Table 12.1*, 12.5
  group accounts, 9.2
  historical cost figures, 3.5, *Table 12.1*

  production cost, 12.5.2
  purchase price, 12.5.1
  revaluation reserve, 3.5, 12.5.3
annual accounts, *Appendix A*, *Appendix B*
  Companies Act 2006, 2.2, 3.1
    basic approach, 2.2.1
    implementation, 2.2.2
    small companies regime, 2.2.3
  contents, 2.5, *Table 2.6*
  definition, 12.1.2
  group accounts, 12.1.2, *Appendix A*
  medium-sized company, 8.10.1
  for shareholders, 6.2
  SI 2008 No. 409, 12.1.2
  as statutory accounts, 12.1.3
  'true and fair' view, 3.3
  see also group accounts; individual accounts
annual report, 2.5
  contents, 2.5, *Table 2.6*
  definition, 12.1.1
  see also directors' report
approval and signing of accounts, *Appendix A*, *Appendix B*
  abbreviated accounts, *Table 8.1*, 8.7
  accountants' report, 3.11
  auditors' report, 3.11, 14.1.5, *Table 14.2*
  balance sheet, 6.9, 6.9.1, 8.5
  Companies Act 2006, 2.3
  directors' report, 3.11, 6.9.1, *Appendix B*
  directors' statement, 6.9, 6.9.1
  FRSSE, *Table 10.3*
ASB *see* Accounting Standards Board
assets
  abbreviated accounts, *Table 8.3*
  awaiting disposal, 12.3.1
  balance sheet
    assets awaiting disposal, 12.3.1
    exclusions, 3.4
    format, *Table 6.4*
  current *see* current assets
  definition of 'financial asset', 12.4.2
  fixed *see* fixed assets
  FRSSE, *Table 10.2*, *Table 10.3*
  intangible
    balance sheet format, *Table 6.3*, *Table 6.4*
    FRSSE, *Table 10.2*, *Table 10.3*
  profit or loss on disposal, 12.2.23
  securitised, 12.8.2
  tangible, balance sheet, *Table 6.3*, *Table 6.4*, 12.3.3, *Appendix C*
associated undertaking
  definition, 12.6
  see also group accounts; undertaking
associates
  balance sheet, 12.3.6
  definition, 12.3.6
  FRS, 9 *Table 4.2*, *Table 10.2*, 12.3.6
  FRSSE, *Table 10.2*
  see also group accounts; joint venture
assurance report, *Table 11.2*, 11.7, 14.6

Index

audit
   accountants' report, *Table 11.2*
   banking company, 11.3
   Companies Act 1985, 2.4
   Companies Act 2006, 2.3, 2.4, *Appendix A*
   exemption *see* audit exemption
   insurance company, 11.3
   liability limitation agreements, 2.3
   non-statutory, 14.6
   public companies, 11.3
   public sector companies, 2.4
   right to require, 11.5
   special register body, 11.3
   see also auditor; auditors' report

audit exemption, 1.1.1, 1.1.2, 3.2, 5.4, 6.2
   abbreviated accounts, *Table 11.1*, *Table 11.2*
   accountants' report, *Table 11.2*
   charitable company, 2.4, 11.2
   conditions, 11.2
   determination, 11.6
   directors' statement, 6.9.2, 7.5, 11.8
      dormant company, 7.5, 11.8
   dormant company, 3.2, 6.2, 6.10, 7.1, *Table 7.1*, 7.4, *Appendix A*
      Companies Act 2006, 7.7
      conditions, 7.1, 7.3
      directors' statements, 7.5, 11.8
      excluded companies, 7.4
   excluded companies, 11.3
      dormant company, 7.4
   FRSSE, *Table 10.3*
   group companies, 9.8, 11.4
   non-statutory audit and assurance reports, *Table 11.2*, 11.7, 14.6
   preparation of accounts irrespective of audit, 11.1
   right to require audit, 11.5
   size criteria, 3.2, 11.2, 11.6
   turnover, *Table 11.1*, 11.2, 11.4
   vetoed by shareholders, 11.2

audit report *see* auditors' report

auditor
   appointment, *Appendix A*
   directors' statement as to disclosure of information, 6.9.4
   functions, *Appendix A*
   liability, *Appendix A*
   reappointment, 14.3
   removal, resignation, etc, *Appendix A*
   remuneration
      disclosure, 6.12
      profit and loss account, 12.2.13
   senior statutory auditor, 2.4
   see also audit; auditors' report

auditors' report, 3.9, *Table 11.2*, 11.7, 14.1
   abbreviated accounts, 3.9, *Table 8.1*, *Table 11.2*
      special report, *Table 8.1*, *Table 8.2*, 8.9, *Table 11.2*, 12.1.3, 14.4
   appropriate legislation, 2.4, 14.1.2
   approval and signature, 3.11, 14.1.5, *Table 14.2*
   cash flows, 14.3
   Companies Act 2006, 2.4, 14.1.3, *Table 14.1*
   duty of care to third parties, 14.3, 14.4, 14.5
   elements, 14.1.2
   example, 13.4, *Table 14.1*, 14.3
   form of report or emphasis, 2.4, 14.1.2
   group account exemption entitlement, 9.7
   ISA (UK and Ireland) 700, 14.2
   non-statutory audit and assurance report, 14.6
   reappointment of auditors, 14.3
   relevant reporting framework, 2.4, 14.1.2
   report to shareholders, 14.3
   requirements, 3.9
   'true and fair' view, 2.4, 14.1.2
   website publication, 14.3
   see also audit; auditor

balance sheet, 4.2, 6.5
   abbreviated accounts, *Table 8.1*, 8.2, *Table 8.2*, 8.3, 8.4, 8.7, 12.1.4, *Appendix D*, *Appendix E*
      formats, *Table 8.3*
   accruals, *Table 6.4*, 12.3.10, *Appendix D*
   approval and signature, 6.9, 6.9.1, 8.5
   assets
      awaiting disposal, 12.3.1
      current, *Table 6.4*, 12.3.5
      exclusion, 3.4
      fixed, *Table 6.4*, 12.3.1
      format, *Table 6.4*
      intangible, *Table 6.3*, *Table 6.4*
      tangible, *Table 6.3*, *Table 6.4*, 12.3.3, *Appendix C*
   associates, 12.3.6
   bank loans and overdrafts, *Table 6.3*, *Table 6.4*, 12.2.14, 12.3.4
   capital and reserves, *Table 6.4*
   cash at bank and in hand, *Table 6.4*, 10.4, *Table 10.4*, 12.3.4, *Appendix D*
   creditors, *Table 6.3*, *Table 6.4*, 12.3.10
   current assets, *Table 6.4*, 12.3.5
   debtors, *Table 6.3*, *Table 6.4*, 12.3.10
   development costs, 12.3.1
   directors' signature, 6.9, 6.9.1, 8.5
   directors' statement, 3.11, 6.9, 6.9.1
   excluded items, 3.4
   'exercise of significant influence', 12.3.6
   fixed assets, *Table 6.4*, 12.3.1
   formats, 3.4, *Table 4.1*, *Table 6.1*, 6.2, *Table 6.2*, 6.4.3, *Table 6.4*, 6.5, *Table 8.3*, 12.3, *Appendix C*, *Appendix E*
      abbreviated accounts, *Table 8.3*
      Arabic number sub-headings, *Table 6.3*
      Format 1, *Table 6.2*, *Table 6.4*, *Table 8.3*, *Appendix C*
      Format 2, 5.2, *Table 6.2*, 6.4.3, *Table 8.3*, *Appendix C*
      FRSSE, *Table 10.3*
      less detailed, 6.4.3
   goodwill, 12.3.2
   group accounts, 9.5.3

353

Index

intangible assets, *Table 6.3*, *Table 6.4*
investments, *Table 6.3*, *Table 6.4*
  group accounts, 9.5.3
  less detailed, 6.4.3
liabilities, *Table 6.4*, 12.3.8
loans, *Table 6.3*, *Table 6.4*, 12.2.14, 12.3.4
notes to the accounts, 6.7, *Appendix D*, *Appendix E*
participating interest, 12.3.6
preliminary expenses, 12.3.1
prepayments, *Table 6.4*, 12.3.10
provisions for liabilities, 12.3.8
reserves, *Table 6.4*, *Appendix C*
share capital, *Table 6.4*, *Appendix C*
SI 2008 No. 409, *Table 4.1*, 6.4.3, 6.5, 9.5.3
  abbreviated accounts, *Table 8.2*, 8.4
  goodwill, 12.3.2
  tangible assets, 12.3.3
social security, 12.3.9, 12.3.10
stocks, *Table 6.3*, *Table 6.4*, 12.3.7
tangible assets, *Table 6.3*, *Table 6.4*, 12.3.3, *Appendix C*
taxation, 12.3.9, 12.3.10
total *see* balance sheet total
balance sheet total
  group exemption qualifying condition, 9.2
  qualifying as a small/medium-sized company, 1.1.1, 5.2
bank *see* cash at bank and in hand
bank loans and overdrafts
  balance sheet, *Table 6.4*, 12.2.14, 12.3.4
banking company
  audit, 11.3
banking partnerships, *Appendix B*
benefits
  directors *see* directors
bill and hold arrangements, 12.9.2

capital instruments
  FRS 4, 12.4
  FRSSE, *Table 10.2*
cash
  definition, 12.3.4
cash at bank and in hand
  balance sheet, *Table 6.4*, 10.4, *Table 10.4*, 12.3.4, *Appendix D*
  cash, definition, 12.3.4
  FRSSE, 10.4, *Table 10.4*
cash flow statement, 4.2, 4.3
  abbreviated accounts, *Table 8.2*
  accounting standards, *Table 4.2*, 4.3, *Table 10.4*
  disclosure, 10.4
  exempted companies, 4.3, 4.5
  format, *Table 4.1*, 4.3, *Table 10.4*
  FRS 1, *Table 4.1*, *Table 4.2*, 4.3, 4.5, *Table 10.2*, 10.4, 12.3.4
    cash, definition, 12.3.4
  FRSSE, 4.5, *Table 10.2*, 10.4, *Table 10.4*
  voluntary disclosure, 4.3, 4.5, 10.4

charges
  profit and loss account format
    interest payable and similar charges, 12.2.14
    other external charges, 12.2.8
    other operating charges, 12.2.9
charitable company
  audit exemption, 2.4, 11.2
  charity law compliance, 2.3
  Companies Act 2006, 2.3
  company accounts, 12.1.5
  IAS accounts, 12.1.5
charitable donations, *Table 6.6*, 6.8.2, *Table 10.3*, *Appendix E*
Companies Act 1985, 1.2
  audit, 2.4
  directors' report, 3.7
Companies Act 1985 (International Accounting Standards and other Accounting Amendments) Regulations 2004 (SI 2004 no. 2947), 1.4, 4.6.2, 4.6.4, 12.10.1, 12.10.3
Companies Act 2006, 1.2, 2.1–2.5, 11.1
  accounting standards, *Table 4.1*, 4.4.3, *Appendix A*
  adequate accounting records, 3.2, *Table 3.2*, 3.10, 6.1
  annual accounts, 2.2, 3.1
    basic approach, 2.2.1
    implementation, 2.2.2
    small companies regime, 2.2.3
  application, 1.2, 2.2
  approval and signing of accounts, 2.3
  audit exemption for dormant companies, 7.7
  auditing and auditors' reports, 2.4
    liability limitation agreements, 2.3
  auditors' report, 2.4, 14.1.3, *Table 14.1*
  bases of accounting, 12.5
  charitable companies, 2.3
  company law review, 2.1.1
  directors' benefits, 2.3
  directors' liability for false or misleading statements, 2.3
  directors' report, 2.3, 6.8, 6.9.1, *Appendix A*
  early acceptance of regime, 2.2.2
  early adoption of provisions, 1.2
  filing and circulating accounts, 2.3
  FRSSE and, 10.1.1, 10.1.4, 10.2.2, 10.5, 10.8.3
  group accounts, 3.1, 3.8, 6.2, *Appendix B*
    small groups, 9.5.1
  implementation, 2.2.2
    examples, *Table 2.2*
  liability limitation agreements, 2.3
  main changes, 2.3
  medium-sized companies, 2.3
  quoted companies, 2.2.1
  'small companies regime', 1.1.1, 1.1.2, 2.2.1, *Appendix B*
    annual accounts, 2.2.3
    application, 5.1
    exclusions, 5.1

Little GAAP, 4.4.4
main changes, 2.3
minimum disclosure, 6.2
thresholds, 2.3
substance of transactions, 12.8.1
'think small first' approach, 1.1.1, 2.1.1, 2.2.1
'true and fair' view, 2.3, 2.4, 4.4.1, 4.4.2, 6.3, 10.2.2
company law, 1.1.2
reform, 2.1
review, 2.1.1
revised regulatory framework, 2.1.2
'true and fair' view requirement, 4.4.2
consignment stock
definition, 10.7.2, 12.8.2
FRS, 5 12.8.2
FRSSE, *Table 10.3*, 10.7.2
substance of transactions, 12.8.2
consistency
accounting principle, 3.5
consolidated accounts
FRSSE, *Table 10.2*, *Table 10.3*, 10.5
group accounts, 3.8, 9.1–9.8, 10.5
subsidiary undertakings, 3.8
contingent liabilities and assets
FRSSE, *Table 10.2*, *Table 10.3*
continuing operations, 12.2.16
contracts for services
revenue recognition, 10.12, 12.9.2, 12.9.3
cost of sales
profit and loss account, 12.2.2
credit
directors' benefits, 2.3, *Appendix B*
creditors
abbreviated accounts, *Appendix D*
accruals, 12.3.10
balance sheet, *Table 6.3*, *Table 6.4*, 12.3.10
notes to the accounts, 6.7
taxation and social security, 12.3.10
trade creditors, 12.3.10
currency *see* foreign currency
current assets, *Appendix E*
abbreviated account format *Appendix D*
alternative accounting rules, *Table 12.1*
assets awaiting disposal, 12.3.1
balance sheet, *Table 6.4*, 12.3.5
definition, 12.3.1, 12.3.5
FRSSE, *Table 10.3*
investments, *Table 10.3*
valuation, *Table 12.1*
current cost
alternative accounting rules, 3.5, *Table 12.1*, 12.5

debt factoring
FRSSE, *Table 10.3*
substance of transactions, 12.8.2
debtors
abbreviated accounts, *Appendix D*
balance sheet, *Table 6.3*, *Table 6.4*, 12.3.10
notes to the accounts, 6.7, *Appendix E*
prepayments, 12.3.10
trade debtors, 12.3.10
defective accounts, revision, *Appendix A*, *Appendix B*
deferred tax, *Table 10.2*, *Table 10.3*
defined benefit retirement schemes, *Table 10.3*, *Table 10.7*, 10.9.1, 10.9.2
defined contribution retirement schemes, *Table 10.3*, 10.9.1
depreciation
FRSSE, *Table 10.3*
goodwill, 12.3.2
derivative financial instrument
definition, 12.4.7
derivatives
definition, 12.4.7
fair value accounting, 3.5
development costs, *Table 10.3*, *Appendix E*
balance sheet, 12.3.1
directors
advances, 2.3
benefits, 2.3, *Appendix B*
notes to the accounts, 6.7
Companies Act 2006, 2.3
credit, 2.3, *Appendix B*
disclosure of interests, 2.3
guarantees, 2.3, *Appendix B*
liability for false or misleading statements, 2.3
loans and transactions with, 10.8.2
FRSSE disclosures, 10.8.3
remuneration *see* directors' remuneration
'true and fair' view requirement, 6.3
directors' remuneration, *Table 6.7*, 6.11, *Appendix B*
disclosure, *Table 6.7*, 6.11, *Appendix E*
FRSSE, *Table 10.3*
SI 2008 No. 409, 6.11
directors' remuneration report, 3.7
directors' report, *Table 2.6*, 6.8, 12.1.1, *Appendix B*, *Appendix E*
abbreviated accounts, 6.8.3, *Table 8.1*, *Table 8.2*
approval and signature, 3.11, 6.9.1, *Appendix B*
business review, 2.3, 3.7
Companies Act 2006, 2.3, 6.8, 6.9.1, *Appendix A*
consolidated report, 3.7
contents, 3.7, *Table 6.6*, 6.8.2, *Appendix B*, *Appendix E*
disclosure of directors' interests, 2.3
drafting considerations, 6.8.3
duty to prepare, *Appendix B*
entitlement, 6.8.1
FRSSE, *Table 10.3*
group directors' report, 3.7
medium-sized company, 3.7
requirements, 3.7
research and development, *Table 6.6*
SI 2008 No. 409, *Table 6.6*, 6.8.2
SI 2008 No. 410, 3.7
directors' statement, 6.8.2, 6.9
abbreviated accounts, 8.5

355

Index

audit exemption, 6.9.2, 7.5, 11.8
   dormant company, 7.5, 11.8
balance sheet, 3.11, 6.9, 6.9.1
directors' responsibilities, 6.9.3
disclosure of information to auditors, 6.9.4
preparation, 6.9.1
SI 2008 No. 409, 8.5
signature, 6.9, 6.9.1
statutory accounts, 12.1.3

disclosure
accounting policies, 6.7, *Appendix D*
auditors' remuneration, 6.12
cash flow statements, 10.4
directors' remuneration, *Table 6.7*, 6.11, *Appendix E*
directors' report, 6.8.2
directors' statement, 6.9.4
FRSSE, 10.4
liability limitation agreements, 2.3, 6.7
notes to the accounts, 3.6
   concessions, 6.2
parent company, 8.8
reduced requirements, 3.2, 6.2
related party disclosures, *Table 10.2*, *Table 10.3*, 10.8.1
related undertakings, 9.3, 12.7, *Appendix B*, *Appendix E*
SI 2008 No. 409, Schedule 1, 3.6, 6.2
simplification, 1.1.2
transactions with directors, 10.8.3
turnover, 12.2.5
voluntary, 4.3, 4.5, 10.4

discontinued operations, 12.2.18
discounting
FRSSE, *Table 10.8*, 10.11
invoice discounting, *Table 10.3*

disposal
assets awaiting, 12.3.1
profit or loss on, 12.2.23

distribution costs
profit and loss account, 12.2.3

dividends
classification of preference dividends, 12.10.2
GAAP, 12.10.3
notes to the accounts, 6.7
presentation, 12.10.3
SI 2008 No. 409, 12.10.1
tax on, *Table 10.3*
treatment, 12.10.1

dormant company
abbreviated accounts, 6.10
accounts, 5.4.1, 6.10
   example, 13.3
acting as agent, 7.6, *Appendix D*, *Appendix E*
audit exemption, 3.2, 6.2, 6.10, 7.1, *Table 7.1*, 7.4, *Appendix A*
   Companies Act 2006, 7.7
   conditions, 7.1, 7.3
   directors' statement, 7.5, 11.8
   excluded companies, 7.4
definition, 7.1, 7.2
directors' statements, 7.5, 11.8
electronic filing, 1.5.1, 1.5.3, 7.8
unaudited accounts, example, 13.3

e-filing *see* electronic filing of accounts
electronic filing of accounts, 1.5
abbreviated accounts, 1.5.1, 1.5.3
dormant company accounts, 1.5.1, 1.5.3, 7.8
WebFiling
   benefits, 1.5.3
   dormant company, 7.8
   template, 1.5.2
XBRL development, 1.5.4

employees
numbers
   group account exemption, 9.2
   size qualification, 5.2
profit and loss account, 12.2.10
staff costs, 12.2.10

equity instrument, 12.4
definition, 12.4.4
settlement in own equity instruments, 12.4.2, 12.4.3

equity instrument granted, 12.4.5
European law
application of international accounting standards, 4.6.1, 4.6.4
'true and fair' view requirement, 3.3, 4.4.2

exceptional items
profit and loss account, 12.2.19

extraordinary items
profit and loss account, 12.2.20

factoring of debts
FRSSE, *Table 10.3*
substance of transactions, 12.8.2

fair value accounting, *Appendix E*
defined benefit schemes, *Table 10.7*
definition of 'fair value', 12.4.6, 12.9.1
derivatives, 3.5
financial instruments, 3.5, 12.4.6
format of accounts, *Table 6.1*
FRSSE and, 10.1.1, 10.1.3, *Table 10.2*
notes to the accounts, 6.7, *Table 8.4*
revenue recognition, 12.9.1

fellow subsidiary undertaking
definition, 12.6
see also undertaking

filing of accounts, 2.3, 11.1, *Appendix B*
abbreviated accounts, 2.3, *Table 8.1*, 8.3
electronic *see* electronic filing of accounts

Finance Acts 1998 and 2002
'true and fair' view, 4.4.1

financial instruments, 12.4
definition, 12.4.1
derivative, 12.4.7
equity instrument, 12.4
   definition, 12.4.4

Index

settlement in own equity instruments, 12.4.2, 12.4.3
equity instrument granted, 12.4.5
fair value, 3.5, 12.4.6
financial asset, 12.4
  definition, 12.4.2
financial liability, 12.4
  definition, 12.4.3
  shares, 12.4
FRSSE, *Table 10.2*, *Table 10.3*, 12.4

Financial Reporting Council (FRC), 2.1.2
accountancy regulation structure, *Table 2.1*
'true and fair' view, 4.4.1

Financial Reporting Standard for Smaller Entities (FRSSE), 1.1.2, 1.3, 1.4, 4.4.3, 6.2, 6.4.3, 10.1.1
abbreviated accounts, 10.1.1
accounting policies, *Table 10.2*, *Table 10.3*
accounting principles, 3.5, *Table 10.3*
accounting standards and, 10.2.3
accruals, *Table 10.3*
acquisition and mergers, *Table 10.2*
adoption, 1.1.1, 10.1.1
application, 1.3, 10.1.1
approval and signing of accounts, *Table 10.3*
associates and joint ventures, *Table 10.2*
audit exemption, *Table 10.3*
balance sheet format, *Table 10.3*
basis of preparation under, *Table 10.1*
capital instruments, *Table 10.2*
cash at bank and in hand, 10.4, *Table 10.4*
cash flow statements, 4.5, *Table 10.2*, 10.4, *Table 10.4*
Companies Act 2006 and, 10.1.1, 10.1.4, 10.2.2, 10.5, 10.8.3
companies legislation and, 10.1.3
consignment stock, *Table 10.3*, 10.7.2
consolidated financial statements, *Table 10.2*, *Table 10.3*, 10.5
contingent liabilities and assets, *Table 10.2*, *Table 10.3*
corresponding amounts, *Table 10.2*
current asset investments, *Table 10.3*
current tax, *Table 10.2*
debt factoring, *Table 10.3*
deferred tax, *Table 10.2*, *Table 10.3*
delivery of accounts to registrar, *Table 10.3*
depreciation, *Table 10.3*
development, 10.1
directors' remuneration, *Table 10.3*
directors' report, *Table 10.3*
discounting, *Table 10.8*, 10.11
dividends, tax on, *Table 10.3*
exclusions, 10.1.1
fair value accounting, 10.1.1, 10.1.3, *Table 10.2*
financial instruments, *Table 10.2*, *Table 10.3*, 12.4
fixed assets, *Table 10.3*
  impairment, *Table 10.2*
  investments, *Table 10.3*
  tangible, *Table 10.2*, *Table 10.3*
foreign currency translation, *Table 10.3*, 10.10
format of accounts, *Table 10.3*
FRSs and, 10.1.1
  FRS 3, *Table 10.2*, *Table 10.3*, *Table 10.5*, 10.6
  FRS 17, 10.1.3
  FRSs 1–29, *Table 10.2*
FRSSE (effective April 2008), 1.3, 10.1.2, 10.1.4, 12.10.2
FRSSE (effective January 2005), 10.1.2
FRSSE (effective January 2007), 1.3, 10.1.2, 10.1.3, 12.10.2
going concern basis, *Table 10.3*
goodwill, *Table 10.2*, *Table 10.3*
  impairment, *Table 10.2*
government grants, *Table 10.3*
group accounts, 4.3, 9.5.2, *Table 10.2*, 10.5
history, 1.3, 10.1.1
intangible assets, *Table 10.2*, *Table 10.3*
investment properties, *Table 10.3*
invoice discounting, *Table 10.3*
leases, *Table 10.3*
Little GAAP, 4.4.4
loans and transactions with directors, 10.8.2
  disclosures, 10.8.3
long-term contracts, *Table 10.3*
objective, *Table 10.3*
'one-stop shop', 1.3, 10.1.2
outline, 10.3, *Table 10.3*
pensions and retirement benefits, 10.1.3, *Table 10.2*, *Table 10.3*, *Table 10.7*, 10.9, 10.9.1
  defined benefit schemes, *Table 10.3*, *Table 10.7*, 10.9.1, 10.9.2
  defined contribution schemes, *Table 10.3*, 10.9.1
post balance sheet events, *Table 10.3*
preference shares, 12.10.2
preparation of accounts under, *Table 10.1*
profit and loss account format, *Table 10.3*
provisions, *Table 10.2*, *Table 10.3*
  discounting and, *Table 10.8*, 10.11
prudence, *Table 10.3*
related parties, definition, *Table 10.6*
related party disclosures, *Table 10.2*, *Table 10.3*, 10.8.1
related party transactions, 10.8
reporting financial performance, *Table 10.2*
reporting the substance of transactions, *Table 10.2*, 10.7
research and development, *Table 10.3*
revaluation reserve, *Table 10.3*
revenue recognition, 10.1.3, *Table 10.3*, 10.12
scope, 10.1.3
share-based payments, 10.1.3, 10.13
small groups, 9.5.2, 10.5
small subsidiary within large or medium-sized group, adoption by, 10.1.1
SORPs and, 10.1.1, 10.2.3
SSAPs and, 10.1.1, 10.2.3
stand-alone document, 1.3, 10.1.2
start-up costs, *Table 10.3*

357

Index

statement of total recognised gains and losses (STRGL), *Table 10.3*
status, 1.3
stocks, *Table 10.3*
subsidiary undertakings, 10.1.3, *Table 10.2*
substance of transactions, reporting, *Table 10.2*
taxation, *Table 10.2*, *Table 10.3*
'true and fair' view, 1.3, 10.1.1, 10.2.1, 10.2.2, *Table 10.3*
UITF abstracts and, 10.1.1, 10.1.2, 10.2.3
value added tax (VAT), *Table 10.3*
voluntary disclosure, 4.3
write-downs to recoverable amount, *Table 10.3*
Financial Reporting Standards (FRSs), 3.5, *Table 4.2*, 4.4.3, *Table 10.2*
application, *Table 4.2*
concessions, *Table 4.2*, 4.5
exemption, 10.1.1
FRS 1 *Cash flow statements*, *Table 4.1*, *Table 4.2*, 4.3, 4.5, *Table 10.2*, 10.4, 12.3.4
  cash, definition, 12.3.4
FRS 2 *Accounting for subsidiary undertakings*, 3.8, *Table 4.2*, *Table 10.2*
FRS 3 *Reporting financial performance*
  FRSSE and, *Table 4.2*, *Table 10.2*, *Table 10.3*, *Table 10.5*, 10.6
  statement of total recognised gains and losses, *Table 4.1*
FRS 4 *Capital instruments*, *Table 4.2*, *Table 10.2*, 12.4
FRS 5 *Reporting the substance of transactions*, *Table 4.2*, *Table 10.2*, 10.7.1, 10.12, 12.8.1, 12.8.2, 12.9.1
  consignment stock, 10.7.2
FRS 8 *Related party disclosures*, *Table 4.2*, *Table 10.2*, *Table 10.3*
FRS 9 *Associates and joint ventures*, *Table 4.2*, *Table 10.2*, 12.3.6
FRS 17 *Retirement Benefits*, *Table 4.2*, 10.1.3, *Table 10.2*, *Table 10.3*, 10.9.1, 10.9.2
FRS 18 *Accounting policies*, 3.3, 3.5, *Table 4.2*
FRS 25 *Financial instruments: disclosure and presentation*, *Table 4.2*, *Table 10.2*, *Table 10.3*, 12.2.14, 12.4, 12.10.2, 12.10.3
FRSs 1–29, *Table 10.2*
FRSSE and
  FRS 3, *Table 10.2*, *Table 10.5*, 10.6
  FRSs 1–29, *Table 10.2*
medium-sized company, application to, *Table 4.2*
small companies, application to, *Table 4.2*, 6.4.3
financial services companies, 1.1.1
financial statements
ASB *Statement of Principles for financial statements*, 4.1
basic contents, 4.1
consolidated *see* consolidated accounts
definition, 4.1
notes to, 4.2
objective, 4.1
primary statements *see* primary statements
summary financial statements, 2.3, *Table 2.6*, 3.12, 11.1, *Table 11.1*, *Appendix B*
'true and fair' view, 4.1
financial year, *Appendix B*
fixed assets
abbreviated account format, *Appendix D*
accounting principles and, 3.5
assets awaiting disposal, 12.3.1
balance sheet format, *Table 6.4*, 12.3.1
definition, 12.3.1
depreciation and diminution in value, *Appendix E*
development costs, *Table 10.3*, 12.3.1, *Appendix E*
notes to the accounts, 6.7, *Appendix E*
preliminary expenses, 12.3.1
valuation, *Table 12.1*
see also assets
foreign currency
FRSSE and, *Table 10.3*, 10.10
losses, 12.2.14
notes to the accounts, *Appendix E*
translation, *Table 10.3*, 10.10
format of accounts, 3.4, *Table 6.1*, *Table 6.2*, 6.4
abbreviated accounts, *Table 8.3*, *Appendix D*
adoption, 3.4
balance sheet, 3.4, *Table 4.1*, *Table 6.1*, 6.2, *Table 6.2*, 6.4.3, *Table 6.4*, 6.5, 12.3, *Appendix E*
  abbreviated accounts, *Table 8.3*
  Arabic number sub-headings, *Table 6.3*
  directors' statement, 6.9
  Format 1, *Table 6.2*, *Table 6.4*, *Table 8.3*, *Appendix C*
  Format 2, 5.2, *Table 6.2*, 6.4.3, *Table 8.3*, *Appendix C*
  FRSSE, *Table 10.3*
  less detailed, 6.4.3
  SI 2008 No. 409, *Table 4.1*, 6.4.3, 6.5, *Table 8.1*, 8.4, 9.5.3, 10.5
  small group accounts, 9.5.3
cash flow statement, *Table 4.1*, 4.3, *Table 10.4*
changing, 3.4
departure from, 3.4
fair value accounting, *Table 6.1*
FRSSE, *Table 10.3*
notes to the accounts, *Table 6.1*, 6.7, *Appendix C*
profit and loss account, 3.4, *Table 4.1*, *Table 6.1*, 6.4.3, *Table 6.5*, 6.6, 12.2, *Appendix C*, *Appendix E*
  choice of format, 6.6, 12.2
  depreciation, *Table 6.5*, 6.6
  FRSSE, *Table 10.3*
  gross profit or loss, *Table 6.5*, 6.6
  SI 2008 No. 409, *Table 4.1*, 6.4.3, *Table 6.5*, 6.6
SI 2008 No. 409, 3.4, *Table 6.1*, 6.2, 6.4.1–6.4.3, 6.6, *Appendix C*
SI 2008 No. 410, 3.4

Index

statement of total recognised gains and losses (STRGL), *Table 4.1*
statutory formats, 3.4, 6.4.3
FRSs *see* Financial Reporting Standards
FRSSE *see* Financial Reporting Standard for Smaller Entities

Generally Accepted Accounting Practice (GAAP), 3.5, 4.4.4, 4.6.2
  abbreviated accounts, *Table 8.1*
  Big GAAP, 4.4.4
  Little GAAP, 4.4.4
  presentation of dividends, 12.10.3
  'true and fair' view, 3.3, 4.4.1, 4.4.4
  XBRL development, 1.5.4
gift vouchers, 12.9.2
going concern
  accounting principle, 3.5
  FRSSE, *Table 10.3*
goodwill, *Appendix E*
  acquired, 12.3.2
  balance sheet, 12.3.2
  depreciation, 12.3.2
  FRSSE, *Table 10.2, Table 10.3*
  impairment, *Table 10.2*
  rules regarding, 3.5
  SI 2008 No. 409, 12.3.2
government grants
  FRSSE, *Table 10.3*
gross profit or loss
  abbreviated accounts, *Table 8.5*
  format of accounts, *Table 6.5*, 6.6
group
  definition, 12.6
  related undertakings disclosure, 9.3, 12.7, *Appendix B, Appendix E*
group accounts, *Table 2.6*, 3.8, 9.1, *Appendix B, Appendix E*
  abbreviated accounts, 8.3, 8.8, 9.4
  alternative accounting rules, 9.2
  annual accounts, 12.1.2, *Appendix A*
  audit exemption, 9.8, 11.4
  auditors' report, entitlement to group account exemption, 9.7
  balance sheet, 9.5.3
  Companies Act group accounts, 3.1, 3.8, 6.2, 9.5.1, *Appendix B*
  consolidated accounts, 3.8, 9.1–9.8
    small groups, 10.5
  directors' report, 3.7
  disclosure requirements, 9.3, 12.7.2
  exemptions, 12.1.2
    auditors' report, 9.7
    availability of small audit exemption, 9.8
    entitlement, 9.7
    parent company of small group, 4.3
    qualifying conditions, 9.2
    related undertakings disclosures, 9.3
  filing, 9.4
  form and content, *Appendix E*
  FRSSE and, 4.3, 9.5.2, *Table 10.2*, 10.5
    small subsidiary within large or medium-sized group, adoption by, 10.1.1
  IAS group accounts, 3.1, 4.6.2, *Appendix B*
  individual profit and loss accounts, *Appendix B*
  joint ventures, 12.6, *Appendix E*
  medium-sized companies, 9.1, 9.6
  parent companies, size qualification, 5.3, 9.2
  parent company *see* parent company
  profit and loss account, *Appendix B*
  requirements, 3.8, 9.1
  SI 2008 No. 409, *Table 2.3*, 3.8, 9.2, 9.4, 12.1.2, 12.7.1, 12.7.2
  SI 2008 No. 410, 3.8, 9.5.1, 12.1.2
  small groups, 5.4.1, 9.5, 9.5.3
    balance sheet format heading for 'Investments' 9.5.3
    Companies Act 2006, 2.3, 9.5.1
    FRSSE and, 9.5.2, 10.5
  subsidiary, exclusion from consolidation, 3.8
group directors' report, 3.7
group undertaking
  definition, 12.6
  participating interest, 12.6
  shares in, 12.6
    income from, 12.2.11
  see also undertaking
guarantees
  directors' benefits, 2.3, *Appendix B*
  notes to the accounts, 6.7, *Appendix E*

historical cost accounting, 3.5, *Table 6.1*, 12.5, *Appendix E*

IAS *see* international accounting standards
IASB *see* International Accounting Standards Board
IFRS *see* International Financial Reporting Standards
income
  profit and loss account formats
    other operating income, 12.2.6
    participating interests, 12.2.12
    shares in group undertakings, 12.2.11
income and expenditure account
  definition, 12.1.2
income statement *see* profit and loss account
indebtedness
  notes to the accounts, 6.7
individual accounts, 12.1.2, *Appendix A*
  Companies Act individual accounts, 3.1, *Table 3.1, Appendix B, Appendix E*
  IAS individual accounts, 3.1, *Appendix B, Appendix E*
  SI 2008 No. 409, *Table 2.3, Table 6.1*, 6.4.2, 12.1.2
individual determination
  accounting principle, 3.5
information disclosure *see* disclosure
insurance company
  audit, 11.3

Index

intangible assets
  balance sheet format, *Table 6.3*, *Table 6.4*
  FRSSE, *Table 10.2*, *Table 10.3*
interest payable and similar charges
  profit and loss account, 12.2.14
International Accounting Standards Board (IASB), 1.4, 4.6.3
  IFRSs, 4.6.3
  SME project and Exposure Draft, 4.6.5
  standards, 4.6.3
international accounting standards (IAS), 1.4
  adoption by British companies, *Table 4.3*
  Companies Act provisions and, 4.6.2
  EU Regulation, 4.6.1, 4.6.4
  fair presentation, 3.3, 4.4.1, 4.4.2
  group accounts, 3.1, 4.6.2, *Appendix B*
  IAS accounts
    abbreviated accounts, 8.3
    change to, 4.6.2
    definition, 12.1.2
    incorporated charities, 12.1.5
  IASB SME project and Exposure Draft, 4.6.5
  individual accounts, 3.1, *Appendix B*
  option to choose, 4.6.2
  quoted companies, 4.6.1
  smaller enterprises and, 1.1.1, 4.6.2, 4.6.5
  'true and fair' view, 3.3, 4.4.1, 4.4.2
International Financial Reporting Standards (IFRS), 1.4, 4.6.3
  'IFRS for Private Entities', 4.6.5
  'true and fair' view, 4.4.1, 4.4.3
International Standards on Auditing (UK and Ireland) 700 *The Auditors' Report on Financial Statements*, 14.2
International XBRL Consortium, 1.5.4
investment properties, *Table 10.3*
investments
  abbreviated account format *Appendix D*
  balance sheet, *Table 6.3*, *Table 6.4*
    group accounts, 9.5.3
  current assets, *Table 10.3*
  fixed assets, *Table 10.3*
  notes to the accounts, 6.7, *Appendix E*
invoice discounting
  FRSSE, *Table 10.3*

joint venture
  definition, 12.6
  FRS 9, *Table 4.2*, *Table 10.2*, 12.3.6
  FRSSE, *Table 10.2*
  group accounts, 12.6, *Appendix E*

Large and Medium-sized Companies and Groups (Accounts and Reports) Regulations 2008 (SI 2008 No. 410)
  abbreviated accounts, 8.1, 8.2, *Table 8.2*, *Table 8.5*, 8.9, 8.10.2, 12.1.4
  accounting principles, 3.5
  accounting standards exemption, 4.4.3, 4.5

  directors' report, 3.7
  format of accounts, 3.4
  gross profit or loss, *Table 8.5*
  group accounts, 3.8, 9.5.1, 12.1.2
leases
  FRSSE, *Table 10.3*
liabilities
  abbreviated accounts, *Table 8.3*
  balance sheet, *Table 6.4*, 12.3.8
  contingent, *Table 10.2*, *Table 10.3*
  financial liability, 12.4, 12.4.3
  provision, 12.3.8
liability limitation agreements, 2.3
  notes to the accounts, 6.7
loan transfers
  definition, 12.8.2
  substance of transactions, 12.8.2
loans
  balance sheet, *Table 6.3*, *Table 6.4*, 12.2.14, 12.3.4
long-term contracts
  contract for services, 12.9.2
  FRSSE, *Table 10.3*
  revenue recognition, 12.9.2

medium-sized company
  abbreviated accounts, 3.2, 6.2, 8.1, 8.10.2, 9.1, 11.1, 12.1.4
    contents, 8.2, *Table 8.2*
    filing requirements, 8.3
    profit and loss account, *Table 8.2*, *Table 8.5*, 8.10.3
    transitional determination of qualification, 8.11
  annual accounts, 8.10.1
  auditors' remuneration, disclosure, 6.12
  Companies Act 2006, 2.3
  directors' report, 3.7
  Financial Reporting Standards (FRSs), application of, *Table 4.2*
  group accounts, 9.1, 9.6
  IASB SME project and Exposure Draft, 4.6.5
  qualifying conditions, 5.2, 5.4.1, *Appendix B*
    balance sheet total, 1.1.1, 5.2
    decision chart, 5.4
    employees numbers, 1.1.1, 5.2
    parent companies, 5.3
    size qualification, 5.3, 5.4
    turnover, 1.1.1, 5.2
  see also Large and Medium-sized Companies and Groups (Accounts and Reports) Regulations 2008 (SI 2008 No. 410)
mergers
  FRSSE, *Table 10.2*
modified accounts *see* abbreviated accounts

netting, 3.5
non-statutory accounts
  auditors' report, 14.6
  publication, 3.12

notes to the accounts, 4.2, *Appendix B*, *Appendix E*
  abbreviated accounts, *Table 8.2*, *Table 8.4*, 8.6, *Appendix D*, *Appendix E*
  balance sheet, 6.7, *Appendix D*, *Appendix E*
  creditors, 6.7
  debtors, 6.7, *Appendix E*
  definition, 12.1.2
  departure from 'true and fair' view, 3.3
  directors' benefits, 6.7
  disclosures, 3.6
    concessions, 6.2
  dividends, 6.7
  fair value accounting, 6.7, *Table 8.4*
  fixed assets, 6.7, *Appendix E*
  foreign currency *Appendix E*
  format, *Table 6.1*, 6.7, *Appendix C*
  guarantees, 6.7, *Appendix E*
  indebtedness, 6.7
  investments, 6.7, *Appendix E*
  liability limitation agreements, 6.7
  profit and loss account, 6.7
  related undertakings disclosure, 9.3, 12.7, *Appendix B*, *Appendix E*
  reserves, 6.7
  share capital, 6.7, *Appendix E*
  SI 2008 No. 409, 3.6, 6.7
  turnover, 6.7, *Appendix E*
notes to financial statements, 4.2

operating and financial review (OFR), *Table 2.6*, 3.7
operations
  continuing, 12.2.16
  discontinued, 12.2.18
ordinary activities
  profit and loss account, 12.2.15
other external charges
  profit and loss account, 12.2.8
other operating charges
  profit and loss account, 12.2.9
other operating income
  profit and loss account, 12.2.6
overdrafts *see* bank loans and overdrafts
own work capitalised
  profit and loss account, 12.2.7

parent company
  abbreviated accounts, 8.8
  auditor's remuneration, disclosure, 6.12
  disclosure, 8.8
  exemption, 4.3
  individual profit and loss account, 12.1.2
  profit and loss account, 12.1.2
  size qualification, 5.3, 9.2
  see also group; group accounts
parent undertaking
  definition, 12.6
  see also group accounts; undertaking

participating interest
  balance sheet, 12.3.6
  definition, 12.3.6, 12.6
  group undertakings, 12.6
  profit and loss account, 12.2.12
pensions and retirement benefits
  accounting for, 10.9.1
  defined benefit schemes, *Table 10.3*, *Table 10.7*, 10.9.1, 10.9.2
  defined contribution schemes, *Table 10.3*, 10.9.1
  FRS 17, *Table 4.2*, 10.1.3, *Table 10.2*, *Table 10.3*, 10.9.1, 10.9.2
  FRSSE, 10.1.3, *Table 10.2*, *Table 10.3*, *Table 10.7*, 10.9
PFI (Public Finance Initiative) contracts, 12.8.2
political donations and expenditure, *Table 6.6*, 6.8.2, *Table 10.3*, *Appendix E*
post balance sheet events
  FRSSE, *Table 10.3*
preference shares, 12.10.2
preliminary expenses, 12.3.1
prepayments
  balance sheet format, *Table 6.4*, 12.3.10
  as debtors, 12.3.10
primary statements, 4.2
  abbreviated accounts, *Table 8.2*, 8.3
  formats, *Table 4.1*
  see also balance sheet; cash flow statement; financial statements; profit and loss account; statement of total recognised gains and losses
prior period adjustments
  profit and loss account, 12.2.21
private company
  appointment of auditor, *Appendix A*
  filing accounts, 11.1
production cost
  definition, 12.5.2
  determination, *Appendix E*
profit and loss account, 4.2
  abbreviated accounts, *Table 8.1*, *Table 8.2*, *Table 8.5*, 8.10.3
  acquisitions, 12.2.17
  administrative expenses, 12.2.4
  auditors' remuneration, 12.2.13
  continuing operations, 12.2.16
  cost of sales, 12.2.2
  depreciation, *Table 6.5*, 6.6
  discontinued operations, 12.2.18
  disposal, profit or loss on, 12.2.23
  distribution costs, 12.2.3, *Appendix C*
  employee costs, 12.2.10
  exceptional items, 12.2.19
  extraordinary items, 12.2.20
  foreign currency losses, 12.2.14
  format, 3.4, *Table 4.1*, *Table 6.1*, 6.4.3, *Table 6.5*, 6.6, 12.2, *Appendix C*, *Appendix E*
    choice, 6.6, 12.2
    depreciation, *Table 6.5*, 6.6
    FRSSE, *Table 10.3*

361

Index

gross profit or loss, *Table 6.5*, 6.6
SI 2008 No. 409, *Table 4.1*, 6.4.3, *Table 6.5*, 6.6
gross profit or loss, *Table 6.5*, 6.6
  abbreviated accounts, *Table 8.5*
group accounts, *Appendix B*
income from participating interests, 12.2.12
income from shares in group undertakings, 12.2.11
individual, 12.1.2
interest payable, 12.2.14
interest payable and similar charges, 12.2.14
notes to the accounts, 6.7
ordinary activities, 12.2.15
other external charges, 12.2.8
other operating charges, 12.2.9
other operating income, 12.2.6
own work capitalised, 12.2.7
parent company, 12.1.2
participating interests, 12.2.12
prior period adjustments, 12.2.21
profit or loss on disposal, 12.2.23
realised profits, 3.5
selling and distribution costs, 12.2.3, *Appendix C*
SI 2008 No. 409, *Table 4.1*, 6.4.3, *Table 6.5*, 6.6
SI 2008 No. 410, *Table 8.5*
staff costs, 12.2.10
total recognised gains and losses, 12.2.22
  see also statement of total recognised gains and losses
turnover, 12.2.5
proper accounting records *see* adequate accounting records
provisions
definition, 12.3.8
FRSSE, *Table 10.2*, *Table 10.3*, *Table 10.8*, 10.11
prudence
accounting principle, 3.5
public companies
audit, 11.3
laying of accounts and reports before general meeting, *Appendix B*
Public Finance Initiative (PFI) contracts, 12.8.2
publication of accounts, *Appendix A*, *Appendix B*
non-statutory accounts, 3.12
purchase price
definition, 12.5.1
determination, *Appendix E*

qualifying as a small company, 5.1–5.4, *Appendix B*
abbreviated accounts, 8.11
balance sheet total, 1.1.1, 5.2
decision chart, 5.4
employees numbers, 1.1.1, 5.2
number of employees, 5.2

parent companies, 5.3
size qualification, 5.3, 5.4
turnover, 1.1.1, 5.2
quasi-subsidiaries, 12.8.2
quoted companies
accounts, *Appendix B*
audit concerns, *Appendix A*
Companies Act 2006, 2.2.1
definition, *Appendix B*
directors' remuneration report, 3.7, *Appendix B*
GAAP and, 4.4.4
International Accounting Standards, 4.6.1
International Financial Reporting Standards, 4.4.3
operating and financial review, 3.7

realised profits
definition, 3.5
records *see* adequate accounting records
related party transactions
disclosures, *Table 10.2*, *Table 10.3*, 10.8
FRSSE and, *Table 10.2*, *Table 10.3*, *Table 10.6*, 10.8
loans and transactions with directors, 10.8.2
transactions with directors, 10.8.3
related undertakings disclosure, 9.3, 12.7, *Appendix B*, *Appendix E*
research and development
costs of research, 12.3.1
development costs, 12.3.1
directors' report, *Table 6.6*
FRSSE, *Table 10.3*
reserves
abbreviated accounts format, *Appendix D*
balance sheet, *Table 6.4*, *Appendix C*
notes to the accounts, 6.7
see also revaluation reserve
retirement benefits *see* pensions and retirement benefits
revaluation reserve, 3.5, *Appendix E*
alternative base of accounting, 12.5.3
definition, 12.5.3
FRSSE, *Table 10.3*
revaluation surplus, 4.2
revenue recognition
areas of specific guidance, 12.9.2
basic principles, 12.9.1
bill and hold arrangements, 12.9.2
contracts for services, 10.12, 12.9.2, 12.9.3
fair value, 12.9.1
FRS 5, 10.12
FRSSE, 10.1.3, *Table 10.3*, 10.12
gift vouchers, 12.9.2
long-term contracts, 12.9.2
turnover, 12.9.1, 12.9.2
UITF 40, 10.12, 12.9.2, 12.9.3
revision of defective accounts, *Appendix A*, *Appendix B*

362

sale and repurchase agreements
  definition, 12.8.2
  substance of transactions, 12.8.2
SAP *see* Statements of Standard Accounting Practice
securitised assets
  substance of transactions, 12.8.2
selling and distribution costs
  profit and loss account, 12.2.3, *Appendix C*
service contracts *see* contracts for services
share capital
  abbreviated accounts format, *Appendix D*
  balance sheet format, *Table 6.4*, *Appendix C*
  notes to the accounts, 6.7, *Appendix E*
share-based payments
  cash-settled transactions, 10.13
  choice of settlement method, 10.13
  equity-settled transactions, 10.13
  FRSSE, 10.1.3, 10.13
shares
  abbreviated accounts, *Table 8.4*
  financial liabilities, 12.4
  group undertakings
    definition, 12.6
    income from, 12.2.11
  preference shares, 12.4, 12.10.2
short period accounts, 1.2
signature *see* approval and signing of accounts
'significant accounting transaction'
  meaning, 7.2
Small Companies and Groups (Accounts and Directors' Report) Regulations 2008 (SI 2008 No. 409), 2.2.4, 9.5.1, 11.1, *Appendix C, Appendix E*
  abbreviated accounts, 8.1, 8.9, 9.4, 12.1.4, 13.2, *Appendix D*
    balance sheet, *Table 8.2*, 8.4
    form and content, 8.2, *Table 8.3*
    notes, *Table 8.4*
  accounting principles, 3.5, 6.4.3
  annual accounts, 12.1.2
  balance sheet, *Table 4.1*, 6.4.3, 6.5, 9.5.3
    abbreviated accounts, *Table 8.2*, 8.4
    goodwill, 12.3.2
    tangible assets, 12.3.3
  contents and structure, *Table 2.3*
  determining the substance of transactions, 12.8.1
  directors' report, *Table 6.6*, 6.8.2
  directors' statements, 8.5
  disclosure of directors' remuneration and benefits, 6.11
  dividends, 12.10.1
  dormant company acting as agent, 7.6
  format of accounts, 3.4, *Table 6.1*, 6.2, 6.4.1–6.4.3, 6.6
  FRSSE and, 9.5.2, 10.1.1, *Table 10.1*, 10.3, 10.5
  goodwill, 12.3.2
  group accounts, *Table 2.3*, 3.8, 9.2, 9.4, 12.1.2, 12.7.1, 12.7.2

  individual accounts, *Table 6.1*, 6.4.2
  notes to the accounts, 3.6, 6.7
  profit and loss account, *Table 4.1*, 6.4.3, *Table 6.5*, 6.6
  related undertakings disclosures, 9.3
  'true and fair' view, 10.2.2
social security
  balance sheet, 12.3.9, 12.3.10
special auditors' report on abbreviated accounts, *Table 8.1*, *Table 8.2*, 8.9, *Table 11.2*, 12.1.3, 14.4
staff *see* employees
start-up costs
  FRSSE, *Table 10.3*
Statement of Principles for financial reporting, 4.1
statement of total recognised gains and losses (STRGL), 4.2, 12.2.22
  format, *Table 4.1*
  FRS 3 and, format, effect on, *Table 4.1*
  FRSSE, *Table 10.3*
  revaluation surpluses, 4.2
Statements of Recommended Practice (SORPs), 4.4.4
  FRSSE and, 10.1.1, 10.2.3
Statements of Standard Accounting Practice (SSAP), 3.5, *Table 4.2*, 4.4.3, 6.4.3
  application to small and medium-sized companies, *Table 4.2*
  concessions, *Table 4.2*, 4.5
  disclosure, 12.9.2
  exemption, 10.1.1
  FRSSE and, 10.1.1, 10.2.3
  research and development (SSAP 13), 12.3.1
statutory accounts, 1.1.1, 1.2
  definition, 12.1.3
stocks
  balance sheet, *Table 6.3*, *Table 6.4*, 12.3.7
  valuation, 12.3.7
  see also consignment stock
subsidiary
  consolidated accounts, exclusion, 3.8
  definition, 12.6
  FRS 2, *Table 10.2*
  FRSSE, 10.1.3, *Table 10.2*
  meaning, 12.6
  quasi-subsidiary, 12.8.2
  related undertakings disclosure, 9.3, 12.7, *Appendix B, Appendix E*
  'wholly-owned subsidiary', definition, 12.6
  see also group accounts
substance of transactions
  accounting principle, 3.5
  consignment stock, 12.8.2
  determination, 12.8.1
  factoring of debts, 12.8.2
  FRS 5, 12.8.1, 12.8.2
  loan transfers, 12.8.2
  PFI and similar contracts, 12.8.2

Index

principle of 'substance over form', 3.3, 4.4.1, 10.7.1, 12.8.2
quasi-subsidiaries, 12.8
reporting, *Table 10.2*, 10.7
sale and repurchase agreements, 12.8.2
securitised assets, 12.8.2
SI 2008 No. 409, 12.8.1
summary financial statements, 2.3, *Table 2.6*, 3.12, 11.1, *Table 11.1*, *Appendix B*

tangible assets
  balance sheet, *Table 6.3*, *Table 6.4*, 12.3.3, *Appendix C*
taxation
  balance sheet, 12.3.9, 12.3.10
  as creditor, 12.3.10
  current tax, FRSSE requirements, *Table 10.2*
  deferred, *Table 10.2*, *Table 10.3*
  on dividends, *Table 10.3*
  FRSSE, *Table 10.2*, *Table 10.3*
  VAT, *Table 10.3*
'think small first' approach, 1.1.1, 2.1.1, 2.2.1
total recognised gains and losses
  profit and loss account, 12.2.22
  see also statement of total recognised gains and losses
trade creditors, 12.3.10
trade debtors, 12.3.10
transactions
  with directors, 10.8.2, 10.8.3
  'significant accounting transaction', meaning, 7.2
  substance of *see* substance of transactions
  see also related party transactions
'true and fair' view, 3.3, 6.3, 11.1, 12.1, *Appendix B*
  abbreviated accounts, 8.2
  accounting standards, 4.4.1, 4.4.3
  auditors' report, 2.4, 14.1.2
  Companies Act 2006, 2.3, 2.4, 4.4.1, 4.4.2, 6.3, 10.2.2
  company law and, 4.4.2
  departure from, notes to the accounts, 3.3
  directors' duties, 6.3
  European law, 3.3, 4.4.2
  Finance Acts 1998 and 2002, 4.4.1
  Financial Reporting Council, 4.4.1
  financial statements, 4.1
  FRSSE and, 1.3, 10.1.1, 10.2.1, 10.2.2, *Table 10.3*
  GAAP and, 3.3, 4.4.1, 4.4.4
  IAS accounts, 3.3, 4.4.1, 4.4.2
  IFRS, 4.4.1, 4.4.3
  meaning, 3.3

  override, 3.3, 4.4.1, 4.4.2
  SI 2008 No. 409, 10.2.2
  special circumstances, 3.3
turnover
  abbreviated accounts, *Appendix C*
  audit exemption, *Table 11.1*, 11.2, 11.4
  bill and hold arrangements, 12.9.2
  disclosure, 12.2.5
  group exemption qualifying condition, 9.2
  notes to the accounts, 6.7, *Appendix E*
  profit and loss account, 12.2.5
  revenue recognition, 12.9.1, 12.9.2
  size qualification, 1.1.1, 5.2

unaudited accounts
  accountants' report, 14.7
  dormant company, example, 13.3
undertaking
  associated undertaking, 12.6
  Companies Act 2006, *Appendix A*
  definition, 12.6
  fellow subsidiary undertaking, 12.6
  group undertaking, 12.2.11, 12.6
  joint ventures, 12.6
  parent undertaking, 12.6
  subsidiary, 12.6
United States
  accounting standards, 4.6.3
unlimited company, 11.1, *Appendix A*
Urgent Issues Task Force (UITF) abstracts, *Table 4.2*, 4.4.3
  as accounting standards, 4.4.3
  concessions, *Table 4.2*, 4.5
  exemption, 10.1.1
  FRSSE and, 10.1.1, 10.1.2, 10.2.3
  nature and application, *Table 4.2*, 4.4.3
  revenue recognition and service contracts, 10.12, 12.9.2, 12.9.3

valuation
  alternative methods *see* alternative accounting rules
Value Added Tax (VAT)
  FRSSE, *Table 10.3*
  see also taxation

WebFiling *see* electronic filing of accounts
website publication of accounts, 14.3
write-downs to recoverable amount
  FRSSE, *Table 10.3*

XBRL (eXtensible Business Reporting Language), 1.5.4